MORAL

SPECTATORSHIP

MORAL SPECTATORSHIP

TECHNOLOGIES

OF VOICE

AND AFFECT

IN POSTWAR

REPRESENTATIONS

OF THE CHILD

LISA CARTWRIGHT

Duke University Press

Durham and London

2008

© 2008 Duke University Press
All rights reserved
Printed in the United States of
America on acid-free paper ∞
Designed by Amy Ruth Buchanan
Typeset in Sabon by Achorn
International, Inc.
Library of Congress Cataloging-in-
Publication Data appear on the last
printed page of this book.

FOR FRANCESCA PERRIER

CONTENTS

ACKNOWLEDGEMENTS

Many people have contributed to this volume in conversations and in other helpful ways. The chapter on Deaf cinema began when Mark Betz, then of the George Eastman House film archive in Rochester, New York, suggested that I take a look at the film *Mandy*. Joe Wlodarz and Dan Humphries contributed to my work on that chapter in different ways. The chapter on facilitated communication would never have been written without the inspiration of Linda Ware, who introduced me to disability studies. I am grateful to Douglas Biklen for being so generous with his time during our many conversations about the FC method. My friends and colleagues at the University of Rochester's Susan B. Anthony Institute for Gender and Women's Studies and the Program in Visual and Cultural Studies, particularly Janet Berlo, Douglas Crimp, Marilyn Lambert-Fisher, and Mary Fox, provided a fabulous intellectual support network during the early research for this book. Rochester remains an ideal place for the cultivation of new ways of working across the disciplines.

I am enormously grateful for the intellectual support of my colleagues at the University of California at San Diego, and in particular my chair, Dan Hallin, whose optimism is a treasure. I am most grateful for the insight and collaboration of Brian Goldfarb, David Benin, Val Hartouni, David Serlin, and Morana Alač, the people with whom I have worked most closely at San Diego. Brian, David, and Val read versions of these chapters and worked with me on parallel projects in forging the ideas developed here at different stages of the project; I could not have completed this book without working through the thoughts and feelings of these friends of the heart and mind. Marq Smith, editor of the *Journal of Visual Culture*, deserves a very special thank you for coaching me through ideas that found their way into portions of this book at points when I had many pressing reasons not to write. His encouragement kept my thinking alive. It was my good fortune to have had Elizabeth Wilson and Jonathan Metzl as close and attentive readers of drafts of this book near the end of the project. Their wit and incisive intelligence were a gift that carried this project through to its end.

To Marie-Luise Angerer, Eva Warth, Astrid Deuber-Mankowsky, Jackie Stacey, Annette Kuhn, Jose Van Dijck, Kristen Ostherr, David Serlin, and Lucy Fisher I am grateful for providing me with especially fruitful opportunities to develop the ideas in this book in dialog with colleagues and graduate students at different phases of this project's development. Marie-Luise and Jackie deserve special thanks for sharing their own work in progress during this process.

As always, the professional assistance of archivists and librarians deserves mention. David Baker and Dorothy Gruich of the Archives of the History of American Psychology deserve special thanks.

My biggest debt is to Brian, Nilo, and Sabina Goldfarb and Lori Boatright.

SPECTATORSHIP, AFFECT,

AND REPRESENTATION

The concept of spectatorship proposed in this book is indebted to previous work on the spectator and identification in film theory.[1] Thinking through the psychoanalytic and philosophical traditions that have prevailed in feminist psychoanalytic film theory, I propose a model that takes into account aspects of the theories of affect developed by the French psychoanalyst André Green (1999a) and the American cognitive psychologist Silvan Tomkins (1962, 1963, 1980, 1991, 1992; Sedgwick and Frank 1995). Until recently feeling has been a touchy subject for feminist theory. This book is an attempt to develop a theory of spectatorship and affect's relationship to representation without reproducing the sentiments it analyzes. My aim has been to track, through film texts about Deaf female subjects and through the interpersonal relationship of facilitated communication among people with communication disorders, the connection between representation and that more elusive psychical entity, affect. Work on affect is brought into dialog, in this book, with the writings of Melanie Klein, Donald Winnicott, Heinz Kohut, and a set of child psychoanalysts working on the question of ego development and narcissism in infants and children with sensory and cognitive impairments. From the writings of these child psychoanalysts and object relations theorists I adapt a set of concepts including projective identification, introjection, incorporation, and potential space for use in conjunction with theories of affect and representation. I suggest some ways of theorizing the subject that move us into the domain of nonnormative concepts of self and ego in processes of identification and spectatorship.

A second line of thought introduced in this book follows ideas about spectatorship and the sort of empathy at play in moral perception. Heinz Kohut defines empathy as the capacity to think and feel oneself into the inner life of another (Kohut 1984). I propose the concept of empathetic identification as an alternative to the model of identification that has presided in film theory for more than two decades. That model, I explain, has been tacitly based on the idea of feeling what the other feels, imagining oneself to be the other. I argue in the first section of this book that empathetic identification, in which I do not necessarily feel the other's feelings or imagine myself in his or her place (Vetlesen 1994, 8), but rather recognize and even *facilitate* the otherness of the other, is a crucial but overlooked aspect of identification that deserves to be considered in film theory. I stress throughout this book that empathetic identification must be understood as a radically intersubjective process, and not one that is most significantly produced in the individual spectator or film character, or between those two, but which is more radically intersubjective and multisensory in its enactment. I read the concept of empathy historically through writing by the Scottish moral philosopher Adam Smith on the subject of the spectator (1966), suggesting that his concept offers much toward understanding the fragmentation and intersubjectivity of the experience of spectatorship. I also draw on concepts of the self and empathy developed by Kohut (1971, 1984) and other psychoanalytic theorists whose writings have previously been bypassed because of their focus on that much maligned liberal concept, the self. My intention is not to resurrect this concept, but to draw on some useful aspects of the work of its theorists in order to further develop ideas about the subject in film theory. This book expresses political caution regarding one of its own key concepts, empathy. To articulate this caution, I draw from the German philosopher Hannah Arendt (1963), whom I consider in conjunction with the thinking of French pragmatic sociologist Luc Boltanski (1999). *Distant Suffering*, Boltanski's monograph on morality, media, and politics, is an important tacit reference throughout this book. My thinking on this latter set of authors is developed at greater length in a companion book, *Images of Waiting Children* (Cartwright forthcoming). That book was written in conjunction with this volume, and they were one project until the very last stage. For this reason, *Moral Spectatorship* makes reference to that book and the ideas developed there on occasion as more than an artifact of the two volumes' origins as one work.

Thinking about affect relative to representation, agency, and the constitution of the subject is at the core of this book. I consider representation beyond the boundaries of visual culture, in the realm of audiovisual expression. Working within the field of disability studies for the past ten years, I have not been able to put down the question of how we can think about how subjects form when the faculties of sight, hearing, and speech are impaired. I have tried to work against the deficit model that would understand sensory impairment as constitutive of absence or lack of those very abilities understood to be basic to ego development and subject emergence. This line of thinking drew me into elaborating a model of spectatorship that takes into account theories about how subjectivity takes form with differences of sensory, mental, cognitive, and physical ability. With few exceptions, psychoanalytic feminist theory has elided these categories of subjectivity except in cases where they are interpreted as constitutive of lack. This has produced a tacit aversion to the figure of the sensorily disabled subject. The political and historical nature of this problem and some possible reasons for it are elaborated in the first section of this book.

The interconstitutive nature of human subjectivity is also a strong concern throughout this volume. My intention was to try to develop a model that accounts for the complexities of intrapsychic life while also accounting for the intersubjective production of feeling, action, and agency. The literature on intersubjectivity is vast and varied across fields. That which concerns me here is drawn primarily from two sources: psychoanalytic theory of affect and objects relations theory; and the philosophy of the subject introduced by Emmanuel Levinas, especially in his interpretation of Maurice Merleau-Ponty's phenomenological thinking about intersubjectivity (Levinas 1993). At the basis of this entire book is a concept of intersubjectivity that Levinas develops, in which the copresence of two hands, belonging to the same body, is extended to the other person. This idea of intersubjectivity as the other person and I as "elements of one incorporeity" and as a "borrowing of myself from the other" (Levinas 1993, 100, alluding to Merleau-Ponty) is demonstrated over and over in *Moral Spectatorship* as a relationship into which always enters the problematic of "hands" that cannot always reach, feel, and express in ways that are intended and desired by either the I or an other. The "intropathy of intellectual communication" theorized by both philosophers is idealized on the basis of a whole body that has the capacity to reach, to touch, and to feel in normative ways. This model continually fails in the face of what we might call sensory deficits, or emotional deficits—or, rather, differences in the organization of the sensory and emotional pathways within and between subjects. What I emphasize throughout *Moral Spectatorship* is that the "touching" described by Levinas and Merleau-Ponty is in fact also and importantly feeling, as Eve Kosofsky Sedgwick so beautifully demonstrates in *Touching Feeling* (2003). Produced in the breakdown of the ability to touch is not egological isolation or failed communication. Rather, it is a heightening of dependency and a rerouting of intersubjective pathways. The result is new dynamics of experiencing this "borrowing" of myself from the other. As I will show throughout this book, to borrow oneself from an other in order to have voice in the world has been regarded with suspicion, has been pathologized, because it proposes a model of subjectivity that flies in the face of the liberal autonomous subject. Dependency and nonisomorphic relationships of power are anathema to notions of the autonomous individual.

Feeling is a suspect area of research for media and film scholars, who, since the time of Brechtian distantiation and Althusserrian apparatus theory, have worked to institute models that allow us to resist the seductive pull of the medium as it moves us to feel for the other. For this reason film theory thus far has not paid very close attention to aspects of spectatorship linked to moral sentiment and affects expressed in the public sphere, except to critique them. A related concern: the paradigms of sexual difference, pleasure, and fictional narrative have dominated the field of film and media study, if only as models against which to base categories of spectator based on race, nationality, and other categories of identity. *Moral Spectatorship* does not offer a new category of identity or spectator group. It is not a contribution to disability identity or resistance politics, though I hope the book will be viewed as a contribution to disability studies. Rather, it addresses instances in which texts interpellate a full range of viewers or listeners in ways that, in some cases, elicit moral responses that are deeply felt as personal, sentimental, and inner-directed, but which elicit a sense of responsibility for an other—responsibility that, to borrow a line from Levinas, "is also the stern name of love without lust" (Levinas 1999, 129). The kind of love for the other discussed in this book is not most productively read through the paradigms of either sexual difference or identification in the conventional sense. C. Fred Alford notes that for the psychoanalyst Heinz Kohut it is not desire that splits the ego but faulty empathy (Alford 1991, 31–32). The texts and human relationships considered in *Moral Spectatorship* are analyzed in the registers of human empathy and care—not in order to restore these qualities, but to consider them as constitutive factors in the formation of the human subject in sociality. The chapters that follow propose a model of a spectator that emphasizes links between affect and empathy. If desire is always the desire for an other, then empathy is the process of movement between the one and the other. Empathy is posited not as a quality or condition that one might or should have possession of, but rather as a force that moves desire. In the model of empathetic identification put forward in this book, I attempt to account for both the intrapsychic and, most important, the intersubjective and multimodal, multisensory forces that constitute the subject not only as one who looks and is seen, but also one who listens and is heard, touches and is touched, caught in the movement of a multisensory gaze that is constituted through empathetic identification. The concept of projective identification, elaborated in the first chapter of this book, will be an important term in putting forward a model of this intersubjective process.

Regarding identification more closely, my proposition is that identification with screen characters is a film theory concept that currently requires more careful material disaggregation and analysis than the kinds of textual and shot analyses we have done before, in order to better understand identification beyond its manifestations in film-viewing. Laplanche and Pontalis (1973) explain that for Freud identification is "not just one psychic mechanism among others, but the operation whereby the subject is constituted" (206). They distinguish between forms in which the subject identifies his self with others (heteropathic) and those in which the subject identifies the other with himself (idiopathic). But they also mention a more complex form in which both tendencies are present at the same time, "one which is sometimes invoked to account for the constitution of a 'we'" (206). The term "we" is a complicated one regarding identification, because it carries the weight of a feeling of belonging. Too, it can suggest patronizing assumptions that violate one's status as a distinctive, boundaried subject, as in the doctor's query "How are we today?" Throughout this book I will be elaborating a way of thinking about identification that is organized not about a "we," but about the complex, intersubjective coproduction of the "I."

Voice is a central concept throughout this book that is linked to this coproduction of an "I." The term "voice" has a wide range and mix of meanings. The most important one for this work is the political use of the word "voice" as a figure of speech connoting agency and power. *The Voice*, a British weekly paper by and for black British subjects, is but one example of this use of the term. "Coming to voice" is a figure of speech in a range of political movements connoting the achievement of agency, usually belatedly or through a political struggle before which the individual or collective subject who speaks is understood to have been "silent" or "invisible." The concept of voice developed throughout this book is indebted most specifically to work that brings together this concept of voice and/as agency in feminist writing that interrogates the material history and practices surrounding technologies through which voice and/as agency is materially achieved in the world. There are many sources on the concept of voice in this regard that could be cited here; however, I am indebted most directly to Kaja Silverman's *The Acoustic Mirror* (1988) and Mary Ann Doane's writing on voice in the context of psychoanalytic theory of the cinematic apparatus (1986). These works on voice were written during a period when feminist film theory was centrally engaged with Lacanian psychoanalysis. *Moral Spectatorship* is more broadly in dialog with the extensive work of the 1980s and 1990s in Lacanian psychoanalysis, but I hold important reservations about Lacan's influence. These reservations are discussed in the first chapter of the book, where I introduce a new paradigm through writings on affect and representation by André Green, a student of Lacan's and a figure whose usefulness to feminist thinking about the subject and representation, I argue, was overlooked in the Lacanian turn.[2]

The first chapter of *Moral Spectatorship* returns to early feminist psychoanalytic theory to ask why object relations and affect theory were spurned in favor of work on representation and language. I propose a new use of these areas of psychoanalytic theory congruent with earlier work on representation. A new way of thinking about identification is proposed.

The second chapter of *Moral Spectatorship* considers some of the meanings assigned to speaking (or not), listening (or not), and Deaf oral speech and sign language in social-problem melodramas about Deaf and nonverbal girls and young women produced for hearing audiences during a period of technological innovation in film-sound instrumentation (the transition to magnetic and stereophonic sound). Rather than routing this discussion through apparatus theory alone, I combine a historical approach to sound technology with work about the register of affect and its theorists. My hope is that this approach might suggest for readers a new direction to turn in psychoanalytic thought about film, the body, and the subject.

The second chapter is also devoted to maternal melodrama. It offers extended intra- and intertextual readings of the place of voice and of touch in films that take mute girls as social problems requiring a particular sort of talking cure. I consider the multivalent textual and technological meanings of gendered deafness, sound, and listening in the postwar historical moment of the major transition in sound technology that followed the Second World War. The films I consider include *Johnny Belinda* (Warner Brothers/First National/Jean Negulesco, United States, 1948), *Mandy* (U.S. release title *Crash of Silence*, Ealing Studios/Alexander Mackendrick, England, 1952), the documentary *Thursday's Children* (Lindsay Anderson and Guy Benton, England, 1954), the Helen Keller biopic *The Miracle Worker* (United Artists/Arthur Penn, United States, 1962), *Children of a Lesser God* (Paramount/Randa Haines, United States, 1986), and the Australian feature *A Test of Love* (Gil Brealey, 1985). In these films female voice, child voice, and the act of listening are assigned complexly layered meanings and politics relative to agency and power in the postwar era. I introduce the listener-spectator as a subject in an empathetic audiovisual field who is hailed by the image of the "nonverbal" child as she comes to voice through the ministrations of hearing maternal caregivers. I consider the appropriation of the "mute" female figure by feminist theorists as a figure who embodies the trope of voice as (thwarted) agency; the Lacanian trope of muteness as an expression of repressed desire; and the technology of acoustics and the embodied experience of sound rather than voice as the medium through which girls who do not speak enter the transitive space of agency by gaining "voice" through caregiver mediation. Crucial to my discussion is a focus on the film text as a site of public fantasy where the social issue of deafness and/as women's voice is repetitively acted out and worked through.

The third chapter of *Moral Spectatorship* interprets facilitated communication as a technological practice. This practice allows me to think through the extent to which intersubjectivity is acknowledged (or not) as a model of agency and expression in children with communication disorders that preclude speech and writing, but who achieve "voice" through writing facilitated by humans and machines. It is in this chapter of the book that the concept of intersubjectivity is most fully elaborated. Facilitated communication is a process in which children with communication disorders based in motor or cognitive impairments are physically and emotionally supported by caregivers in the use of computers to communicate by writing. I review a discussion of a landmark legal case in Australia in which the legitimacy of this technique as a means of bringing the child to voice was brought to public attention in forms including a popular autobiography and a popular motion picture (Gil Brealey's *A Test of Love*). The chapter then turns to a reading of the introduction of facilitated communication in the United States with children with autism, and the impassioned professional and legal challenges to the method's legitimacy that ensued from the bombshell of allegations of sexual abuse typed by children who previously had not spoken or communicated. I read this saga through a variety of historical lenses including the "memory wars" of the 1990s (Campbell 2003), and Sigmund Freud's "A Child Is Being Beaten" (Freud 1955a). At stake in debates in education, psychology, and law about facilitated communication is the question of whose memory is recounted in these narratives; who the author is of the writings attributed to these children, the child itself or the adult caregiver who supports the arms and wrists of the typing child to stabilize its movements. Most crucially of interest is the insistence of some public and professional discourses that this affective relationship between child and caregiver is neither a legitimate interpersonal bond nor a trustworthy mode of communication because of the potential for intense countertransference. Of great interest to me in this debate is the projective identificatory power attributed to facilitators in allegations of their authorship of autistic children's communications. That perception of manipulation of the child by the facilitator in response to these cases has invoked intense contempt and fear in many professional and public spectators. These spectators discredit the technique, using it as a prime example of bad science, and malign the facilitators, casting them as hysterics or obsessional neurotics unwittingly playing out their fantasies through the vehicle of the hapless child. Also of interest in this chapter is the debate about the nature of autism that comes to the fore in the debates about facilitation. Autism was defined during the period in question as a disorder characterized in part by cognitive differences in the feeling and expression of empathy and the ability to attribute—to project—a concept of mind to others. The controversy over facilitated communication was embroiled in a controversy that still rages about the nature of autism. Vying perceptions of the child's ability to experience empathy and affect and to conduct transitive relations have been at the center of this controversy. Empathy and affect are, however, also prominent features of adult behavior in this context, demonstrated in the concern showered upon the autistic child on both sides of the debate. Facilitated communication thus is one site where questions about transference and countertransference in the communication-disordered child's belated coming to voice could be performed and negotiated in the public eye.

Although this book's title emphasizes the moral aspects of spectatorship, it could well take the term "empathetic" to describe the sorts of relationships of identification it elaborates. When Kohut (1984, 82) described empathy as a kind of "vicarious introspection" in which one thinks and feels oneself into the inner life of another person, he was referring to the psychoanalyst's necessary relationship to a client in the process of a cure. This is a fundamentally moral relationship. It is this type of caregiving that structures the relationships of identification and spectatorship discussed in the chapters that follow.

CHAPTER ONE

MORAL SPECTATORSHIP:

RETHINKING IDENTIFICATION

IN FILM THEORY

*Paths not taken: Object relations and affect
in early feminist film theory*

Which psychoanalysis was taken up in feminist film theory, and what can
we learn from revisiting some psychoanalytic notions and practices that were
not? In *Psychoanalysis and Feminism* (1973), Juliet Mitchell provided a rationale for the choices made by feminists taking up psychoanalysis at that moment. She recalls the opening claim of psychoanalyst Melanie Klein in *Envy
and Gratitude* (1957) in which the leading proponent of object relations theory explained her reasons for focusing on the infant's relation to the mother.
Mitchell explains that what Klein intended as an analytic description was, in
the climate of the time, taken for an ideological prescription for mothers to
perform in a manner adequate to the production of a sound subject. The welfare state of postwar and cold war Britain fostered a milieu in which "the cult
of the mother and child went its relentless way" as psychoanalysts grappled
with rebellious youth culture, delinquency, child psychosis, and problems of
the family at the expense of the study of a feminine psychology that ventured
outside the figure of the mother (Mitchell 1975, 227–231). It is not surprising
then that reception of Mitchell's book in Anglophone feminism emphasized
her contribution to the interpretation of Lacan and Freud and not her reading
of R. D. Laing and his contribution to the study of schizophrenia.[1]

In her introduction to *Psychoanalysis and Cinema* (1990), E. Anne Kaplan also reminds us that the women's movements in the United States and Britain were strongly motivated to reject Freudian psychoanalysis as well as object relations theory. Lacanian psychoanalysis, however, "seemed immediately relevant to analysis of representation in film." Language was an apt model for interpreting filmic systems of meaning; concepts such as the mirror phase seemed apt analogs for the screen-spectator relationship (Kaplan 1990, 10). As Kaplan notes, the construction of the subject and the circulation of desire were regarded by academics studying literature, art, and film as important issues that could be usefully discerned through psychoanalytic theory, not only that based in clinical practice and the analysis of individuals but also that which was already applied to the analysis of literature and the visual and plastic arts. It was in this context, which emerged under the interdisciplinary rubric of *representation*, that the concept of the feminine, another concern of Lacan's, was further developed outside the paradigm of the mother-child relationship. Thus the turn to representation was accompanied by a return to the subject of feminine psychology, a topic that Mitchell had noted was all but abandoned by psychoanalysis after the 1930s.[2]

But Lacan was not the only post-Freudian theorist available for appropriation in the construction of theories of femininity and representation in the late 1970s. To understand the turn to Lacan and away from other options in the late 1970s and early 1980s, I begin by looking back on some conversations about the status of *the subject* in film theory. In 1991, David Rodowick looked back to remind readers that, "contrary to film theory's emphasis, psychoanalysis is not a theory of the subject" (Rodowick 1991, 67–68). He cites Juliet Mitchell and Jacqueline Rose to support this point, recalling Mitchell's contrast of object relations theory, with its emphasis on "ego's deviations and returns to 'norms' of self-identity and coherence," to Lacan's antihumanist insistence that the subject is incommensurable with any notion of unity or coherence. Positions of masculinity and femininity are built on fantasies that engage figurations of identity unification (through others/objects) (Rodowick 1991, 67–68). Robert Stam, Robert Burgoyne, and Sandy Flitterman-Lewis made the same contrast a year later in their *New Vocabularies in Film Semiotics*: "While ego psychology seeks to bolster the unified subject by reinforcing the perception of a coherent self, Lacanian psychoanalysis implies a critique of this idealist unity" (1992, 135). Object relations, in this formulation, is not the right psychoanalysis because it emphasizes the ego's "return to coherence" rather than the unitary ego's status as artifact of liberal humanist philosophy.

These interpretations of object relations, void of examples and author references, are both far too general and off the mark. They conflate different varieties and periods of object relations theory and ego psychology. The popular psychology of Erik Erikson (1965) may be faulted for offering a relatively unitary model of a self. D. W. Winnicott (1965, 1971a, 1971e) and Melanie Klein (1952a, 1952b, 1955, 1975a), however, stress the divisions that are constitutive of the self. Klein, especially, based her work in the sustained function of splitting as an essential protective measure (enacted through projection and introjection) in defending against the disintegration that threatens the organization of the self. And the proposition of Heinz Kohut, theorist of self psychology, that it is not desire and lack but failures in empathy that split the ego (Kohut 1971 and 1984; Alford 1991, 31) has yet to be mined for its implications regarding the fundamental fragmentation of the ego relative to processes of identification.

Film theory's writing off of object relations theory and self psychology for their supposed investment in a subject that comes too close to the liberal notion of a unified self left us without the variety of useful concepts and tools that object relations theory offered. It may be true that *some* objects relations theory of the late twentieth century became the domain of a popular psychology of the liberal self and a means of shoring up the traditional role of the mother (e.g., Erikson 1965), but the empirical ego psychology of Freudian psychoanalyst René Spitz and object relations theory as proposed by Klein, Winnicott, and later psychoanalysts who drew from a range of approaches, most notably André Green, were for the most part not guilty of these mistakes. These psychoanalysts introduced concepts that support film theory's interest in a subject model that veers from the various normative, ideal, and unitary forms offered in liberal humanist political and psychological theories. I will be arguing throughout this book that this body of work provides concepts and models that can help us to get past some of the impasses created by the Lacanian model's adherence to language.

To begin with, Klein's object relations theory views the subject as being constituted in a manner that is deeply divided intrapsychically, as well as being fundamentally intersubjective in its formulation. Intersubjectivity, however, is not emphasized in the Freudian model of the psyche. Film theory, despite its emphasis on splitting as constitutive of the ego, has yet closely to consider splitting and fragmentation as processes that shift and change according to relationships with others in the world, rather than as ontological states achieved at some developmental moment then held and reenacted within the subject throughout adulthood. For Klein, the spectrum of experiences of fragmentation and splitting is not retrogressive, harking back to some primitive moment in childhood, but rather is a densely layered process that continues into adulthood, unfolding throughout a lifetime.

The matter of intersubjectivity must be emphasized here. Laplanche and Pontalis (1973, 278) recall Spitz's point that Freud throughout his writings viewed the libidinal object solely from the view of the individual subject (cathexes, object choice), with one exception: his *Three Essays on the Theory of Sexuality* (1905), in which he addresses the mutual relationship between mother and child. Subject production in the object relations theory of Klein and Spitz (1959, 1965) is fundamentally interconstitutive beyond the binary of mother and infant, including radical fragmentation at the level of object fantasies. Object relations theory thus can help film theory to model the action of film as agent upon and through the subject in an interconstitutive process that takes form at the level of fantasy. This process involves a complex arena of part-objects, bodies, and subjects, through visceral projective processes that are radically multiple and fractured, carrying forward throughout adulthood without being regressive in nature.

The historical resistance to object relations theory in the 1970s and 1980s, I propose, had to do in part with a strategic aversion—perhaps even a political abhorrence to certain kinds of work: to work on psychosis, developmental delay, cognitive disorders, the infant/child-maternal relationship, and, most of all, to work on the body (figured as maternal) outside the linguistic-symbolic register through which we came to interpret representation.[3] In an interview with Juliet Mitchell and Jacqueline Rose published in the British feminist theory journal *m/f* in 1983, Parveen Adams and Elizabeth Cowie asked these leading feminist scholars: "What has happened to the Oedipus complex in Lacan's later texts?" Mitchell's response brings us directly to psychosis, infancy, and object relations theory:

> I think the reason why the concept of the Oedipus Complex has disappeared in favor of the castration complex, so to speak, is that in Lacan's return to Freud, his re-reading of Freud, he is stressing that one can, as an analyst, only treat neurosis and not psychosis. And it is only in the positioning in the symbolic, in other words after the castration complex, that neurosis or "normality" start to have any meaning. So Lacan

is attacking all the work subsequent to Freud and by that I don't mean simply all those who wrote after his death, but all the work of object relations theorists, Kleinians, etc. Lacan argues that these analysts are only dealing with the resolution of or the failure to resolve, the shattering of or the failure to shatter the Oedipus Complex. (Mitchell in Adams and Cowie 1983, 9)

Klein, in a theory proposed in 1946 and modified by 1952, identified the Oedipal situation as a process that begins much earlier than Freud posited. She described the infant's normal development as entailing a paranoid-schizoid phase, characterized by destructive impulses and projection of fantasized objects and parts objects during the second quarter of the infant's first year, giving way to a reparative depressive phase characterized by awareness of the mother as an object that can be lost, destroyed, and mourned. Mitchell states that Lacan is critical of object relations analysts' focus on the Oedipus complex. This point is perplexing because Klein and others explicitly shifted the boundaries and its terms, locating it much earlier in the life of the subject, and extending it, as well as rethinking its implications. As Michelle Boulous Walker notes, Lacan, in his "On a Question Preliminary to Any Treatment of Psychosis," takes to task psychoanalyst Ida Macalpine (without mentioning her coauthor Richard Hunter) precisely for *not* interpreting Freud's patient Daniel Schreber's psychotic fantasy properly within the terms of the symbolic structure of the Oedipal complex—the resolution of it, or the failure to resolve it (see Boulous Walker 1998, 58–64; Macalpine and Hunter 1956; and Lacan 1977b, 127–225). In the essay that Lacan critiques, Macalpine and Hunter do indeed argue that Freud, "in his determination to attribute Schreber's illness to unconscious homosexual wishes . . . had discounted Schreber's central theme of *soul murder*," mistaking Schreber's idea of *unmanning* as emasculation and connecting the latter with castration and homosexuality. This error, they note, was perpetuated in translations of Freud's paper (Macalpine and Hunter 1956, 40). They emphasize the theme of ego coherence and its failure—in a word, the failure of cohesion that results in psychosis—as the more crucial content of the Schreber case.

If, as the passage from Rodowick suggests, objects relations theorists really cared most about subject coherence and ego emergence, it can easily be demonstrated that those of Klein's generation and those who followed her work closely spent their energy attending to situations where the normative formation of the ego had not or could not properly occur, and the places where ego formation comes closest to failing. For example, Spitz, a Freudian psychoanalyst working both prior to and alongside Klein, closely observed the failure of the institutionalized infant to move through normative developmental stages toward symbolization, speech, language, and the law. He saw much more at stake prior to and outside linguistic symbolization—notably, the requirement of transitive human contact—for ego formation and the emergence of a coherent subject.

But to return for the moment to the conversation that ensues from this statement by Mitchell: Rose at first challenges Mitchell's claim that Lacan failed to see psychosis as analyzable and refuted those post-Freudians who did address psychosis. But she quickly changes her mind and concurs with Mitchell, even augmenting her point. For Lacan, she concludes, psychosis is the foreclosure of the symbolic. Even in his famous paper in which he discusses Freud's Schreber case and presents his own account of psychosis, Lacan (1977b) understands psychosis as "the *default* of the symbolic, not any idea of failure *within* it" (Rose in Adams and Cowie 1983, 10). From psychosis, and the foreclosure of the symbolic and the transitive relation to the analyst that this condition refuses, we again swing back to the infant and young child, who are similarly foreclosed from analysis because they have not yet entered into symbolization. Rose reminds readers of Klein's case of Little Dick (Klein 1975b), discussed by Lacan in his first seminars (1988). The four-year-old Dick had the language ability of an eighteen-month-old toddler and showed limited affective ability to bond. Lacan, Rose explains, applauded Klein for giving her client Dick a means, belatedly, through which to organize language, a structure through which, in Rose's words (describing Lacan 1988), "the child starts speaking."[4] But Rose is quick to agree with Mitchell's sense that Lacan's description of this case as a narrative that climaxes in the child's belated entry into language performance is off the mark. Lacan "changes what Klein meant," making the analyst's observations about Dick's imagery, action, movement, and behavior into an account about the analyst giving the child a means of entering language (figured in the moment when Klein helps Dick imagine himself as a train entering Mommy). Mitchell concludes that Lacan "equates language and symbolization." Rose agrees, adding that we must keep in mind the distinction between parole and language: "the fact that he (Little Dick) is using speech doesn't mean there is the structure of language" (Adams and Cowie 1983, 10–11).

This distinction is even more crucial as we now realize that this is not a matter of distinguishing between psychotic and normal language development: Dick was in fact likely to have been autistic and not, as Klein inferred, schizophrenic. The distinction is crucial: theories of autism would come to emphasize problems in praxis, the cognitive aspects of affect and empathetic identification with others, as a distinctive feature of the disorder.[5]

In Lacan's perspective (1988), Klein gives Dick a system of symbolization, a "letterbox" through which to organize language. But if this interpretation is not quite accurate, then what may we analyze in the absence of organized transitive language? Or, what might the analyst give the analysand if not the gift of organized, transitive symbolization ability? On this point, Rose remarks that this absence "is why someone like André Green wrote his book *Le discours vivant* (Presses Universitaires de France 1973). He thought that affect was the concept through which you could re-insert, against Lacanian psychoanalysis, a non-symbolic domain" (Rose in Adams and Cowie 1983, 11).

Affect, object relations theory, psychosis, infants, what lies outside language and the symbolic: all are threads mostly not pursued in feminist film theory of the 1980s. Published ten years prior to this exchange between Rose and Mitchell, the extensive account of affect in *Le discours vivant* was issued in its first English translation (Green 1999a) a long fifteen years after the conversation between Rose and Mitchell that I recall here, and four years after Eve Kosofsky Sedgwick and Adam Frank introduced affect to feminist theory in *Shame and Its Sisters*, their 1995 publication of a selection of writings by Silvan Tomkins, the American experimental psychologist who offered an extended empirically based theory of affect.[6] After mentioning Green's book, Rose turned immediately to a set of theorists concerned with the social inscription of the female body: Michèle Montrelay and Luce Irigaray, psychoanalysts who, like Green, studied with but broke away from Lacan. "Femininity to these post-Lacanians [Montrelay, Irigaray] is what psychosis was to post-Freudians [Klein, Maud Mannoni]: It is the 'other' which has not been sufficiently articulated by the theory" (Rose in Adams and Cowie 1983, 11).

That conflation of work on affect with work on psychosis and the feminine was one step in the tainting of affect as an aspect of study. Rose would again align Green with Irigaray and Montrelay in a more extended and obviously critical treatment. In *Sexuality in the Field of Vision* (1986), Rose describes a reading of *Hamlet* by Green that draws on Donald Winnicott, for whom creativity arises "out of a femininity which is that primordial space of being which is created by the mother alone." Green describes this state of being as anterior to the self, "au-dela [sic] de la répresentation" and "before the coming of the sign" (Green quoted in Rose 1986, 137–138). Having again aligned Green (wrongly) with object relations theory because of his reference to Winnicott, Rose also repeats her alignment of his ideas with the writings of Irigaray and Montrelay, this time to emphasize their mutual interest in the physical embodiment of the symbolic. Contrasting Green's *Hamlet* reading to an interpretation by Lacan, who reads the play in the registers of language and the symbolic, Rose takes Green to task for reproducing a negative representation of femininity in which the maternal (as embodiment or ground of creativity) is held responsible for failing to uphold the order of language (Rose 1986, 136–140).

We might surmise that Rose aligned Green with Irigaray and Montrelay because she believed he took the (female) body as the basis for a theory of meaning, suggesting he might fall within the realm of that soon-to-be-overwritten impasse in feminist theory, essentialism.[7] Critiques of essentialism had been circulating since the late 1970s. Monique Plaza's influential polemic "Phallomorphic Power and the Psychology of 'Woman,'" which appeared in *Ideology and Consciousness* in 1978, helped to launch debates about the questionable political investments and implications of Irigaray's use of the body within a year of the original French publication of *Ce Sexe qui n'en est pas un.*[8] Debates about essentialism thus would have been quite familiar to readers of Rose's discussions of Green in 1983 and 1986. Her readers required no further explanation of why work on affect should be handled with kid gloves, if at all.

But my concern is not just that Rose was mistaken in implying that Green might, like Irigaray, suggest that the body is a source to mine for a morphological basis of symbolic meaning. She overlooked the fact that his engagement with affective processes and their bodily course led him to think more closely about the routes through which affect functions both intrapsychically and intersubjectively in relationship to representation. In this project, he was far from advancing essentialist arguments about language and the body. Green emphasized throughout his 1973 book that affective experience is internally routed, "tied to the body" (Green 1999a, 346). However, because this tells him very little of use, he maintains a rigorous concern with the relationship between affect and representation, affect and perception, affect and analytic knowledge and, above all, with the intersubjective routes through which intrapsychic affect processes are projected and transformed in material action.[9] Though tied to the body and internal in its movement, "affective experience," he maintained, "is none the less subjective experience, that is to say, intentional and relational."[10] Affect is "primarily a process that tends to diffusion and extension outside the frontiers of the psyche" (Green 1999a, 295). Yet despite its outward reach, affect's perceptibility by others does not necessarily tell us anything we can directly know by observation. "Nobody," he asserts, "would dare to maintain that the part of the affective phenomenon that is externalizable is enough to give an idea of the internal processes that accompany it" (Green 1999a, 346).

It is this relational model that brings me back to object relations theory—not Green's primary affiliation, but one of the sets of work to which he later returns to modify his ideas on the question of affect and representation (Green 1999a). The problems identified in works labeled essentialist included not only the emphasis on the biological body as a source of meaning morphologically inscribed (as Irigaray proposed in Irigaray 1985b), but also the proposal of a developmental schema that situated the female body as the support of a primitive or infantile stage of the subject prior to language (as some object relations theorists including Klein suggested). Development comes into play in the latter set of works insofar as the feminine inhabits the prelinguistic world not as infant but as maternal space or supportive ground in the intersubjective maternal-infant relationship through which language may emerge in and through the child subject. It is the infant/child's subjectivity and not the mother's that Klein articulates. But what about the other subject in this relationship, the mother? In the work of Nancy Chodorow (1978), Klein's account of the mother's identification with the child is misunderstood as a process of "maternal regression." In Chodorow's view, it is as if the dynamic movement of object relations, the internal-external play of unconscious fantasy, should cease with maturity but does not in the case of the mother. For Klein, however, it is not only normal but also inevitable that the dynamic of object relations extends into adulthood.[11]

To be associated with the world of object relations wrongly understood as an infantile space, and to be constituted as mere facilitative ground of fantasized part-object relations and ego emergence for the child subject, was clearly of potential damage to women in a social movement geared to advancing women's public agency and voice. Rose addressed at length the writings of Julia Kristeva, a theorist whose concept of the semiotic also invokes the extralinguistic and the feminine-corporeal but explicitly rejects the developmental schema. Rose is no less cautious, though, about Kristeva's evocation of psychosis.[12] She expresses relief that Kristeva never offered psychosis as a revolutionary ideal even as she articulated a theory of avant-garde self-negation in which was at stake "the subject's very ability to hold itself together in speech" (Rose 1986, 148, describing Kristeva 1984). Kristeva's maternally connoted semiotic, a space of negativity and "the reject" (Kristeva 1984) and, later, horror and the abject (Kristeva 1982) was troubling to Rose because it situated the feminine outside psychic normalcy and in proximity with psychosis. As Rose points out, Kristeva became problematic for feminism when she concluded that the unconscious could not be politicized, for to engage politically requires communication and performance within linguistic, behavioral, and psychic norms (Rose 1986, 150, referring to Kristeva 1982). For feminism to renounce its allegiances to linguistic and psychic normativity would require women to forgo claims to political agency. The feminine-and/as-maternal trope was dangerous enough, critiques of work on embodiment seemed to suggest, but to elaborate the feminine-as/and-psychosis trope was political suicide—for madness, as Green notes in his work *On Private Madness*, is the "worst shame of all" (Green 1986, 116).[13]

What was at stake, I propose, was the need to preserve for women a position of dignity, which entailed a position within both language and normative psychic models. Social movements require a degree of pride in self (think of the movement paradigms "black pride," "gay pride"),[14] a comportment of respect toward the self-identity category that resists the self-abnegation that is inherent in shame. Respect in the concept of self was not problematic for a liberal feminism based in an ideal of human freedom (a concept that, I will soon explain, is fundamental to Tomkins's concept of affect), but was incongruent with an antihumanist feminism grounded in the notion of the unified subject as anathema, a by-product of fantasy and a tool of patriarchal ideology. Though pride and self did not reconcile with a radical feminism that challenged a humanist paradigm of the self, madness and psychosis were no less troubling paradigms through which to think through a political position for feminism. To think the feminine through the model of the nonnormative psyche was equally problematic. It was only in 1974 that the American Psychiatric Association officially relieved homosexuality of its stigmatizing medical classification as a psychiatric disorder (American Psychiatric Association 1974; Spitzer 1981). To claim an interest in the feminine through models that emphasized the nonnormative aspects of the psyche would risk losing such hard-won shifts that had brought women as well as gays and lesbians into the realm of the norm and rights. At the same time, the potential to look to object relations theory was also foreclosed due to the theory's supposed figuring of the subject as unitary, as already noted, and its reduction of the adult female subject, the mother, to the human subject's facilitator and receptacle for fantasized relations.[15]

This formulation is not too far from Emmanuel Levinas's concept of the rights of man as originally the rights of the other and not of the self. These are the rights upheld through a pathologically passive attachment to the other that grants the other priority over me (Levinas 1999, 149). Affinities with theories that brought feminism too close to the overworked figure of the selfless mother, along with the biological or neural substrate concepts tainted with links to the ideologically troubled body-bound theories of hysteria, were better avoided.

It is not surprising, then, that a relationship within normative developmental phases—passage through the mirror phase and castration, ego/language acquisition, and sexual differentiation—would be grasped as the tacit constitutive bases of a politically useful model of the subject in feminist (film) theory. This was a split subject, but a normatively split one with the capacity to speak and to act within the terms of the law. And it comes as no surprise as well, then, that object relations theory, with its focus not only on modalities other than language and subject states, other than knowledge and being, and including not only infancy but also negatively coded psychotic and depressive states, would be less than attractive to a political feminism. Klein's fundamental developmental conditions of early human life, with the depressive position of the second half of the first year constitutive of the basic form of the ego, would be less than useful to a politics that as a matter of survival was obliged to take as its model a normative if divided subject, and that must refuse for women the roles of service to another and responsibility for the other's survival. Klein's focus on the mother at the service of another's ability to emerge as subject, as the psychic entity on whom depends the violent object and part-object relationships constitutive of the infant's ego, was a concern of criticism so much that theorists neglected what she and other post-Freudian psychoanalysts had to say of potential use. Yet she had much of value to say regarding the infant and what happens along the way when a subject *does* fail to cohere—not only to fail to "hold itself together in speech," but to fail properly to pass normatively through those developmental phases requisite to entering into transitive symbolic language and action requisite for the subject to emerge as anything more than a promise of itself.

Green gives us a means through Freud to approach what was passed over in the turn to speech and language other than a vague notion of something outside of or anterior to the symbolic. What Green offers in his engagement with the concept of affect is a means of theorizing the relationship between affect and representation, and among the body, movement, and space in the cinema—the relationship of the spectator to film world, film object, and film character. Theories of affect, with object relations, can tell us something about the transitive and mobile nature of intrapsychic and intersubjective processes in subject formation, issues that are key to understanding processes of primary and secondary identification. In order to understand what Green might offer, it is necessary to revisit the concepts *identification* and *representation* in relationship to affect.

Empathetic identification

It is a given of poststructural psychoanalytic theory that identification is the operation whereby the human subject is made. Rodowick (1991) observed that a crucial and unresolved problem in film theory's encounter with psychoanalysis remains. This is "the question of sexual identification and sexual difference in spectators—above all through the problem of enunciation or 'subject-positioning.'" He continues: "Despite the achievements of psychoanalytic film theory and textual analysis in the past twenty years, I would insist that all claims made about processes of identification in actual spectators, powerful and important as they may be, are speculative" because "they can tell us nothing definitive about the forms of sexual identification, or the potential meanings, produced with respect to actual spectators." Therefore "one must accept fundamentally that these positions exist only as potentialities that are ultimately undecidable with respect to any given spectator" (Rodowick 1991, viii).[16] Without evidence of the production of meaning in any given spectator, claims about identification are projections, perhaps group projections shared and revised among theorists—speculative theories about categories of viewers to which we also, importantly, belong.[17]

Rodowick's argument is about the impossibility of verifying claims about the meanings produced on the route from any given representation to any given spectator. This amounted to a dead end in film theory around processes of identification and the related problem of dealing in the register of representation. This was as profound an impasse as that identified in the term "essentialism." By returning to the psychoanalytic concept of identification, but not through Lacan, my project follows through on some missed conceptual openings for working through rather than closing down the project that emerged around both identification and representation.

First, I propose that *the concept of filmic identification may be reworked by shifting the discussion from identification to a related term: empathy*. By "empathy," I mean the reflexive experience of awareness of the thoughts, emotions (from the Latin *movere*, linked to movement), or concerns of an other or others. Freud, in a letter of May 1897 to Fliess, described identification as a mode of thinking about objects (cited in Perelberg 1999, 174). More recently, psychoanalyst Rozine Josef Perelberg repeats the formula that this mode of thinking lies at the origins of the constitution of the subject, is an unconscious process that takes place through fantasy, and is fluid in its movement between the masculine and feminine poles (Perelberg 1999, 174–175). The oscillation she describes is consistent with the understanding of identification's fluid movement across gendered positions proposed by Rodowick (1982, 1991), Mary Ann Doane (1984), and Miriam Hansen (1986). But the concept of empathy suggests a different model of identification from that of oscillation among gendered positions. In their handbook of film theory terms Stam, Burgoyne, and Flitterman-Lewis are emphatic that it is absolutely necessary to maintain a distinction between identification and empathy. "Psychoanalytic identification," they explain, "is concerned with unconscious processes of the psyche rather than with cognitive processes of the mind." "Consciously experienced empathy," they continue, "has very little to do with identification in the psychoanalytic sense." They summarize the difference this way: Whereas the formula "empathy = I know how you feel" relies on knowledge and perception as structuring categories, "identification = I see as you see, from your position" relies on vision and psychic displacement to organize its terms (Stam, Burgoyne, and Flitterman-Lewis 1992, 150–151).

Let us put aside the surprising emphasis on knowledge and the absence of the term "emotion" in this definition of empathy, and the puzzling idea that empathy is closer to cognition and consciousness. Stam, Burgoyne, and Flitterman-Lewis do allow that empathy and identification "interanimate."[18] It is this zone of "interanimation," I will argue, the transitive domain of the affects, that can help us to identify "something definitive" about the movement within and among agents active in a field of subjects and technologies of transitivity in which identification occurs. It is in this interanimation that we can begin to consider the movement between identification and expressions and perceptions, between identification and objects, and between unconscious and conscious processes. I will argue that in empathy there is a force in that moment in which I feel that I know how you feel, a welling up and bursting forth of emotion about the object of regard, that is not held solely in the register of conscious perception and expression. In my empathy with you, in thinking I know how you feel, I do not need to know about you or identify with you (or any given object of my attention such as an image of you). I do not see from your position (and it is necessary for me not to, in order to achieve the distance required for pity). I do not identify with myself in a state of self-perception, to recall Metz's famous concept (Metz 1982, 48–50). Rather, in empathy, I will propose, my knowledge comes from the force of the object ("you," the image, the representation), and my reciprocal sense that *I recognize the feeling I perceive in your expression.* "You" move me to have feelings, but the feelings may not match your own. In the model of empathetic spectatorship, we may downplay the factor of knowledge in the experience "I know how you feel" and analyze the nature and experience of that projective relationship in which I am myself "made to feel" and subsequently act "on your behalf." Importantly, you may not reproduce in me the same feelings that I witness in you. Take the example of witnessing grief. Your grief may make me feel surprised, sorry, or angry at its imagined source. Or, I may feel in some sense *responsible* for your grief—not because I believe I have directly caused it, but because I feel that I might, or should, intervene or help—that I can *make a difference* for you. However, I may not necessarily know about or share your experience, much less your grief. I may even acknowledge that I cannot know what you feel from my own experience, even as I "feel for you."

My second proposal is that *projection and the concept of projective identification can be important aspects of empathetic identification.* Introduced by Melanie Klein in 1946, the term "projective identification" describes a form of identification that establishes the prototype of an aggressive object-relation in which hatred against parts of the self are directed toward, and projected into, the mother (Klein 1952a, 102). What is projected is not the hated object or part per se, but a fantasy of an object relationship.[19] Laplanche and Pontalis carefully outline the distinctions among the various connotations of projection and between projection and projective identification. They emphasize the psychoanalytic definition of the term "projection" that refers to a defense of primitive origin whereby qualities, feelings, wishes, and objects that the subject refuses to recognize in itself are projected from the self and located in another subject. Projection always appears as a defense, and as an attribution to another person or thing of qualities repudiated in the self (Laplanche and Pontalis 1973, 349–353). Green emphasizes that projection is an externalization of *a danger* believed to exist in something judged undesirable, or something excessively desired (Green 1986, 85). Projection plays an important part in the development of the distinction between ego and outside world.

Adopting Sandor Ferenczi's term "introjection," Freud rendered this process more flexible in its directionality when he described the subject taking into itself of pleasurable objects, and the expulsion (projection) of whatever within itself has become a source of displeasure to the subject—a dynamic expressed in the language of the oral instinct (Laplanche and Pontalis 1973, 349–353).

Schreber's case is an important one for the development of the concept of projection for the cinema. In Freud's reading, Schreber's intolerable feeling of homosexual love is explained as being repressed inward, transformed into its opposite, and projected outward into the world. Using the example of Schreber, Laplanche and Pontalis compare psychoanalytic projection to cinematic projection: the subject sends out into the world an image of something that exists in himself in an unconscious way. Projection is a mode of refusing to recognize within oneself an unbearable quality or object that is then recognized in an other/outside into which that quality has been projected (Laplanche and Pontalis 1973, 354).

Laplanche and Pontalis offer another understanding in which projection is not "not wanting to know" but "not wanting to be" (Laplanche and Pontalis 1973, 354). They summarize the cinematic mode of projection as confining projection to illusion, and the "not wanting to be" (the "not me but him!") mode as being rooted in subject/outside world-object distinctions. I suggest that in the case of projective identification the two categories of projection they describe are mixed. But knowing and being are not the only modes at stake in projective identification. Neither concept gives us a model adequate for thinking through the modes of, for example, "[not] wanting to possess," "[not] wanting to enter," "[not] wanting to inhabit," "[not] wanting to touch [or be touched by]." *To possess, to enter, to inhabit, to control, to animate, or to touch the other is, crucially and firmly, not to (want to) know or to be the other*. The uncanny charm of ventriloquism, the theatrical convention of *speaking for*, animating a mute other, rests precisely in the difference between controlling and becoming the other. In this relationship we find traces of the concept of interanimation used by Stam, Burgoyne, and Flitterman-Lewis. This process of speaking for will resonate throughout the chapters of this book.

In Klein's "Notes on some Schizoid Mechanisms," the term "projective identification" describes forms of identification that establish the prototype of an aggressive object relation (Klein 1952b, 300). It is in this concept that we may find models that allow us to consider relations with the other that include touching from within, entering, inhabiting, controlling, succumbing to, being engulfed by, and animating (bringing to life) an other. Projective identification's prototype is in the paranoid-schizoid position that is basic to Klein's model of the infant's psychic development during the first year. This process is not abnormal but basic to development and repeated throughout life as a mechanism of fantasy. The subject projects hatred against split-off parts of its self into the mother's body, to phantasize control over her and/ or the infliction of hurt from within. We might say the mother, in Klein's concept, becomes a benign receptacle of evil. Interanimation, however, is an important aspect of the process. Projection always takes two subjects, and we should not assume the recipient to be passive. Even in the child's fantasy, there is the illusion that the mother is in control and may come to life, retaliating and projecting back.

Discussing the role of identification in projection, Laplanche and Pontalis note that it is unclear whether there is a valid distinction to be made between those modes of a process where the subject makes himself one with the other, and those where he makes the other one with himself (Laplanche and Pontalis 1973, 357). They frame this problematic in terms of the internal identificatory experience for the subject who projects. But they stop short of asking the questions of whether and how projective identification impacts the subject who is the recipient of the projection, and whether "making one-self one with another" can be an adequate description of a relationship that may include the dynamic of engulfment or destruction of the other. As I have already suggested above, making one—unity—may not be the most accurate concept to describe the volatile and mutable subject-object relationship in projective or introjective identification.

C. Fred Alford takes account of the complexity of projective transference in a discussion of Heinz Kohut's concept of the splitting of the ego. He notes that for Kohut it is not desire that splits the ego but faulty empathy. The part of the self not empathetically responded to by the other goes underground, where it "acts on its own." The mature part of the ego rationalizes the pursuits of the part of the self that seeks satisfaction in destructive ways. In the therapeutic relationship, the analyst who offers empathetic acceptance is also the "dustbin" for projected bad parts in a negative transference relationship (Alford 1991, 32). Alford emphasizes the intersubjective aspect of this splitting, which always occurs in reference to an other. He asks, what parts of the self are given up to others? How extensively? In what type of practice or process, and in relation to what other processes? These are, Alford point out, essentially questions about the social contract. Who contracts with whom? What is given up, what is retained? Can the contract be rescinded? For Alford, projective identification is a central aspect of social relations (Alford 1991, 33–34).

Green emphasizes the importance of the role of mediation and appearance (representation) in this interanimated relationship between subjects in projective identification. "The relationship of projection to reality via the medium of appearance," he states, is a basic unresolved relationship in the concept of projective identification (Green 1986, 84). Projection, inextricably linked to perception, he explains, entails a double inside-outside split: the first being that between the subject and object, and the second an intrapsychic split into the preconscious-conscious, on the one hand, and the unconscious, on the other (Green 1986, 85). He uses a cinematic metaphor to describe this relationship. The screen is "the other in reality," something like a "movie" to which the subject's eyes are glued. The subject's eye (his "bad eye") is projected into the image on the screen, where it is made an integral part of the subject's projection. The eye is "screen and projection all in one" (Green 1986, 85–86). Here we may recall his idea that the representation "is no more than the avatar of the eye as look and of the look as eye that looks at it" (Green 1999a, 227). The paranoid psychotic is not conscious of the split that occurs in projection. In this he differs from the neurotic, who retains the ability to distance himself and see himself seeing (as in one of Metz's versions of the spectator). With the repression of the reality of the split and without the distancing perspective of an internalized other eye, the struggle is shifted into the real—that is, into the resonant field of interactive social space that encompasses the ego and the other. Green likens psychotic paranoia in the narcissistic relationship of subject to object to the correspondence between projector and screen.

Green introduces a third subject to the subject-object relationship of projective identification. His example is the position of the older brother as imago between subject and father. The small difference between the subject and the brother is never eliminated, he explains, frustrating the subject's wish to reach the brother's envied position of being the more beloved son. "Such is the other, my fellowman," writes Green of the brother (1986, 98). This position is compared to Donald Winnicott's concept of the transitional object. For Winnicott, the transitional object is the first non-ego possession. It sits on the "having" side, as a "not-me possession" and not on the "being" side. Here we arrive at a model of the relationship of possession: not knowing and not being but influencing through a mediating transitional object in a potential field. Green states that for him, however, the double is on the being side. The double is the first object with which the subject changes place. The projection required to constitute the double and become the other allows the eye to tear itself from the screen (Green 1986, 98–99). My interest, however, is to stay with Winnicott's other as an object *to be had*, through which one may exercise influence transitively. His concepts of the potential field, the transitional object, and the ability to be with an other will all come into play throughout my discussions of film texts and intersubjective experience in the chapters that follow.

What is the impact upon the object, the recipient of projective identification? The psychoanalytic sociologist Simon Clarke notes that revisions to Klein's work on the concept have emphasized that projective identification is intersubjective and communicative. Projective identification affects the recipient (Clarke 2001b, 1). Clarke describes the route of the projection's path into the recipient in terms that suggest that the passage of psychical objects (such as "feelings") may impact the recipient quite powerfully (Clarke 2001a). "Projection *per se* may not be damaging as the recipient of the projected thoughts may be blissfully unaware," Clarke explains. "Projective identification may, however, involve a forcing of such feelings into the recipient" (Clarke 2001b).

Clarke, like Green, describes the subject who projects feelings as a *projector*. I will pursue the connection to the cinematic technology that also takes this appellation. Metz's famous claim about the spectator's self-identification happens to invoke the figure of the projector in this way. Equipment, Metz explains, is both metaphor and real source of mental processes (1982, 51). The statements "I take no part in the perceived, on the contrary, *I am all perceiving*" and "it is I who make the film" (48) are directly followed by an explanation that destabilizes the singularity and unity of the all-perceiving I, suggesting its dependence upon an other that is, precisely, the projector: "I know that I am really perceiving" in the cinema because "there is a projector" facing the screen. In this model, the projector is the other on whom I depend for my sense of all-perceiving unity. Metz makes this point clear in his statement that "it is not I who am projecting, or at least not [I] all alone" (48). What is projected is "deposited in me as if on a second screen"; "I am the place where this really perceived imaginary accedes to the symbolic." What the projector gives the subject is an imprint or trace, an entity that is also described parenthetically as an introjection (50). It is only after affirming the place of the projector that Metz makes the oft-quoted controversial claim that "the spectator *identifies with himself*, with himself as a pure act of perception (as wakefulness, alertness): as the condition of the possibility of the perceived and hence as a kind of transcendental subject, which comes before every *there is*" (48–49).

Metz's evocation of a transcendental self was abhorrent to readers of the 1980s seeking to theorize the subject in terms of its constitutive splits. This claim of the cinema's power to produce in the subject a retrograde sense of self-unity, no matter how "radically deluded" the spectator is understood to be (52), was not appealing to film theory at a moment that was moving toward an understanding of the subject as being self-aware of and even reveling in its basic condition of fragmentation and reduplication. The concept of a deluded subject suffering from false consciousness or collective psychopathology was not adequate to this newly emergent postmodern subject. One might say that the film theorist's response to the self-perceiving subject was first "not I!" then "not them either," and finally "if them, so what?" (Žižek 1992). Focusing on, and rejecting, Metz's surprising suggestion that the cinema could be a machine for producing fantasized self-unity and transcendence, film theorists overlooked another important shift in context and frame at this point in Metz's discussion. As the spectator "identifies with himself as look," Metz continues, he "can do no other than identify with the camera, too." The camera, however, is absent. Standing in for the camera (the instrument of the look) is the projector, the instrument of transitivity. It is at this point in the text that Metz reminds us of the body in its relationship to the work of fantasy: the projector is positioned "behind him [the spectator], *at the back of his head*, precisely where fantasy locates all vision" (49). Attached to this statement is a footnote to an essay by André Green (1970), with which, Metz explains, his own discussion happens to coincide.

The cast of characters and theories invoked expands even further. In a parenthetical reference that makes a rare exception to the Lacanian model employed throughout his book, Metz brings in Melanie Klein to make a point about vision. *All vision, Metz posits, consists in the double movement of projection and introjection* (1982, 50). If we take Klein as the source of these concepts, then all vision involves processes of projection and incorporation of fantasized part-objects. This is exactly not to say that the subject identifies "with" the part-objects projected, much less with the projector-apparatus or with himself. Rather, the spectator participates as recipient in the volatile dynamic of object relations, a concept that situates the subject and in which signification is only a partial aspect, and may not fully be in place. Cinematic space is potential space, and it is also *projective* space (Young 1994).

Here a crucial disinction needs to be made. Robert Young notes that for Kleinian analysts, psychoanalysis is solely about internal objects. Winnicott's notion of potential space and his use of the concept of transitional objects emphasizes an intermediateness—neither internal nor external—that is absent in Kleinian thinking. Young writes, "[This] sense of intermediateness is exactly what I feel sitting in a theatre, listening to music, reading, watching a sunset. I cannot say where my hopes, dreams and longings end and what I am taking in from the experience begins. There is a merging, a congruence, a suspension of boundaries. I am in the theatre, *in* my mind and *in* the cultural experience—all at once" (Young 1994).

But Metz does not take us far enough with his reference to projective identification to reach the point where we might see what identification would be like in a model that places the subject in a system that takes seriously the Kleinian meaning of projection. Nor does Metz's account recognize Winnicott's expansion of and break with it into the concept of potential space that Young describes above. Metz quickly absorbs the concepts of projection and introjection, along with Green's discussion of projection (which is imbued with his focus on the movement of affect), into the Lacanian concept of identification as a series of mirror effects organized in a signifying chain. The spectator, Metz rapidly concludes, *duplicates* both the projector and the screen. The film is "what I receive, and it is also what I release." Finally, "I am the projector, I am the screen" (1982, 51). Secondary processes cover for primary, and the cinema, "chain of many mirrors," is after all *like* the body, *like* a tool, *like* an institution: "it is really all of these at the same time" (51). Here we arrive at the mirror model of identification

taken up by film theory, a model of the replication of the subject as being
and knowledge of being.

Green's break away from Lacan was in part a rejection of the reduction
of all to discourse, all institutions to the discursive pattern of isomorphism,
the endless "chain of many mirrors" in a process like signification (Metz
1982, 51). The concept of projective identification tells us nothing about
how the image might function between projector and recipient, how mediation of projected part-objects occurs, and what are the forms taken by
part-objects other than dream-like representations of body parts to which
cling the values "good" and "bad." I suggest that we turn back to Metz's
(Green's) concept of identification to mine it for its implications regarding
projection and introjection, recalling Althusser's concept of interpellation
as summarized by Silverman (1983, 48–49) in which it is noted that the
"others" that hail us (projectors) may be instruments and images, texts and
technologies. The first change I propose to this model is to dissociate the
projector from the spectator—to allow that introjection does not necessarily entail becoming (one with) the projector, but rather to be "filled in" or
emptied out (gutted, as in "the image wrenches my gut") by the projector.
Second, we should allow that the inductive process is reciprocal and moves
between spectator and projector. The spectator and the projector oscillate in
their roles as actors upon one another, but their actions may differ and may
entail passive aggression. In my discussion of empathy earlier in this chapter,
I noted that when I respond to your projective look or call, I do not need to
"see as you see" or "feel as you feel" in order to recognize what you feel, or
to "feel for you" and act on your behalf. The next modification is to recognize the role of nonisomorphic intersubjectivity in cinematic projection. The
observations of Clarke and Young about the recipient of projections for
the most part assume the projector to be a human subject, and the medium
is tacitly taken to be present, bodily performed interpersonal communication (the therapeutic situation that involves two people, for example, or the
oft-cited example of the mother and child). Their points about projective
identification beg some questions about the recipient that are remarkably
like the questions addressed by effects research with regard to the media
audience member who is influenced by the mass media message: Might the
spectator-recipient of the projection notice that she has been "projected
into"? Might she know what hit her? Does she recognize the status of the
projection's representational content as "only" fantasy? Can the projection
act upon her? How might the recipient contribute, even passively (through

appearance or gaze direction, for example) to the constitution of the other's projection? Does the projection require some degree of recipient consent or invitation (such as the look or the smile of the mother), even if passively and unconsciously delivered? What are the effects on the spectator-recipient, whether she is cognizant of the projection into her or not? Does she act in response to the projection and how might we observe and describe her responses with accuracy?

Relevant here is an observation made by media effects theorists Paul Lazarsfeld and Herbert Menzel (1963) that challenged models of communication flow such as the hypodermic needle and limited effects (Klapper 1960). Lazarsfeld and Menzel observed that audience opinion is filtered through several levels of opinion leaders in addition to being influenced by media texts (Lazarsfeld and Menzel 1963, 295). We can surmise from this point that significant if overlooked elements in the formation of recipient response to projections are the internalized views of others and body-to-body relationships and the spectator or recipient's observation of facial and performative affect in the speech and behavior of those influential "opinion leaders" (parents, teachers, therapists, social problem film narrators) to whose judgments the spectator is beholden. In an era dominated by the scholarly claim that the media shape opinion and ideology, we would do well to remember that what also moderates media reception is observation of other people, and immersion in the affective relationships that pass between bodies and among communities, on screen and off.

Effects research addresses information, behavior, and opinion. Affect, the quality that comes heavily into play when we engage in person-to-person interaction, carries influence in the personal moderation of projected "messages." But since there is nothing unambiguously to measure or to represent in affect, it has gone largely unremarked upon in media effects research. We might describe as a sort of "media research" the attempts of Tomkins and his colleagues and successors to produce a scale of infant and adult expression on film and video (Izard 1982). Object relations theory, like theory of affect, has provided little toward an understanding of what constitutes the object outside the ideational representations of fantasy as it exists in the mind of the human projector. This gap in theory requires us to think also about affect as it interanimates with ideational representation. This is precisely the domain of much of Green's work, and a question to which he returned at the end of the century (Green 1999b). Klein emphasized part-objects as the elements of projection, postulating that the projector and recipient traded in a moral system of imagined part-objects drawn out of and thrust into one another's bodies. The part-body images are imbued with moral value. Winnicott (1971) gives us a concept of objects in their material investments. Transitional objects are real-world entities (blankets, stuffed animals) invested with meaning through the wear and tear of intensive bodily use to the point of their attachment and incorporation as parts. The child pulls, strokes, licks, and drools upon the blanket, projecting itself into the object and taking the object into itself. Intermediate objects such as vomit and feces help to complete the picture of the object as an entity that materially channels the body's overflows and influxes of feeling.

What is distinct about the concept of projective identification is the emphasis it places on the directness of this psychic impact from human subject to human subject: the original model is the proximal relationship between mother and infant. As recipient, I may be touched by the force of sound and image, but this is not to be confused with the direct look, appearance, and physical contact of another human subject. Winnicott's transitional objects come close to providing a model of mediation such as that provided by theories of cinematic representation, but his theory takes us a step further by emphasizing the physicality of the mediating object. We might ask not only *did* the recipient feel the projection, but also *how* did she feel it—that is, by what route was she touched (in her heart or her gut, for example),[20] whether she registered the projection consciously or not. It is this force and the change effected by it through the spectator-recipient who reacts that distinguishes between projection, which may consist and remain "inside" the projector as "harmless" fantasy, and projective identification, which entails intersubjective mobility and material transitivity—in which projection is acted out relationally. The latter is a communicative dynamic that may be conducted in words, gestures, expressions, actions—and in media texts and through media and communication technologies—in the empathetic field. Fantasy may thus be brought into the realm of transitive mediation and transformative action, in potential space that is, importantly, not solely psychical. This change in the model, recognizing the recipient as an active agent who may respond in ways much more complex than to notice or not, enjoy or not, or "resist" or passively accept the invitation offered by the projection to introject it, makes of the identificatory process a complex network of forces that pass among subject, recipient, others and/as objects, and fields of engagement.[21]

To put this in clearer terms: projective identification requires a better theory of communication than a subject-object model of knowing and being in the world. It is inadequate to rely on a model that gives us a line of force both directed inward and "expressed" outward (through bodily appearance, gesture, expressions, words) and interpreted at the point of its perception, as in "When I see your expression I know how you feel." No longer adequate is the model of the screen or mirror as agent for feeling communicated and mirrored back, isomorphically, by the other, as in "I see how you feel and I feel your feeling too," or in the other's passive role as unwitting screen (in which the object unwittingly mirrors the projector's feeling).[22] To be absolutely clear, I am arguing that the projection may produce not precisely misidentifications, misrecognitions, or oscillations in identificatory orientation, but reciprocal, nonisomorphic affective processes in the recipient. He or she may then act, or not, in ways that are unpredictable and based on the set of intrapsychic and intersubjective forces introduced in the empathetic field of action. In that field, representations may have a materiality and autonomy (the "freedom of objects" described by Tomkins, discussed later in this chapter) not typically acknowledged in post-Kleinian psychoanalytic theory.[23]

What concerns me in the complexity of the mediation of the empathetic process, then—the intersubjective and introjective-projective movements through which I feel that I "know how you feel" and in which I am moved by your appearance or your image to "feel for you" (and perhaps even to speak for you) but not to imagine myself to "feel as you feel" or "do as you do." Green describes the relationship between the projecting subject and the recipient as one of isomorphic or homologous mirroring (Green 1986, 86, 92–94). His model is from the standpoint of the projecting subject: "I am him, he is me" (Green 1986, 92). Swinging around to the empathetic viewpoint, I propose a different take: both the projecting subject and the recipient of the projection may "feel for" the other. But this is not to be the other or to feel "like him" (to feel as and what he feels). Perhaps what Rodowick cautions us against ultimately is the empathetic mode of film theory that says of spectators "I have knowledge about how you feel," for knowledge claims about film spectatorship are ultimately empathetic in nature, constituting spectators as within a class or subcategory of identity (female, black, lesbian, Asian spectatorship, and so on) even if empathy is not what film theory was after in studying identification. It is precisely this response, "I know how you feel," that Sedgwick counters in her critique of axiomatic claims about fantasy and sexualized subject positions (Sedgwick 1990, 1–63). Moreover, the affective aspects of identifactory responses may be transient and mercurial. Malcolm Bowie (1991) gets at this when he writes: "A long gaze at the Pacific may be taciturn at one moment and loquacious the next" (199). I am suggesting that we consider a method that allows us to analyze the individual intrapsychic specificity of empathetic identification, and also the varied representational expression of empathy in different experiential moments shaped by the intersecting conditions of group and personal life.

Lacan suggests that the ego is "a hodgepodge of identifications," misrecognized images of self-identity (cited by Stam, Burgoyne, and Flitterman-Lewis 1992, 147). I wish to suggest that we consider the aspects of the psyche that are constituted through a hodgepodge of affective forces that are intersubjective and recognized as nonisomorphic but reciprocal, in a field of empathetic resonance whose material sites may include not only the body of an other but also the photograph, the cinema, and the networked computer, between subjects and through intersubjective, communicative mechanisms of fantasized object-projection and introjection. Fantasy moves us and takes objects into its path, externally as well as internally. "One always says," Green observes, "there is representation and then one must not forget that affect accompanies it." We might analogize this understanding of affect to the sound track as accompaniment to the cinematic image, or the left hand's role in producing chords for the right hand's melody in the performance of a composition for piano. Why not the contrary, Green proposes: "*the profound nature of the affect is to be a psychical event linked to a movement awaiting form*" (Green 1999a, 268, his italics). The film text is, in this model, a movement to be traced for the material routes by which it elicits feelings in spectators, and not only a representation to be mined for its possible meanings with regard to being and knowing.[24]

Green suggests that we imagine the affective process as "*the anticipation of a meeting between the subject's body and another's body.*" The psyche is also defined in terms of this relational model: "*The psyche is the relation between two bodies one of which is absent*" (Green 1999a, 312, his italics). This model may remind readers of Lacan's formula of desire as that which emerges in the space between subject and object. It is not to be confused with this formula, however. For Lacan, desire is situated in the distance or difference that separates the subject from the object it seeks but which it will never meet. As Mary Ann Doane reformulates this in her rereading of the Oedipal complex and/as the subject's advancement to sexual difference, "distance from the 'origin' (the maternal) is the prerequisite to desire"

(Doane 1982, 12). What constitutes and fills in that distance or difference, insofar as we can know it, is language. For Green, that gap is less clearly explained. It continues to be the focus of a study of representation in its relationship to affect (Green 1999a). Green's affect is a set of processes active at both the conscious and unconscious levels of a psychic topography. Affect may include the drives. Affect works in conjunction with representation (perceptions) and other subjects in ways not yet fully understood. As unfixed as it stands in relationship to the term "representation," his concept of affect gives us important insights into how we might understand what constitutes the empathetic field of identification that includes both of those entities, representation and affect. Thinking through affect, I will argue below with Green, allows us to understand how that overworked entity of film theory, representation, is mobilized—is vivified and rendered transitive and materially transformative—consciously and unconsciously, internally and between subjects, and through actions and impressions that include vocal sound, expression, and gesture, and mediating technologies.[25]

Affect and representation: André Green's Le discours vivant (1973)

Green suggested in 1973 (1999a) and 1986 that affect, even as it "commands a large part of our [psychoanalysts'] efforts," is evasive. Affect constitutes a "challenge to thought." Moreover, affect has been spurned from Freud to late-century psychoanalysis in favor of work on psychic representation (Green 1986, 174). Returning to the topic of affect and representation in 1999, he identifies the same problem: "One [still] meets in certain analysts a great deal of resistance to conceiving of psychical states in which affects and representations are simultaneously present in a mixed form in the unconscious" (Green 1999b, 293). In 1986 he provided a backstory to this resistance. He described the battles that raged in French psychoanalytic circles during the 1970s over the respective functions of representation and affect, and the consequent divergences of method and interpretation that resulted. His mentor Lacan's act of "standing up against the entire psychoanalytic community," returning to the word of Freud by giving precedence to speech and language, is noted as a crucial move (Green 1986, 6). But the Lacanian school that emerged, Green observed, consequently emphasized representation at the expense of affect, "showering sarcasm on all who refer to it [affect]." The Lacanian school's use of Freud's statute of representation, he further charged, not only emphasized representation over affect but rendered representation "disincarnate" (Green 1986, 234), reducing discourse to the representational register alone and spurning *le discours vivant*, that is, affect.

Central to Green's understanding of affect is his perception that a career-long split can be identified in Freud's writing between the concepts of representation and affect. Freud "remained faithful" throughout his work to the opposition of representation and affect, moving alternately between the two terms even as he understood the two registers to be interdependent and interconstitutive of the human subject (Green 1986, 212). But in *The Interpretation of Dreams* (1900), Green observes, Freud made a fateful move. He organized psychic space between two poles: perception (the psychic screen of the dream) and motility (downplayed in *The Interpretation of Dreams* because of the relative paralysis of sleep). Freud's theory of the psychic apparatus, Green argues, was achieved in this text. However, Green concludes, this achievement was "at the price of a fascination with representations, to the detriment of affects" (Green 1986, 180).

Two things must be emphasized regarding this narrative of affect's neglect. First, affect is defined by the dominant psychoanalysis of the time, according to Green, in a binary system that situates it as a mobile, internally directed force, and as the rival of perception and representation, which are apprehensible and outwardly oriented. For a theory of film, this splitting of "shy" movement and "gregarious" perception is both a troubling and interesting historical legacy to reflect back upon. If representation, the pole of Freud's interest emphasized by Lacan, allowed film theory to theorize perception with great specificity, then did we lose sight of a concept that might have been helpful in theorizing film in terms of its place in relationship to movement—not as depicted action, but as psychic motivation—might we say, drive? Second, if we follow Green, affect/movement appears to Freud in *The Interpretation of Dreams* as an absence (sleep as "relative paralysis")[26] and loses Freud's attention, which turns to the more alluring, discernible site of representation: the dream scene/screen, memory contents, ideational representatives. Not only is affect elusive (fleeting, hard to see, hard to document), then; it is also an object of disdain, spurned first by Freud, then by Lacan.

Green speculates that Freud's spurning of affect in favor of representation may have been strategic: perhaps Freud anticipated that an account of affect might be more readily dismissed by those whose approval he sought in order to gain legitimacy for psychoanalysis as a science. The system of psychic representation, oriented in perception, generates more demonstrable and objective evidence (dreams, performances, utterances that can be described and quoted). The affect system, described in terms of the quantitative trope of unmeasurable, inner-directed, neuronal forces and charges relative to fleeting and transitionally apparent objects was not an easy target to study, much less to describe. If Freud wanted to garner scientific respect for his method, affect would not be the easiest concept to model in 1900.

Whether or not this was Freud's line of thought, and whether or not Green is correct that this choice of representation over affect was a matter of political strategy and professional pride, Green's account is significant. It accurately identifies a split between two terms, "affect" and "representation," and a favoring of the latter over the former—a relationship that is emphasized by Lacan and inherited by film theory, as well as by "certain analysts" alluded to by Green. We thus inherit an overdeveloped concept of representation (which has run its course, as the turn to affect in film theory demonstrates) and an underdeveloped, shady concept of affect along with allied concepts such as internal movement, force, emotion, instinctual impulse, abreaction, and drive. It is easy to turn away from the seemingly bottomless well in which we catch glimpses of the rent between affect and representation. The task of disaggregating the form and content of that space is paralyzing.

Green notes that, ironically, the aim of proving psychoanalysis as a science was not in fact achieved in Freud's turn away from affect to representation. Freud succeeded in "attracting to himself" not men of science but their opposites: "men whose vocation was to respond to human suffering," analysts who recognize the "determinisms at work in their own psyches" as inseparable from their practice and their thirst for knowledge. This response to something called "human suffering" will be at the center of the concerns laid out in *Images of Waiting Children* (Cartwright forthcoming), where I make a crucial detour into the nonpsychoanalytic terrain of sociologist Luc Boltanski's theory of the spectator of human suffering (Boltanski 1999). However, I must first set out with some clarity the place of Green's concept of affect in this discussion.

What is relevant about Green's reading of Freud on affect is not only the fact that Freud is argued to have favored representation, but that the spurned register, affect, is identified as the basis of another professional split: that between a soft humanist and a hard, scientific, antihumanist approach to the treatment of psychic life. Affect, Green suggests, was subject both to professional scorn, in the case of the antihumanist Lacanian response, and to strong professional identification, in the case of those men attracted to Freud—men who cared about human suffering, men who were cognizant of their own psychic implication in a transitive social process that shaped their practice and knowledge. Affect "from this moment on," from *The Interpretation of Dreams* forward, holds an "ever uncomfortable position" in psychoanalysis (Green 1986, 181). Affect is uncomfortably placed not only because it is elusive and therefore hard to speak of, but also because analytical awareness of it implicates the analyst in an uncomfortable proximity both to his subject and to his own affective state.

If the purpose of psychoanalysis is to treat and to cure mental disturbance, then it is something of a paradox that psychoanalysis emerged within medical practice (psychiatry) as one of the few clinical treatments that involved diminishing physical contact over its history after its incorporation into medicine.[27] The nonproximal, virtual relationship between analyst and analysand, conducted through words, is reinforced by the classical talking-cure model that positions the analyst as listener removed from the body and from the day-to-day movements of the analysand, who lies or sits immobilized. In recognizing their own affective responses, analysts enter into the troubling terrain of their own psychic investments and identifications, their own appearance and bodily reactions shielded from the analysand's view in the classic mode, or confronting the analysand in the face-to-face conversational mode of analysis. That affect is associated with "feelings," emotions, and expressions, not "ideas," representations, and perceptions, is perhaps one reason why it was avoided in a phase of psychoanalytic theory, from Freud to Lacan, that emphasized knowledge. Perhaps also this is why representation became such a cornerstone not only of twentieth-century psychoanalysis, a practice whose choreography in its early years entailed the avoidance of the interocular look in the analytic context, but also of film theory, a discourse that, in Martin Jay's view, developed out of a "denigration of vision" in philosophical thought—a mentality of casting the eyes down from the body, as if in shame, that can be traced through to the end of the century in critical theories of film and visual culture that take representation as their object of critical analysis (Jay 1993).

Green's agenda is not to achieve balance by turning to affect as the object of isolated study. Representation and affect, he asserts, cannot be studied separately. Tracing the development of the concept of affect in Freud's work, Green notes that for Freud affect has always been bound up with the concept of discharge—with a process in action and movement, but with that movement directed "towards the interior of the body" (Green 1999a, 8). Much of Freud's writing on the concept was articulated through descriptions of situations where affect is brought into check, intercepted, or routed inward, only to erupt outward in symbolic activity. Like hysteria, an inward process whose outward expression is captured in the static frame of the photographic serial motion study so famously produced by the neurologist-photographers of the Salpêtrière, affect could be tracked only in its representational effects. The "Studies on Hysteria" (Freud and Breuer 1957) were in fact Freud's earliest engagement with the concept of affect. They give an account in which affect, linked to traumatic memory, is blocked. Affect is the force behind that blockage which mobilizes representation. Affect, an interior force, erupts in disorganized motor activity, divesting the body of the force of the charge (Green 1999a, 13–19). Or, affect is abreacted through speech acts, "pouring out" verbally. "Language," Green explains, "not only allows the load to be unblocked and experienced, it is itself act and abreaction by words" (Green 1999a, 15).

Green notes that in these cases, one should not give greater emphasis to memory or ideational representatives over the forces of the id and affect, for affect is a requisite condition of both. Similarly, "language cannot be shifted to the side of representations, for it is itself a form of abreaction, equivalent to the act" (Green 1999a, 16). Green's point is that the two are interdependent in producing the performed speech-act, and not that affect is prior to language. His model of affect described below should clarify this point.

Green identifies Freud's "Project for a Scientific Psychology" as another important source of Freud's development of the concept of affect. It is in this reading that we find two concepts crucial to *Moral Spectatorship*, communication and the moving image. They are articulated in ways that will resonate throughout these chapters. In discussing satisfaction as the first model of desire, Green explains, Freud identified communication as "a secondary function of highest importance" in the fulfilling of need by satisfaction through an external object (another subject): "The initial helplessness of all human beings is the primal source of all moral motives [Freud, *SE* I, 318]. One can hardly stress too strongly this primary link between discharge through emotivity and motricity, and the function of communication, from which language springs" (Green 1999a, 24).

Having asserted that in this period of Freud's work the link between emotive discharge and communication (the drive to satisfy oneself through an other) functions as the source of language, Green goes on to associate satisfaction with the inner movement of desire, the internal aim of the affect ("inner discharge") and a perception of the object that aroused desire. From now on satisfaction will be associated with the image of the object that first aroused it and the moving image of the reflex movement that allowed its discharge. *"This is a new relationship between perception of the object and internal discharge (through its trace in the image). Moving image and affect are therefore linked"* (Green 1999a, 24, my italics).

Thus affect is hardly just the emotional state of the primitive experience mirrored on screen. It is its reproduction in a form that brings together the inward, inner movement of affect as tension and discharge in and through the subject's body with the perception of, and also communication toward (in the form of a signal), the subject who arouses desire. This second subject, I will propose, may be the spectator apprehended by the projective force of the image, who may be apprehended bodily, and who may be "moved" in this process. Affect may take the projective form of communication through language and bodily signification, and through "the moving image of discharge" (Green 1999a, 24).

Green's own model of affect is constructed in comparison to graphic models of the psychic process in the constitution of the subject offered by Lacan (taken from Lacan 1977b, 193) and Klein in her theories of the schizoparanoid and depressive processes that occur during the infant's first year (see Green 1999a, 220). Green notes that Lacan, by his own admission, installs narcissism at the center of his reading, whereas Klein emphasizes the structuring roles of the good-bad dyad in constituting the ego through object relations. His own model brings together four terms: conjuncture, event, object, and structure, connected by what he calls "a circuit" (Green 1999a, 222).[28]

Desire and identification occupy one side of the circuit, affect and negative hallucination the other. Green's concept of object is of special importance here, because for Green its first property is to be constituted by desire and identification (Green 1999a, 222–224). Affect is situated on this model as the pivot. It is "at the place of an encounter between the effects of the tensions aroused by the object and the event," a "zone of interpenetration" and also a "point of turning back." Affect is the point at which the vectors amass their effects as force and as subjective experience. Affect, thus, plays a conjunctive role. It is the "pivot of the system" (Green 1999a, 226).

Having outlined a model of the psychic process in which affect is the centerpiece (replacing narcissism in Lacan and the good-bad dyad in Klein),

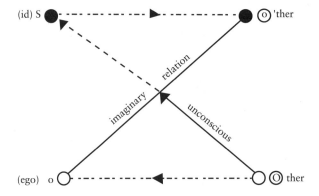

1. Lacan's model of the psychic process in the constitution of the subject.

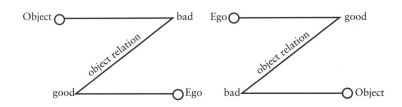

2. Klein's processes of the schizoparanoid and depressive positions.

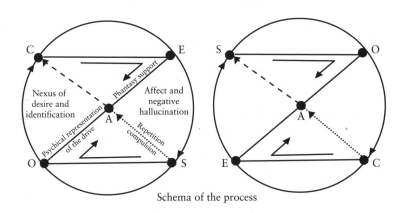

Schema of the process

3. Green's model of affect. Figures 1–3 reprinted from André Green, *The Fabric of Affect in the Psychoanalytic Discourse.*

Green makes two further points that are relevant to my later discussions. The first is that affect is not only conjunctive but also disjunctive. Earlier, Green had noted that affect, when it breaks the screen of consciousness, is "the epiphany of the Other for the subject" (Green 1999a, 215). In this breaking through there is a subversion of the ego. The subject is driven to the brink, "the old background of childhood is reborn," and the subject "becomes the other." In this process affect "becomes a power of loss, even in elation, orgasm, triumph" (Green 1999a, 216). Referring back to this breakthrough of affect to consciousness, Green posits that an effect of the breakthrough to consciousness is to abolish or replace representation in the form of negative hallucination (Green 1999a, 226). Typically defined as *not* hearing, tasting, smelling, seeing something right before us, negative hallucination in this sense seems to engage repression. But negative hallucination, Green argues, entails neither lack or deficit of representation nor repression, but rather is a condition of representation's possibility. The representation "is no more than the avatar of the eye as look and of the look as eye that looks at it" (Green 1999a, 227). This concept of negativity is useful to film theory because it suggests we might approach negativity as something other than motivation for a reading of latent meanings, structuring absences, or evidence of repressed or subjugated voices and meanings.

Green notes that affect has, in psychoanalytic theory, occupied the privileged place in conceiving "the return" as the process of turning against oneself and into the duality of the pleasure-unpleasure principle. He proposes a further theoretical mode of the field in which the subject is defined as *process*. This term reflects the first publication of this text in 1973, during a period dominated by structural thought, and seems akin to Kristeva's concept of the intertextual construction of the subject-in-process that negotiates an other from within itself.[29] "Process" is defined not only in the sense of movement, development, and progress, but also in the legal sense, as the production of an outcome of a conflict determined by examination and judgment (Green 1999a, 228). I will shortly be interpreting this concept of the subject in light of Adam Smith's concept of the spectator. Green explains his rationale for this juridical concept of process by comparing Lacan's emphasis on pleasure with his own interest in suffering, the quality he observed in the men attracted to Freud not for his science but for the awareness of the affective register that his work evoked in them. "Psychoanalytic experience teaches us that, although it is the absence of [Jouissance] 'that makes the universe vain' [Lacan 1977a, 317], it is through suffering that the truth of the subject is attained" (Green 1999a, 228). Analysis, Green concludes, is a process that aims at control of the affects of suffering by "detachment" from the drives that cause it (Green 1999a, 229). My next step is to put Green's thoughts on affect that I have stitched into a loose patchwork here into dialog with some of the observations about affect drafted by Tomkins.

Silvan Tomkins: Affect wants to be free

Silvan Tomkins could easily be the "nobody" in Green's admonition "Nobody would dare to maintain that the part of the affective phenomenon that is externalizable is enough to give an idea of the internal processes that accompany it" (Green 1999a, 346). For Green, the aim of work on affect is to help the subject who suffers to come to terms with the forces of affect, to help the subject control (which does not mean to inhibit) the dissolution that the ego is threatened with in its anticipation of a "meeting between the subject's body and another body" (Green 1999a, 289). Tomkins's writing on affect, slightly in advance of Green's, never enters into the domain of psychoanalytic treatment. Though they both write extensively on affect, the two seem to have failed to sound each other out. But their mutual omission is understandable. Whereas Green had his sights set on clinical analysis and the psychoanalytic literature, Tomkins dedicated his efforts to looking and recording his observations on the evidence of affect in the bodies of subjects including himself and those around him. His was a psychological theory of affective process, Green's a theory geared toward clinical treatment.

Tomkins's daring strategy of staring affect in the face and attempting to describe and classify it is worth investigating for film theory for many reasons, not the least of which is to mine his idea that *affect wants to be free*. His observation-based materials supplement Green's theory-rich but example-poor text.

Reading Tomkins on Freud's concept of affect, we come away with a heavily depleted term compared to that offered by Green. Freud, in the view of Tomkins, was not concerned with affect proper at all. Rather, Freud's concern was primarily with the drives. Tomkins uses a cybernetic metaphor to describe the relationship between the two terms. Affect is "a motivational system of great complexity." The complexity of this system makes possible varieties of freedom. By contrast, the drives are "a motivational system of little freedom" (Tomkins in Sedgwick and Frank 1995, 34). He compares the affect system to the computer, which can perform the operations of scanning all relevant information and determining and following through on appropriate operations, and the adding machine, whose function is limited to addition on numbers fed to it. "Both systems are determined," he explains, "but one is freer" (Tomkins in Sedgwick and Frank 1995, 35; see also Wilson 2002).

A living system is, moreover, a feedback system that becomes freer as its wants and its ability to satisfy them grows. "The freedom of a feedback system, we argue, should be measured by the complexity of its 'aims' and the frequency of their attainment" (Tomkins in Sedgwick and Frank 1995, 36). Affect is a motivational system that differs from the drives in its potential to be controlled in the process of satisfying aims, thereby maximizing human freedom. Affect, unlike the drives, has a degree of competency and complexity that affords it the relative ability to motivate the human to greater degrees of freedom. For freedom is measured quantitatively, in degrees of cognitive competency and complexity. Tomkins even proposes a principle for freedom, suggesting Freud's pleasure principle as the model. He calls it the information, complexity, or "degrees-of-freedom principle" (Tomkins in Sedgwick and Frank 1995, 35). Drives, on the other hand, are handicapped in their limited cognitive competency and complexity. Drives score low on the scale of degrees of freedom/information/complexity and are therefore unlikely to be of use in facilitating human freedom.

Readers will be familiar by now with Stewart Brand's quip, famously circulated among freeware advocates, "Information wants to be free." It is interesting to hear that in 1962, not only information but also human affective processes were believed to be motivated by this desire for freedom. But let us put aside the mid-century cybernetic metaphor that constructs freedom in terms of quantity and information access. In his discussion of freedom of the affect system Tomkins methodically lists the ways in which affect performs its freedom. Unlike the drives, which increase in intensity until satisfied, affects vary in rate of intensity over time. The "density tolerance" of affect, its intensity times duration, varies as compared to the density tolerance of drives, which have low density tolerance where survival is at issue. In the drive for air, "low density" may result in death, for example (Tomkins in Sedgwick and Frank 1995, 51). Affect, according to Tomkins, is free to invest in possibility: "Yesterday's pain is not painful today." Memory is part of a learning response in which remembering does not necessarily evoke the original affect, as in the case of the burnt child who learns from the surprise of the burn to fear the flame. Tomkins devotes considerable attention to the ways in which affects link to objects with a freedom not characteristic of the affects activated by drives. Masochism and Puritanism and the ability to love the object that is death, and to hate the object that is life, are Tomkins's examples of the freedom of objects in the affect system (Tomkins in Sedgwick and Frank 1995, 52–55).

This concept of "freedom of the object" in affect has relevance with regard to Rodowick's claim that "processes of identification in actual spectators, powerful and important as they may be, are speculative" (Rodowick 1991, viii). The object (image) that fills me with disgust may fill you with pleasure; I may respond in ways that are not congruent with the responses predicatively linked to my identity category. Identification is something we cannot track, because fantasy is interior to the psychic life of the individual and therefore is subject only to speculation, and in any case may not be based in isomorphic identification.

But empathy is something we can track by shifting our focus to a nuanced model of affect that accounts for intersubjectivity, transitivity, and the flexibility or "freedoms" of the affect system described by Tomkins. The notion of freedom merits articulation. The object to which I impute a characteristic may evoke affect, but the evocation of affect may in turn restructure the object within the terms that I seek. This formulation is in keeping with the psychoanalytic idea that the object is a cause of desire as well as a condition of desire's existence. The term "desire" implies that we are dealing in degrees of pleasure. Taking this into the realm of film theory, it is the image that causes my desire and that is also a condition of my desire. I may impute qualities I desire to the image; however, I may also restructure the image's qualities, investing it with qualities I desire it to have in order that it may serve my interests. The possibilities for using the image in the production of desire are thus quite fluid.

Compulsory compassion

However, the concept of desire, even when conceived in terms of *degrees* of desire, does not account for all that the object may ask of the spectator, or all that the spectator may ask of the image/object. The image may "give me" something that I want, or it may "thrust upon me" something else. I may invest an object (which I imagine to be an object of beauty, of banality, of horror, or of shame) with the capacity to *give* me pleasure today, and still this same object may *make* me sick tomorrow. Although Tomkins does not put it this way, the object of affect (which may be a person, an image, a material artifact) is always subject to projection, and can be subject to projective identifications that may animate and anthropomorphize the object in the narrow sense by giving it the power to "make me" feel. In this interpretation, Tomkins's freedom of the object places the subject who experiences affect in the same position as Levinas's subject who grants priority over the self to the other (Levinas 1999, 149)—to the "face" that interpellates him, *projectively.* Fantasy and projection are essential, then, to the freedom of the object in the affect system. Whether the image *gives* or *makes me* depends on what it is I believe I have asked of it, and whether it is an image that has the "freedom" to make demands of me that override my own demands of it. In either case, I may continue to look—because I feel compelled, because it feels better to look, because I feel I should, or because I believe that I choose to look even against my pleasure. Or, I may turn away in moral repugnance, or in shame, or out of my own pride or respect for the other. I may feign performance of any of these responses because I think you expect a particular response of me, and I feel I should comply because you are morally right, or because I wish to go unnoticed in the group, or to save face. I may turn my eyes from an object of "beauty" out of jaded boredom, out of disgust toward its interpellative draw, in shame over my attraction to it, or in disciplined self-denial of pleasure. It may be my pleasure to hoard my "beautiful," "shameful," or "compelling" objects/images and look at them later. Or, I may feel compelled to share them with others (endlessly on the Internet or the Web, for example). I may continue to look in the face of an image that makes me sick because the image makes a demand I feel compelled (or "choose") to act upon, even as and precisely because the image pains me. I may act on that demand even if I do not really feel compelled in my heart to do so, because I believe others would expect me to. Would this be compulsory compassion? This concept has yet to see the analysis it deserves, alongside compulsory heterosexuality, as a problem that cannot be resolved through the twin paradigms of choice and inner feeling.

Further still, there is much more between those two poles of being pleased and being sickened—more possibility (more "freedom" in the object's course in relation to the spectator). I may feel tender compassion for the object that hails me. Or I may feel burning compassion, or dispassionate. I may feel some other sentiment, or nothing. What is free in this formula is not the object alone that moves along its many possible routes of investment in the spectator, but also the subject's negotiation in putting the object to work through investments of fantasy, to act on its behalf, or to engage it in some way that may be other than resistance or pleasurable engagement. In this sense, freedom is not a matter of the will (of the object or the spectator), but of the limitations of both desire and choice as they vie with other forces. This occurs in an empathetic field of spectators and objects. Demands are asked for, made, and accepted at the levels of the conscious and the unconscious, intrapsychically and intersubjectively.

"It is this somewhat fluid relationship between affects and their objects which offends human beings, scientists, and everyman alike," Tomkins explains. This fluidity has led to "suspiciousness and derogation of the study of the feeling life of man" (Tomkins in Sedgwick and Frank 1995, 55). In the end affect is "free" in the same sense that information is "free." Like information that spontaneously seeks a unique, unpredictable route through the Internet, affect follows the principle of degrees of freedom in which inhibition or resistance (blockage) results in the seeking out of a new route for affect's expression. Affect may freely "pour out" in a torrent of words or gestures, or it may be directed inward, as in the case where my face remains a controlled impassive mask while others cry or cry out in response to the object, even as the object may wrench my gut. Or, unmoved by the object-image, I may crease my brow and draw in my breath just so, in order to comply with what I perceive to be a social expectation that I should feel (and involuntarily exhibit through my body) a degree of anxious concern. What is also "free," then, is my ability to control the expressive and signifying modalities of affect, even as I may not be free to control the feeling that courses through me. "Repression" is not the operative term here. To control affect is not to keep it in check but to perform its outward signs in ways that may not conform to the logic of isomorphism between performed expression and inner feeling. This is not solely a matter of conscious manipulation. My neurological makeup may incline me to *involuntarily* perform the "wrong" affective response irrespective of my "true feelings," as in the case of the individual with a compulsive speech disorder who may be compelled to say "the wrong thing," or to make "the wrong face" in response to a motivating scene.

Tomkins helps us to perform a crucial shift that takes us back to the beginnings of structural film theory and the observational psychology of the filmology movement. He gives us a model in which we may put the spectator, rather than the film image, in the position of subject of the theorist's observational gaze. In film theories that focus on the image we encounter the problem of representational isomorphism that, I propose, is at the heart of work on affect. The "freedom" of the spectator-subject to play with the signifying and expressive registers of affect, willfully or not, has profound impact on the ability of the observer of affect, Tomkins, to make claims about the meaning of observed expression. Tomkins provides compelling descriptive detail about the appearance of affect and its possible meanings and relationships to inner feeling and, to a lesser degree, to neural processes. But it is Green who offers an account of representation in its relationship to affect, allowing us to steer clear of the one-for-one claims about bodily appearance and meaning that rightfully are anathema to visual theory.

Throughout this book, my attempt has been to articulate with care the qualities and conventions of the empathetic field in which affective processes motivate identifactory processes that are mapped onto the bodies of screen characters, and are projected into the body of the spectator. Recall the formulas: empathy = "I know how you feel" and identification = "I see as you see, from your position" (Stam, Burgoyne, and Flitterman-Lewis 1992, 150–151). My concern is not with what knowledge "I" (the spectator) believe myself to gain when "I know how you feel," but with the feelings and actions effected "in me" when "I" think I know what "you" (the object or image that I contemplate) feel. My feelings are not isomorphic with yours (I do not feel as you feel) any more than my knowledge or standpoint is isomorphic with yours (I neither believe myself to see as you see nor apprehend myself in the act of seeing/knowing). Rather, knowing "how you feel" produces feelings "in me" (the spectator) and acts through me. Of concern throughout *Moral Spectatorship*, then, is the problematic of motivated action: how "I" (the spectator) *respond* when I believe that I "know how you feel"; what is produced "in me" when feelings are projected through representations; and how I act in response to that process, whether I am cognizant of my affective response or not.

Film theory has been attentive to sexual pleasure, addressing it by reading films that live in the negatively coded registers of horror and anxiety as well as in the positively coded registers of sexual love and affection. The classification of affects offered by Tomkins is useful to film theory in its elucidation of the range of registers we might consider. In the class of "positive" affective experiences Tomkins names only two categories: interest-excitement and joy-enjoyment. The transitional category of "resetting" holds the sole affect surprise-startle. Negative affects are more numerous:

distress-anguish, fear-terror, shame-humiliation, contempt-dismell, disgust, and anger-rage (Tomkins in Sedgwick and Frank 1995, 56–57, 109–250).[30] My strategy throughout this book has been to retain the categories but to downplay the binary value-schema. I prefer to see affects not as value-fixed but subject to the varied forces, if not "freedoms," of attachments, historical determinations, responses of other bodies, and transitional objects such as photographs, television and film images, and computer keyboards and displays.

CHAPTER TWO

THE (DEAF) WOMAN'S FILM
AND THE QUIET REVOLUTION
IN FILM SOUND: ON PROJECTION,
INCORPORATION, AND VOICE

Listeners and speakers

This chapter mines the historical terrain of film representations of deafness in postwar British and North American film melodramas. I offer textual readings of films that posit the belated achievement of speech as the social birth of the Deaf female child as subject. Deaf girl characters and the medium of voice were invested with particular meanings relative to subjectivity and agency in melodramas produced during the decades of the twentieth century after the Second World War. In the United States, this period saw a transition in dominant deaf educational methods from oral instruction to sign language and mixed approaches. Technological changes included the introduction of smaller hearing aids and developments leading toward experimentation with cochlear devices by the end of the century. Even as American and British Sign Language gained status and recognition as languages in their own right, deaf oral speech gained ascendancy in the popular imagination through advances in technologies like the cochlear implant. At the same time, the postwar period was marked by significant transitions in film sound technology that coincided with changes in the meanings and function of sound, listening, and voice in postwar public culture in Britain and the United States. The sound revolution of the late 1920s is a familiar chapter in film history. Stereophonic and magnetic sound systems used in post–World War II film production and exhibition, I propose, represented important changes not only in the industry's technological practices but also in the cultural meanings and practices involving sound and voice on- and offscreen. The period of the 1940s and 1950s saw a relatively silent revolution in film sound—silent in the sense that it was subject to very little press promotion and has received relatively minimal attention by film scholars. By focusing on postwar melodramas featuring Deaf girls who come to voice through oral speech and signed English, I enter this terrain of the silent revolution in film sound through a historical context that situates sound technology as a component of the moral systems through which ego and agency are socially constituted.

The films considered in this chapter include *Johnny Belinda* (1948); *Mandy* (U.S. release titles *Crash of Silence* and *The Story of Mandy*, 1952); the documentary film *Thursday's Children* (1954); the Helen Keller biopic *The Miracle Worker* (1962); and, finally, *Children of a Lesser God* (1986). In reading these films and their original, spin-off, and sister texts my thematic focus is the status of sound and voice as affective media of agency and subjectivity. I consider the ways in which changes in the technologies and meaning of sound and voice were worked through textually in the postwar British and North American maternal woman's film, the popular subgenre of melodrama well known for its depictions of mothers and daughters.[1] My focus is a subdivision of the maternal melodrama: films that feature Deaf girls who undergo a "talking cure" and come to voice with maternal caregivers. The films I consider mix documentary elements from the social problem film and the biopic forms into the conventions of the maternal melodrama. They rehearse stories about female agency and subject formation in the intersubjective production of agency across the bodies of girls and the maternal caregivers (mothers, as well as other caregivers, such as doctors and teachers, male and female) who bring them to voice.

Projection and containment of vocalization—working through to the ability to perform the social function of projecting oneself in vocal sound and containing the vocal expression of another—are the key processes I will be considering. As Michael Renov (2004) has explained, documentary film can be a medium through which trauma and loss are worked through (120–128). Deafness is figured in these hybrid-genre films in terms of a crisis of the subject that entails a working through to voice as agency, in this emotional sense. We might imagine hearing and speech, or the hearing child, to be the entities represented as "lost" in these texts. I will explain below that it is the ability to serve as a projector and container of voice, along with the social performance of listening in the sense of obedience, and not simply the ability to hear or to produce speech in the sense of orally expressed language, that figure most powerfully as the loss these narratives seek to address. To project and contain vocal sound, and to perform the discipline of listening, are the literal and metaphorical media of child agency and subjectivity projected in these films. The fantasy these melodramas enact is the belated emergence of the child as subject—as autonomous being who comes to voice, and who may choose to listen within the terms of the law, belatedly and through a particular sort of medium: the selfless maternal caregiver, who performs these roles of projector and container with and for the child.[2]

In my use of the concept of *listening* below, I regard the verb through the etymological roots it may share with the term "lust" (Ayato 1990, 325–326). Listening is, in this etymological sense, connected to desire. This incidental notion, a coincidence of possible shared origins, lingers in the term's leanings away from the passive shadings of "hear" and toward the active connotations of "obey," a word that suggests compliance through action. Though archaic, this possible connection between listening and lust is helpful to recall in considering the role of listening relative to desire in the formation of a self who achieves a sense of belonging and self-representation through compliance with familial and national terms. Compliance has a passive connotation. The connection of these words, "listening" and "lust," to the adjective "listless" is significant in this regard. A child who is listless is without lust for life. He or she might lack the desire, or moreover the ability, to listen—that is, to comprehend and to obey. Whereas refusal to listen connotes the pleasurable assertion of an ego exercising independence in its act of choosing not to obey, lack of ability to listen suggests an inability to recognize oneself as being the subject of a command and to sublimate the desires of the self to the will of another and answer the command, as in some cases of selective mutism.[3] "Listless" is a term used to characterize the child who does not seem to possess either the will or the ability to listen and to articulate its desires in the form of behavior that answers a command, despite having the sensory and cognitive ability to hear and to speak. Two aspects of the verb "listen" converge, then, in the space between ability and desire: for the child, to listen is not only to hear and comprehend the demands of adult authorities, but also to be able to both recognize and sublimate the self in answer to the demands of another.

My objective, in identifying as subgenre a Deaf "woman's film," is not simply to bring to light the underconsidered presence of deafness and Deaf characters in the mid-twentieth-century sound-film maternal melo- drama, a genre closely studied in feminist scholarship. Rather, as a hearing spectator—as a listener of these texts about Deaf girls and their caregivers, my objective is to uncover some of the meanings assigned to intersubjective re- lationships between Deaf and hearing caregiver characters in texts produced for hearing audiences during a period of dramatic technological innovation in theatrical film-sound instrumentation. Postwar sound innovations were implemented not only in hearing technologies for the Deaf (the refinement of hearing aids and the development of cochlear implants during this period, for example) but also in the film industry, where the postwar years saw in- novations including stereophonic sound projection and magnetic recording. In addition to investigating the meanings of deafness and Deaf characters in these films, I also consider the multivalent textual and technological mean- ings of sound and listening in the postwar historical moment of the transi- tion in sound technology that followed the Second World War. In the films I consider, sound, and especially the act of listening, is assigned complexly layered meanings and politics relative to gender and power in the postwar world, but not most crucially with reference to language and the word. The Deaf female child body in the maternal melodrama is one location where the meanings and politics of sound were played out for a hearing viewing public. But the drama played out is not precisely one of coming to voice in the sense of entering language. Rather, these films dramatize the intersubjec- tive process of achieving the ability to project and contain vocal sound, and the ability to control one's status as a receptive medium—a status that I link also to the concept of listening.[4]

The main goal of this chapter, then, is not to interpret a thematic or suggest a new subgenre. The films I discuss are vehicles through which I develop a set of arguments about the nature of screen characters relative to the problematic of projective identification and containment, or incorpora- tion, relative to voice in spectatorship theory. My emphasis, as in the previ- ous section, is on the relationship between affect and representation, and between empathy and identification. Although I do not discuss the direct relationship of the spectator to the screen image and to film sound directly in much of this portion of *Moral Spectatorship*, I do describe at length the textual interrelationships of screen characters as they are constituted in image and sound. My proposition is that screen characters, like human subjects, are always constituted as viable and cohesive models of human subjects through intersubjective and multimodal relationships of projection and incorporation. This process of constituting the subject, on-screen and off, occurs through a range of technologies of appearance, voice, and interaction.[5] The technology of the gaze, as Mladen Dolar (1996) and the film theorists discussed in this chapter note, is enacted not only in sight but also in sound. By technologies, I mean not only instruments and artifacts but also and most importantly bodies. The bodies I consider engage in caregiving and the reception of care; in teaching and learning; and in dialogic interactions performed in attempts toward speech that entail nonverbal aspects of vocalization, gesture, touch, movement, and eyesight—all elements of the gaze.

In accordance with this understanding of the body as a site of technology, I propose that we think about the close relationship between the two meanings of the term "speaker." A speaker is a technological instrument of sound incorporation and projection. It is also a human incorporator and projector of vocal expression with and for another. The affective and projective dimension of speakers in the human sense is made clear by Tomkins in his writings on the concept of the amplification of affect (1980, 1962). In what follows, the two meanings of speaker are intertwined.

As noted in the previous chapter, identification with screen characters is a film theory concept that requires more careful material disaggregation and analysis. I recalled the brief description offered by Laplanche and Pontalis (1973) of a complex form of identification that is both heteropathic and idiopathic, "invoked to account for the constitution of a 'we'" (206). The central concern of this chapter 2 is this interconstitutive and multidirectional, multimodal form of identification as it is enacted in relationships between characters and through technologies of voice and agency on-screen. What is produced, I propose, is not exactly the collective unit "we" suggested by Laplanche and Pontalis, but rather a way of being a subject together with, and through, others. I borrow from Melanie Klein the concept of projective identification, introduced in chapter 1, to build an idea of intersubjectivity. This concept is brought into the realm of this interconstitutive model of subject formation on-screen. I make a case for understanding the subject as always intersubjectively and multimodally constituted with human and technological others.

Film theory offers a range of approaches for understanding the spectator's shifting and multiple identifications with either characters or with the apparatus, but is less instructive about how screen characters are constituted as entities harboring a unitary identity, and how this takes places across bodies, objects, and technologies in the narrow sense. Little has been said about how screen characters are constituted as viable and compelling models of human subjecthood with which spectators might identify. The pages that follow provide an account of screen character formation and spectatorship that picks up threads of apparatus theory. Though this chapter is filled with many points and claims about the history of postwar Deaf melodrama, affect, and voice, the single most important idea it puts forth is this discussion about screen character emergence and the projective and incorporative modes of identification modeled there. In reading these films as I do below, through the framework of empathetic identification and affect introduced in the first chapter of this book, I will be emphasizing the intersubjective and multimodal nature of identification and subject formation represented within and between characters in these texts.

To make claims about affective responses produced in the bodies of film spectators is notoriously tricky, as I noted in the previous chapter with reference to Rodowick's cautionary point about an impasse in spectatorship theory.[6] This chapter of *Moral Spectatorship* attempts a different route to understanding identification and psychic aspects of subject formation enacted on-screen, through an account of the material constitution of screen characters as viable models of human subjects and as emotionally compelling objects of identification. This has relevance to questions of spectatorship insofar as it is never the character alone with which spectator-listeners identify. Rather, agency is forged between and among characters and/as technologies in an intersubjective and multimodal field, and it is in this field that spectator identification occurs (Alač 2005, Latour 1999).

The film analyses included in this chapter are empirically descriptive and detailed microanalyses. I consider representations of physical contact between bodies, facial expression, gesture, sight and control and direction of eye gaze, and hearing and speech among characters, as well as technologies of sound and voice as they are embedded in character constructions across figures and technologies of interaction on screen.

One last contextual aspect of this chapter requires mention. Like chapter 3, which is on autism and facilitated communication, it is directly engaged with ongoing work in the relatively new field of disability studies. One of the many contributions of this field is the alternative it proposes to the deficit model of physical, cognitive, and sensory impairment. I consider representations of impairment of sensory abilities in screen characters (blindness, deafness) as sites where the production of human subjects occurs in ways that vary from norms, rather than regarding representations of impairment as ciphers of lack or absence of human subjectivity, signification, and meaning. As I will note below, previous work in feminist film theory has most often posited sensory impairments as ciphers of lack. This approach has been tacitly normativizing. I shift this orientation to suggest deafness and blindness as conditions that are always constitutive of particular sorts of relationships of subjectivity and as particular sorts of identificatory models. Deafness and blindness involve different routes to subjectivity and different ways of constituting agency that deserve to be read in more subtle ways. My intention is to avoid identity-based claims about disability, instead contributing to theoretical models for understanding aspects of identification and multimodal subject formation, using the insights of the psychoanalysts introduced in chapter 1.

Repetition and working through in the Deaf melodrama

Christine Gledhill reminds us that the melodrama form is founded on plagiarism (Gledhill 2000, 225). The subgenre of the Deaf woman's film is, true to this formula, rife with copies and copies of copies. To read maternal melodramas that feature Deaf girls as original texts or as an exceptional subgroup within the genre would be misleading, for they have been typical of the melodrama's patterns, and particularly that of generic proliferation. The repetition of the Deaf-girl-who-comes-to-voice theme in the sound cinema has been an important means of collective, public working through of the social meaning of deafness in the hearing world. In this section I detail some of the ways that repetition informs the practice of working through that is enacted across the Deaf melodrama and its sister texts over time.

The repetition mode of the melodrama joins with the social problem form as a vehicle of working through in the Deaf melodrama. The two concepts *compulsion to repeat* and *working through* require some discussion in order to ground their use here. These concepts appear together for the first time in Sigmund Freud's essay "Remembering, Repeating, and Working Through" (Freud 1958a). Freud describes the analysand as compulsively repeating the same action, acting out rather than working through unconscious and repressed entities. Freud emphasizes that "the patient does not *remember* anything of what he has forgotten and repressed, but *acts* it out," reproducing it "not as a memory but as an action" without knowing that he is performing repetitively (Freud 1958a, 150). Freud describes the compulsion to repeat as a "playground" for the therapeutic situation. Admitted into the transference, the playground of compulsive repetition allows the neurosis to be granted a new, indeterminate, "artificial" and more transparent meaning situated between fantasy and action in the world. Through the repetitive enactments played out over and over in the transference-neurosis, a transition can be made from acting out to working through (Freud 1958a, 154). For Freud, working through rests on the side of verbal vocalization. The cure is achieved through talking. But we might also look to nonverbal vocalization, gesture, gaze, and touch—all present in the field of play—as important means through which acting out and working through are carried forward between analysand and analyst. The social problem–melodrama hybrid form, I propose, functions a bit like the transference-neurosis "playground." The hybrid genre is situated not between fantasy and action in the world but between conventions of fiction and nonfiction, between the cinema as space of fantasy and other spaces of social interaction in the world, and between screen characters and spectators. In this transitional space between the melodrama and the social problem film forms, we see staged the acting out and working through of social issues that are otherwise largely left unspoken, subject to stigma and shame in the public culture of the postwar period.

Any description of a shared psychical space as playground must acknowledge Donald Winnicott's building on Freud's term with his concept of transitional space: the arena of relational embodied experience that resides between the internal psyche and the external other (Winnicott 1971d). For Winnicott, to play is to engage in creative, intersubjective experience. Only in playing, Winnicott states, "is communication possible, except direct communication, which belongs to psychopathology *or to an extreme immaturity*" (Winnicott 1971b, 54, my italics). I am interested in the ways that maternal melodramas, using campy fiction as material ground, play out an idea of "direct communication" that belongs to the "extreme immaturity" often associated with the world of the child and imputed to the mental world the mother inhabits with it. My concern throughout will rest in this intersection: the movement between acting out ("immature," as if "direct," communication between characters) and working through as maternal and child subjects come to voice in the communicative "playground" of the intertextual, intersubjective experience in and across film text, context, technology, and the historical world of audiences. In this playground we hear familiar stories that resonate in forms including the remake and the copycat film. The Deaf melodrama stages the process of coming to voice in the space between child and maternal bodies, a site associated with direct communication, immaturity, and play as a means of materially rehearsing (and thereby acting out and working through) intersubjective models of subject formation that are imagined beyond the screen. They are, in a word, invaluable bad copies without an original.

In the early writings of Gilles Deleuze, repetition is a movement generative of simulacra, not of an original myth or narrative (Deleuze 1995, 92, 123–125). We might call these sorts of copies "bad," not only because they do not have the status of an authentic source but also because they are so often maudlin and tawdry. The melodrama's status as bad copy is part of its appeal. Repetition of the same old story may drive the listener to distraction, like the tape recorder stuck on playback or the voice of the nagging mother. Melodrama is thus a kind of demon repetition technology. Green (1999b) notes that it is the demonic aspect of the repetition compulsion that is most often overlooked in discussions of the concept (29–30). Fictional repetition can be demonical in the senses of "bad" described above. My concern is with the psychically "demonic" connotations given to doubling and bodily control imputed to the maternal figure–Deaf child pair on film. As we shall see in my discussion below of, for example, the Helen Keller–Anne Sullivan pair, and especially in the cases of facilitated communication considered in chapter 3 of *Moral Spectatorship*, repetition and doubling are subject to widespread mistrust and consternation because of the perceived threat to independent subjecthood they present.

Acting out and working through occur not only through the film text but also across the public personas of particular performers (via news stories and biographies) and typecast roles, as well as across originals and "bad" (tacky, infidel) remakes (serial novels, plays, films, and made-for-TV movies). The texts I consider below constitute an interknit set of series, the sentiments and meanings of which resonate among genres, titles, and the lives of performers and fictional characters. As instances of a repetition text continually undergoing reinscription and reinterpretation, the Deaf melodrama has been subject to revivals and shifts in produced and received meaning. In the case of the performers in these films, what is repeated is not simply the story line from role to role, but the characters' involvements in a set of texts and contexts that allow them to oscillate between the reciprocal roles of daughter and mother, victim and caregiver. For the listening audience, too, there is the experience of identificatory oscillation (between the positions of child and caregiver, for example). Through these texts, cultural anxieties about sound and voice relative to the process of women and Deaf children acquiring agency in the public sphere are acted out and worked through by audiences witnessing these dramas in a larger national and historical context. It is in this sense that the filmic text becomes a public "playground" where repetition and playback build national bodies through identification and fantasy.

Intersubjective play in the transitional space between shame and pride is familiar territory in the maternal melodrama. The psychologist and theorist of affect Silvan Tomkins describes "joy" and "shame" as terms that are mutually constitutive and which are the basis for social interaction.[7] A familiar figure in film studies is the character Stella Dallas, standing (at the end of the eponymous film) outside an upper-class home gazing in through a window at her daughter, who stands radiant, the object of admiration on an upper-class society dance floor. The child subject's narcissistic-exhibitionistic enjoyment is approvingly mirrored and confirmed in the gleam in the mother's eye, a reflection that the psychoanalyst Heinz Kohut identifies as a moment in the constitution of the child's self[8] (Kohut 1971, 116). Although the child does not witness her mother's proud look, her performance is conducted wholly according to the script her mother has imagined with her. In her mind's eye, she basks in the approving gaze of the mother. But Stella's pride and joy in her daughter don't displace for either the shared shame that has motivated this upward class transition. Rather, pride and joy reside alongside shame, and are heightened by its copresence in the framing of the mother-daughter pair. The daughter projects joy back out to the mother, who takes this projection in. The mother identifies with her daughter, but not isomorphically. Pride and shame are fluid and move across the transitional space between them in a manner that interconstitutes them as subjects. We arrive at a screen articulation of that complex subject unit, the "we," with whom spectators might identify.

Viewing once again this climactic selfless-mother instance in *Stella Dallas*, a moment compulsively repeated across maternal melodramas, their remakes, and writings about them, we might recall the sense of attachment and responsibility to another that is characterized by the philosopher Emmanuel Levinas as "love without lust" (1999, 129), the passionate "attachment to the other in his alterity to the point of granting him a priority over oneself" (Levinas 1999, 149).[9] I propose that we read this moment in *Stella*

Dallas and other maternal melodramas not solely within the terms of a paradigm of selfless maternal masochism but also in terms of an enactment of the reciprocity and attunement of affect (Stern 1985, 142–144). Affect is attuned when psychic states are coproduced in a shared social field. We might also see this moment as an instance of the form of identification in which is articulated the complex production of the identificatory "we" noted in passing by Laplanche and Pontalis. Linda Williams has written about the effect of multiple identification in the soap opera form, in which the spectator is divested of power but empathy is increased (Williams 1990, 153). I mean the "we" unit to remain more narrowly among a set of characters and spectators who constitute one another simultaneously.

The psychoanalyst Daniel Stern introduced the concept of affect attunement to describe intersubjective psychical states of emotional resonance in which the feeling state but not the overt behavioral manifestation of the feeling is mirrored. Stern takes pains to distinguish affect attunement from the isomorphism and synchrony that are implied in the terms "mirroring," "mimicry," and "echoing." "Mirroring implies that the mother is helping to create something within the infant that was only dimly or partially there until her reflection somehow acted to solidify its existence," he explains. The term "mirroring," as used by Lacan (1977a), Mahler with Furer (1968), and Kohut (1971), suggests a process in which the mother-as-mirror consolidates the child-as-other. With the concept of affect attunement, Stern proposes something close to my concept of empathetic identification, although he insists that his concept shares only some aspects of empathy. "Attunement takes the experience of emotional resonance and recasts it into another form of expression," he explains. Attunement, however, "need not proceed toward empathetic knowledge or response" (Stern 1985, 145). My interest lies in the empathetic resonance that takes place in the repetition that occurs in these texts not only between mothers and daughters but also across characters and remakes. These films are the "playground" in which we see empathy attunement played out.

By tracing in detail the network of repetitions and doublings that characterizes this set of films and their characters and performers, as I do in the next section, I demonstrate two points. First, through these films' repetitions and doublings melodramatic fiction merges with documentary form to render the films socially relevant in a way that is different from other film and genres of the period that perform a similar crossover to their contemporary milieu. This crossover occurs not only in and between the film texts and their various remakes for stage and screen, but also in the larger social context that includes the screen roles and the public lives of these films' key performers. Repetition and doubling enacted at the textual and technological levels come into play in the controversies about oral speech as the paradigm of voice that is at the core of these film texts and the life stories they evoke explicitly or indirectly.

Melodrama, textual repetition, and doubling
in the Deaf woman's film

Material evidence of repetition within and across the films considered in this chapter is abundant. *Johnny Belinda*, originally a short-run Broadway play (Harris 1988) about a Deaf miller's daughter in a remote fishing village, saw its screenplay recycled into three made-for-TV movies, most recently in 1982 (directed by Anthony Harvey, starring Rosanna Arquette). It was then revived in a stage adaptation of the film script (Harris 1988). *Mandy* (1952) was based on a 1947 novel by Hilda Lewis titled *The Day Is Ours*. The film was described by a *Variety* reviewer, at the time of its U.S. release, as copying *Johnny Belinda*'s theme. *Mandy* clearly influenced the production of *Thursday's Children*, the 1954 British documentary short about children in the Margate School for the Deaf, who, in the rhyme recited on the film's soundtrack by narrator Richard Burton, "have far to go" before they achieve voice and enter the hearing world of postwar Britain.[10] Scenes from that documentary fall in line remarkably with school scenes in the earlier fiction film *Mandy*. In *The Miracle Worker* (1962), Arthur Penn brought to the screen the original cast of the successful 1959 William Gibson Broadway stage play of the same title. The play had started out as a television script in 1956. It is in *The Miracle Worker* that we see most vividly the doubling and repetition that takes place across the life and work of the performer beyond the film itself. In the 1957 *Playhouse 90* series live television broadcast, Teresa Wright won an Emmy for her performance of Anne Sullivan. Like Marlee Matlin, the Deaf stage performer turned screen and television icon, Wright was a former child star. Introduced to the public as a dazed "ex-schoolgirl,"[11] Wright built on her persona as the actress who had played the seventeen-year-old "good daughter" to Bette Davis's evil perimenopausal mother in *The Little Foxes* (1941). Wright's image ricochets between "special child" and devoted mother throughout her career. In 1942 she appeared in the role of girl-bride twice, first in the Academy-Award-winning role of wife to Lou Gehrig, the hero whom she selflessly supports to his death through the progressive and fatal neuromuscular disease, amyotrophic lateral sclerosis (ALS, aka Lou Gehrig's disease), in the biopic *Pride of the Yankees*; and then to a teenaged pilot who marries Wright, the high-born British girl next door, in the U.S. film adaptation of the prewar British newspaper serial *Mrs. Miniver*. In the latter maternal melodrama, a film that served as an important stylistic reference point for the postwar *Mandy*, Wright, at the age of twenty-three, played the orphaned society girl who is one of the two Mrs. Minivers referenced in the film's title. As the younger Mrs. Miniver, Wright dies in the arms and gaze of the other Mrs. Miniver, her husband's mother (whose eyes predictably gleam with pride and sorrow), tragically sacrificed by a stray bullet. This maternal melodrama, which features the Mrs. Miniver duo as a mother-daughter pair of selfless caregivers in national war work, is credited with winning the U.S. public's support for military involvement with sister-country Britain.[12] Wright's association with patriotic caregiving continued in her part as the compassionate teen fiancée of a disabled war veteran whom she rallies to save from shame and despair in the postwar *Best Years of Our Lives* (1946). By 1957, Wright had more than secured her identity as the life-giving caregiver, making her a natural for Anne Sullivan's role in the 1957 television *Miracle Worker*. She would carry this persona into her final screen roles (e.g., in *The Good Mother*, 1988).

The Miracle Worker came back to life in two television remakes following the *Playhouse 90* television production and motion picture. The first television version (directed by Paul Aaron) aired in 1979, and the second was a feature production for ABC's *Wonderful World of Disney* (directed by Nadia Tass in 2000 and starring "Pepsi Girl" Hallie Kate Eisenberg as Helen Keller). The latter version is widely in distribution, both commercially and as part of a teacher's educational media package. Patty Duke, like Mandy Miller, the hearing child star of *Mandy*, who dropped her surname in screen credits after her performance of the Deaf child made her star persona synonymous with the character she had played, took over the part of Helen on stage and film from another Patty (McCormick), the actress who had played Keller in the 1957 television broadcast. Duke became closely identified not only with Keller but also with the duplicative process: its premier medium, television, and one of its premier psychological manifestations, manic depression. Having won, at age sixteen, an Oscar with Anne Bancroft for their performances as Keller and her "miracle worker" Anne Sullivan in the 1962 Penn screen feature, Duke followed Wright's lead. She ricocheted from child to mother, playing Sullivan in the 1979 television remake. By that year, Duke had already secured her place in the public eye as iconic teen, capitalizing on melodrama's copycat mode by performing the tricky double role of identical girl cousins Patty and Cathy Lane, replete with discrete British- and American-accented voice dubbing in *The Patty Duke Show*, the popular ABC television serial (1963–1966) dubbed, like *Mandy*, with the appellation of its child star. Perhaps television listeners will recall the show's indelible lyrics about the two-of-a-kind cousins played by Duke: "They laugh alike, they walk alike, at times they even talk alike—you could lose your mind. . . ." The actor's two coauthored autobiographies assure the reader that for Duke, whose given name was not Patty but Anna, "losing one's mind" through the maddening process of media duplication and maternal-child mediation was no joke. In *Call Me Anna* (Duke and Turan 1988), a title that refers to Duke's given name (as well as Anne Bancroft's—she was born Anna Maria Louisa Italiano), Duke recounts her childhood experience of being split by her mother between stage life and real life, stage name and birth name. *A Brilliant Madness* (Duke and Hochman 1995) recounts Anna/Patty's life as an adult with manic depression—a condition tied, the book implies, to the childhood trauma of splitting her identity between stage and screen. Duke's official fan Web site impresses readers with the importance of respecting the identity of the original child, instructing readers to refer to Duke by her given name, Anna, and to ignore screen credits. This gesture seems to be performed in affirmation of the right of the child to regain the authentic identity, the nascent child self lost in the remake that was her stage life. [13]

A detail cited in few sources about Anne Sullivan's history notes that she too bore a stage name of sorts. Born Johanna Mansfield Sullivan, she assumed the role of her mother, Alice Cloesy, at age eight, after Cloesy's death from tuberculosis. The newly christened "Anne" assumed her dead mother's adult labor as caretaker of her father, Thomas Sullivan. Thus, ironically, the "Anne" that restored Duke to something like her given name Anna on screen and brought the child Helen to authentic self-expression was in fact the bearer of a surrogate name and identity that cast her as a maternal substitute even in childhood. Under the familiar form of this name, "Annie," Sullivan achieved the status of national icon of selfless maternal caregiving. Indeed, like Little Orphan Annie, the patriotic institution whose popularity spanned nearly a century through comic syndication (starting in 1924), popular films (1932, 1982), and a Broadway hit (*Annie: The Musi-*

cal, 1977–1983), "Annie" Sullivan was an American institution with an institutional past, an orphan forced to grow up too soon, raised in a poorhouse and serving the role of refracting gendered social values concerning self-sacrifice and giving.

The journalist Cynthia Ozick describes Keller, not Sullivan, as "the infrastructure of an institution" (Ozick 2003, 192). The *Miracle* biopics were indeed only a fragment of the vast interlocked Keller-Sullivan industry of textual remakes, emerging as they did against a perpetually expanding body of literature that includes Keller's declassified FBI files, one of the best sources on her activism in the realms of socialism, birth control, and Black civil rights (Pelka 2001). The proliferation of regionally inflected remakes of Gibson's *Miracle Worker* stage play, adapted for specific age groups and hearing, Deaf, and blind audiences, and a cottage industry of documentaries and books about Keller and Sullivan shows no signs of letting up, with two centennial reissues of the Keller autobiography, *The Story of My Life,* appearing in 2003. What troubles some authors reviewing this body of work is the intersubjective production of this oeuvre, and specifically the strength of Sullivan's voice as caregiver, teacher, and interpreter. Her influence over and mediation of Helen's authorial voice is at the heart of the concern. As Ozick notes, Keller's writings, the product of quasi-collaborative composition with Sullivan and others, were subject to charges of plagiarism and appropriation of the words and mental images of sighted, hearing authors she had read, a phenomenon that drives home the problem of drawing lines among original, interpretation, and copy in an era increasingly characterized by technological reproducibility and problems of narrative fidelity.

Ozick observes that the noted phenomenologist and psychologist Thomas Cutsforth spoke out against what he perceived as the inauthenticity of Helen's reports of experience. His objections came in 1933, coinciding with the appearance of Walter Benjamin's "The Work of Art in the Age of Mechanical Reproduction" (1992), an essay that marked the failing status of the authenticity of the original in works of art and lived experience. Cutsforth, who was blind, was incensed by Keller's dependence on metaphors drawn from registers of sensory experience other than her own. He took issue with her willingness to believe that legitimate experience of sound and the visual could be had indirectly and intersubjectively, through mediated representations, copies that leaped the tracks of form from body to body or from image and sound to printed word. His objections were not only about sensory inauthenticity, but also about mediation as a source of inauthenticity. He perceived the interconstitutive doubling of the Keller and Sullivan pair as a grave ethical problem relative to authorship and experience. "Her teacher's ideals became her ideals," he complained, "her teacher's likes became her likes, and whatever emotional activity her teacher experienced she experienced" (quoted in Ozick 2003, 194). His objections evoke the frustrating virtual doubling that would be the basis for humor in Duke's television serial ("they walk alike, they talk alike"). Keller, he charges, sold out her authentic "birthright" of blindness to copy the words of sighted and hearing others.

Ozick discusses the troubling nature of this call for sensory authenticity. Taken from her perspective, Cutsforth's charge would seem out of character given his own professional interests, which included synaesthesia, the mind's projection of representations in one sensory mode in response to a stimulus in another. Kevin Tyler Dann (1998) writes that Cutsforth believed synaesthesia to be a universal and not rare mode of cognitive experience (see also Cutsforth 1925). Keller's insistence on writing in visual and aural metaphors would seem to be entirely in keeping both with the era's cultural embrace of reproduction and intermodal form-crossing as legitimate and historically necessary mechanisms of expression. Cutsforth's own theories of mind and perception are in keeping with ideas about cross-modal sensory experience. But it is important to look beyond Ozick's reading to see that Cutsforth's critique concerned his perception that Keller made her own sensory experience secondary, emphasizing instead an intersubjective linguistic form that translated the sensory experience of others, depicting her sensory world in linguistic terms. This accommodation to descriptive language, he felt, diminished the place of the sensory experiences that were her birthright as a blind and Deaf person. His objections to her assimilation were part of a larger politics in which, in the words of Jacobus tenBroek (scholar of law, political science, and speech and founder of the National Federation of the Blind), Cutsforth held that "the conditions imposed by blindness" make inevitable neurotic distortions of personality that take the form of hysteria or "compulsive compensation." The latter behavior produces "lopsided personalities, monstrosities or geniuses" (tenBroek 1951). Keller, in Cutsforth's analysis, would be precisely a neurotic, compulsively accommodating personality in her striving to replicate the linguistic representational form of sighted culture.[14] In other words, for Cutsforth, Keller failed by succumbing to the ethos of bad simulacra, the compulsion to repeat that, for him, characterized the worst features of the new era.

But neither Cutsforth nor tenBroek considered the relationship between Sullivan and Keller as an entity unto itself worthy of note. The attunement through which they achieved recognition was the object of deep skepticism. Feminine doubles, child/adult charge-and-caregiver partnerships like that of Sullivan and Keller continue to be the object of mistrust and discomfort, as we shall see most clearly in the third chapter of this book.

This detailed rehearsal of the doubling that occurs in and across these film texts was undertaken here prior to discussion of the texts to emphasize the degree to which this genre and its texts, performers, and real-life sources are structured throughout with repetitions cast as demonic, compulsive copies that do not simply echo or mirror one another (they are bad simulacra, after all) but which are products of a kind of textual and intersubjective attunement of feeling. These texts, their themes, characters, performers, and even their technologies play off of one another with a rhythm and pattern that feature human proximity and intersubjectivity. What is reproduced with each repetition is not precisely a mirror copy of content, of one subject in another, but rather an expressive empathetic resonance between and across subjects, texts, and technologies.

Historical repetitions, resonances, and dissonances also require some consideration. Second-wave feminism, and feminist film theory's revival of the mid-century melodrama, coincided with transformations in Deaf education and public culture regarding recognition of sign languages as distinct language groups and identity cultures. There is a major and paradoxical difference in the status of voice between these two social movements; for the women's movements, however, oral speech, the articulation of the word and (in second-wave psychoanalytic feminism especially) the meaning of oral speech relative to human subjectivity, occupy a key place in concepts of women's agency and liberation. For Deaf advocates of sign language and/as culture, such reverence for oral speech as performance and symbol of human agency would evoke the repressive "oral speech or nothing" approach that kept sign language instruction out of schools for the Deaf until the 1970s.

Before turning to close discussion of the film texts, I recount the historical backgrounds to these two strands of history, keeping in mind that the purpose of this chapter is not to provide full accounts of these respective social histories but to interpret a set of films and film theories in light of these historical intersections.[15]

Feminism, Deaf activism, and voice

A familiar narrative of women's history is that the period following the Second World War was one of relative silence for women and the women's movement as men resumed jobs and their place as public figures and women returned to the home, launching a period of "doldrums" from which women would emerge on the wave of the civil rights movement. In one of the few accounts of women's political activity from 1945 to the 1960s, Leila Rupp and Verta Taylor (1987) challenge this model, unearthing evidence of women's mid-century political activity through more conventional routes such as women's clubs and party politics. These involvements might not be described as activist; however, as Rupp and Taylor show, these women did advocate for women's rights and for their place in the public sphere during a period of relative political conformity. The films considered in this chapter, with one exception, were produced during this "doldrums" period and can similarly be viewed as texts that channel concerns about the place of women during a period when relatively few venues existed for political expression.

The maternal melodrama was revived for critical analysis by authors whose politics ranged from liberal feminism (Haskell 1973, for example) to poststructural psychoanalytic feminist writings referenced later in this chapter. The latter set of writings intervenes in a cycle of reproduction not of stereotypes and images (Haskell's concern) but, more important, of the means of production of male and female subject positions. The conventional process of reading narrative and character construction is supplemented by consideration of the technical means of production and viewer positioning through, for example, close examination of the shot, editing, sound, and character point of view. To expose the means of production and reproduction was, in theory, to destabilize the social order of which it is a part. As participants in a Freudian and Lacanian theory tradition, these writings drew on a base of theory that afforded privilege to language and speech, a fact that sits oddly with the focus on the film image in the earliest key texts (Mulvey 1975, for example). Women's voice and film sound became a concern in a second wave of feminist film scholarship, in part as a response to the overemphasis on the image track in earlier writings on the audiovisual medium, and in part inspired by cautious consideration of the writings of French psychoanalytic feminists on the meanings of women's voice and body (Hélène Cixous, Luce Irigaray) and of male psychoanalysts (Guy Rosalato, Didier Anzieu) who analyzed the gendered meanings of voice.[16]

The metaphors of voice and silence abound in all periods and sectors of feminist writing, from the nineteenth-century rhetoric and performance of the abolitionists Sarah and Angelina E. Grimké[17] to Carol Gilligan's psychological theory of women's development, *In a Different Voice* (1982), to name one of dozens of books across various sectors of second-wave feminism using or analyzing this trope. Angelina Grimké's histrionics and her 1836 "appeal to Christian women" ("Where woman's heart is bleeding, /Shall woman's voice be hushed?" [Grimké 1836]) echoes uncannily across the spectrum from liberal to left to radical feminist discourse in the 1970s and 1980s.

The place and meaning of voice in Deaf communities during these periods differs in important ways. At mid-century a medical model of deafness prevailed in the United States and England. From roughly the 1880s until the 1970s, deafness was regarded as a condition to be addressed optimally through training in speech methods. Residential schools for the Deaf were regarded as the humane educational programs of choice for Deaf children with urban middle- and upper-class hearing parents, because they were equipped to train children to lip-read and thus be better situated to perform in hearing culture. In many schools for the Deaf until the 1970s, sign language was forbidden in favor of rigorous training in lipreading and oral speech. Oral speech was difficult to master, especially among students with little or no residual hearing. Yet many educators regarded oral speech as fundamental to the Deaf child's entry into public life and the workforce. Communication through sign often was prohibited in these schools as a means of ensuring the child's compliance with the oral method (Padden and Humphries 2005).

Among advocates of the oral tradition, as in feminism, speech and voice functioned both symbolically and literally as the imagined means of emancipation into the public sphere. Douglas Baynton explains that historically the connection between oralism and the women's movement politics of voice and emancipation was played out in Deaf pedagogy, placing women on the side of oralism: "While most manualist teachers were predominantly men, most oralists were women, which in the context of the nineteenth-century suffrage movement and the struggle for the right to speak in public, gave them different perspectives on the worth of 'possessing a voice' " (Baynton 1996, 9).

Baynton (1996) writes that oralism was linked to women educators and cast in the light of progressive reform, its advocates portraying Deaf children as requiring freedom from the clutches of manual educators and giving them access to a normal life in the hearing world. Like women, this logic would seem to imply, Deaf children could be educated to achieve voice and win a place in the public sphere. But for Deaf children in Deaf schools, and for Deaf communicators in sign language, the imperative orally to speak was repressive, blocking existing or more logically acquired forms of language and communication—namely, manual sign language. For some Deaf children of hearing parents sent away to acquire oral speech without having any previous exposure to sign, life in a residential school provided an introduction to a community where children could acquire sign language through covert student-to-student communication, these "lessons" passing under the radar of hearing teachers and the official instructional program in relatively hard-to-monitor spaces like playgrounds and dormitories. The oralist method reigned as the normative method in classrooms and in the hearing public mind until the constellation of events around the movement in education and public culture that took shape following the publication in the United States of *Sign Language Structure* (Stokoe 1960), a linguistic analysis that gave scholarly visibility to the argument that American Sign Language (ASL) is speech, a language in itself, and not a substitute for oral speech (as is signed English). Among advocates of sign language education, then, "coming to voice" involved acceptance of sign as a means of agency, and recognition of deafness as linguistic and cultural difference not medical problem.

If, as contemporary psychotherapist Neil S. Glickman and J. C. Carey (1993) propose, Deaf community and identity develop along the lines of minority identity, then it is easy to see the place of Deaf politics parallel to various other identity movements of the period: Black civil rights, women's liberation. This parallel makes the differences between feminism and Deaf politics with regard to the meaning of "voice" all the more troubling. As Carol Padden and Tom Humphries show, the emphasis on oral voice as a signifier of agency and subjectivity in hearing culture was consistently challenged by Deaf speakers of American Sign Language, who continued to speak in sign and who maintained the right to keep alive a language around which had risen a deep and broad culture, history, and politics (Padden and Humphries 2005). Feminism, with its emphasis on oral speech as a primary means and signifier of agency, has never fully recognized the problematic nature of this model of agency.

Mandy and *Miracle Worker* give us a window onto public conceptions about the link between hearing women (as mothers, educators) and the conservative politics of oralism during the period of the feminist doldrums, after suffrage and prior to the second-wave women's movement. The oralist concept of agency permeated not only the postwar maternal melodrama, produced as it was during the period dominated by oralist methods and conservative gender politics, but also, anachronistically, the body of film theory that revived and analyzed melodramas in the eighties and nineties. In the woman's film of the late forties through the early sixties, women characters' relationship to speech and oral expression can be interpreted to uncover the dynamics of working through the problematic of women's access to public voice, the same problematic that had concerned abolitionist- and suffrage-era women. This genre was revived in feminist film theory of the late 1970s, 1980s, and early 1990s as a methodological strategy, pre- cisely to consider the gender dynamics the films perform and in which they engage their spectators relative to female image and filmic body, voice, and agency. Films featuring mothers and daughter units were obvious concerns, with essays emphasizing, for the most part, the figure of the mother. The postwar *Mildred Pierce* (Michael Curtiz, 1945) is an example of a heavily revisited text, with studies ranging from Pam Cook's 1978 essay to Andrea Walsh's 1986 historical-sociological account in her book on women in films of the Second World War period to Linda Williams's psychoanalytic and historical reading of both the film and the earlier literature (anthologized in 1988).[18]

Like Freud's original psychoanalytic case studies (Dora, Little Hans, the Wolf Man) revisited by scholars of psychoanalysis, these Hollywood films and their earliest studies were revisited in scholarly treatments that were, in effect, remakes—not only because they told something more or different each time, but also because the films and their readings had become shared public space, a collective and familiar screen memory where scholars and students could further refract the spectrum of issues and theories laid out in the earlier version, the "original." In this sense, the articles themselves participated in the melodramatic mode of doubling and replication, rework- ing not only the films but also familiar "plot lines" in theory and method. Through these essays the films and the genre were given new reception contexts, new meaning and use-value, not only among audiences of film scholars but also among a generation of students in fields such as women's studies, film studies, communication, and disability studies. In the realm of the popular, they were remade in the postmodern wave of nostalgic revival of old movies, a boom coincident with postwar buyouts of studio libraries,

advances in home video markets for old movies (1980s), and digital sound
and image restoration technologies (1990s).

This revival, though, renewed the implicitly oralist gender politics of the
era. Deaf female characters, present in a few of these melodramas, posed
particular issues in the domains of film speech and voice that feminist film
theorists were equipped to consider through a psychoanalytic framework
that on the one hand emphasized language on the model of speech, and on
the other hand linked silence and meaning performed visually through the
body with infantile, prelinguistic stages of development and with a troubling politics of the female body (a politics forwarded in Irigaray 1985a and
1985b, for example). In returning to the genre of the woman's film, then, I
return to the concerns and contributions of feminist film theory of the 1980s
and early 1990s, recycling this canon in keeping with the melodramatic
habit of remaking familiar texts, in this case scholarly as well as filmic, to
revive "missed" meanings of sound technology and of Deaf and "mute"
screen women and the meanings of voice. I will revisit key essays on sound,
voice, and the female body by Mary Ann Doane (1986) and Kaja Silverman
(1988), attempting to put a new spin on some ideas from these authors' older
writings that hold much of value and meaning for a contemporary critical
exchange between feminism and Deaf cultural studies in the 2000s.

Listening and the postwar film sound transition

Sound in film and public culture had historically specific meanings in the
postwar period. This was true for public culture and for film culture. World
War II was not only physically and visually devastating, it was deafening, leaving many veterans with hearing loss.[19] In postwar Britain and the
United States, industrial technology continued to proliferate, qualitatively
transforming urban and suburban landscapes and soundscapes. While some
industries produced noise as an artifact of postwar construction of, for example, homes, factories, roadways, and telephone lines, other industries
worked to refine sound's expanded potential as a medium of communication, information, and entertainment for a redistributed population. It is
common to regard the postwar years as a period in which visual media
culture ramped up its assault on the senses, with the growth of advertising,
the introduction of home television, the expansion of movies into previously
undeveloped spaces in the form of suburban theater and drive-in development and new technologies of widescreen, for example. But we would be

mistaken to overlook the fact that it was *audio*visual media that proliferated during these years. Sound film and television, like the telephone, privileged hearing subjects. But the ramping up of acoustic media was ironic, for the distracting cacophony of everyday life made it harder for the hearing to hear, to be attentive listeners.

Listening and participation in technologies of communication were featured tropes of participatory citizenship in Britain at mid-century. This is demonstrated nowhere more clearly than in national cinema and documentary. The historian John Trumpbour (2001, 119–120) notes that film was assigned great power in shaping the fortunes of empire in Britain at mid-century, holding an important place alongside cable as an international technology of communication in which the country was staking its future. *Listen to Britain*, the 1942 Ministry of Information documentary by Humphrey Jennings, hailed British citizens as a hearing public. The film invited its audiences to regard listening as a form of national participation, safety, and salute. Sounds of everyday Britain—fighting troops juxtaposed against women working factory machines, for example—are montaged in this film's celebration of a national culture acoustically both enriched and imperiled by modern industrial, war, arts, and communications technologies. The film coincided with the emergence of the concept of the British welfare state in 1941, a social program girded by the Beveridge report, a text that would become both a freak bestseller and the model for the postwar British state. Under the guidance of this program that set out to undo the report's cited evils of "Want, Disease, Ignorance, Squalor, and Idleness," film was a means of education toward eradicating these ills. Listening connoted voluntary participation in this national effort. In a country where accent is so closely tied to class identity, to listen is to recognize and conform to the social order. In this climate deafness could be interpreted as failure to engage in the public act of being an attentive listener and learner, to perform one's place as active and informed citizen. Deafness could thus be identified as a problem to be managed through the burgeoning realm of social and workplace habilitation at the public health level.[20]

In a world increasingly invested in social management through voice and sound, then, deafness took on new valences of meaning. The postwar U.S. government responded to "hearing casualties" among veterans by pouring funds into research on hearing aid technology, initiating a shift in focus from augmentation to restoration and capitalizing on wartime advances in technologies that were at the same time benefiting the film sound industry.

Whereas before the war hearing aids were external devices designed to augment residual hearing, by 1945 the marketing of smaller batteries made the devices small enough to be worn "at the ear"—not quite invisibly inside the body, but nearly there, expanding the imagined potential for incorporating and naturalizing the technology. Funds for research after the war resulted in the design of some hearing-aid models powerful enough to be used with some effect by some profoundly deaf people, widening the industry's imagined framework of consumers available for conversion to hearing practices. Although these changes did not impact the experience and education of a large percentage of deaf people, they did impact industrial and public imagination about the technology's potential to conform lives to a hearing standard. These postwar shifts set the ground for the late-twentieth-century sets of ideas and problems that surrounded the introduction of surgically implanted aids and, ultimately, the controversial cochlear implant. This technology, discussed briefly later in this chapter, allows some deaf individuals physically to become listeners—even if the sounds they hear cannot readily be decoded as language because of the missing childhood years of linguistic training and experience.

At the same time, within the postwar film industry voice—its control and meaning, and its means of reception relative to narrative space and other sounds—was a particularly vexing concern, raising problems from production to exhibition. This point, largely undocumented in secondary historical accounts of the film industry, requires elaboration here in order to ground the claim that deafness held historically specific meanings relative to film sound at mid-century.

Following World War II the U.S. and British film industries underwent a second, quiet (that is, less publicly hailed) revolution in sound technology with the introduction of magnetic recording tape, stereophonic sound recording and projection technologies, and the conversion of the foreign-language version sound-dubbing studios into discrete sets for sound recording in the new era of postdubbing technology. These innovations held out promise but also wrought havoc behind the scenes among industry sound technicians who, in Hollywood, had been engaged since the 1930s in an interstudio cooperative, ongoing struggle (under the auspices of the American Academy of Motion Picture Arts and Sciences)[21] to improve and standardize optical, monaural sound practices from production to exhibition. The reason: synchronous sound and "the talkie" had become rudimentary possibilities by 1930, but the studios were far from the capabilities they desired to make quality sound film recordings and to render recorded sound acceptably audible and realistic to listeners in the space of the movie theater. Simply put, it was one thing to introduce a new set of technologies and quite another for a listener accustomed to one system of signification to understand a new, experimental one as intended. Film historian James Lastra notes that "during Hollywood's transition to sound, technicians' duties often seem to have been split almost evenly between working on the set and theorizing about sound representation" (1994, 203).[22] Likewise during the early decades of sound, technicians devoted much collective time to imagining and discussing representational models for sound: how sound should sound was a question newly opened, not solved, with the introduction of sync. Their concerns centered on what constitutes quality and realism in sound. Standards and technologies to uphold these ideals across the industry and across production, postproduction, and exhibition could not be established without a desired voice for film, a collective industry goal. Reading through industry technical journals with an eye to sound production and management during the decades of the 1930s through the 1950s, one detects a quiet ongoing hysteria about the perpetual resurfacing of problems in realizing ideals and maintaining control over film sound quality in the face of ongoing technological innovation throughout the decades between the watershed of 1929 and the Dolby transition of the 1970s.

Sound was particularly vexing for engineers with regard to controlling and standardizing the reproduction of speech, particularly in a production context where sound engineers were newly vying with image experts for authority on the set (Lastra 1994, 215–216). To make voice and body cohere ultimately required a technology that separated voice and body temporally, spatially, and materially in the production process even more dramatically than they had been in the so-called silent era, only to more firmly and seamlessly join them upon exhibition. Voice and its control—being heard on film, being able to hear film—was of course not only a technical problem but also a social and political issue even in the realm of industry technology research and development. Technological responses to the problematic of sound were an expression of broader cultural anxieties about sound relative to agency and control. It is well known that synchronized sound was instituted as a standard component of popular cinema in the late 1920s. Synchronized voice (singing, speech) was the most compelling aspect of that shift, accounting for "talkies" as the technological watershed and not the introduction of sound on film (or disc) per se. For the presound cinema was hardly silent, involving as it did live musical accompaniment, sound effects, and vocal narration and, in the 1920s, nonsynchronous and synchronous recorded sound effects and music. These sounds were easier to implement than the synchronous voice of the talkie. It is the shift to a successful means of producing synchronous speech in 1928–1929 and not the standardization of sound use (music, effects) in general that marks the break agreed upon by historians as the watershed between the silent and sound cinema eras. It is no coincidence that some of the key early contributions to film sound were made by researchers at Bell Telephone Laboratories, a locus of hearing aid technologies and a company founded by oralism's most influential U.S. proponent (Lastra 1994, 205–208).[23]

Control over sound beyond technical concerns proper was also a concern of the industry. The management of noise outside film sets and theaters was a problem amplified by expanding industry and travel, exacerbated by mid-century expansion of roadways, airports, and other forms of development. Technicians implemented control through measurement of elements such as audience noise in theaters to assess the cause of low film dialog intelligibility, use of mixed-studio test reels to assess sound qualities and audibility in theaters nationally, and reliance on data from the 1939 World's Fair Hearing Tests to determine reasonable expectations for audience hearing abilities. Technicians designed set and theater architecture innovations (such as more efficient sound insulation) to mask noises encroaching from outside the theater. Makeshift interventions were implemented like the policy of floating an orange balloon four hundred feet above a set as a signal to pilots to stay clear of films in production, or filming on weekends when traffic on the burgeoning roads hemming in studios would be less heavy, hence less apt to be picked up as artifact on the sound recording.[24] Pioneer automatic dialog replacement engineer Paul Zydel describes the problem of sound's invasiveness: When an airplane flies through a scene, the camera can frame it out "but the microphone hears it."[25] Whereas in other industries sound control was regarded in part as a public health issue, in film, an industry notoriously derided and debated for its tantalizingly unhealthy effects on moral and mental health, the management of extraneous sound was ultimately in the service of making quiet "space" for the production and exhibition of a bigger, fuller, more acoustically powerful film experience. This was hardly toward the goal of aural health (protecting the public from the onslaught of noise under urbanization) but rather about sealing off cinematic space, the set and the theater, as discrete sound envelopes.

Noise as artifact on the optical recording medium itself was another concern. Optical sound tracks included unwanted noise not only from ambient
sound penetrating the set but also from variations in sound projection speed
(causing an artifact technicians variously called "wow" and "flutter") and
scratches and ambient dust particles floating in the recording field, catch-
ing light and registering as hiss. Evidence of noise artifacts, like germs, was
everywhere to be seen: even the grain of the optical film emulsion could introduce noise. Similar concerns about noise artifacts and background noise
concerned users and manufacturers of hearing aids.

It is a paradox of the film industry that less than two decades after the
introduction of synchronous, direct sound recording the studios gradually
converted to an economy of postdubbing, a system that was in effect an even
more dramatic separation of image and sound in the production process
than the separation of the two registers that had existed in the silent film
era. Postdubbing was economical, but it introduced more than a little anxiety about how to achieve the effect of sound-image matching. The postwar
introduction to the industry of magnetic recording facilitated multiple-track
recording and mixing (a process previously attempted at great cost and
effort with optical sound recording and playback experiments in, for example, Leopold Stokowski's work on Disney's *Fantasia* and its Fantasound
system).[26] Multiple-tape or triple-track tape (one strip holding three discrete
sound stripes read by a triple sound head) and more complex sound editing
and mixing systems facilitated the sharper division of sound into discrete,
separately tracked categories (music, dialog, and effects) and subcategories.
This refinement of the sound process required more specialized and carefully orchestrated experimentation and practice in the production, recording, mixing, and exhibition of sound within and across dialog, music, and
effects.

Postdubbing introduced an economy of production that separated image
and body from sound and voice—temporally, spatially, and epistemologi-
cally. This abstraction of vocal sound and image was as dramatic an epistemological shift in film logic relative to body, sound, and meaning as the
introduction of shooting out of sequence and analytical editing had been
earlier in the century.

Stereophonic sound also ushered in significant changes in the meaning
and experience of film sound for audiences. A fallacy regarding the word
"stereo," perpetuated by the standardization of two-speaker systems in
home radios and phonographs in the fifties, is that "stereo" means two

speakers, approximating the body's two ears. From its inception in the forties, stereo output in film theaters involved four or more speakers, and a distribution of sound recorded from multiple sources within and outside the set. With multiple tracks moving among multiple speakers, stereo posed exciting possibilities for enhancing film's illusion of dimensional space and enveloping audiences in a rich, complex acoustic field. But stereo also posed problems of control.[27]

Volume and directional space control, as well as viewer's expectations based on previous monaural listening practices, challenged sound technicians and engineers as they tried to produce viable new formulas for "bigger" sound not only for multiple-track sound recording and mixing but also for speaker systems in movie theaters. It was one thing to imagine that the placement of multiple speakers dedicated to different sorts of sound would create a better semblance of space and a richer sensory experience of sound, quite another to arrive at recording and speaker dedication formulas that would deliver a credible and palatable narrative sound experience to listeners accustomed to monaural sound conventions.

What is curious about the handling of stereo potential is not that the medium is suddenly regarded as less self-limiting and therefore requires more control, but that imagination and desire changed regarding what should count as "quality" sound. Before stereo, loudness was equated with tinny noise and incomprehensible speech. With stereo, "more" and "bigger" sound was a goal. The metaphor of deafening sound comes to mind, along with articles in the trade press following the Dolby (1977 onward) and digital (1990s onward) booms about the assault of loudness in film theaters. Whereas in the 1940s, patron and external noise were the problems of note, by the 1990s film sound itself did become an esthetic and even a public-health-risk concern within the industry regarding auditory damage. Sound artist Randy Thom, CAS, answering the question "Are movies getting too loud?," asserts that it is not technology that makes movies loud, but directors who use the technology to this end:

> The proliferation of digital movie houses with high fidelity amplifiers
> and speakers has provided Directors with a powerful set of instruments
> which they can use wisely or foolishly. The trend recently has favored
> the foolish. So when a movie is too loud, don't blame the hardware
> or the people whose names at the end of the credits are only seen by
> those who clean the theater. Ask the Auteur why he designed his roller

coaster to do nothing but go a hundred miles an hour, downhill all the way, frantically, numbingly, nowhere.[28]

Sound level recording, then, was seemingly without limits at the dawn of the digital decade of the 1990s. This was also the case with the introduction of stereo in the late 1940s and early 1950s. But what is limited is the ability of listening bodies to hear at these extremes, much less to find meaning and pleasure in the sound. The body's technical limits, set in part by cultural expectations and habit, were a check on the sound fantasies of the 1940s and 1950s industry, creating for it anxieties about the limitations imposed by patron bodies which could only take so much.

Changes were determined in part by the issue of how different sound conventions might fit with previous filmic narrative conventions. Magnetic stock, postdubbing, and stereo required a reconsideration of previously relatively smooth conventions of cinematic time and space, sound-image relationships, and the new range of meanings that could be carried by sound as a potentially bigger, fuller, more precise medium of meaning. As in the first sound revolution, it was not the music and effects domains but dialog, the spatialization and embodiment of voice and speech, which was most crucial yet most recalcitrant. Like color film stock, lauded for making images spectacular but derided by designers such as Natalie Kalmus (codeveloper of the Technicolor process, executive head of the Technicolor art department, and film color consultant on all Technicolor films from 1933 to 1949) for its decorative, candy-box-color flattening of narrative space, music and effects were domains where early stereo excelled as vivid audio spectacle, but wrought havoc with conventional narrative flow. Narrative logic required a signifying system different from the tone, rhythm, and pattern systems of music (which might be compared to Freud's "primary" or preverbal processes, which as I argued in chapter 1 are not as simplistic as language-based psychoanalysis would have us believe). Immediately after the introduction of magnetic playback systems studio sound departments grew more diverse and specialized in the realm of music recording and mixing.[29] Oral dialog, requisite of the talkie after 1929 and tied to the diegetic field, was the sound domain where problems of narrative verisimilitude, palatability, and control were confounding and persistent.

Thus, as with the sound transition of the late 1920s, and as with widescreen and 3D innovations of the 1950s, the postwar sound technologies threw a wrench into the relatively smooth works of the classical "silent" (visual) Hollywood system by technologically tying sound to the image—but also potentially letting sound get out of control and making it a potential arena of novelty and noise (nonmeaning), acoustic pyrotechnics needing to "grow up" into the formal maturity of organized signification.

All of these circumstances and the discussions about them make it clear that the production of sync sound may have been achieved in 1929 but the problems of audibility and clarity so crucial to understanding dialog persisted well into the century, with every new solution bringing its own set of sound problems, and a revised set of sound practices and meanings. A similar problem persisted in Deaf education, with the recognition by the 1970s that, despite advances in technologies for training in acoustic phonetics and hearing aids, oral speech did not seem to improve standards of speech production in Deaf speakers.[30] Just as in the cinema, where representing speech did not guarantee audible and comprehensible speech, so in Deaf education, training in speech did not always result in learners able to produce speech that would be understood by listeners unaccustomed to the qualities of Deaf voice.

There is no doubt, then, that questions of sound, voice, technology, and the hopes attached to them were buzzing in the air during the postwar years, and that the linking of sound, bodies, and meaning was crucial not only to the studios but also to a broader world where technological augmentation of speaking, hearing, and listening were crucial components of social subjectivity during these years. It was in this context of women made silent, the Deaf made orally to speak, deafened war veterans, and the promise and problems of new hearing and sound technologies in the cinema and in Deaf education that *Johnny Belinda* and *Mandy* were released as "firsts" in the postwar group of Deaf melodramas, to which I now turn.

Mandy *(1952) and* Miracle *(1962): On voice and listening*

Deaf and mute female characters in the sound-era woman's film have not gone unnoticed in feminist film theory. Sarah Kozloff writes: "Because they appear with surprising frequency in Hollywood cinema, mute characters have attracted the attention of numerous critics. . . . Bridging the gap from silence into sound is repeatedly thematized by American films, as if the medium compulsively needs to repeat the transition of the mid 1920s" (Kozloff 2000, 77).

Silverman (1988, 67–71) notes that in melodrama the "mute" role is prominent among women characters. She describes *Johnny Belinda* as a "'talking cure' film with a difference" in which Belinda, who learns sign language, is prompted to "speak" through her vagina, issuing forth a child whose inarticulate cry is Belinda's surrogate and inarticulate voice. I discuss Silverman's account of this film at length later but for now wish to note that in the melodrama the "mute" role is far more prominent among girl characters than among adult women. Belinda, though she becomes a mother, is cast as a girl by dint of her age and her position as a daughter living sheltered within the paternal home, as well as her naïveté regarding all things sexual. In the woman's film, Doane wrote in her classic account of the genre, "little is left to language" (Doane 1987, 85). Kozloff states, in an apparent contradiction to these earlier claims, that melodrama is the domain of outspoken women, women who talk *too much* (Kozloff 2000, 77),[31] a factor of interest to theater managers concerned about the volume of patron noise making film dialog all but inaudible (Mueller 1940, 48). In the films I consider, both Doane's and Kozloff's observations are shown to be accurate, with daughters and mothers in shifting, interconstitutive roles in relation to speech and silence. The two roles are clearly modeled in the 1952 film that takes as its subject problems of gendered voice in the coming of sound, *Singin' in the Rain*. In this film, the harsh-voiced silent-era star Lina (Jean Hagen) is voice-dubbed into the sound-film era by Kathy (Debbie Reynolds), a female figure that is not only esthetically pleasing in voice but also morally upright, a good citizen. She stands in contrast to Lina, whose gnarly voice signifies her crass working-class immigrant origins. Her voice is a signifier of her trashy insubordination: like her voice, Lina can't be trusted. It is not a surprise that in 1952 Kathy's confident screen voice could comment that silent film acting is "a lot of dumb show," or that Lina might ask Kathy, "What do you think I am, dumb or something?" equating, as Steven Cohan (2000) has observed, "one meaning of 'dumb' ('muteness') with another ('stupidity')" (56). In 1952, the year of *Mandy*'s release, to be orally silent was to be disempowered. But not all female voices could win public right of place.

As discussed above, for the semiotically and psychoanalytically informed feminist film criticism of the 1970s and 1980s, speech and voice were both literally and symbolically linked to women's access to power and place. If as Tania Modleski argues the melodrama is "fundamentally about events that do not happen; and . . . above all the word that was not spoken," the Deaf melodrama is about precisely that struggle to articulate "the word" as a literal expression of the female subject's emergence into the public sphere (Modleski 1987, 326–338).

Mandy is about precisely this problematic of articulation of the word as the means of the female subject's emergence. The film tracks Mandy as she emerges from her lonely, mute existence in the sheltering Victorian home of her grandparents to her experience acquiring oral speech in a school for the Deaf. She is accompanied and supported by her mother, Christine Garland (Phyllis Calvert), who functions both as narrator and as joint lead protagonist who also comes to voice both publicly and sexually through the tribulations of her daughter. Reading *Mandy* in light of this connection of "the word" with female agency, Marcia Landy writes that "by centering on the issue of hearing and speaking, the film exposes the strategy whereby women are rendered powerless" (Landy 1991, 459). It is not only the child character of *Mandy* for whom access to speech/power is at issue, but also and more important, Mandy's mother, Christine Garland. Landy continues: "Though the film ostensibly presents the child as the one in need of acquiring language, it is the wife who must gain access to it in order to free the child" (Landy 1991, 458).

Whereas for feminism, speech is both symbolic of and requisite for power, for advocates of sign language use, mandating oral speech entailed compromise and submission. Certainly it is through a quest to acquire the ability to speak that Mandy achieves liberation from the isolation of the domestic sphere. But for a child of six, separation from family and home and immersion in the public life of an institution would be experienced as trauma. If there is liberation in *Mandy*, Landy, Annette Kuhn (1992), and Pam Cook (1986) all agree, it is the liberation of Mandy's hearing mother Christine, and not of the girl.

Douglas Baynton writes that the reform movement against the teaching of and in sign language and in support of exclusive instruction in lipreading and oral speech gained momentum in the late nineteenth century, reaching its peak of influence after World War II, precisely the time of these two films' release in Britain and the United States. At this time, Baynton notes, an estimated 80 percent of Deaf children in the United States were taught entirely without sign language, up from 40 percent at the turn of the century (Baynton 1996, 5).[32]

In *Mandy*, oralism is front and center: The film is set in the public contexts of urban postwar Britain and the country's network of Deaf schools. Margaret Deuchar explains that Britain's schools for the Deaf were free and compulsory, oralist, and largely residential. This was despite the fact that the Education Act of 1944 mandated some integration of Deaf students into nonresidential schools. *Mandy* is set in this moment of educational reform. If the Victorian British child was to be seen and not heard, by the post–World War II period the "deaf and dumb" child, to use the language of *Mandy*, was a social problem requiring intervention by a Labour Party state educational system that had inherited a structure of public institutional management from the prewar regime. The idea that the education of Deaf children was the responsibility of the state was part of the broader postwar ethos of state responsibility for workforce habilitation. British Sign Language (BSL) thrived informally in communities outside schools, Deuchar explains, as well as in some of the many schools established by evangelical and Church of England missions to the Deaf, where sign language was sometimes accepted and even promoted as a means of religious instruction (Deuchar 1984, 33–35).[33] But the emphasis was on speech training for as many Deaf subjects as possible.

Mandy was conceived as a fictional melodrama, though produced by a studio (Ealing) and director (Alexander Mackendrick) with deep experience in the social problem film genre. As noted above, the script took as its basis *The Day Is Ours*, a British romance novel of 1947 by Hilda Lewis. The novel, set in postwar England, chronicles the psychic life of Christine Garland, a wanton socialite raising a Deaf daughter whose birth she experiences as punishment for her war-era promiscuity. Vain and materialistic, Christine is a simulacrum of Mrs. Miniver, the protagonist of the prewar novelization and 1942 film about British maternal morality in the war era. In *The Day Is Ours*, Christine, shamed for lasciviously entertaining the troops, is branded by husband and doctors as a hysteric who talks too much and who produces her child's deafness: the obstetrician is obliged to use his forceps to extract the head of the infant from the pelvis of his noncompliant patient. Christine's resentment about her future role as mother is such that she refuses to push. The mother redeems her social standing, however, by competently putting the child, whose deafness she describes as punishing, through speech education in a school for the Deaf.

In the film, which follows the novel by half a decade, moral degradation is no longer a strong feature of Christine's character. She is cast from the outset as morally righteous and without guilt. Though the film does portray her as narrowly avoiding an affair with the Deaf school's dashing renegade headmaster, the flirtation is represented as part of her own coming to independent voice, and their bond over Mandy's oral speech education makes their union fall on the side of what is moral and good. The cause of Mandy's deafness is left uncertain rather than being attributed to the mother's behavior. Mandy is saved from the "silent world" her mother imagines out loud through the efforts of a fully competent Christine (played by Phyllis Calvert), a woman who risks her marriage and reputation to bring her daughter to voice. In the analysis of sound in *Mandy* that follows, I consider the relationship between mother and daughter as they together form an intersubjective identificatory figure for postwar British hearing audiences. Christine is a political figure who advances in the new welfare state through a public role carved out there for women: as moral caretaker. Regarding women's relationship to citizenship in emergent welfare states including England's, policy theorist Ruth Lister explains that central to those debates were "issues of maternal and child welfare as women in a wide range of countries strove to translate their private responsibilities as mothers into public citizenship claims" (Lister 1998, 177). Christine's function in this regard is not unique. Literary historian Alison Light notes that between the world wars the romance genre narrowed to signify fiction for working women and girls and veered toward mass entertainment (Light 1991, 160). *Mandy* followed the pattern of *Mrs. Miniver*, the British pre–Second World War newspaper romance serial turned popular U.S. weepy (MGM, 1942) as war propaganda. Light, referring to the serial as "the snuff of a nation in arms," quotes Roosevelt's comment about the film version: "*Mrs. Miniver* did more for the allied cause than a flotilla of battleships." How did it become possible, Light asks, for "the mediations of a middle-class, middlebrow woman to speak for a nation?" (1991, 113–115). Similarly we might ask how Christine Garland makes the transformation from the novel's "loose" wartime hysteric and negligent mother to the standard bearer of the postwar welfare state's maternal ethic of caring and responsible citizenship.

Mandy gives us a child body without a voice and, through maternal voiceover early in the film, a maternal voice without a body. Silverman notes, "Because her [the mother's] voice is identified by the child long before her body is, it remains unlocalized during a number of the most formative moments of subjectivity. The maternal voice would thus seem to be the original prototype for the disembodied voice-over in cinema . . . [that has] become the exclusive prerogative of the male voice within Hollywood film" (Silverman 1988, 76).

In a flashback, typical of the maternal melodrama, that grants the mother narrative agency, Christine speaks directly to the viewer in the film's opening scene. She introduces her baby Mandy to film listeners in voiceover. In shot after shot during this early portion of Christine's voiceover monologue, the image track shows the baby Mandy in close up. Christine is visible for the most part only in frames that include her hands lovingly attending to the baby. Her place offscreen, but for her administering hands, and her authoritative, caring voiceover in the opening minutes of the film, evoke the style used in the films of child experts Margaret Mead, Arnold Gesell, and René Spitz. These authorities demonstrate their theories of child development and maternal caring through an instructional voiceover that, like Christine's, directs our attention to the child's body. Voiceover is a pointedly ironic means of representing the mother in a film about a child who, listeners will soon learn, is "stone deaf."

In 1980, Doane (drawing on the writings of psychoanalyst Guy Rosolato) asked the question, "In what does the pleasure of hearing consist?" (in Doane 1986). One answer she offered is that pleasure is situated in the divergence between present experience and the memory of early satisfaction. Her example is infant memories of sound, precisely the sorts of memories we are invited to understand as lost to the child Mandy. Traces of "archaic desires" stemming from this early experience of hearing the maternal voice are never annihilated in the adult subject, Doane explains. "Memories of the first experiences of the voice circumscribe the pleasure of hearing and ground its relation to a phantasmatic body." For the child, she continues, physical space "is defined initially in terms of the audible, not the visible" (Doane 1986, 342–343). This point has yet to see the kind of interrogation it deserves relative to the film soundtrack. Doane goes on to describe female voice-off and voiceover using the metaphor of a "sonorous envelope" (Doane 1986 338–340). The term, which she draws from the writings of Didier Anzieu (1976) and Guy Rosalato (1974, 33), refers to the acoustical containment of the listening body in a spatial field. This envelope of sound space is akin to the field in which the infant experiences the voice of its mother, which is "the first model of auditory pleasure" (Doane 1986). Doane emphasizes the experience of viewer containment and safety as deriving from the memory of this early prelinguistic experience.

Kohut, the psychoanalyst of the self whose concept of the infant's self-recognition in the gleam in the mother's eye was discussed earlier, introduced a similar idea about the constitution of the blind child's sense of self through sound. He introduces the concept of the tape recorder as an analogy to the mirror in the development of the child's sense of a self.[34] This is put forward through an observation of a child caught on a film made by Anna Freud's partner Dorothy Burlingham and the psychiatric social worker James Robertson. In the film, Kohut explains, the expression of a child who is blind lights up at the sound of her own voice played back to her on a tape recorder. Kohut suggests that the tape recorder acts as a mirror, reflecting the child back to itself in a manner typically performed by the mother (Kohut 1971, 118). This relationship of maternal mirroring is of course familiar to film readers through Lacan's concept of the mirror phase. It is important to note that whereas Lacan's child is about eighteen months old, Kohut describes a child old enough to manipulate a recorder and understand its function. This child is therefore likely to be much older, making this an example of a much later experience of this narcissistic self-recognition. Like the "gleam" in the mother's eye that is constitutive of the child's emergent self, the mirroring response supports the child's narcissistic pleasure in witnessing its own physical performance, an enactment that is fundamental to the emergence of a cohesive self. The vocal function of the maternal voice is an auditory self-playback technology that facilitates the development of the blind child's sense of self. Further, if we note that the girl in Burlingham's film is in fact an institutionalized child living without a mother, we might speculate that the technology of maternal mirroring finds an acoustic surrogate in the audio recorder.[35] Ironically, the child has been removed from the home in part because she could not engage with the mother in the visual process of mirroring considered so essential to its development. The institutional context provides a surrogate system of maternal care.[36]

Three years after the release of Penn's film version of *The Miracle Worker*, Burlingham published an influential article on ego development in blind children that would evolve into a book on blind and sighted children in circumstances such as twinning that also uniquely impact ego development. Burlingham, lifetime collaborator of Anna Freud in work with homeless and war-displaced children in Vienna and England, based her essay on observations at the Hampstead Nursery for Blind Children, which she ran after the war through the middle of the 1970s. She considered problems of communication and pleasure, both from the side of the mother and the side of the child: "Blind infants need more than the usual stimulation from the mother to respond to her," she noted, adding that "acoustic and tactile sensations do not seem to have the same arousing effects on the [sighted] infant as visual ones" (Burlingham 1972, 327). Her point is not the stereotypical one about the primacy of vision; lack of vision in itself is not the problem she wants to highlight. Rather, her concern is about synaesthesia: vision stimulates the other senses, prompting the senses of hearing and touch to develop along with sight.

Vision also comes into play as a problem, Burlingham suggests, for sighted subjects interpreting the expressed affect of the blind child. Blind children's expressions, Burlingham explained, tend to be hard to read because they are not confined to the face as would be expected but rather are dispersed over the whole body: "The blind child uses his body and musculature to express pleasure . . . in a manner which is more appropriate for the toddler stage, before communication of affect is confined to facial expression" (Burlingham 1972, 327). The implication is that the routing of affect primarily through facial expression, a process that was so much the focus of the work of Tomkins, is simply not present in the blind child in the same way or to the same degree as it is in sighted children.

The North American physician Van Spruiell, in an unpublished paper recounting his experiences working as a visitor at the Hamstead Nursery for Blind Children, emphasized that the Hamstead analysts were especially taken with the question of narcissism among the blind children. "By thinking about congenitally blind children," he explained, "we might come to think new thoughts about normal narcissism." And "by thinking about narcissism we might 'see' blind children in new ways." He goes on to explain that what they learned was less about narcissism than about the inadequacy of the concept to describe ego formation. In these children, he wondered, "was there any self at all—self to love?" (Spruiell 1972–1973). His conjecture, rather than leading him to wonder *if* the blind child develops an ego properly, steers him to question the value of the very term "narcissism" which is so central to psychoanalysis from Freud to Lacan, with its connotations of visual perception as a constitutive necessity of self, an idea suggested in Lacan's concept of the mirror phase and in Kohut's suggestion that the most significant interactions between mother and child occur in the visual area, with the child's bodily display "responded to by the gleam in the mother's eye," which is exultant and suggestive, we might even say projective, of an image of the child in its unity and totality (1971, 115–117; see also Winnicott 1971a). Burlingham's account of the blind child's development stresses what the blind child *does* do toward constructing a concept of self in the world, rather than constituting its blindness as a condition of developmental lack that must be habilitated, coaxed into a state of becoming.

It is not only children who require mirroring technologies of accommodation in an increasingly specular culture that makes appearance a mandatory constituent of the subject's emergence. The sonorous or acoustic envelope concept introduced to film theory in Doane's essay of 1980 (Doane 1986) appeared much earlier in the film industry context. In 1941, at about the time that the "self-playback" film described by Kohut was shot by Burlingham and Robertson, a film industry trade essay described a playback system that was dubbed an acoustic envelope. This system was piloted with the singer and film actor Paul Robeson (Burris-Meyer 1941). The sound technician author of this essay explains that Robeson found that he could no longer hear himself sing in the new, larger theaters into which he was booked to hold his burgeoning audiences. His voice was lost to himself in these cavernous spaces.

As Doane notes, sound unlike image is simultaneously emitted and heard by the subject. The maternal function of "playback" described by Kohut is the medium through which the child comes to recognize itself as the source of the sound it witnesses.[37] Narcissism is thus, importantly, not an immediate relationship with the self but a mediated, proximal, and intersubjective relationship. But the vast spaces designed for mass audiences afforded no inherent mechanism for this kind of proximally mediated sound reflection. In effect, Robeson lost his self in losing track of his own voice. The acoustic envelope filled this breach in the acoustic mediation of self to self, offering to performers the experience of an invisible, intimate, and resonant acoustic field in which they could hear themselves sing within the cavernous space of a large theater. In the acoustic envelope the speaker or singer is safely ensconced in a field in which his or her own voice remains intimate and available for self-perception even as that voice is given over to a vast audience. In other words, this is an acoustic mirror, an instrument of reassuring self-perception that accommodates the alienating, eradicating effects of mass-audience performance technologies.

I cite this example of the acoustic envelope technology because it suggests that performer self-perception was not always or easily achieved on a film set where the technologies of architecture, miking, and the increasingly used strategy of postdubbing and playback interfered with this necessary narcissistic cycle of self-perception. Cavernous theaters and location shooting, sets where external sound broke in—all interfered with the reversibility of the voice required for the performer to situation him- or herself in character. In Doane's account, the infant's self-perception requires the voice of the mother as a device that defines and situates the infant within a world, a concept that echoes Kohut's (1971) description of the mother as mirroring playback system.

In *Mandy*'s opening scene the viewer is invited by Christine's voice into a secure narrative space, just as Mandy herself would be expected to derive a sense of secure orientation from the voice of the mother within the diegesis. But *Mandy* offers a similar situation of breakdown of this acoustic logic not unlike the breakdown of performer self-perception that Robeson's acoustic envelope technology was designed to fix. The two-year-old Mandy, the audience will learn shortly after this idyllic opening set of shots, cannot hear her mother's voice. Hence she cannot have oriented herself through sound to pass through stages of attachment to the mother and development in ways imagined to unfold relative to maternal voice. Christine's competent voice may lead the audience through the narrative, but it is lost on the screen mother's most important audience, the child.

Mandy fails to begin to speak as her mother believes she should have by age two. The symbiotic pair is then separated on the image track. We see Mandy alone as Christine's voiceover assumes an anxious edge, describing her daughter's failure to speak. Doane remarks in a footnote that there are two kinds of disembodied voices: theological and scientific (Doane 1986, 347). In a strategy that will be repeated in *The Miracle Worker*, Christine's voiceover tone shifts from solicitous to clinically descriptive as she discovers Mandy's deafness in the opening scene, then offers a few brief updates on her child's progression to speech in the remainder of the film. The occasional voiceovers that punctuate the film after the opening scene documenting the discovery of Mandy's condition have the feel of a documentary-style medical progress report.

Christine's progress reports are the viewer's first hint of the film's affinity with the social problem film, the style in which many reviewers saw it, and in which Landy places it in her classic *British Genres* (1991, 458–459). In the typical social problem film, the ubiquitous voices of famous men narrate didactic commentary on social issues. Pascal Bonitzer has described the voiceover as representing a transcendent power, an authority that emanates from outside and over the image: "The voiceover is assumed to know: such is the essence of its power."[38] In Britain and the United States at mid-century, we find the convention of using celebrities as moral pedagogues, public intellectuals of a sort who expound on social problems. A disembodied James Agee, for example, performed the voiceover narration for *The Quiet One* (Janice Loeb and Sidney Meyer, 1948), a melodramatic documentary about a troubled African American boy from Harlem who is mentally ill and has fallen mute, reportedly as a psychosomatic response to neglect and abuse by his grandmother. Agee's urgent voiceover provides a poignant yet authoritative medical-educational narrative about the boy's history and his recovery of speech. The boy comes out of his shell when placed in a rural residential home, where he is nurtured by a male social worker. In Britain, Richard Burton performed the voiceover for *Thursday's Children*, a documentary about a residential shool for the Deaf designed to show children "breaking into communication,"[39] just a few short years before Burton and director Anderson themselves would break into their own political voices as two of Britain's notorious "Angry Young Men." *Thursday's Children* brought Anderson directly into the world of national child welfare and moral regeneration: following this film he made three neorealist-influenced spots for the National Society for the Prevention of Cruelty to Children. Male voiceover in all these documentaries about child voice and agency walks the line between intimate, empathetic storytelling and distanced factual register of medical-pedagogical progress: The "quiet one," the boy of the U.S. documentary's title, finally comes out of his pathological state of withdrawal and speaks; Britain's "Thursday's children" acquire oral speech and, as Burton assures us, thereby gain access to Britain's hearing working world.

In *Mandy*, it is the fictional Christine whose first-person voiceover leads the viewer along this borderline between sentimental fiction and clinical document, from doldrums to cure, making the film appear almost like an instructional film in some respects—an effect replicated ten years later in *The Miracle Worker*. If Christine's maternal voice is inflected with the authoritative tones of the social-problem film in order to drive home the hard fact of Mandy's deafness, then it might also be said that the social problem film's male narrators mimicked the poignant and emotional cadences of the female voice in maternal melodramas like *Mandy* aurally to stir the emotions of their listeners.[40] Their tones urged audiences into a position of empathetic pity for and perhaps even humanitarian action on behalf of children like those depicted in these films. This humanitarian appeal is achieved at the level of sound and voice, and attached to silent child images. The films are strongly set up to encourage empathetic identification at the level of sound (voice), affording a response of pity with the child as image.[41]

In both *Mandy* and *Miracle*, it is mothers not doctors who diagnose their children's deafness. Christine, following her sharp observations of the child, performs impromptu sensory tests to prove Mandy's deafness to her husband, engaging him as assistant in deductive experiments. This examination is conducted through a process that splits sound and image. When Mandy's head turns to look up from her crib as her father enters the room, Harry Garland is assured that his daughter must have heard him enter the room. Christine, however, notes that it was a visual cue—a shadow—that had caught Mandy's attention and not the sound of her father's steps. "Harry," Christine commands, "make her hear something she couldn't possibly have seen." Mandy, gazing blankly at the camera, does not flinch as the listening audience undoubtedly does as Harry loudly crashes a metal tray to the ground behind his daughter's back. Harry follows this failed experiment by hysterically calling out his daughter's name, a performance that garners no response. By separating sound from image in Mandy's perceptual sphere, Christine proves to Harry the fact she states with finality to her film audience: *Mandy cannot listen.* She pronounces the girl "really stone deaf" and predicts "she'll be dumb, too." A subsequent scene in a doctor's office where Mandy's deafness is confirmed is superfluous, for Christine has already proven the fact empirically.

This display of maternal diagnostic acuity is repeated in *The Miracle Worker* ten years later. In the film's opening scene, Kate Keller (Inga Swenson) ministers to her toddler daughter Helen, who is convalescing in the nursery following a respiratory illness dismissed by a visiting doctor as a routine childhood ailment. In a high-key close-up that renders her lovely face a fright mask, Kate coos ironically in a sarcastic voice to the off-screen baby that Daddy should print an article in the newspaper he publishes heralding the marvels of the modern medicine that has failed to name his daughter's illness.

In both of these films' opening scenes, the children's status as deaf and, in Helen's case, blind elicits first horror then shame. The shaming of the child in the eyes of the mother, Tomkins suggests, is at the origin of the taboo on mutual looking between two subjects (Tomkins in Sedgwick and Frank 1995, 146). He identifies as the paradigm of this kind of looking the interlocked gaze of the mother and infant, the adoring mutual stare. Spitz noted that, in his film footage of nursing babies, "the nursing infant does not remove its eyes for an instant from the mother's face until it falls asleep, satiated" (Spitz and Wolf 1972, 109).[42] Proximity, epitomized in the contact of the breast inserted in the mouth (for Spitz [1955] a "primal" cavity), is the object of the taboo, not looking. We should take careful note of this as a counterpoint or supplement to Lacan's important point about the child's later (mis)apprehension of itself in the mirror.[43] Film theory has been highly attentive to the mirror moment, its replication in circumstances including the cinema, and the misrecognition and splitting that it models. But we have been less than observant in noting the evidence of negativity (not the same as misrecognition) on the part of the mirror in this moment. The pride of the caregiver in the child's newfound ability and her own responsibility in giving the child this ground for the subject's formation may be evident, but we may also observe disappointment in the mirror-eyes of the caregiver, say, if the child fails to perform within the terms of that ego-constitutive paradigm of recognition and misrecognition. The mother may see in the child the mirror image of her own failure to inspire (mis)recognition in the child, and hence may instill in the child a sense of shared shame over its lack of self-control and mastery.

Kate Keller's address to the baby is, of course, purely for the benefit of the listening audience, which is privileged with knowledge the screen mother does not yet have: the child neither sees nor hears her. Kate's monologue is thus, in effect, a voiceover insofar as it has no diegetic receiver. Michel Chion expands on the imagined relationship of infantile security "inside" the space of female voice, the maternal acoustic envelope discussed earlier. He puts a sinister spin on the control over the spectator-as-infant this model implies. Chion describes the intimate, closely miked female voice as a "uterine nightmare" in which the listener is trapped, suffocating. Silverman, describing this sadistic twist to the metaphor as a fantasy construction shared across film theory and film texts, quotes from Chion:

> In the beginning, in the uterine night, was the voice, that of the Mother. For the child after birth, the mother is more an olfactory and vocal continuum than an image. One can imagine the voice of the mother, which is woven around the child, and which originates from all points in space as her form enters and leaves the visual field, as a matrix of places to which we are tempted to give the name "umbilical net." A horrifying expression. . . . (Chion 1982, 57, quoted in Silverman 1988, 74)

Chion's metaphor of the uterine nightmare as deadly trap is an apt one for describing *The Miracle Worker*'s representation of Helen and Kate in a state that borders on madness. The psychoanalyst Robert Fliess, in *Dream, Symbol, and Psychosis*, makes the astute observation that Freud very belatedly admitted the existence of delusions in dreams when he opened a chapter of his 1940 *Outline of Psycho-analysis* with the statement that "the dream, then, is a kind of psychosis" (Fliess 1973, 203). Kate's mock-comforting maternal voice, its dry wit matched in this scene with her frightfully lit face, dissolves into hysterical cries that resonate with the inarticulate screams of Harry Garland in *Mandy* ten years earlier. Kate's cries, like Harry's, are expressions of horror and consternation motivated by her observation of her daughter's lack of response. Helen's eyes had remained motionless during her mother's dramatic ministrations. The fictional space of a comforting blanket of maternal voice as theorized by Silverman and, earlier, by Rosolato and Doane—the tone and proximity that initially had lulled listeners, breaks down as listeners must come to realize that the parent's performance has gone unnoticed by the screen child, who remains blank. With her shrieks, expressive vocalization that is not speech, Kate Keller pulls listeners down with her into a nightmare fantasy that imagines the mind of the prelinguistic child as one destined to be lost in a world of nonmeaning for far too long because of her loss of the senses of sight and hearing. The child imagined in this fantasy may never emerge as a subject insofar as, when the time comes, she will neither see herself as the gleam in her mother's eye nor hear herself in the playback mechanism that is the mother's enveloping voice. In short, she will remain without a self-image and without a sense of herself as having voice and/as agency. This impending failure of the ego properly to form in relationship to image and sound is the anticipated tragedy set out in this scene of the film. As in *Mandy*, this opening scene sets up a narrative movement toward the talking cure that will be performed by maternal surrogate Anne Sullivan in the remainder of the film.

I emphasize with Silverman that this idea of a "uterine night" is a construction evident in film and culture, in which the mother is imagined to share the child's undeveloped sensory and communicative abilities. These undeveloped or lacking abilities are imagined to exist across the mother-child couple and not just in the child. This transposition is repeated in Chion's use of the concept. Silverman writes:

The opposition of the maternal voice to the paternal word attests to a quite remarkable sleight of hand, although one which has become so frequently effected within recent theory as to have become almost transparent. It attests, that is, to the displacement onto the mother of the qualities which more properly characterize the newborn child. The conceptualization of the maternal voice as a "uterine night" of non-meaning effects a similar displacement: once again the infant's perceptual and semiotic underdevelopment are transferred onto the mother. (Silverman 1988, 75)

In pulling Kate into this space of semiotic underdevelopment imputed to the deaf and blind child, the film also pulls its listeners into this world. Spectators are given a glimpse of the imagined nightmarish qualities of sensory impairment. *The Miracle Worker* in this way sets up its narrative objective: to deliver the child, and with her the caregiver and the viewer, from a nightmare of nonmeaning and to enter (with) her into the intersubjective public space of maternal playback and social signification. In both *Miracle* and *Mandy*, it is the mother's responsibility to thus deliver the child. For the remainder of these two films, the mothers struggle to save their daughters from their silent worlds, belatedly bringing them up with the help of professional doubles, maternal surrogates.

Focusing on sound, thus far I've suggested that *The Miracle Worker* invites the listener to identify empathetically with the grief and shame of the grief-stricken mother. Her narrative voice pulls the listener down with her and her daughter into the space of a uterine nightmare in which deafness and blindness are the conditions of a fundamental tragedy in which the child cannot develop a normative ego. But I have overlooked vision and the image, the question of Keller's blindness, and a reading of affect that might bring us somewhere other than into the uterine nightmare the film seems to want listeners to experience. Jumping tracks in *The Miracle Worker* from sound to image, we see that throughout the opening scene, the baby Helen is never shown on screen. Her offscreen presence is indicated by the direction of Kate Keller's gaze. Kate's face, bathed in light, gazes into the offscreen space where lies the implied subject of the reverse shot that never comes. The baby for whom Kate's look is intended is incapable of receiving this expressively powerful look, an affirmative affective projection that is so crucial to the emergence of the child's ego, if we follow the lessons of child psychoanalysis. What can we do with those cornerstones of film theory, the mirror stage, the theory of suture, and the visually based theorization of subsequent phases of entry into language, when a deaf and blind infant subject is constituted as absence, and as a subject without the ability to constitute herself in the world? If we follow the lead of Chion, the screen child's failure to hear and to see leads the viewer to imagine a tragic failure of subject emergence.

The very basis of subject formation and of filmic identification, spectatorial unity with the maternal body and the subsequent formation of the ego through a process of separating from that oneness of infant and maternal bodies, is suspended in this splitting of on-screen mother and offscreen, invisible child. Helen needs to be part of an intersubjective unit through which she may come to life before she can gain voice and agency in the film. The agenda of these films, to give voice to mother and child, becomes focused in this process of splitting of sound and image, mother and child. Narrative tension in this film centers on the listener's anticipation that Mandy and Helen will, to use a term introduced by Helen's brother Jimmie, be "opened" to dialogic speech.

Mandy and *Miracle* each pick up their stories about six years later, with girls now of school age, who, the films imply, have remained locked in the shadow worlds of their domestic spaces and infant egos. They are unprepared to enter the public sphere insofar as they have not achieved the ability properly to listen, to speak and, in Keller's case, see. Keller is particularly noncompliant, performing like the proverbial wild child who communicates her desires through gesture, physical force, and tantrum.[44] Christine's story resumes with her bitter statement that Mandy spent "the next five years being sheltered," and we see that the family has indeed gone back in time to a version of the uterine nightmare, moving from their bright, modern flat to the dark and drab Victorian home of Harry's parents. The latter home fully captures the stereotype of postwar England as a smothering and defensive domestic space. Christine and Harry face a crucial decision: should Mandy be kept in this dreary home under the tutelage of an elderly finger-spelling nurse-governess and doting paternal grandparents, as her father wishes, or should she be sent away to a modern residential school for the Deaf, where she would be taught to lip-read and possibly to speak in order to prepare her for life in the hearing world, as her mother desires? The mother's desires win out, casting her for the remainder of the film as the champion and representative of all that is moral and good about Britain's modern welfare state and its humanitarian reforms.

Debates about Deaf residential schools were very much "in the air" in postwar Britain. Discussions following the Education Act of 1944 proposed some integration of Deaf students into nonresidential schools.[45] That institutionalization is the film's moral response to Mandy's circumstance is made clear for viewers through a series of short vignettes set in the Victorian paternal home. Through these quick segments we witness Mandy dangerously compromised by her inability to listen and to communicate in this space. Viewers are expediently aligned with Christine and residential education as the modern, humane choice in a series of scenes that posit life at home as endangering to Mandy's social welfare and life.

In one of these segments we see Mandy in a medium close-up looking longingly through a wired-over gap in the wall framing the Garland yard, where she plays protected and alone. We cut to a shot, filmed from Mandy's point of view, of children noisily at play across a rubble-strewn lot, presumably the site of a home destroyed in an air raid during the war. The camera then returns, in a forlorn reverse shot, to Mandy. In a 1992 reading of *Mandy*, Annette Kuhn wrote that the domestic chasm where the children play in this scene symbolizes the gap between Mandy and other children caused by her inability to speak. Mandy's longing gaze across the chasm is not returned because she cannot hail those children with her voice. When Mandy later in the film utters her first word, Christine comments that it is like "seeing the door of a cage open," and it is Mandy's escape from this fenced yard into the social world of play with hearing children that we are meant to visualize. The backyard chasm scene is recalled at the end of the film, Kuhn reminds us, in a climactic scene where we see Mandy gazing across the same breach again, having returned home after a year at a residential school for the Deaf. But this time she enters the postwar playing field as a listener and a speaker, reading the lips of the child who asks her name and using her voice to hail her peers, to name herself, affirming her own identity and thus bridging the gap symbolized by the bomb chasm.

Kuhn reads these scenes within the terms of this metaphor of voice as emergent agency. I will give her reading closer consideration, but I first wish to consider what was at stake regarding listening in England during the war. In a vignette coupled with the chasm scene, the family dog runs into the street. Mandy leaps from the doorway into the path of a car to pull the dog from its path. Point-of-view shots from Mandy's perspective establish clearly that Mandy has seen the danger and makes the choice to risk her own life to rescue her pet. But the scene nonetheless is folded into a series of cases demonstrating the dangers posed to children who cannot hear the warning sounds of modern urban culture, such as the car horn, in places where technology increasingly encroaches upon private domestic space. The driver blares his horn, screeches his brakes, and hollers at Mandy in a tirade that fades to a faint hum on the soundtrack, putting listeners in Mandy's auditory point of view as we see her shamed face in close-up. The scene is clearly set up to suggest that Mandy requires special training and protection to survive in a postwar climate of urban development.

During the Second World War listening for air-raid sirens, planes, and strikes was a critical means of survival for hearing citizens. Deaf workers relied on visual and physical cues set up in advance with hearing coworkers. Accounts of experiences among Deaf citizens help to put the meanings of *Mandy*'s chasm and car scenes into perspective. Accounts like the one quoted below suggest that the chasm in *Mandy* would have had a meaning for Deaf British viewers of the film very different from those of film listeners. This is the account of one informant, a Bristol woman who ironically worked manufacturing munitions:

> I worked in Yate, just outside Bristol, in an ammunition factory, making shells. One night I was working when suddenly I noticed the power was failing on my machine. . . . I looked up and the woman opposite me pointed above her head and said *Jerries above*. . . . Suddenly the lights went out. . . . We were told to go and wait in a field away from the factory. . . . I looked over toward Bristol and saw nothing but a sea of flames. I . . . watched the fire and cried. I was only 19.
>
> When I finally got home I couldn't get into the house because the front door was locked. I . . . climbed over the garden wall where the bomb shelter was because I thought maybe my parents didn't know it was safe to come out. They were not in the shelter and I began to get very worried. In the end I broke a window to get into the house. They had slept the whole night through and had not known there was a raid. We all looked at the piece of string tied to my mother's toe. It had snapped.
>
> . . . There was a hearing foreman who got on very well with Deaf people, and he could communicate with me, using a special set of gestures that we had worked out between us. The foreman always worked on the same shift as I did so he could keep an eye on me. The foreman ran up to me and said (in our special gestures) *run for your life!*

There was a wall along my route to the shelter that should have protected me, but I was in a panic and ran along the wrong side of the wall where I could be seen. An aeroplane followed me, shooting me with its machine gun. . . . as I came to a gap in the wall, he [the fore-man] grabbed me and pulled me to the shelter on the other side. We saw a bomb land directly on the factory.[46]

Education toward the goal of survival in and service to a hearing world that was increasingly utilizing sound not only for communication but for workplace, home, and public safety helped to justify ongoing curricula in lipreading and speech. It is precisely this controversy surrounding sign (represented in Mandy by the signed English of the elderly nanny, not British Sign Language) versus oralism that is the broader tension driving the film's plot forward, lifting the text from sentimental melodrama and metaphor and placing it squarely into the real-world domain of the social problem film. The controversy is cast in postwar terms, foregrounding listening as a means of public safety and civic participation.[47] For the postwar milieu of Mandy, to become a listener is fully to become a subject and/as citizen.

Acoustics in Mandy (1952): The Deaf child as speaker

To become a speaker in the social sense of that term is to perform with the independence required of the public citizen. A speaker in the technological sense is an instrument that converts electrical energy into sound energy. It contains an amplifier, a public address system. In an essay about Helen Keller and the symbolic and literal meanings of her hands, Diana Fuss (2004) writes that the telephone was the first technology with which Keller was associated (135). She was introduced to it by Alexander Graham Bell at the 1893 World's Fair, where at the same time she was introduced to the phonograph. Keller, Fuss observes, most often appears in photographs as the passive receiver of the manual alphabet pressed into her hand by her interlocutor. Fantasies of Keller as a receptive medium extend to representations of her interest in the technology of radio (136–137). I mean to suggest here that Mandy, in her transition from the uterine space of the Victorian home to the residential school, performs this public function. She becomes a facilitative technology of voice, and not simply of reception. Through Mandy and her mother the nation may recognize itself as having the ability to confer agency, to extend to its citizens the ability to speak and to listen.

Like the psychoanalytic projector, the figure whose emanations enter the recipient with force, the speaker is a figure whose emanations amplify affect from screen to audience. If we take the view of Tomkins (1980), that affect is a form of *amplification*, then we can understand how the Deaf film child Mandy came to embody the potential voice of its audiences.

Mandy is set, as previously noted, in the fictional Bishop David School for the Deaf, a location probably meant to suggest a private Church of England mission school. The bulk of the film was shot at the real-life public Royal Manchester School for the Deaf. At this institution are set scenes that feature Mandy's emotionally grueling acquisition of lipreading and oral speech performance in her sixth year, a process witnessed by viewers through the perspectives of Christine and the female teachers who help Mandy achieve oral speech. The children with whom Mandy interacts on screen were actual residents of the Manchester school, untrained actors whom director Alexander Mackendrick coached to perform in the film.[48] They themselves would have been undergoing the oral training we see Mandy undergo on screen. Press coverage and the film's credits established the documentary status of these scenes for the film's audiences, ensuring that the public understood the real and present social importance of the melodrama's message regarding speech acquisition among the Deaf. A *London Times* film reviewer describes these scenes as going "straight to the heart and nerve-centres of emotion" (*London Times* 1952, 9).

Published in 1992, Annette Kuhn's essay "*Mandy* and Possibility" recalls the film theorist's own experience viewing the movie as a girl in a British cinema theater shortly after its release. Kuhn's mother had taken her to see "this picture everyone is talking about," a film about a girl, Kuhn explains, "who could so easily be myself" (Kuhn 1992, 233). It is not surprising that *Mandy* had a child audience, for in postwar Britain youth film culture thrived through the vast Odeon and Gaumont-Britain Children's Cinema Clubs, which had a collective membership of over 400,000 children ages seven to fourteen (one in ten British children in this age group) at the phenomenon's height, all sworn to an oath of "good and honourable young citizenship."[49] Ealing Studios would have been aware of this civic-minded young audience, suggesting the possibility that *Mandy* was indeed a film for girls. Kuhn explains to her readers that *Mandy* left its mark on the child Annette in the form of intense, emotionally charged memories of identification with the character Mandy during moments when the girl struggles to perform oral speech. Kuhn's identification with Mandy is interesting in a film that is so overtly designed to establish Christine, not Mandy, as narrative authority. After recounting her experience, Kuhn fast-forwards to a memory from 1980 when, as a film professor, she seized the opportunity to reconsider this film that had drawn from her such a strongly affective response years before. She recounts having an incongruous tearful outburst as an adult during a discussion about the film with a colleague. For Kuhn, revisiting *Mandy* is the catalyst not only for remembering, but also for taking seriously such affective responses to film (Kuhn 1992, 236–237). *Mandy*, Kuhn explains, "speaks to the child in both the child and the adult" (Kuhn 1992, 237).

My concern is, first, with the term "in." Might not the child-figure Mandy also speak to or call forth an adult female subject "waiting" in the girl who is the spectator of Mandy? In other words, might the film not also speak to the woman who the girl will someday become? And by what mechanism does Mandy call forth the child "inside" the adult spectator? My hypothesis is, first, that this process occurs in the complex form of the "we" form of identification, the sort that involves reciprocity and an interconstitutive process in subject formation. I also posit that that uniquely self-reflective and feminine affect, shame, is a major factor in the intersubjective processes of projective and incorporative identification.

Kuhn's choice of terms here—*Mandy speaks*—is of course deliberate in discussing a film where speech acquisition drives the plot. But the focus on Mandy as speaker is perplexing, for throughout the film the child Mandy does not acquire the framework and use of oral language, understood within psychoanalytic terms as entry into the symbolic, but rather acquires the initial ability to name. She speaks exactly two words by the end of the film: her own name, and "Mummy." These names are uttered with intense difficulty. In Kuhn's reading, Mandy's agency crystallizes in the moment in which the Deaf girl speaks her own name out loud, announcing herself with this single word as a subject in a social world of oral speakers as she joins hearing children to play in a field of domestic ruins. The child Annette, Kuhn tells her readers,

> desperately wants Mandy to triumph. At the end of the film, showing the world she can now "listen," can understand ("Lend us your ball," shouts a boy among a group of children at play. Mandy offers it to him with a smile. "What's your name?" he asks). Mandy makes the supreme effort to utter her name. With an equal intensity of concen-

tration, the girl in the audience wills the sound to come from those silently mouthing lips; inwardly, urgently, speaks the name for her; feels
such release when Mandy at last, in flat uninflected tones, manages to
achieve the two syllables. (Kuhn 1992, 234)

In psychoanalysis and in much of feminism, to speak the word is to enter
the social space of paternal law. Kuhn writes as the everygirl of postwar British listeners who gained voice and agency "with an equal intensity" along
with the screen child, naming herself as properly listening postwar subject,
a girl preparing to enter the public playing field of adulthood through the
second-wave women's movement in the decades to come. But the matter of
liberation is a complex one. Kuhn's essay was published well into the period
of the reform of Deaf education toward inclusion of sign language and during a period of wide recognition of sign language in Deaf culture.

I wish to shift the focus of analysis from the utterance of the word by
the autonomous Mandy as signifier of her emergence as agent in language
and the law, to the significance of the intersubjective production of vocal-
ized sound, not word-sound but a simple phoneme, as signifier of a different sort of developmental moment. This utterance, I will show, is achieved
intersubjectively, between Mandy, her teacher, and her mother. The scene I
have in mind is noted by the film's contemporary reviewers to describe their
cathartic experience via Mandy's entry into speech and the hearing social
order. This is a classroom scene during which Mandy first utters a letter
sound. This scene was singled out in the era's journalism for its "documentary fidelity." I turn to this scene so highly regarded as faithful to the real as
a means of moving away from the privileging of "the word" and language
as mediators of the subject's place in the law. I suggest two deviations from
Kuhn's focus. First, I wish to shift the emphasis from word to phonetic
sound. Second, in this scene Mandy's coming to linguistically meaningful
phonetic sound is a profoundly moving and even traumatic process that
secures her place not as an independent agent, but as a participant with a
maternal other in the physical pleasures of dialogically produced embodied
sound. I wish to highlight this moment of phonetic vocal expression as the
one the film seems to indicate as the climactic passage into subjecthood for
Mandy and her mother together, as a necessarily interdependent pair.

In her dissertation on phonosemantics Finnish scholar Margaret Mannus
(2001) proposes that the phoneme carries meaning; the morpheme is not the
smallest unit of meaning. In the case of oral speech this would mean that

sound, prior to its place in a word, may hold meaning. I wish to go with this claim for the purpose of this analysis. The phoneme holds the *promise* of the word.

This scene includes a highly analytic montage, shot in close-up, in one of the school's classrooms. Comprised of thirty close shots of Mandy and her teacher, Miss Stockton (played by the teenaged Australian actress Dorothy Allison), this sequence performs something akin to a serial motion study of the two figures as they negotiate the production of Mandy's phonetic utterance. Its analytic intensity reveals in stark detail the trauma Mandy experiences in achieving voice. Sound and image are fractured just as Mandy herself is torn by the struggle, violently thrust into the role of phonetic speaker. I will propose that this role allows her to transcend her state of silence, encoded as shameful, and enter symbolically into a position of access to public agency and hence pride. It is through uttering a phoneme that Mandy emerges belatedly into one who may contain speech.

Affect figures importantly in the process of coming to voice. The scene features an experiment in which Mandy comes to understand her own body as an instrument that transfers feeling and allows her feelings to be acoustically channeled and communicated into her female teacher and, importantly, her mother. Instrumental to this process are the teacher as maternal surrogate, and transitional objects (Winnicott 1971d, 1971e)—in this case, a container that substitutes for that primary form of the container that is the maternal body. The transitional objects featured in this scene are first a doll, a hollow of the human form tailor-made for the child to fill with projection, and then a balloon, a supple, responsive body pared down to porous skin and hollow container, waiting to be touched and filled with the resonance of intersubjective voice.

The scene begins in a classroom where a little girl plays with Mandy, mouthing to her the word "baby" with her lips as she holds a baby surrogate, a doll. Mandy presses her lips together, silently copying the "b-b-b" sound—keeping the sound, as it were, inside her mouth. Viewers look in on this scene along with a nervous female teacher positioned as voyeur at the classroom door. This teacher is not a lovely young woman like Dorothy Allison but an older, cynical instructor who could be described as homely. She happens to pause to look in at this scene as she passes by the doorway during her preparations to leave the school and the profession. Importantly, this teacher with whom we watch this scene is a skeptical viewer caught in the act of turning away: in a previous scene we watched and listened to her

outburst as she revealed to the school's headmaster her intense shame and
bitter resentment over her own inability to help these children speak. Her
outburst, fraught with bitter cynicism and defensive negativity about her de-
feat, was the classic response of turning away in impotent shame: she stated
her wish to leave the school and the thankless job because she had failed. She
is positioned inside the film as the moral witness, the distant, critical, external gaze before which the shame that is a child who cannot listen and cannot
speak may be played out and worked through for the film's spectators, an
audience caught during this crucial historical turn in the act of turning away
from the social problem of Deaf education. Like the teacher, the audience is
positioned as witness to the scene. Their invisibility and distance, requisites
of pity, allow the audience to sustain its look in the face of Mandy's pain,
and thereby to work through that moment when the spectator's eyes lower
from another's pain to afford them privacy. Importantly, by positioning the
spectator outside the door with the skeptical teacher double, this scene at
first asks nothing of the spectator except to act as distant witness.

When Mandy silently mouths the labial sound b-b-b, Miss Stockton no-
tices immediately. She rushes over to Mandy's side. In a move that will
be replicated with a difference in *The Miracle Worker* ten years later, the
teacher takes the place of the playmate, making the scene into a playground
of repetition—a kind of object-relations play therapy. Miss Stockton thrusts
into Mandy's hands a b-b-b-balloon, a phonetic substitute for b-b-b-baby.
Like the baby doll, the balloon is a hollow body, a transitional, scooped-
out object waiting to be filled with the resonant exchanges that will pass
between female teacher and girl child. This is a crucial transitional passage
in which Mandy moves from listener to speaker. With these quick transitions in player and object, the scene shifts gears formally into a pattern of
serial close ups and extreme close ups, shot-reverse shots of the teacher-
child pair physically linked through their manual and labial contact with
the resonant transitional object positioned between them, the balloon. Miss
Stockton presses her hands and lips to the balloon, uttering a staccato series of b sounds on its surface. As if performing an externalized display of
the transitional zone described in Spitz's work on the primal cavity (1955),
she transfers her voice from her mouth out onto the surface of the balloon, where it is mediated into the balloon's interior space, and then on to
Mandy's own lips and hands. "Feel the vibration," Miss Stockton instructs
Mandy as the sound passes into her body. The camera cuts in to an extreme
close-up of Mandy's hands and lips pressed against the balloon's surface as

4. Mandy and Miss Stockton, eyes locked, pass sound
vibration mouth to mouth in a resonant field of looks.
Mandy (1952).

Miss Stockton's b-b-b utterance is looped on the soundtrack, first louder,
then distorted in the wowing sound of stretched magnetic tape. The looped
playback is then slowed to a gradual stop. The b-b-b sound drops out and
a high-pitched string instrument whine cuts in. This single, high-pitched
tone is sustained and matched to Mandy's face, suggesting that it is meant
to signify Mandy's interior auditory and tactile experience of the sound.
The abstract string-instrument vibration gets louder then drops out as the
camera cuts between Miss Stockton and Mandy negotiating the balloon that
is now firmly established as a connective acoustic field between them. The
spectator-listener witnesses a negotiation in which Mandy at first resists and
then succumbs to the transference and incorporation of the teacher's letter-
sound into her own body. Mandy literally takes in that sound.

   René Spitz, the psychiatrist who pioneered the use of Freudian psychoanalysis to empirically chart ego development in the first year of life, developed the concept of the mouth as a "primal cavity" in directions that will
be useful here.[50] Spitz identified certain transitional oral zones that mediate
between inside and outside, between peripheral sensory organs (such as
the skin) and visceral ones. These transitional organs and zones include the
tongue, the laryngopharynx, the soft palate, the inside of the cheek, where
they intersect with the peripheral zones: the lips, the chin, the nose, and
the outside of the cheek surface (Spitz 1955, 1965, 44–45). In my discussion of Mandy's passage into acoustic space below, these transitional zones
are both replicated in, and are extended and facilitated by, the transitional

objects of doll and balloon (and later, in *Johnny Belinda*, by another hollow instrument, the fiddle). For Spitz, the transitional zones that mediate between inside and outside also play an anaclitic function: They form a bridge between coenesthetic (autonomic, visceral, unconscious) and diacritic (conscious, cognitive) functions in the experience of the subject. In my discussion below, the balloon is a mediating, transitional object that anaclitically props up—we may go so far as to say prosthetically extends—the transitional zones of the body described by Spitz. Mandy's incorporation of Miss Stockton's labial phonemic utterance depends on this facilitative skin, the balloon, that forms a bridge between their bodies, but which also, for Mandy, forms a bridge between the visceral and the unconscious, on the one hand, and the conscious and cognitive, on the other. The balloon's mediation allows her experience to move from feeling to meaning, from affect to representation, and from incorporation to introjection.

I have used the term "incorporation," not "introjection," thus far for particular reasons. Distinction between the terms requires clarification here. Laplanche and Pontalis explain that orality is the prototype of incorporation, making incorporation "the matrix of introjection and identification" (1973, 212). Freud first used the term "incorporation" in his earliest discussion of the oral stage, during which he began to emphasize the importance of the object (the breast). Previously, in his 1905 "Three Essays on the Theory of Sexuality," he had emphasized the activity of sucking. But in his 1915 writings on the oral stage of the organization of the libido, Laplanche and Pontalis remind us, the subject's act of obtaining erotic mastery over the object entails the destruction of the object (Laplanche and Pontalis 1973, 212). The destructive tendency of projection features strongly in Klein's discussions of projective identification. Maria Torok makes a distinction between the terms incorporation and introjection.[51] Her distinction helps us to better understand the significance of introjection for this scene in *Mandy* and the moment in subject formation it models. Torok proposes that incorporation tends toward compensation for loss, and involves the taking in whole of a traumatically lost entity. Introjection is a very different process, tending toward development and growth rather than compensation. Introjection is a gradual process in which instinctual promptings are transformed by naming into desires and fantasies of desires, and are thus given the right to exist in the external world. Incorporation is much more immediate and internally organized, operating by means of representations, affects, and bodily states. Incorporation occurs relative to a loss that constitutes an insurmountable obstacle. The naming that transforms instinctual promptings into fantasies in introjection is absent in incorporation (Abraham and Torok 1994, 113). "While the introjection of desires puts an end to objectal dependency, incorporation of the object creates or reinforces imaginal ties and hence dependency" (114). Finally, like myth, incorporation may "state the desire to introject" even as it does not achieve the naming of the unborn desire it disguises (115).

Torok's point that incorporation proceeds by way of representations, affects, and bodily states but not by ways of naming (the word) or articulation of fantasy (narrativization) is a crucial one for our purposes. Her distinction opens up a space for analysis of what comes before naming, before the word, but still within the realm of representation and bodily states. Incorporated entities can be observed and described, even if the subject does not engage in practices of naming and narrativization. Incorporation is a process that proceeds as if magically and instantaneously, presupposing a lost object and taking it in without giving it the means to exist in the world. But this process, when modeled in screen characters, can nonetheless be described—named and narrativized—by spectators.

The lost object that I am proposing in my reading of Mandy is not her hearing but her voice or, more precisely, the child with a voice who Mandy's mother imagined Mandy might have become, but for her deafness. By incorporating Miss Stockton's projected voice, by swallowing it whole and spitting it back out with expulsive force, Mandy puts herself on the path to the introjection of the word (the ability to name, to narrativize, to speak the word). But she is not yet there.

In incorporating Miss Stockton's vocalization, Mandy allows her body to be used as potential space for the movement of sound that is the basis for dialogic speech. We might consider the process of identification to be one in which the subject recognizes herself not only as one who is (or, who is mirrored in) the other *in* potential space, but as part of the potential space itself through which communication moves. She is an extension of the mediating balloon that is at once both transitional object and potential space. For Winnicott, a transitional object may be an entity such as a blanket or toy given to the child by the mother. The transitional object is a container for what passes between mother and child, substituting for the direct physical contact of body to body, mouth to breast. The balloon allows the child to invest her feelings away from the body of the mother and into the field inhabited also by an intermediate other. The balloon, like the doll she had been playing with earlier in this scene, is a contained entity that abstractly duplicates the body of another, allowing the body to enter into the field of play. The balloon's hollow interior offers the openness and containment of an acoustic field through which communication, moving sound, may resonate. This is a potential space waiting to be inhabited. It is a space waiting to take in and hold a projection.

The soundtrack is, in a metaphoric sense, also an empty space of potential interconnection. It waits to be filled. Silence fills a few key moments of this portion of the scene in which Miss Stockton and Mandy struggle over what passes between them in the acoustic space contained by the balloon. A rarity in sound-era cinema, absolute silence makes these moments stand out to listeners, who would have been acutely aware of the pregnant pause's intended significance as Mandy's acoustic viewpoint, her supposedly "blank" aural experience, waiting to be broken and filled. Abruptly, sound floods the acoustic field of the theater. Listeners are jolted out of Mandy's aural perspective with a piercing shriek that, confusingly, is Mandy's own voice. This shriek is accompanied by a deafening shatter that is synched with a shot of a china cup and saucer crashing to the floor, shot from Mandy's optical point of view. This abrupt transition in sound casts the listener from a deep involvement with Mandy's "silent" inner distress, her metaphorical absence, into the surprise shock of breakthrough to powerful sound emanating from her previously silent body. An extreme close-up on Mandy's face reveals that she is crying. These are not tears of shame or anguish, but of confusion, relief, and pride. The careful sequencing of events leads the spectator-listener to read this flood of sound and tears as dam-breaking relief, signaling a transition that will follow from shame to pride and joy.

What is staged in this moment of breakthrough is Mandy's belated achievement of a mirror-stage developmental equivalent. Mandy *feels* sound pass through her and, in taking it in, (mis)recognizes it as her own. Sound fills her to bursting, causing a tension that forces deafening expulsive projections: the smashing of the china and the scream. But at this moment of sonic excorporation, Mandy's signifying orifice, her mouth, is ironically hidden from view by the balloon pressed to her lips. Her mouth is out of sight; however, listeners can hear her utterance, her loud and frantic b-b-b-b, resonating through the potential space of the balloon that had linked her to her teacher. The physical transference of agency from caregiver to child is complete as the child gives back sound, completing the passionately affective feedback loop that is empathetic identification. Mandy has not become "like" Miss Stockton, nor does she learn to speak words like her; rather, she has taken in and spit out a part-object—the phonemic sound Miss Stockton has quite literally projected into her.

Here is the lesson in affect regulation and modulation modeled in this scene: Mandy, feeling the sonic impact of the cup and saucer as they crash to the floor, stands frozen, startled and overwhelmed by her loss of control over excitations. Surely someone will disapprove of this destructive behavior toward the object. Miss Stockton defies the logic of the normative six-year-old superego and lets Mandy have the babyish tantrum. She drags Mandy over to another cup and saucer set and gestures to her to repeat her forceful expulsion that produced such damaging effects. Mandy's transition out of shame through the emergency affect of rage is thus effected in the medium of sound and the destroyed object as she crashes a second cup to the floor. This scene echoes an earlier scene, in which the father, Harry Garland, in an emergency state of fear and denial regarding his discovery of his daughter's deafness, crashes a metal tray to the floor. At that moment the father's aggressive act of aural signification—the crash of the tray a command to his toddler daughter to *listen*, to look his way—is utterly lost on the daughter's deaf ears. She does not respond to the command to listen (to look). This confirms in him and in the film's spectator-listeners the shattering reality of Mandy's deafness, her tragic inability to become a listener in a world defined by hearing.

Through the passage of letter-sound from Miss Stockton and into Mandy via the balloon, and in the projection of sound into Miss Stockton that Mandy performs in return, Mandy's shameful, devastating silence is transformed into an intersubjective achievement of becoming the potential space through which sound passes and is shared. This is the social space of intersubjective communication. Filled to bursting with sound, Mandy is also filled to bursting with anger, fear, and finally pride and joy in her imagined sense of self-control over production, containment, and expulsion of sound. Just as the toddler apprehends itself in the mirror and imagines itself in command of the figure it spies, proudly reflected in the gleam in its mother's eye, so the child Mandy belatedly achieves a sense of mastery over her body as the bounded space through which communication may pass, regulated by her movements.

Given the sense of self-mastery conveyed in this scene, it is striking that in the remainder of this scene Mandy's mouth is never visible on screen as she repeats the labial phoneme whose incorporation and excorporation she has mastered. What matters is not Mandy's speech performance, but her embodiment of sound—and, as we shall now see, her engagement with its responsive echo in the body of another. Green notes that "the most primitive expression of subjectivity needs to find an echo in another in order to receive its meaning" (Green 1999a, 297). Mandy, upon recognizing herself in sound, immediately seeks out her affirming echo. Not surprisingly, she finds this in the body of her mother. Following the performance described above, Mandy urgently signs to her teacher to take her to her mother—and it is here in the act of signing, that we first see Mandy as speaker. Miss Stockton answers by rushing Mandy from the room to a vast hall where her mother stands waiting to receive her. In the triumphant shot that concludes the scene, the performance of sound-incorporation and excorporation between teacher and child is repeated—but with two crucial differences. In the place of the teacher stands the mother. And in the place of the transitional object, the balloon, stands Mandy's own body as transitional space. Mandy grabs her mother's hand and places it upon her own chest, through this gesture inviting her mother not to hear but to feel the "b-b-b" sound resonating inside her body. The sound that passes directly from daughter's hollow chest cavity through the mother's hand and into the mother's own body echoes with improbable loudness against the hard, reflective walls of the entry hall, as if that space were the interior of Mandy herself. This expansive hall is the ideal theater for Mandy's grand entrance into sound. Mandy, the projector (amplifier) of sound, is born as listening subject in this moment of the film. We feel her feeling the sound emanating from within herself out into the theater space. We feel her projecting it into the body of her mother through that medium of (as-if) direct transmission of feeling that is the hands. As Mandy recognizes sound as an object produced within her, she expels and projects it into her mother, who lovingly takes it into herself. The intersubjective, affective feedback loop of communicated sound-feeling is complete.

Or is it? Mandy has become a speaker, an acoustic playback medium that performs and amplifies her own voice, asserting her agency and control over the body in a kind of late-breaking mirror-stage performance. But for Mandy fully to experience pride of self in her performance, she must be able to hear herself speak. Recall Doane's observation that whereas we appear to others without appearing to ourselves, we at once emit and hear the vocal sounds we produce. Sound is routed as if immediate, as if without medium. But Mandy, like Robeson in the field of the acoustic envelope described earlier in this chapter, has no capacity to hear herself. Mandy requires an acoustic envelope, a playback mechanism. It is helpful here to recall Kohut's description of a scene in a film of the 1940s by Burlingham and Robinson, in which a girl who is blind lights up with joy at the experience of being a listener to her own voice on a tape recorder, a machine whose playback function Kohut likens to the mirroring function of the mother (Kohut 1971, 118). It is the mother's face, in this final shot of this pivotal scene in *Mandy*, that functions as Mandy's reciprocal playback device. The mother's face is a machine that registers delight, delivering in and to Mandy the ego-constitutive thrill of seeing the sound of her own voice received. Christine's face, fully visible to spectators while Mandy's mouth remains out of sight, reflects Mandy's performance back to the girl and to spectators. The face, along with the conductive hand that connects the two bodies, forms a sensory loop in which Mandy sees and feels the pleasure her sound performance confers to others even as she cannot hear it herself. For the film listener-spectator, the mother and her surrogate, the teacher, are empathetic pathways to Mandy.

I noted in chapter 1 that Green suggests that we imagine the affective process as "*the anticipation of a meeting between the subject's body and another's body*" (Green 1999a, 312, his italics). He repeats this phrase some twenty-five years later with the proviso that the object may be "imaginary or present" (Green 1999b, 289). Imaginary or present: this phrase makes a world of difference. In this scene from *Mandy*, the adult listener's object of anticipation is the child, or more precisely the *present* child's *anticipated* voice as *imagined* representative (delegate) of agency—both the adult's agency and the child's. But to hear the child's voice, and to see the child narcissistically experience—*feel*—its own voice is not to witness the emergence of the subject *in language*, for "b-b-b" is not language. Rather, the relation through the transitional object facilitates an understanding of the means of induction, command, and interpellation that are basic to becoming one who *can* listen, one who *will be* listened to—and one who experiences representation and affect as necessarily interconstitutive, not separate processes.

To return to my initial claim about the transitional object and potential space, we might imagine the affective process a little differently now. Altering Green's statement, we might imagine affect as *the anticipation of one's body as the potential space through which the subject's body and another's body may meet.* What I am proposing is that what may be incorporated is not simply the object or part-object in its imagined materiality, but the incorporative process itself, fantasized as ability and control. Taking in and emitting are fundamental to all sensory ability and function, whether we understand this to happen automatically or through will or desire.

Thus far I have emphasized the intersubjective relationship between two subjects. I conclude this section on *Mandy* by returning to the figure of the teacher who looks on at Mandy and her mother from the corner of the entry hall. The scene sets up a triadic structure of gaze and voice as well, a structure that will be essential in my discussion of facilitated communication in the next section of this book. To discuss this triadic structure, I return to Tomkins on the system of shame. Most of his formulations were built on a dyadic structure of interpersonal communication and interocular looking, emphasizing parent and child relationships. But he did also write about a more multivalent model even where only two subjects are involved. In this model, which he calls a "hall of mirrors of shame," the self is experienced as "two-headed." "I hang my head in shame," when, for example, I witness another person who appears to be ashamed of me. But the self is also three-headed, as in the case where I hold within my mind a third, internalized self that hangs its head in shame (Tomkins 1963, 214; see also Benin and Cartwright 2006, 5–6). The figure of the teacher who looks on from the corner of the hallway, apparently unseen by Mandy and Christine but witnessed by the spectator, externalizes this internal witness whose head hangs in shame. We might substitute pride for shame in the formula Tomkins describes: Mandy raises her head in pride when she witnesses a person (her mother) whom she imagines to be proud of her. The teacher constitutes the "third head" that performs the transformation taking place across herself, Mandy, and Christine. She changes posture from one of shame (hung head and facial countenance) to the open, radiant face of pride—in Mandy, in the method of coming to voice, in her own stature as an instructor in this community. Here shame may have been the trajectory to community, but pride is the constitutive emotion of sustaining that belonging. Oscillations between shame and pride make community formation dynamic and fluid.

Miracle Worker *(1962): Hunger, touch, and violent play*

The scenes of Mandy's first utterance of phonemic sound establishes a theme that links play to oral speech breakthrough. This resonates with Penn's *Miracle Worker* ten years later. Following the diagnostic opening described earlier, *The Miracle Worker* is composed, like *Mandy*, of a series of vignettes demonstrating Helen's progress toward dialogic communication ability. Helen does not, of course, acquire oral speech. Rather, the film climaxes with Helen "coming to voice" in being interpellated into Sullivan's finger-signed alphabet, accepting the interaction of a vibrating throat pressed into her hand, and performing speech through a human mediator. My focus, in the discussion of this film that follows, is the relationship between touch, play, and a new element—hunger—in this film narrative of the child Helen's emergence as a social subject with her teacher, Anne Sullivan.

Helen's progress to transitive communication is mapped, in the film, as a study in the escalation of corporal discipline that revolves around control over eating and the satisfaction of hunger, an affective condition that I interpret (after Rado 1956) as being linked fundamentally to the hunger for attachment with others. Hunger, I propose, is a key component of what drives Sullivan as well as Helen in their steps toward a fully intersubjective relationship. Throughout the film, eating and drinking are coded as rituals of belonging and submission to the law of the family.

Laplanche and Pontalis note that, for Freud, sexuality and nourishment are closely connected (Laplanche and Pontalis 1973, 212). For the most part, this has been interpreted to mean that nourishment stands in as metaphor for displaced or repressed sexual drives, in dreams and fantasies. In what follows, I wish to emphasize the fundamental literal place of eating and hunger, not restricted to nourishment, expressed somatically through the intersubjective performance of eating rituals. Nourishment is instinctually linked to aspects of love that are not limited to the sort of sexual love euphemistically called genital. Keller's submission to Sullivan's authority is achieved in the film, I will demonstrate, through manipulation of the pleasures of eating, only part of which is in response to the need for satiety. The pleasure of eating freely is typically moderated by an inner sense of the need for restraint, an inner moral spectator that regulates intake: one should not eat past the point of being "full" and/or achieving appropriate levels of nourishment. As we will see below, not just the need to be full, but also the desire for a surplus or excess that brings added pleasure beyond the state of satiety, the sugary reward that is dessert, is an important aspect of the child's experience of eating. Dessert is associated with reward, surplus satisfaction, and pleasures—both guilty and pure. Sullivan's achievement of control over Helen and the bringing of Helen to "voice" are achieved, in the film, in large part through regulation of her food intake, and climacti-

5. Mandy shares sound with her mother in a visually
and acoustically resonant field. *Mandy* (1952).

cally through the use of dessert as reward and punishment in a sadistic
game. I focus on two scenes in which the pair spars over food. Helen is not
the only one fed in these scenes, I propose. Anne's hunger for attachment
is also sated. I will be describing this relationship of screen characters in a
manner that allows me to articulate the deeply physical aspect of their bond
while avoiding the reductive view that this indicates a sexual subtext in their
lifelong relationship. The erotic dynamic I describe is not best served by the
concept of sexual love.

A set of concepts developed through Winnicott, Green, and others will be
referenced in this discussion of the attachment between Keller and Sullivan.
I have already described the film terrain using the psychoanalytic concept
of the playground, a space situated between the psyche and the external
world and between fiction and real life. The film is a site where psychic
problems may be acted out and worked through for a public that dares not
speak of these problems outside the family, the school, and the health and
rehabilitative therapy context. In what follows, I read *The Miracle Worker*
as a text that dramatizes the psychic playground. I propose that Sullivan, as
caregiver, stands in for the analyst as the figure of authority in overseeing
a transference relationship in which the disordered child is turned into a
listener and a social subject in this transitional space.

Some historical background is required to ground the interpretive claims
I will make below. As is well known, Keller was born in 1880 to a wealthy
Alabama family and, following an interview with oral education advocate
and eugenicist Alexander Graham Bell, was tutored from age six onward by

Sullivan. An orphan reared in a poorhouse in Tewksbury, Massachusetts, and (later) at the residential Perkins School for the Deaf in Boston, Sullivan left her institutional home at the age of twenty-one to take up her post with the Keller family. My account will suggest that Sullivan's role in the film version of this early pedagogical relationship is a study in the replication of institutional discipline and rituals of forming attachment. She engages in child-to-child caretaking. Sullivan was a young woman prematurely turned surrogate mother. She met Helen when the girl was the age that she herself was when she lost first her sight (which was later partially restored) and, soon after, her mother. Thus Sullivan lost the two things Kohut tells us are essential for the maternal-mirror transference so fundamental to the emergence of a self (Kohut 1971, 116–119). What better teacher for the blind girl than a girl who has herself experienced the loss of her own "playback unit," her mother, as well as her sight? Sullivan, as we shall see, resorts to touch in the absence of sight and sound to mirror Keller, echoing the smaller girl's slaps and shoves with equally forceful, projective, and affective gestures. Issues of identification and projection between Sullivan and Keller were undoubtedly complexly played out in this relationship in real life, as Robert Young and Hanna Segal suggest in their interpretations of the Keller biography (Young 1994, Segal 1981). My aim, to be clear, is not to analyze the actual relationship of these two women in their real lives or their authored texts, but rather to consider the filmic revival and restaging of this narrative for a 1960s viewing public in the midst of a Black civil rights movement and on the cusp of second-wave feminism, the disability rights movement, and heightened awareness of child abuse as a social problem requiring study and intervention.

Miracle portrays Helen's steps to becoming a listener most vividly through two scenes in which Anne aggressively controls Helen's access to food. Hunger and its fulfillment surely were major issues for Anne as a child growing up in the Tewksbury poorhouse. Rado (1956) describes the borderline personality disorder of the individual whose emotional need for attachment went unmet in childhood and who later experiences a profoundly deep, insatiable sense of need that he calls *affect hunger*. "Attachment hunger" is a phrase in psychology used by Jung and others to refer to a hunger for love and care that is linked to the pre-Oedipal period and to dependency. I use the term loosely here, not as a diagnostic term but as a descriptive term, to characterize the relationship between hunger and attachment, and between attachment hunger and the more-than-symbolic status of food as not only signifier but also a concrete, physical form of love, as these are cast by the film. In the film the desire for food and fulfillment of physical hunger are symbolic of a power struggle over submission to a relationship of dependent love that will strongly institute Sullivan in the role of caretaker and mediator. Through Helen is performed Sullivan's own "rebirth" as a social subject. Keller's obedience is rewarded with food, supplying a satisfaction that, in the film, is central in weaning her away from her mother, whose disciplinary tactics are represented as weak and ambivalent, and to the adversity-steeled Sullivan. Keller's transference relationship to Sullivan is intense, not despite the control and force used upon the girl by the caregiver but because of it. This relationship, I propose, is built upon a fundamental violence. This is the violence that Arendt links to a political compassion that "speaks only to the extent that it has to reply directly to the sheer expressionist sound and gestures" of suffering's audibility and visibility (Arendt 1963, 82). Control over food and physical force are used as means of getting Helen to become firmly attached and compliant, to subordinate her will to Anne and to make her the figure upon whom life depends. Both scenes described below involve use of physical discipline, an audiovisual ritual of bodily force that fuses Anne and Helen in physical proximity and in synchronous image-and-sound unity that optically and sonically figures the production of the two, through ritual perversions of sadistic feeding and play.

Let us turn to the film. Early in the narrative, Sullivan makes a demand to Helen's father, Captain Keller. Her demand sets things straight regarding who will embody the law for Helen in this newly reconfigured psychic world: "I want complete charge of her," Sullivan demands shortly after her arrival to the Keller household. In a performance so infamous that National Public Radio chose it from among Bancroft's many lines to remember her upon the occasion of her death, Bancroft (Sullivan) proceeds from this statement to outline a list of the child's bodily and mental rituals and processes over which she wants control.

Tomkins describes the shaming of the child as the event at the origin of the taboo on looking. This typically first occurs in the situation where a child is shamed in the presence of a guest who is a stranger to the child (Tomkins in Sedgwick and Frank 1995, 146). The first scene in *The Miracle Worker* that explicitly enacts the attachment hunger process is a scene in which Anne is positioned precisely as a stranger who witnesses Helen's shame. However, it is Anne and not Helen's parents who perform the role of the shamer. She does so with a physical intensity worthy of a martial-arts film.

The setting is the dining room of the Keller home. Through Anne's point of view the camera tracks Helen as the girl moves along the periphery of the dinner table where the rest of the family and Anne are assembled before their plates. Impervious to the bodies seated at the table, Helen feels her way from seat to seat, dipping her hands and face into each family member's plate to stuff into her mouth whatever food her fingers encounter. She satisfies her physical hunger with greedy gusto, without generating any response from or engagement with the person at each setting. As if blind to the girl scrounging off of their plates with her hands as she gropes past their seats, Captain Keller and his adult son Jimmie heatedly discuss politics. It is obvious that Helen need never feel hungry, for her access to food is without boundaries. She revels in the process of taking it in, stuffing herself with exuberance.

Anne's eyes alone track Helen's movements at the periphery of the table. Outraged at this uncouth performance of eating, Anne is equally shocked at the inattentive permissiveness of the parents, who take no notice. This scene can be compared to Tomkins's description of a similar family drama. Because his account is, conveniently, published in 1963, shortly after the film's release, we may look to it as an example of the scripts of shame at play in the film's immediate social context. In Tomkins's narrative, a boy called Little Robert eats "greedily" at the dinner table. His mother scolds him, shaming him into a passive posture of nonaffect. Robert covers over his emotions with a mask of nonfeeling and stops eating with gusto. The scolding mother, Tomkins explains, "defends the elementary decencies upon which Western civilization rests." Tomkins mimics the stun-gun impact of the disdainful mother who deflates Robert's ego with one barbed comment, reducing his eager comportment at the dinner table to that of a limp rag doll with the exasperated line "Oh, Robert, you'd think you hadn't eaten in a week, really!" (Tomkins in Sedgwick and Frank 1995, 164). In this narrative, the content behind Robert's shaming is the status of his actual hunger relative to his performance of sating hunger beyond the point of being full, his enactment of desire for the satisfaction of taking in more than enough. To act hungry when one is not, to seek to satisfy one's desire to introject the object food enthusiastically and with pleasure, is infantile, and therefore shameful.

In a manner that is similar to that of the scolding mother in Tomkins's account of Little Robert, Anne seizes control of Helen, and attempts to instill in her a sense of shame with regard to her performance of desire to take in food. Because Helen cannot hear Anne's disciplining words or see her re-

proachful looks, touch becomes the crucial medium of the shaming practice
played out between the two. Convincing the family to leave her and Helen
locked alone in the dining room, Anne launches an interaction covered in
a brutal eight minutes of film that track Helen's first lesson in attachment
hunger and self-shame. Helen responds with surprise and apprehension to
her entrapment in the dining room alone with Anne. She desperately strokes
her own face, a self-soothing but communicative gesture that typically summons her mother to her side. When this call for the mother fails, Helen tries
to escape, desperately seeking a route up the chimney. A series of rapid
swish pans track the movements of the pair as Anne chases Helen down,
tackling her and pinning her to her chair over and over again. Anne grabs
Helen's jaw and forces open Helen's mouth, cramming in a serving spoon
of mashed potatoes. Helen neatly projects the force-fed mouthful back into
Anne's face. Anne returns the blow, throwing a pitcher of water into Helen's
face. When Helen obstinately continues to eat with her fists not her spoon,
Anne grasps the girl's jaw and squeezes, forcing her to disgorge the mouthful
of potatoes that she has just taken in. Throughout this scene, blows to the
surface of the body and physical manipulation of the other's incorporation
and excorporation of food replace conversation in shot-reverse shot volleys,
making the scene a motion study in relays of projection, incorporation,
and excorporation. We see modeled on the screen the force with which the
subject may project, the force with which the receiver of a projection may
resist incorporation and spit back the projection, and the force with which
the subject may repeatedly insist on control over the other's cycle of projection and incorporation.

   Essential to this therapeutic process is Sullivan's bringing about in Helen
a sense of a "psychic playground," a mental potential space that is internal to both figures, and which both operate together. Sullivan fosters the
production of this mental space by arranging for sustained physical experiences of confinement and isolation of the caregiver-child unit, spaces
that become sites for private therapeutic interactions in which touch (in
the form of pushing, slapping, grabbing, forcing food onto and into the
other) and physical care (feeding or withholding food, dressing) replace the
typical therapeutic and caregiving media of voice and the look. In the film
set's confined domestic spaces where Anne and Helen spar, the transference
required for Helen's (and Anne's) entry into language and social belonging
are achieved. I emphasize that this working through is achieved not only for
Keller, who famously came to communicate through Sullivan's tough-love

ministrations, but also for Anne, who acts out and works through her own hunger for attachment in demonic repetitions and in identifications of her own childhood pain projected violently out onto the startled body of the deaf-blind child she tutors.

Anne's work is accomplished through the object of food not once but twice in the film. (Another time it will be a doll and, in the climactic scene, water.) Anne eventually breaks Helen's unbridled pleasure in satisfying hunger, instilling in her the regulatory gaze of Smith's "inmate of the soul" (Smith 1966). Shame in taking socially unmitigated pleasure in incorporating food, love, and the tactile pleasures of unregulated touch are brought into check. Anne establishes a complete intrusion upon the psychic integrity of the child's infantile narcissism, forcing Helen to rally forth the primitive defenses and to project, excorporate, and incorporate in response to her own orders.

Green describes the wish of the subject to identify with another as an intersubjective "project" (Green 1986, 99). The link between project, which he describes as synonymous with wish, and projection, which we may understand as being the putting into action of the wish, is not to be overlooked here. The contest over food and shame enacted in this scene is the pair's project, its shared enactment of a wish, in this sense. That is, together Anne and Helen engage in an *inter*projective contest of desires, the outcome of which will be a sense of self for both Anne and Helen, a self produced through this physical practice of shaming through touching, slapping, hitting, and pushing. Shame is a category of practice that, for Tomkins, is fundamentally constitutive of sociality in the human subject.[52] The "project" of bringing Helen to voice is, fundamentally, a project of bringing Helen to shame (and thus pride) through physical force in the place of the looking and the listening that are off limits to Helen.

Tomkins describes numerous scenarios of parental-child shame performances, all of which are described in terms of looks and bodily performance read visually. To a lesser extent, the spoken word is also involved, as is clear in the example of Little Robert's mother's shaming accusation. The child's behavior, heard and observed by strangers, guests and teachers, shames the parents; the parent's shaming words and looks cow the child into a posture of shame; the parent's physical expressions of shame may be internalized and revived in the child's mind's eye where he or she remembers and reenacts the same offense later, witnessed by the self in place of the parents. Even the negative, head-hanging posture of shame—the child's face and limbs hanging limp, for example, after being shamed for eating with too much verve and gusto—may instill further shame in the parents. Here the child is taught that not only is it projective of shame to visibly express any affect (outwardly expressing joy in taking in food is shameful too), but also the erasure of affect from one's body (the hiding of one's joy by hanging one's head in shame, for example) may be a visual cue that projects shame, insofar as the parents too may hang their heads in shame along with the child (Tomkins in Sedgwick and Frank 1995, 164). With these shifts in agency, location, and embodied performance, we see shame (and joy) as something expressed not so much in the individual body, but across bodies. It is a moral system put into practice intersubjectively and multimodally, through the technologies of looking, speaking, and listening (or not). Tomkins's stories of shame being experienced in the form of multiple voices internalized in the mind of the child echo those told by Adam Smith when he brings to life for his readers the concept of the "inmate of the soul," the inner voice that guides moral judgment (1966), and, as we shall see in the next chapter, by Freud when he describes the fantasies of his patients in "A Child Is Being Beaten" (1955a).

Tomkins is clear about the importance of the look in shame processes. But he does not consider closely oral expression—not simply talk, but expressions and qualities of vocal sound, its production and suppression in the other, and the act of being listened to by, and listening to, an other—as a route through which shame and pride are expressed and communicated. I suggest that we go even further and consider the factor of oral touch (sucking, eating, the explorations of the tongue as a sensory instrument) as a component of oral expression. We may understand eating as a form of touch, and the giving of food, in this sense. To eat is to touch oneself inside with objects. To be fed is to allow another to touch oneself inside. René Spitz suggests as much in proposing his concept of the mouth as the primal cavity. "With its equipment of tongue, lips, cheeks and nasopharynx," he writes, the oral cavity is "the first surface in life to be used for tactile perception" (Spitz 1965, 64; Spitz 1955). Tactile and oral perception, he notes, are usually performed with an other. His example is oral contact during nursing, but we might add that any form of feeding and being fed, as well as the acts of kissing and oral sex, are intersubjective and projective forms of touching. Experience in acoustic space, as I suggested above in my analysis of the balloon scene in *Mandy*, entails both aural and tactile interaction. Importantly, the tactile space of eating bridges the body's exterior and interior. This is captured in the example of the mouth, where food, like vocal expression, is incorporated and projected.

Touch is the sense least discussed by Tomkins. It is to this sensory medium of Helen's socialization that I will now turn once again, using as my example a second scene from *The Miracle Worker*. In this scene, eating and feeding once again come into play.

As we shall see in the reading of *The Miracle Worker* that preceded this one, food is a reward and a punishment. It can be accepted or refused. Negotiations over the production of states of hunger and satiety are enacted through a dialogic cycle of projection and incorporation. Boundaries between self and other blur as the one who offers food projects its objects into the body of the other. The deep frustration and aggression that stir between Anne and Helen over food are productive, not simply of Helen's ability to communicate but of a system of projective identification that radically redraws their respective somatic boundaries. As I will show, play objects foster a kind of relating through identification (Winnicott 1971e) that constitutes *both* subjects, interdependently.

In the film's second prolonged one-on-one discipline scene, Anne again manipulates Helen into submission through control over food. However, in this scene food becomes an element of play. I will draw on Winnicott's concept of transitional space and play as the grounds for communication, noted earlier in this chapter, in my discussion of this scene (Winnicott 1971d, 1971e).

Anne again convinces the Keller parents to leave her alone with Helen, this time in a cabin for two full weeks. Her aim is to make Helen fully reliant on her for all of her needs. The goal of the retreat is to make it impossible for Helen to resist transference and dependency upon Anne—the very things foreclosed for Anne at Helen's age with the untimely death of her mother. Taken as a pawn in this isolation-and-control experiment is Percy, a black boy of Helen's age who is the son of a servant on the Keller plantation. Embodying generations of domestic discipline, Percy functions as the model of compliance and reward in Sullivan's discipline games with the recalcitrant Helen.

Captain and Kate Keller take Helen on a long ride in a horse-drawn carriage, leading her to believe that she has traveled a great distance to reach the cabin that sits on the Keller property. Helen, realizing her mother has left her behind and distraught at the prospect of being alone with Anne, falls into a violent tantrum, tearing the cabin's furnishings to pieces. The extent of her destruction is surveyed in a 360-degree pan of the tight cabin space overlaid with multiple still shots, a montage of short dissolves that reveal in close-up the objects Helen has destroyed in her rampage. Helen and Anne appear collapsed in dead exhaustion amidst the havoc. Sound bites, audio flashbacks of Helen's posttantrum sobbing, are superimposed over floating images of Helen's sleeping body splayed lifeless on the cabin bed, creating an eerie mismatch of temporal zones across sound and image tracks. The dissolve montage on the image track gives way to a shot of Anne asleep in a chair, positioned to keep watch over Helen. Anne abruptly stirs, letting out a series of ambiguously anguished or sexual moans. These agitated sounds are mixed with the sounds of a girl sobbing, a voice that the listener is certain to recognize as quite different from that of Helen, whose cry was heard just moments earlier. The next few shots make it clear that it is Anne as a child whom we hear crying uncontrollably. This is a dream-memory, a flashback. These sobs of the child Anne are the subjective, interior sounds of a dream-memory. The aural affective chain in this sequence is striking: Helen's sobs prompt Anne's dream-memory of her own cries, prompting the adult Anne to sob aloud. Helen's sob is projective, filling Anne with broken part-objects reminiscent of her own shattered past. The image of Anne sleeping gives way to grainy, overexposed shots representing the nightmare of a memory that haunts her: the blurry silhouette of a girl, presumably Anne herself as a child, runs head-on toward the camera. There is an abrupt cut to a reversal in which we see her running away from the camera, toward a door. This sequence is shot in out-of-focus, overlit, and slow-motion jump cuts. We then cut to a shot that reveals what lies beyond the door, the source of Anne's grief: a shadowy corpse laid out on a slab. This is Anne's younger brother Jimmie, the child for whom she played surrogate mother before taking on her maternal role with Helen, whose brother is also, coincidentally, called Jimmie. We saw Anne's brother Jimmie in a previous scene of the film, in which he appears as a memory-image, eliciting her shame by asking her why she had failed to care for him. Jimmie's death is a shame that Anne secretly bears.

Sinister repetitions in the form of surrogacy and name-twinning are rich in this passage of the film. "Johanna" Sullivan went by a name more like her mother's, Anne. At the time of the woman's death the child Johanna was expected to assume not only her mother's name but also her role in caring for her father, Thomas Sullivan. Deemed by the state unfit at the age of eight to care for a grown man, "Anne" and her tubercular brother Jimmie were sent off to live at the Massachusetts state poorhouse in Tewksbury, where Anne would nonetheless assume the role of her mother again, this time to her younger sibling. During this dream about her brother Jimmie's death at Tewksbury, Anne cries his name aloud. Her call inadvertently summons to the cabin window Helen's older brother, also named Jimmie. Anne awakens to this Jimmie-double's response from the window. She spars with him in a conversation that moves from Anne's loss of "the other Jimmie" to flirtation. Anne responds to Jimmie's flirtations comments with defensive barbs, prompting Jimmie to boldly confront Anne about her apparent inability to express her sexual feelings. He charges that Anne hides behind her defiant manner, and her thick glasses.[53] With this placing in the open of the sexual spark between them, and with her propensity to throw cold water on those sparks, the conversation abruptly turns to Helen. Jimmie admonishes Anne once again, challenging her ability to be successful in sharing another sort of love: "You won't open her. Why don't you have some pity and let her be?" Anne's reply reveals her stubborn commitment to unfeeling discipline: "No pity. I won't have it."

Jimmie's suggested expression of pity is to "let her be." He rightly equates pity with distanced remove and the charitable turning away of the gaze. To pity Helen is to leave her alone. Noting that pity is the emotion most commonly found in attitudes toward the blind, Hector Chevigny and Sydell Braverman (1950) analyze pity from a Freudian perspective that defines the sentiment as a sublimation or a reaction formation linked to fear, guilt, sadism, and hostility (148, cited in tenBroek 1999). Kindness is, for Chevigny and Braverman, an expression of beneficence rather than hostility. But kindness, finally, is really nonetheless nothing more than a sublimation of the aggressive drives (Chevigny and Braverman 1950, 149, cited in tenBroek 1999). Chevigny and Braverman, tenBroek concludes, make the point that "all attitudes toward the blind, however apparently well-meaning, are founded on a subterranean rock of antipathy and aggression" (tenBroek 1999).

Read through the lens of Chevigny and Braverman, we might argue that Jimmie's pity is borne of an aggressive contempt for his sister, if we can trace contempt back to its more benign shadings of meaning, through scorn to disregard (recall the lack of notice paid Helen by Jimmie and Captain Keller at the dinner table as she stole their food, unworthy of being lovingly shamed into respectful behavior). What, then, do we make of Anne's tough-love "no pity"? The conversation with Jimmie throws Anne off balance. Exposing her defended sexuality and her potential failure as Helen's rescuer, Jimmie strips Anne of her self-esteem, at once humiliating and infuriating her.

Anne's response is to impulsively and aggressively "open" Jimmie's sister with a vengeance. Therapist Joseph Scalia writes that "just before battering occurs there is an internal explosion by which the subject is imminently threatened," a "rising within of intolerable pressure." This experience, he explains, is akin to what Winnicott described as an unthinkable anxiety of "going to pieces" (Scalia 2002, 63). I suggest that it is this sort of "intolerable pressure" in Anne, triggered by Jimmie's candid exposure of her impaired empathetic state, sets off in her a fit of battering rage that is expressed in a kind of sadistic twist on play therapy. Scalia asks us to think (through Winnicott) of battering as a defense against affect deregulation (Scalia 2002, 21). We will follow this line of thinking below as we move on to the performance of intimate violence centered on food as this scene progresses.

With Jimmie gone, the aroused Anne proceeds to the bed and shakes his sister awake with a startling threat that is spoken as if in answer to Jimmie's challenge "you won't open her." "I will touch you!" Anne tells the bewildered, half-conscious child. Helen recoils from Anne's aggressive grasp, caught in that terrible confusion of being roused from sleep knowing one has become the recipient of another's ugly projection—not knowing what hit her, or why. Anne then summons Percy, the black servant's son, from his sleeping quarters in the mudroom to, in Helen's words, "play a nice game with Helen." Percy is immediately onto the sadistic nature of the game Anne has in mind in this therapeutic playground designed to snare Helen's compliant transference. Unlike Helen, he is quite familiar with the dynamics of projective processes through his experience of racial contempt.[54] He cringes in protest as he reluctantly complies. Once again, food is the transitional object. As Helen grabs the familiar Percy and strokes his face, he cowers: "She's gonna hit me!" His fear of the physical outbursts he has been trained to expect from Helen in this sort of intimate contact is sadistically prolonged with the introduction of the game. Helen engages Percy, finger-spelling the word "cake" into his palm. Like Miss Stockton in *Mandy*, Anne spontaneously seizes the chance to stand in for the hearing child in the game and turn the transitive communication into a more lasting lesson in language acquisition. The game is built around *cake*. Cake is a transitional object that, like the potatoes taken in and expelled in the earlier scene described, lends itself perfectly to modeling caregiver control over the other's incorporation and expulsion. But cake takes us outside the realm of nourishment—indeed, we might even say that cake, a food low in nutrition and high in sugar, stands in moral defiance of the concept of satiety. Typically, cake is ingested to satisfy desire, not the need for nourishment; it is an extra, a reward conferred after one is nourished and full. Cake is a surplus. In using cake to teach Helen this next lesson in attachment and communication, Anne fully exploits the status of cake as a tease, an instrument of control.

The pedagogical intention of this scene is quite overt. The scene demonstrates just how crucial play can be in making communication possible, as Winnicott argued, and just how lacking in banality play can be when the stakes of entering communication are so high. To Percy Anne explains, "She knows how to spell it but she doesn't know what it means. If she doesn't play it with me she'll play it with you. Would you like to learn a new word, Percy?" Ignoring his horrified "No!," Anne pushes Helen aside, taking Helen's place in the finger-spelling game with Percy. When Helen tries to push her way back into the game, Anne shoves her aside again. "Why should I play with you?" she scoffs in a mock child's voice, echoing the taunts of the children who exclude Mandy in that film's chasm scene. Like Mandy, Helen is left out of the social order of play because she does not speak. Anne's move produces a kind of primitive envy in her. Percy plays with Anne dutifully, and the punishment from Helen he fearfully awaits predictably arrives. In a fit of competitive anger Helen slaps Percy and pushes him aside, taking his place in the game. Helen goes through the paces of the game, this time dutifully spelling *cake* into Anne's hand. Anne promptly rewards Helen with cake and milk, which Helen scarfs down as Percy falls asleep on the floor without dessert (a political slight corrected in the Disney remake of the film, in which this scene ends with a shot of Percy seated on the porch with his reward, a slice of cake). Anne rouses Percy and sends him back to the bed, resuming her guard over Helen as she cradles a cat with the gentle affection she failed to lavish on Helen, Percy, and the brothers Jimmie.

The scene I have described depicts play, and this behavioral reward game, as a therapeutic or reparative process. Green, in "Potential Space in Psychoanalysis," draws on Winnicott's notion of potential space to make the point that one of the analyst's tasks is to help the patient achieve the capacity for reparative play in the field of transitional objects. Reparative play is a concept that refers to the use of playing as a form of therapy that repairs the subject rather than as a form of diagnosis or interpretation of causal factors behind pathological or neurotic behaviors. The analyst works with the

6. Anne and Helen engage in feeding lessons.
The Miracle Worker (1962).

patient to act out creative, embodied experience in potential space (Green 1978, 176–180). Green's point is to shift the focus from the analyst's production of analytic interpretation to the intersubjective production of potential space in and for the patient. This is a space where fantasy can be played out as embodied, symbolic, felt experience, in transitive performances of gesture, word, movement, and contact with others. He notes that when the patient concludes the analysis, he may carry with him this schema of potential space, a conceptual arena of sociality that allows for the possibility the subject may coexist with another, of *coupling* (180). Winnicott's reparative potential space, read as a variation on the theme of Freud's analytic playground, is a site where the subject may acquire the capacity to be alone and, importantly, *to be alone with another* (Winnicott 1965). In the scene I have just described, it is this ability to be alone with another that is produced not only in Helen, but in Anne.

The achievement of this ability to be alone with another is demonstrated in the conclusion of the cabin scene. Abruptly and incongruously, there is a temporal ellipse that throws the spectator forward a day or more in time. A montage of shots of the days ahead shows Helen performing as Anne's obedient listener, happily submitting to Anne's care in the space of the cabin. In the short time during which the cabin retreat functioned as the potential space for reparative play, Helen appears to have been abruptly transformed into a child who obediently listens. The marvel wrought by the miracle worker is the delivery of Helen into the law of the family. She has been "opened," to use her skeptical brother Jimmie's language, by force in the perverse play-space that is the cabin, and via the perversely benign transitional object that is the cake through which she and Anne negotiate being with another as that for which they hunger.

Contemporary viewers may be surprised to encounter frank and apparently approving representations of overt physical blows, food deprivation, and force-feeding of a child in a film released in the United States in 1962. As performance artist Terry Galloway and Diane Wilkins suggest in their caustic send-up of the film, *Annie Dearest: The Real Miracle Worker* (2003), the process of bonding and coming to voice as depicted in *The Miracle Worker* entails physical abuse and psychological coercion so blatant as to seem preposterous. But 1962 was a watershed year in the public recognition of child abuse as a social problem in the United States. Historian Larry Wolff notes that this year saw the publication of the medical-professional article that led to wide recognition of child abuse as such. Henry Kempe's essay "The Battered-Child Syndrome," published in the *Journal of the American Medical Association* (Kempe 1962), marked "a revolutionary change in public consciousness," Wolff writes, signaling the need for psychological, medical, legal, and social attention to the phenomenon (Wolff 1988, 61–62). It is possible that *Miracle* escaped notice as a performance of abuse in this year of coming to professional consciousness about child battery partly because of its status as historical biopic representing childrearing in a Victorian-influenced American South.

But there are other factors that may account for acceptance of scenes like the ones described above. Congress would not pass the Child Abuse Prevention and Treatment Act until 1974. Even then it would not be until the 1980s that the "special" cases of alleged abuse of children with communication disabilities by caregivers, a concern addressed in the next chapter, would become a focus of organized legal and governmental action and media attention. The "special" case of Keller would have been understood by audiences of 1962 to require a stern hand and extreme measures designed to save the child from the worse fate of being without dialogic agency in the world.[55]

What Sullivan produces in Helen Keller might be described as the ability properly to enter a field of others where she may engage meaningfully. Transactional analyst Tony White, citing the writings of Schiff and Schiff on the question of passivity, a quality that Burlingham observed to be more prevalent among blind than sighted infants, refines child psychoanalyst Margaret Mahler's term "symbiosis" (Mahler with Furer 1968) in ways that are useful for this reading of *Miracle*.[56] According to Schiff and Schiff, White explains, symbiosis "is experienced by both the mother and the child as a merging or sharing of their needs." The structure of a symbiosis involves two individuals who combine to form one total personality (Schiff and Schiff 1971, 71, quoted in White 1997). "A symbiosis occurs when two or more individuals behave as though between them they form a whole personality. This relationship is characterized structurally by neither individual cathecting a full complement of ego states" (Schiff et al. 1975, 5, quoted in White 1997). In other words, where the ego is concerned, in both parties something is given over but separate egos are not lost in the mix. This concern with subtleties of ego cathexis, the question of what is "given" and what is "lost" in the bonding process—speaks to the problematic of shared authorship some critics of Keller's oeuvre were so concerned with. The concern about identity and agency underlies the question, who speaks? (or, who writes?). It is better articulated in the question of which ego "gives" and which "takes," and which aspects of each discrete ego are given and taken—indeed, which subject, and which parts of which subject, are dependent and which remain independent in the lifelong symbiotic power dynamic. This gets to the problematic that underlies the concept of interanimation discussed in the previous chapter. The subject makes himself one with the other, and also makes the other one with himself.

Sullivan's biographer Joseph P. Lash suggests that Anne was exceedingly possessive and controlling of Helen. It is Anne, we see in the film, who "opens" Helen to language. But we might also note that Helen, as receiver of the "gift" forced upon her, was the member of the pair who gained most in the category of public reward (the Radcliffe degree and international recognition, for example). Anne, who, we might recall, sat by Helen's side through classes and aided her in her coursework, had to wait until 1932, three years before her death, to be conferred a degree, and then only an honorary one from the less prestigious Temple University.[57] The answer to the question of who is in control, and who gains, in this symbiotic state of joint being, is always provisional, complex, and shifts constantly over time.

For White, symbiosis is driven by a desire for attachment rather than an actual state of having the condition of attachment fulfilled. Attachment is not a state a psychologically normal child attains but rather a condition or relation to another that the normal child desires and works dutifully toward. This desire for attachment becomes the model for sexual desire later in life. White notes that analysts Bader and Pearson borrowed from Mahler's well-known concept of symbiosis to propose a developmental model of couple formation.

Bader and Pearson write: "The first stage of couplehood, of 'being madly in love,' we liken to Mahler's second stage of infant growth—symbiosis. Here there is a merging of lives and personalities and intense bonding between two lovers. The purpose of this stage is attachment" (Bader and Pearson 1988, 9, quoted in White 1997).

Though the example concerns the male-female domestic or sexual couple, the concept is useful for understanding the Anne-Helen bond as emphasizing a different aspect of the adult bond of dependency that is not adequately addressed in theories of genital love, apart from work on sadomasochism, anger, and violent sexual relationships—all heavily theorized through the pre-Oedipal stage. Anne's dynamic in the film toward "opening" Helen, "touching" her, making her listen, is fraught with physicality, as my reading of the displacement of sexual tension with Jimmie onto Helen in the cake scene suggests. But my discussion is not meant to suggest that sexual tension therefore drives this relationship, even though it is the spark that ignites the sadistic game. The "marriage" between Anne and Helen produces, among other things, a reciprocal functioning that allows each to operate normatively in the world with the intrapsychic support of the other. This relationship, in which the lines of self and other are continually and radically redrawn, makes possible a semblance of media fidelity in an age that required concerted control of meaning across the registers of sound, image, and text to produce a fully potent public identity. Helen and Anne as a unit were masterful in the production of a symbiotic public persona that moved out into the world with expressive force. This was not because they sublimated or displaced aspects of genital love, or because they stayed down in the dark realm of the Imaginary. Rather, their mutually constitutive performance as public intellectuals was delivered with extraordinarily high symbolic fidelity and clarity. As a couple, Keller and Sullivan managed their synergistic media "industry" exceedingly capably.

Theirs is a relationship "that we speak to children about" (Levinas 1999, 149), as the educational media industry devoted to their story attests. In doing so we do not cover over some underlying, more passionate, sexual or infantile desire. Rather, we uncover a passion for attachment that goes deeper than sex, and whose qualities have been euphemistically softened through the maudlin and the sentimental representations of such couples. The discussion of Anne's pedagogical strategies above is not intended to suggest a moral critique that figures Keller as victim or Sullivan as sadistic abuser or dominator. Rather, it is to suggest that the question of who gives and who takes, who the active agent and true author in the pair is at any given moment, and what the nature of their "individual" subjectivity is, is clearly a complex one with answers as unfixed as the boundary that separates the subject and the object it perpetually seeks and finds living in its own potential space, which is always moving between fantasy and action in the world. The ambiguity of possible answers to these questions is well captured in *fidelity*, that term so at home in discourses of both marriage and sound technology. For either party to gain something, loyalty (trust, constancy, loving fidelity) is essential. Equity (justice) is not. I am once again led to recall Levinas's concept of that gratuitous "responsibility which is also the stern name of love without lust" (Levinas 1999, 129). In the case of *The Miracle Worker*, we have stern love, but we learn that this kind of love for the dependent or the needy is not entirely without lust, even if this desire is not of a sexual nature. It is driven, in certain cases, by a hunger for attachment that drives partnerships deemed in some accounts pathological for the degree of self-debasement of the one to the other that they require.

Representations of Sullivan and Keller tend to emphasize Keller as the disabled subject and Sullivan as her mediator, teacher, and facilitator. I wish to pursue further, finally, an underconsidered aspect of this unit: Sullivan's own sensory and emotional impairments. As I have noted, Sullivan bore the emotional burden of having been an institutionalized child, a fact all the more significant in light of her role as the paid caregiver who made it possible for Helen to escape institutionalization.[58] Sullivan was also herself visually impaired. The film touches on these circumstances formally and in sequences in which we see and hear Sullivan's flashback memories and nightmares of her early life in an institution. Lit in extreme high key, *The Miracle Worker* as a whole is a harsh study in black and white. This is a world filmed as if through the eyes of Sullivan, whose surgically restored, limited vision causes her pain and requires her to wear dark lenses, and whose hard, institutionally circumscribed past leads her to see the world in harsh black-and-white terms. Sullivan's eyesight failed in 1871, when she was about the same age (six) as Helen would be on their first meeting. That Sullivan's personal history is the tutor text for her decisions regarding Helen's training by force is made clear in flashback sequences dramatizing Anne's haunting childhood memories. Overexposed, out of focus, and wrought in blurred slow-motion image and warped sound, these harsh memory segments, scripted as nightmares that intrude upon her during states of wakefulness and sleep, impact Anne's experience of her new genteel world, informing directly each of the two explosive discipline scenes I considered above. These memories seem to motivate Sullivan's choices, explaining the intensive pitilessness with which she forges a strict disciplinary regime for Helen's tutelage.

Dorothy Burlingham held that blind children possess an extraordinary memory, "made more efficient by constant inward looking" (Burlingham 1972, 339). The comment's pejorative implication that those who are blind are prone to narcissism makes it worth recalling for its suggestion of the historical ideology of psychology about the blind that is captured in the film, in Anne's flashbacks and nightmares. These scenes are visually spare, as if to depict the state of her vision prior to the operations she underwent in 1880 (at age fourteen) to improve her sight. Just as blindness was matched with the death of her mother, so the restoration of vision was loaded: the death of her brother coincided with her departure from the Tewksbury poorhouse for the Perkins School, where her vision was partially restored through surgeries. "Possibly," Burlingham speculated, "vision keeps the mind more firmly tied to external reality, while hearing, through its connections with verbal residues, has more links with the internal world. However that may be, we have little doubt from our contact with blind children that they are oriented toward their own inner world and that their minds are constantly preoccupied with going over past experiences" (Burlingham 1972, 339).

Again, I do not take at face value Burlingham's speculation about blind inwardness but rather note it to emphasize the film's similar representation of blindness as a memory state of inward, affective looking-as-feeling, in the optically rehabilitated Sullivan. In the film, Anne's former blindness haunts her. It draws her down into a troubling reservoir of affect-filled memories that border, like the dream state and the uterine nightmare, on psychosis. But blindness is also equated with the dirt and the harshness and sensory deprivation of the institutional home where she spent so much of her childhood. It is worth speculating whether Burlingham's observations about "blind inwardness" may not in fact be accounted for by the deprivations of institutional life that produce similar failures of self-emergence in children housed in them regardless of their states of health and ability.

Psychoanalyst Selma Fraiburg (1977) made major contributions to the empirical study of the relationship between ego development, self-representation, and sight. Her emphasis was on language acquisition. However, she regarded mental imagery as a foundation of language acquisition. One of her foci was the blind child's acquisition of "I" as a correct grammatical form and the correlates of "I" and "you" in representation and play.

This concern was prompted by her observation that a smaller percentage of blind than sighted children achieve accurate usage of "I" and "you" by school age and later. "Blindness," she hypothesized," "imposes extraordinary impediments to the development of a self-image and the construction of a coherent sense of self" (Fraiburg 1977, 149).

Fraiburg discusses a structured play session that, like the scene in *The Miracle Worker* just described, involves dessert. The subject is a three-year-old girl, described as bright. The girl, Kathie, is blind. Kathie approaches an adult caregiver and, sniffing a bit of play dough she has formed into the shape of a cookie, appreciatively remarks, "Play dough." The caregiver asks, "Can I have a bite of the cookie, Kathie?" "You have a bite," Kathie responds as she pops the play cookie into her *own* mouth (Fraiburg 1977, 257). Fraiburg's account leads the reader to understand that Kathie's blindness is behind her inability to understand *want* empathetically, as something that is felt by an other whose needs must be satisfied in a body that is distinct from her own. Like Helen at her father's plate, Kathie is driven to satisfy her own appetite and does not witness the other's wants, the other's hunger, as separate from her own body's, or as an expression of desire that she can respond to without incorporating the desired treat herself. There is no optic for setting out a potential space in which the relation of self to other involves distance and difference. Kathie can know the other only by incorporating the other's desire into her own body.

Here I return to Winnicott's point about direct communication, which for him lies outside of creative, intersubjective experience. In offering the cookie but feeding it to herself, Kathie engages in a kind of creative and intersubjective experience, even if the boundaries of self and other are not firmly secured. Whereas Winnicott's logic taken at its word would attribute this to "an extreme immaturity," I suggest that we try to recognize play as it is enacted on both sides of that border between maturity and immaturity, subject and other, as something other than immature or pathological. By recognizing the integrity of this confusion of self and other and its extension into the world of communication in every case where communication occurs, we can move past the long-troubling question of what constitutes the individual subject by recognizing the continuous and fluid presence of intersubjectivity in its most basic constitution. In a word, the subject concept I propose is not only *internally* fragmented and split, but is also constituted in the space between subject and other. By looking at the performance of acting out and working through of desire and the movement of transitional objects that circulate in the constituted play-space of film, I have tried to demonstrate a different notion of where and in what material relationships the subject resides. In the hunger for affect (Lorber n.d.) the subject is always coproduced intersubjectively to a degree not fully recognized in theories of sympathetic identification.

Johnny Belinda *(1948) and* Children of a Lesser God *(1986): Acoustic bodies, sexual trauma*

In *Mandy* and *Miracle* selfless mothers and female teachers bring girls to voice in the form of oral speech and signed English respectively. In *Johnny Belinda* and *Children of a Lesser God* we find some exceptions to the pattern. In both films, the caregiver who brings the Deaf girl to voice is a male figure. In both cases, these men are feminized in the sense that they are disaffected, "outsider" figures, professional men who are down on their luck and who have opted to stay on the edges of their professions. Their devotion to caring for others seems to stem from an empathy born of their own melancholic state. This male type is present in *Mandy* in the character of the Bishop David School headmaster Jack Searle, a divorcé whose bad-boy charm threatens to distract Christine from her marriage. The Deaf child-turned-woman, in *Belinda* and *Children*, gains agency through a relationship with this sort of emasculated guy who serves as her devoted caregiving medium. In both films, the Deaf girl achieves autonomy through sign language, not speech, and enters a world of emotional intimacy with this feminized man as she takes on sign language. Coming to voice and consciousness are overt themes in both of these films. The director Jean Negulesco's own claim is that *Johnny Belinda* is about "a girl child, deaf and dumb, a young animal becoming aware of life around her and her own feelings, the rebirth of consciousness" (Negulesco 1984, 126).

"Becoming aware" is linked not only to emotional intimacy, but to sexual trauma in both films. In both, the mother figure is notoriously absent or lacking in caregiving skills. In *Johnny Belinda*, we learn that Belinda's mother has died in childbirth and is inadequately replaced by a cold, acid-tongued aunt (played by Agnes Moorehead, who later repeats that persona as the prickly mother-in-law in the television series *Bewitched*). Belinda's identity ricochets from naïf child to mother as she bears a hearing child, Johnny, who is the product of a rape. In both films, whereas sound is eroticized and sexualized, sign language is linked to public politics, truth, and justice.

Johnny Belinda (1948) prefigures *Mandy* (1952) in invoking social realism within a film whose primary genre is melodrama. The film is set in near-present time, and in an identifiable geographic and national context. Though the film is a U.S. production, it is set in Canada. A scene straight out of the geographical instructional-film style used in war newsreels opens the film with a zoom into a map situating the story in a specific village in remote eastern Nova Scotia. Male voiceover narration provides various facts including the community's extreme isolation, its accessibility only by boat even in modern postwar Canada. The realism of the film extends to its actors' training: hearing star Jane Wyman is reported to have plugged up her ears with wax and studied American Sign Language to better understand the role of Belinda McDonald, the daughter of a miller who is mistakenly regarded as developmentally delayed and dubbed "the Dummy" by the rural townsfolk. Wyman won journalistic praise and an Academy Award for her performance.

This film stands apart from *Mandy* and *Miracle* in that the Deaf protagonist is instructed (by a man) in sign language, not signed English, during this period when oral education reigned in the film's location (Canada) and release contexts (North America and Europe). The new town doctor, Robert Richardson, encourages Belinda's father to send the girl to a school for the Deaf at McGill in urban Montreal. The father rejects the suggestion, explaining that the family lacks the money and Belinda's labor is needed at home. The doctor then resolves to rescue Belinda from her isolation himself by teaching her how to sign. Lil Hahn, movie reviewer for *The Silent Worker*, expressed the significance of Wyman's performance in sign language to Deaf viewers: "Perhaps the impression left with me is much deeper and lasting than . . . to the average moviegoer. . . . For the first time in screen history, the sign language is presented with beauty and grace for what it is—a pictorial symbolic language" (quoted in Schuchman 1988, 55).

John Schuchman, in his account of the film, writes: "Director Jean Negulesco did not succumb to the temptation to use the stereotyped ending of both the original script and the stage version, wherein . . . Belinda finally talks, pronouncing, with great difficulty, the name of her son" (Schuchman 1988, 64).

But Negulesco's motivations for making a manualist film at the height of oralism were far from admirable. Schuchman quotes an advisor to the film: "Whether you ever have Belinda speak or not is not for me to say. . . . I don't know which would be worse for the audience: . . . A very attractive deaf girl who cannot speak or the sound of the rattle of a subnormal voice just before the audience leaves the theater" (Schuchman 1988, 55, quoting Bruce Caruthers). The director also expressed fear that the listening audience would find repugnant the Deaf female voice. Better to keep the lovely Wyman silent, he reasoned, than to risk offending the listening audience with the sound qualities of Deaf oral speech (Negulesco 1984, 126).[59]

Belinda acquires sign language through the lessons of a novice professional, the village's melancholic new doctor, and not through the natural process of experience within a community of signers. She appears to be the lone Deaf subject in her remote village. Her tutor, Dr. Richardson (Lew Ayres, who charmed Jane Wyman enough to prompt her to leave her husband, Ronald Reagan)[60] is cast as no specialist in the education of the Deaf, but rather as another sort of specialist. He is trained, in the words of his smitten housekeeper, as "a psy—I can't pronounce it, something important." That Dr. Richardson's unnamable specialty is psychiatry, not psychology, is suggested in that this man has arrived to serve as the town doctor, and apparently as its veterinarian as well. Richardson encounters Belinda when he is asked to act as midwife to a laboring cow on the family's farm. Charmed by the teenaged Belinda's rapt expression as she witnesses the birth of the calf, Richardson, a listless veteran professing disaffection with "the war and all that came after it," brings himself, with Belinda, back to life by teaching her to communicate in the language of sign he'd read about in a medical textbook during his training. He orders an American translation of the handbook describing the method of Charles-Michel (abbé) de l'Épée, the founder of the first regular school for the Deaf in Europe and a major influence on the reception and instruction of sign language in North America, and instructs himself in the method in order to teach Belinda. Sign language thus, for most of the film, becomes a private means of communication for this pair.

The de l'Épée legend holds that he became a teacher of the Deaf after his interest was sparked by an encounter with sisters whose natural manual language intrigued him. Accounts of the legend variously represent these inspirational girls as orphans encountered by chance in nature, and as the daughters of a woman seeking religious instruction for them. De l'Épée became observer and teacher of the Deaf in their use of sign, expanding the group of children under his tutelage from two to sixty and eventually codifying the spontaneous language he observed into a graphic and visual system into which he incorporated an approximation of French grammar.[61]

Though the film does not give this detailed an account of the book's source, the implied parallel is clear between the French almost-priest and his encounter with Deaf orphan girls, on the one hand, and the doctor and his spiritual encounter with a motherless, Deaf miller's teenage daughter "in nature," on the other.[62]

I have stated that, in *Johnny Belinda*, manual sign is linked to Belinda's public agency and sound is linked to her experience of sexual trauma. Echoing a scene in *Mandy* where the child's first word is "mummy," Belinda touches her father's heart by hailing him with the sign for the word "father." Her new words in sign convince him that she's harbored an intelligence and capacity for agency previously masked by her inability to communicate. As in *Mandy*, where Christine is inspired to marital transgression as she passionately embraces the school's renegade headmaster upon hearing Mandy utter the word "mummy," Belinda's signing of the word "father" seems to open the floodgates to sexual encounter. The father-daughter exchange on the grounds of their farm is interrupted by a visit from Loughlin ("Locky") McCormick, the charming village brute who appears at Belinda's family mill to pick up his order of flour. Locky brings with him a hay-wagonload of friends heading out for a night of music, dance, and drink. The exuberant group spontaneously turns the father's spacious barn into an impromptu dance hall complete with fiddler. Belinda looks on from the sidelines in rapt wonder at the dancers, attempting to move her feet like theirs but unable to catch the rhythm. The doctor, charmed by this performance, gets an admiring gleam in his eye. He proceeds to mediate Belinda's experience of the acoustic properties of music, placing her hand on the body of the fiddle so that she may feel the source of the rhythmic vibration she feels passing through the floorboards.

In her 1955 documentary film depicting a day in Helen Keller's domestic life at Arcan Ridge, Nancy Hamilton twice shows Keller pausing to place her hands on the radio console in order to enjoy its vibrations.[63] The fiddle will be the transitional object that brings Belinda the pleasures of feeling sound. Here readers might also recall the scene in *Mandy* in which the lovely Miss Stockton coaxes Mandy into a therapeutic object-relations game in which playmate becomes teacher and baby becomes balloon becomes Mandy's own body as container for transitive expression. As in *Mandy*, what passes between subjects is not language but the material experience of shared sound. The doctor who ushers Belinda into the tactile pleasures of embodied sound, however, functions only as an intermediary. Like the

7. A rapt Belinda touches Locky's vibrating instrument. *Johnny Belinda* (1948).

playmate who proffers the doll to Mandy, and like Percy who spells "cake" with Helen, he is quickly replaced by a figure of greater authority. Belinda, her hand placed on the hollow instrument's body, moves her feet in time to the music, her face aglow with the pleasure of moving in sync with the music and the crowd in the cavernous barn. Like Mandy in her transitional physical encounter with the balloon, Belinda in her contact with the fiddle will be transformed by the physical pleasure of acoustic sound—but not quite yet. This shot is not yet the logical match to the breakthrough moment of Mandy's embodiment of sound. As in *Mandy* and *Miracle* the encounter with acoustic sensation changes tone dramatically when the playmate changes into the more mature, knowing double—a partner who plays harder. The violin, an instrument whose sounds coincidentally lead the musical score behind both the balloon scene in *Mandy* and the cake-and-milk game in *Miracle*, is the transitional object facilitating Belinda's introduction to the pleasures and dangers of *acoustics*. That this word shares etymological roots with "caution" is noteworthy with respect to this scene.

The dance scene described above turns sinister with the intrusion of Locky who, like the doctor, had been eyeing Belinda's legs as she moved her feet to the tune. This sequence of the film provides a rare glimpse into the taboo realm of sexualized disability. Locky and Dr. Richardson find Belinda appealing, not in spite of her deafness but because of it. The isolation imposed upon her as a Deaf individual in a hearing community grants her the sexual innocence of a child contained in a woman's body. As Rosemarie Garland-Thomson argues in her forthcoming book on disability and the look, physical and sensory differences can constitute a certain type of erotic object choice for certain subjects (Garland-Thomson forthcoming). Locky and Richardson struggle throughout the film with their attraction to and repulsion from Belinda, whose silence makes her a convenient screen for their fantasies and projections.

Locky becomes drunk and, later that night, steals the instrument that had given Belinda so much pleasure. He sneaks back to the mill, where he finds Belinda alone binding sacks of flour. Crudely stroking the bow across the stolen violin, he generates a dissonant screech that henceforth becomes his character's leitmotif. The sight of the instrument reels Belinda in. She moves closer to Locky in order to touch it. Sinister cello and bass lines lead on the much-heralded soundtrack composed by Max Steiner.[64] In this moment, Steiner breaks with his romantic style and samples dissonance. Deep and repetitive string notes escalate with urgency as Belinda smiles beatifically and naively down at the instrument, presumably remembering the innocent pleasure it had given her hours earlier.

Locky abruptly chucks the instrument aside. He lunges at Belinda's body in a pursuit accompanied by a staccato volley of high, shrill notes, a warning signal that anticipates the infamous "screaming strings" that Bernard Herrmann would reference years later in his innovative all-string composition for Hitchcock's *Psycho* (1960). In *Psycho* the strings stand in for the absent screams of Marion Crane (Janet Leigh) as she is murdered in the movie's notorious shower scene. Herrmann makes a relevant synaesthetic comment about his decision to use strings only: his intent was to achieve "black and white musical color" to match the cheap television-news image quality of the film.[65] In *Belinda*'s rape scene, high-contrast string tones are similarly matched with a high-key set. Locky bears down on Belinda's body as the screaming strings abruptly cut to silence. The camera zooms in to an extreme close up on Belinda's spotlighted face, which radiates terror. Locky's shadow engulfs the frame, and the screen goes black.

The violent coupling achieved in this scene returns us to that notorious object of incorporation and containment, the baby. What is produced in this exchange is not voice but a child. In the scene that follows, Belinda refuses to perform a sign or utter a sound. She contains her trauma in silence even as she gives birth to Locky's child. Silverman interprets this silence to mean that the results of Belinda's lessons in sign language prior to the rape had been "less than satisfactory," for which reason the psychiatrist, Richardson, seeks another medical consultation for Belinda's deafness and muteness, taking her to a mainland specialist. In fact, the film suggests that it is not because of her inability to speak that Belinda is brought to the specialist but rather to address a medical problem that the psychiatrist has already diagnosed, and which he professes to share with his pupil: "Her problem," he explains, "is loneliness." Silverman's point is that despite the lessons in sign Belinda remains outside language because thus far her knowledge does not include grammar and syntax. "The mute woman," Silverman explains, "does manage to learn a number of significant gestures, but only by identifying each sign with a concrete object, on a one-for-one basis. Because those gestures belong so fully to an interior register, and because they are devoid of the 'presence' which the voice has long been believed to confer, they do not seem capable of revealing Belinda's inner 'reality'" (Silverman 1988, 69).

Grammar and syntax are indeed absent on a large number of the occasions where Belinda signs on film. Silverman also accurately notes that Hollywood cinema tacitly repeats a problematic paradigm of female sexual drives theorized in the writings of psychoanalyst Ernest Jones and advanced by Luce Irigaray's and Michel Montrelay's troubling essentialisms (Silverman 1988, 69–70; Jones 1927, 1935; Irigaray 1985a, 1985b; Montrelay 1978). This paradigm links female articulation to a sort of prelinguistic meaning that is closer to the body than is language, and which is identified with the law of the father. According to Jones, Silverman explains, the mouth is equated with the vagina, an impotent organ hole. Silverman reads the film as an expression of this symbolic paradigm. Belinda's agency is transferred from mouth to womb, she suggests. Belinda is thus discursively impotent. Her baby is a supplement that issues from that other orifice, providing Belinda with a surrogate voice, but one that is infantile, inarticulate. Thus, Silverman explains, that which "the talking cure had been unable to coax out of the female voice is 'spoken' instead through the female body" (Silverman 1988, 69).

It is true that Negulesco offers a film that seems to ask for this sort of interpretation. Deafness is equated with gut feeling in Belinda, making of her a pure affective medium for the spiritual life of the community. This is most dramatically demonstrated in a scene (of which Silverman is quite critical) in which Belinda signs the Lord's Prayer over her father's dead body, interpreted by a chorus of male voices in song, and by the doctor in word.[66] Belinda's character seems to have been to some degree modeled on Negulesco's memory of his mother. "In her simplicity and beauty," he relates, "Mother was a saint" (Negulesco 1984, 15). His charcoal sketches of the pair, "Mother: Portrait of a Saint" (Negulesco 1984, 15) and "Jane" (Wyman as Belinda, Negulesco 1984, 124), portray both women with eyes cast down in chaste, contemplative poses typical of the iconography of female saints, and of shame.

It is worth considering, however, not only the implied association among the female body, deafness, and affective states but also the implication that the male psychiatrist too holds the special power to channel truths of the soul through the self-censoring passivity and receptivity required by his discipline. Just as Belinda is the screen for his projected loneliness, so he is a screen for Belinda. A reflective, empathetic man, the socially disaffected psychiatrist feels a special affinity with outsiders like Belinda. His gift is to mirror her words and feelings through sign interpretation. The similarities between Burlingham's interest in telepathy between mother and child and Sigmund Freud and Helen Deutsch's carefully circumscribed fascination with the idea of telepathy between patient and analyst come to mind with this convergence of student and analyst-as-medium in a symbiotic-telepathic pair that together channels prayer and profoundly moves a room of listeners, and a Deaf and hearing audience (recall Lil Hahn's review, quoted above).[67]

I have suggested that the male psychiatrist's character shades toward the feminine and the maternal. Silverman's reading offered a useful critique of essentialist perspectives on the female body as it is understood organically to speak a sexual politics from within, from a position anterior to language. But in emphasizing the film's essentialist themes Silverman seriously downplays the extent of the role the film assigns to sign language as communication and word and not simply as mute gesture outside language. Belinda does communicate through a means other than her child quite successfully: through sign language, and through a male surrogate speaker who performs dutifully as her interpreter. It is through sign and through the psychiatrist's male voice as medium—as "dummy," reversing the relationship to this derogatory label applied to Belinda in this film—that Belinda enters the public sphere of the mainland Canadian criminal justice system. It is through the medium of Dr. Richardson that the maternal-child unit Johnny-Belinda achieves justice and agency. The role of male voice in the enactment of female agency will be my concern for the remainder of this chapter.

Following the birth scene, Locky reveals his paternity to Belinda's father, enraging him and then killing him in the struggle that ensues. Keeping secret his identity as paternal figure as well as his act of patricide (if we may extend the use of this term to describe the murder of one's child's grandfather),

Locky marries the doctor's housekeeper. This is the woman who could not bring herself to utter the word "psychiatrist" even as she idealized the man. The couple is awarded foster custody of Belinda's child by the town council, whose members judge Belinda an incompetent mother. "A man wants children, and I want him," Locky tells his wife as he marches into the McDonald household to seize Johnny by force. But Belinda, clearly nobody's dummy, stops Locky in his tracks, shooting him dead from behind. Belinda stands trial for the murder. Other interpreters are brought in, but only the trusted voice of Dr. Richardson can interpret Belinda's truth. Duly acquitted on grounds of self-defense and awarded custody of her child, Belinda's rightful place is awarded—an outcome predicted in the compound name, Johnny Belinda, that gives the film its title. Silverman is thus partly correct in stating that it is through the child that Belinda achieves voice and agency. However, the agency Belinda achieves in bringing herself and her child to justice is won through the medium of the psychiatrist. Moreover, what she gains is far more impressive than the achievements of any of the film's male protagonists. Belinda gets justice and a home on the mainland, away from the isolation of the remote family mill. Johnny's and Belinda's fathers both end up dead. Dr. Richardson remains a melancholy and selfless medium for Belinda's happiness, ambivalently bound as surrogate father to the child Johnny and as future husband to Belinda. Like Anne Sullivan, Dr. Richardson grants priority to his charges' desires over his own. Previously unlucky in romantic love and disillusioned by the war, his side comments suggest, his pleasure now can only reside in giving himself over to the compassionate devotion of charitable love in response to the loneliness he sees in Belinda. Hers is a look, as we have seen, that he recognizes as his own. Johnny-Belinda, the film's mother-child unit contained in one film body, never achieves voice literally. However, linguistic agency is gained through her acoustic medium, this male playback instrument or speaker who occupies the feminine role of facilitating caregiver, embodying her words.

Children of a Lesser God *(1986): Male voice as medium*

In *Children of a Lesser God* (Randa Haines, 1986), we see a similar symbiotic pairing of male interpreter and Deaf young woman in the authorship of speech. In this film, as in *Johnny Belinda*, the interpreter is a male professional. In a reversal of the typically dominant place given to male voice as authority in mainstream cinema, the film gives over a large part of William

Hurt's narrative voice in the starring role of James Leeds, former disc jockey and oralist hearing teacher of Deaf children, to mirroring the signed speech of Sarah, the outspoken female lead character played by Marlee Matlin. Hurt talks, throughout the film, as if to himself, bemusedly repeating aloud the lines signed by Matlin.

Plot resonance with the earlier films mentioned is unmistakable. *Children* is set, like *Johnny Belinda*, on a remote coastal island where Deaf children, "children of a lesser god," like the "Thursday's children who have far to go" of Anderson's 1954 documentary, are instructed in oral speech acquisition. As in *Mandy*, *Children*'s location is an oralist residential school for Deaf children. As in *Johnny Belinda*, the plot centers on the attraction of a male professional caregiver to a charming Deaf woman whom he imagines to be isolated, like himself, in her difference. Like Dr. Richardson, he sees his own disaffection and sadness reflected in Sarah's enigmatic looks. As in *Mandy* and *Miracle*, *Children*'s plot centers on the tension around coming to voice. Will Sarah comply with James's insistent request that she learn to speak, or will she remain in her isolated island world, where she works as a custodian of the school where she was formerly a star student, simply because she nei- ther signs nor speaks and therefore cannot function in the Deaf and hearing social worlds of the mainland? James's insistence that Sarah speak, and spe- cifically that she speak his name aloud as they make love, is the figurative core of the narrative tension of the film.

The play and film versions of *Children of a Lesser God*, set in the late 1970s, a period of renewed tension between oralism and ASL instruction in Deaf schools, were important mainstream media texts for Deaf and disabil- ity rights activists. The film brought mainstream attention to the predica- ment of Deaf education at an important historical crossroads of oralism and manualism, as noted earlier in this chapter. It therefore occupies an important place in the history of Deaf culture and politics. The status of a young woman as self-possessed speaker was different in the film's setting of the late 1970s and in 1986, the year of the film's release, than it was in 1948 (the year *Johnny Belinda* was released), 1952 (*Mandy*) and 1962 (*Miracle*). In *Children*, Sarah is ostracized as a signer among the students and hear- ing teachers who attend the oralist school, but she meets with other Deaf activists who communicate in sign. The film grants her a political commu- nity. By the film's end, Sarah has remained staunch in her commitment to communication in sign language, even in the face of a personal commitment to the oralist teacher who is her love interest, and whose passionate demand that she learn to lip-read and orally speak provides the narrative tension that drives the plot forward.

The film's form mirrors this tension. Deaf and hearing audience members are offered different points of entry to the film. Deaf audiences may view Sarah's signed words without mediation, but the voice of the male character Hurt must be close-captioned for them; for hearing audiences, this dynamic is reversed. Listeners experience Sarah's words through the interpretation of James, her male voice double; James's lines require no interpretation. In content and in form, then, the film provided a ground in which to enact the tension between oralism and ASL instruction and practice experienced by Deaf schools and communities of the late 1970s.

The play and the film surprisingly escaped the notice of feminist criticism despite, or perhaps because of, keen attention to voice in the women's movement during this period, and despite Randa Haines's status as successful female director and Matlin's emergence as a mainstream political and media figure with a successful television series of her own. In *Reasonable Doubts* (NBC, 1991–1993), Matlin played the authoritative role of an assistant district attorney. She performed primarily in sign, interpreted once again by a man—a working-class cop hired to serve as her interpreter (played by Mark Harmon, who would later play the hapless fiancé to the hysterically boundary-less mother-daughter duo in Disney's 2003 remake of the studio's 1977 hit *Freaky Friday*). Harmon's lack of skill with sign was, according to one reviewer, as noteworthy as his on-screen and real-life resentment about being cast in the feminized service role of interpreter. (In a *USA Today* publicity photograph, Harmon playfully displays this antipathy toward the star by signing the F-word to her.) Why did Matlin go unnoticed by feminist film and television critics and theorists, despite her on-screen relationship to male characters who serve virtually as assistive technologies, and despite her politically provocative mainstream media presence as an outspoken leader in advocacy of the mainstreaming of ASL? Perhaps film feminism, with its rhetorical emphasis on voice and oral speech as means and symbols of women's entry into the public sphere, and its rejection of women's bodies as silent bearers of meaning, had no place for a woman character and star who in her screen roles and public identity remained (mostly) orally silent, dubbed by a male voice. It is no small irony of history, then, that at the same time that Deaf activists successfully brought sign language to wide public recognition as language and culture, in part through this film and its star, feminism placed such a high premium on oral speech and voice not only as symbols but also as means of agency and emancipation, effectively eliding one of the more outspoken, politically active female stars of 1980s–early 1990s television and cinema.

The political and social question of how to communicate as a Deaf subject, and how to educate Deaf children, orally or through ASL, is played out in the film within the register of sexual psychology. James's demand that Sarah orally speak to him is a demand intended to help Sarah become a social being and achieve a place in the mainstream world. But it is also a demand that she express her feelings for him in the register of voice, a register that he identifies as holding deep emotional significance for him. The film places responsibility for Sarah's refusal to speak not with Sarah but with her mother (played by Piper Laurie). Though the mother appears on-screen only briefly and we are led to understand that she is both geographically and emotionally remote from Sarah, she is nonetheless cast as the figure responsible for Sarah's oral silence. In a monolog directed to the ever-receptive listener, James, Sarah's mother coldly relates that Sarah's speaking voice, when she did use it, was decidedly unattractive. She herself discouraged the girl from acquiring and using oral speech. Like Negulesco in response to the possibility of including a speaking line for Belinda, Sarah's mother found the girl's voice aesthetically offensive, out of keeping with her lovely appearance. Defying generations of melodrama convention, the mother silences the daughter.

The mother's prohibition against speech is linked to an experience of sexual violence. Moreover, this violence is facilitated by a member of the family. As in *Johnny Belinda*, sound is linked to sexual initiation and trauma. In a conversation that requires no translation, Sarah signs to James that she obeyed her mother's injunction to remain silent as she was screwed by a series of boys, an event coordinated by her hearing sister, who "kept a list" of boys to "introduce" to Sarah during Sarah's weekends home from school. The film implies that these factors, the maternal judgment against Deaf female voice and the trauma of serial rape upon the silent child facilitated by the evil hearing sister, are suggested in the film to be strong causal factors in the adult Sarah's stubborn silence and proud resistance to speech. The consternation with which she meets James's attempts to make her want to speak is thus grounded in childhood memories that equate the demand for oral speech with the demand for sexual performance. This pivotal set of conversations in which Sarah and her mother confess to James a shameful past motivates an interpretation of Sarah as a victim, an institutionalized child humiliated in her difference during her brief stays on the mainland. Her political affiliations from this point forward can easily be read as motivated by the violence enacted upon her body. This reading gives us reason to see Sarah as part of a larger series of girls with sensory impairments whose identities are constituted through victim narratives on screen. This group includes not only Belinda but also both Helen Keller, whose training is represented on film as violently coercive, and Anne Sullivan, the pedagogical figure whose failure to respond to Jimmie Keller's advances is represented as an outcome of her own childhood trauma and deprivation.

Let us turn, finally, to the male interpreter, James Leeds. His paternal and professional authority, like Dr. Richardson's in *Johnny Belinda*, is undercut by allusions to his lonely disaffection, his failure to build a stable life in the mainstream. Like Headmaster Searle in *Mandy*, he is cast as a sentimental loser, a "hurt" man who advocates offbeat methods of teaching and learning. "Hurt is the ideal actor," wrote one reviewer of the film, who is "secure enough in his machismo to play an impotent male" (Kempley 1986). James's characterization as impotent throughout the film role is linked to his advocacy of oralism, a pedagogical stance that, as I noted earlier, Baynton links historically to hearing female educators of the Deaf. By 1986, however, oralism had already been losing ground. James's effort to get his students to speak is pitifully inadequate, as seen through the narrative point of view of Sarah, whom we witness at a political meeting with Deaf signers of ASL. Indeed, the bulk of Hurt's own spoken lines throughout the film are woefully shallow and offensive. His greatest charm is his willingness to put his foot in his mouth repeatedly despite Sarah's rebuffs.

Leeds plays with sound technology and its seductive pleasures in his role as classroom teacher. A former disc jockey, he uses the phonograph, a not unusual teaching tool, with a then unorthodox teaching text: rock 'n' roll music. That famously deafening musical form, with its booming acoustics and crass lyrics, is used to woo listless students into desiring the forbidden pleasures of a sort of sound that is outlawed in the halls of the staid school. "Put your hands on the speaker," James dares Lydia, a teenage student. (Matlin was performing in this role in the Chicago stage version of the play when she was discovered for the film.) "Feel that?" Leeds asks Lydia, using his hands to guide her body to the beat as the sound track pumps out corny suggestive lyrics ("My heart can feel ya, close enough to steal ya"). In a scene that resonates with the excitement over the feel of embodied sound generated between Belinda and her dance partners at the hoedown at the family barn, James seduces Lydia into enjoying the physical and intersubjective pleasures of acoustics. But for Sarah, the lesson is double-edged. Her enjoyment of the physical pleasure offered in music is unmistakable in a scene where she dances languorously with James and then alone, eyes closed, shot from James's point of view as he takes her in with agonized desire, to Otis Redding's sexy pop hit "I've Been Loving You So Long."[68] But it is through Sarah's scathing eyes that we watch from the back of the school auditorium as Lydia and other teen students take the stage to dance under James's direction, gyrating to the song whose beat is marked by the approving nods of the students' visiting hearing parents in the audience. Performing as the No-tones, the teens act the part of a rock band to deliver a karaoke-like singing performance of *Boomerang*, an onomatopoeic song that makes a joke about repetition and reverberation in rock lyrics ("ba boo ma rah rah rah").

But the sparring between James and Sarah is not about sound. It is about spoken language and/as sex. "I could teach you how to speak," James insists. "I could teach you how to mop floors," she retorts. Her sharp response makes the exchange reminiscent of the filmic Anne Sullivan's verbal spar with another James, Jimmie Keller, discussed earlier in this chapter. James's male students are more than clear about their understanding of voice and agency in relationship to sex. Asked by their teacher for a list of reasons to speak, one boy responds without missing a beat: "To pick up hearing girls."

I described Sarah's mother's relationship to her daughter's deafness and sound as one constituted through shame. We can also interpret James's longing similarly, recalling some lines from Silvan Tomkins: "If I wish to hear your voice but you will not speak to me, I can feel shame. If I wish to speak to you but you will not listen, I am ashamed" (Tomkins in Sedgwick and Frank 1995, 152).

James, in love with the sound of voice, demands to hear the voice of a woman he loves, but she refuses to listen. He wishes her to hear him, but she refuses to read his lips. Hence he is doubly ashamed or, more precisely, humiliated in that he cannot have that which he desires most. His objective is to hear his name uttered in her voice while they have sex. Her body is thus constituted as an acoustic space, and a potential space, for James. But Sarah refuses the roles of both speaker and listener. Her refusal is part of a politics of language, but also and complexly it is in response to a maternal prohibition to speak, to constitute herself as subject in acoustic space. Tomkins observed that the shaming of the child is at the origin of the taboo on mutual looking between two subjects (Tomkins in Sedgwick and Frank 1995, 146). In this film, in keeping with the parallel of the maternal figure as projective audio playback device discussed previously, I suggest that Sarah's mother enacts this taboo in the register of voice. As Silverman and others have suggested, the space of the voice, like the space of the look, is constitutive in the emergence of the ego and the subject. A taboo on mutual speaking is fundamental to the child's development as an obedient listener. School-aged children know that it is correct to sing together in unison, but it is not good practice to all speak at once. After a certain developmental point, the infant knows there is a temporal distance required after the call, during which one listens for the response. One need only think of the injunction to the child not to speak in the classroom, the church, the library, and the movies to know that the shaming of the child is very much at the origin of a prohibition against speaking in public. We may recall once again Tomkins's anecdote about the bad Little Robert, whose ungainly performance at the dinner table provoked his mother's shame, drawing him into the ritual of mutually projective shame in which Robert imagines himself in the eyes of his mother. Sarah's speech is an ungainly entity in the inner voice imagined by Sarah, the voice of the mother that echoes the shame Sarah's mother expressed for her daughter, and which she has projected onto her. The mother's shame originates in her acoustic fantasy of the reception of Sarah's voice in public space. To speak, then, in the logic of the film's narrative about Sarah's past, is to shame the imagined mother before the listening ears of the public. Just as Little Robert deflated and drew in his body, so Sarah silenced her offending voice.

James is driven to rescue Sarah from a logic that equates oral silence with a deeply primitive shame in the eyes of the parent that is at the root of sexual shame. But he is also driven by shame he feels regarding his own sexualized compassion. In *Johnny Belinda*'s characterization of Dr. Richardson's love for Belinda, the psychiatrist's feelings are rife with ambiguity. The film is unclear about the degree or type of his passion for Belinda. Viewers are left with a weak impression: is the psychiatrist's love for Belinda a sexual, genital sort of love, or is it a love born of charitable feeling about which Freud, Levinas, and Tomkins all speak—the more sentimental sort of love about which we speak to children, and which we confer upon them? In the case of James, this distinction is much more clear. James's love is constituted both ways, hence his awkward shame about his intense attraction to Sarah. It is both sexual and empathetically compassionate. James's fantasies about Sarah are constructed quite explicitly along the lines of rescuing her from a childhood trauma that induced her silence. The film is structured to the beat of James's repeated plea "Why won't you let me teach you to speak?" James projects onto Sarah the need to speak, a need she explicitly and repeatedly denies having throughout the film. James wants Sarah to overcome her shame and work it through to oral speech. Interestingly, however, Sarah holds her own in suggesting that she is in fact quite proud in her command of ASL and her outsider status regarding oral speech. The shame and the need to work it through exist solely on the side of James. His status as pathetic clown derives in part from his apparent compulsion to repeat this scene of rejection in which he commands Sarah to feel a need to speak aloud, a need that burns in him alone.

Here echoes once again "the anticipation of a meeting between the subject's body and another body, imaginary or present" (Green 1999b, 289). James's demand that the anticipated meeting occur in a potential acoustic space, a space constituted in sound, makes the body for which he waits tragicomically imaginary, even as Sarah's physical presence is fully constituted in the world of the film. What gives this film such tragicomic humor is the obviousness of this one-sided fantasy that constitutes the Hurt man.

This circumstance of intense projection of a need that is recognized only with distanced bemusement by the recipient presents an opportunity to read the text more thoroughly through the paradigm of the rescue fantasy that it so obviously invokes, but also to use this opportunity to rethink that concept's typical formulation for film theory. The psychoanalyst Emanuel Berman reads Hitchcock's *Vertigo* through the paradigm of the rescue fantasy in a manner that moves the concept in this direction. *Vertigo*'s protagonist Scottie, Berman recalls, suffers a trauma in which a colleague's attempt to rescue him from danger results in the rescuer's fall to his death. Scottie, Berman proposes, from this point forward strives to undo his humiliation, to rescue himself from chaotic fearful regression. His quest shifts, projectively, to Madeleine, whom he at first refers to a professional for help. Here we hear echoed the scene in *Johnny Belinda* in which the profession cannot be named aloud: "Take her to the nearest psychiatrist, or psychologist, or neurologist, or psychoana. . . ." Scottie begins to say "psychoanalyst" but, as Berman notes, can't bring himself to complete the word (Berman

1997). Berman completes this brief interpretive passage with the statement that Scottie's drama resonates with his own experience as a psychoanalyst. Pursuing the problem of countertransference raised with this identification, Berman traces the concept of rescue fantasy applied to the therapeutic relationship back through Ferenczi to Phyllis Greenacre, who applied the concept to analysts' feelings about clients. Berman's impulse is contrary to Freud's focus on the fantasy as an Oedipal drama, in which we might see the concept as describing an underlying wish to rescue mother from father. Instead, he emphasizes that the object of rescue is "a projected version of the rescuer's own disavowed vulnerability, and the danger from which rescue is needed" (Berman 1997).

Would it be feasible to propose that James, Belinda's psychiatrist Richardson, and *Mandy*'s headmaster Dick Searle also are constructed as harboring a psychic danger from which they want to be rescued, and which they project onto the mute women they wish to rescue from silence? What, then, is their crisis? The films provide slight clues: these are disaffected men weary of the mainstream culture's professional demands, unsuccessful at career, love, and family. In 1986, in the benevolent, ironic voice of Hurt as comic champion of Deaf female agency, we hear echoes of James Agee and Richard Burton, the caring male authorities whose voices carry the moral line in the 1950s humanitarian documentaries about children traumatized into silence and then freed through voice, "quiet ones" who have "far to go" (to echo the refrain invoked by the title *Thursday's Children*). But this benevolence, this insistence to speak on behalf of others who are perceived as unable to speak for themselves, becomes questionable in a Deaf civil rights movement that refuses the narrative of crisis and rescue, and which rejects the political relationship of compassion in which the one speaks for and thus saves the other. At stake is the question of what constitutes speech in the absence of voice during a given historical moment, a question that will be the focus of the next chapter of this book.

I noted earlier that Negulesco elected not to have Belinda speak for fear that the guttural sound of a Deaf female voice would offend listeners. Lennard Davis, in his memoir of growing up as a hearing child of Deaf parents, relates his own childhood interpretation of sexual difference in Deaf voice: "The first aural distinction I made was between my parents' voices. Father's voice was gruff, guttural and unclear. . ." (Davis 2000). Davis's comment implies that maternal Deaf voice might by comparison sound softer, more sonorous, more clear—a voice that would be more pleasing, would better engage listeners in the public sphere, for its more pleasing "female" qualities, perhaps. His decision recalls the esthetic concerns of directors in the sound transition years regarding foreign, regional, and class accents in silent-screen stars that would be dramatized in *Singin' in the Rain* shortly after *Johnny Belinda*. Dick Searle and James Leeds, *Mandy* and *Children*'s surly oralist pedagogues, share in common voices that might be described, like Davis's father's, as rough-edged. These "unaesthetic" qualities add to their appeal as gruff heroes. When female characters' voices carry these qualities, they are used to convey negative personal qualities: Agnes Moore-head, who played a stone-hearted aunt in *Johnny Belinda*, has a voice that is notorious for its edge and its commanding masculine tones. Belinda, Sarah, and Lina (*Singin' in the Rain*) are all barred from speech (Sarah and Lina diegetically, Belinda at the level of scripting decisions) out of concern that their voices would convey rough masculine qualities. Voice esthetics apparently was a strong concern in the production of these films: Marlon Brando was ruled out for the part of Belinda's psychiatrist on the basis of the gruff speech qualities that would become his trademark. Producer Jerry Wald objected, "He doesn't talk. He mumbles" (quoted in Negulesco 1984, 127).

The meaning of male voice across these films is played out not only in the films themselves, but also in the public lives of their lead actors. Gruff-voiced Jack Hawkins, the British actor who played headmaster Searle, gained international prestige as a supporting actor in *Mandy* after a previously mediocre career. With Mandy Miller he shared the experience of launching his acting career as a child (he assumed his first role, at age twelve, as elf king in a 1922 London theatrical production titled *Where the Rainbow Ends*). Like Miller, Hawkins was typecast on the basis of his performance in *Mandy*. He repeated the role of the sharp-tongued, insubordinate renegade liberal for the rest of his career.[69] But in 1966, after establishing himself internationally in this character type, surgery for throat cancer stripped him of his trademark voice entirely. He continued to act in sound films until his death in 1973, but with a voice double (either Charles Gray or Robert Rietty) stepping in to record his lines, which were then postsynchronously married to his image. Hawkins's role in *Mandy* as oralism's hearing spokesperson, then, is both prescient and ironic. In his last seven films, Jack Hawkins may have been a hearing subject, but his film voice was no longer his own.

Turn-of-the-century narratives of listening

Children of a Lesser God has brought us out of the immediate postwar period and into the end of the twentieth century. We might ask: how does voice coincide with listening in the formation of the child subject in a more contemporary context? I close this chapter with a consideration of a few contemporary examples in which Deaf girls and hearing mothers play out modern versions of the repetition-text traced in the film analyses thus far.

The first text I consider is an advertisement. A full-page, sepia-toned, soft-focus photograph of an ocean, waves lapping at the shoreline, where a speck of a toddler stands silhouetted in the sand, spreads in full bleed across the back cover of the *New York Times Magazine*'s July 27, 2003, issue. Across the photograph in large schoolbook typeface floats the boast: "We turned a child who couldn't hear into a typical two-year-old who doesn't listen." Discreetly imprinted with the Mount Sinai Hospital logo, the advertisement completes itself with a small-print story that weaves a late-1990s transnational adoption child-rescue narrative with another story, the 1990s saga of the rescue of the Deaf child from her world of silence via the technology of cochlear implants:

> Two year old Patricia Puia sat on her mother's lap, unable to hear the gentle voice that tried to comfort her. Deaf from birth, her life in Romania was lived in silence. But a month after undergoing cochlear implant surgery at Mount Sinai, the silence was filled with the sounds of a world Patricia never knew existed. "I feel like I've just given birth to this child for the first time," her mother said tearfully. "But this time she hears."

The ad text describes Patricia's adoptive mother weeping joyfully over her experience of the implant surgery as a kind of childbirth. The site of delivery is channeled from birth canal to auditory canal, with cochlear implant surgery substituting belatedly for the missed ritual of a biological birth. Of course, Patricia was "delivered" to this mother once before, through the legal process of adoption—another context pervaded by the metaphor of rebirth that, as I suggest in my forthcoming book *Images of Waiting Children*, is conferred with the adopted child's acquisition of citizenship in a new national context. Of course it is the family not Patricia that is reborn in this little story. Just as the state reproduces itself by reimagining what constitutes its subjects according to changing discourses of rights, agency, and belonging (as in the U.S. Adoption Citizenship Act of 2000, which streamlined the passage from international adoption to citizenship), so the family is made anew through adoption of a child previously born to another nation-state, another mother. Among parents of hearing foreign adopted children, the child's acquisition of English is sometimes noted as a milestone in the child's assimilation, its process of being passed fully into the folds of family and nation. Spoken English language acquisition marks the child's rebirth, its passage from her past and now private worlds of foreign language, experience, and memory into the present and future space of English-language communication, of American citizenship and family life.

But in this advertisement for Mount Sinai Hospital we can discern a second and different sort of birth displacement in the proud clause: "But this time she hears." Patricia is "born" to her adoptive mother, in this narrative, not in the adoption process that delivers her to a new family and a new state, but through an operation that allows her to hear. What Patricia hears, the advertisement tells us, is her mother's "gentle voice." Voice, as Veena Dass and Renu Addlakha explain with regard to disability and citizenship in India, figures importantly in a domestic public sphere in which the disabled subject is constituted as citizen (Dass and Addlakha 2001, 512). Voice is a widely used metaphor in representations of the hearing internationally adopted child's assimilation into a new nation and culture. Adoption literature suggests that the orphan is "without voice"—that is, without adult representation, without access to the privileges of representation that parents and language-group belonging would typically confer to the child. This child gains voice (is legally constituted) through a transnational adoption that paradoxically strips the child of the self-representation that comes with language-group belonging.

Note, though, that it is the mother and not Patricia who literally acquires voice with the insertion of cochlear implants in Patricia's auditory canals. That is, Patricia is regarded by her mother as being "brought to life" with cochlear implants not because she can now speak to her mother (she had not yet learned to do so), but because she can now hear her mother's voice. With hearing, it is implied, comes that cornerstone of liberal democracy, choice—and, specifically, the choice to *listen*. Mount Sinai's text makes the joke that cochlear implant surgery has turned Patricia into "a typical two-year-old who *doesn't* listen." Slippage between listening, an act that connotes personal volition, and hearing, the basic ability ideally conferred with implants, is crucial in this ad's metaphor of birth. For what is "born" is not the child's ability to understand and to speak the language she now may hear with her new implants, for to confer the ability to hear is not to confer the ability to understand spoken language and symbolic sound. What is "born" is the hearing mother's perception that her daughter can now hear her parental voice and therefore may engage in the intersubjective disciplinary practices that constitute the mother-child relationship of interpellation that brings the child to self-mastery. The mother may imagine that Patricia may now become like any "typical" toddler. She may be a good girl and listen to her mother, or she may not listen to, may not obey, the maternal voice that strives to mirror and shape her.

Consider two unstated ironies of this double meaning of listening as comprehending and as obeying. The first concerns the capacity of listening born with implants. As noted, the installation of implants in a person born deaf may produce the capacity to hear, but does not automatically confer an ability to comprehend sounds newly heard. We might look to the work of Marius von Senden, who investigated sixty-three subjects born blind and were operated upon for congenital cataracts between the ages of three and forty-three. Not one of these subjects experienced their gain of sight as a blessing. Though they had gained vision, initially they could not see. Von Senden documents the laborious and painful months and years over which these individuals were trained to see. Some of them never succeeded (von Senden 1932, cited in Spitz 1965, 40–41). The child psychoanalyst René Spitz likens the experience of sensory overload of sound that is perceived as meaningless to the clattering of pebbles and the hissing of waves upon a beach, an image that resonates with the advertisement's portrayal of Patricia on the shore (Spitz 1965, 64). Patricia, as a child older than two who is born deaf, would need to train hard to understand the meanings of the noises that converged in her at the time she was "reborn" to her mother through implant surgery.[70]

Tomkins notes that the content of shame may be morality or achievement (Tomkins in Sedgwick and Frank 1995, 143). In birth, personal achievement figures strongly relative to the act of bringing forth the life of another. Birth also produces the potential for a lifetime of experiences organized through the lens of achievement, from the child's developmental progress to its success in career and family life as an adult. The "birth" of Patricia as a listener through implants is very much the birth of her entry into a framework of achievement. Morality is typically cast in a spectrum of relationships to shame, and its objects situated in relationship to right and wrong. Although

Tomkins does not make this point, it is clear that achievement situates the subject in relationship to success and failure. The term "achievement" in itself is optimistic, situated closer to shame's opposite: pride. Achievement is therefore, along with pride, a term toward which the subject is imagined to move as it develops, and as it learns how to avoid shame.

In the same year that the Mount Sinai advertisement described above appeared, the youth e-journal *Teen Ink* posted an essay by reader Barbie H., a professional American Sign Language interpreter. Barbie's letter provides us with an opportunity to read a hearing narrative of Deaf speech acquisition in which the achievement-shame paradigm figures overtly in the shaping of the Deaf subject's life. Barbie's contribution to the e-magazine's reader series on teen heroes, like the Mount Sinai advertisement, is a narrative about a hearing mother and a Deaf daughter. Barbie's perspective is that of a listening audience-member who witnesses the narrative of a hearing mother and her Deaf daughter through the media, then recasts for readers her own account of pleasure and identification with the characters in the story. Barbie writes:

> Recently, I read the story of someone who I believe is one of the world's bravest women: Heather Whitestone, crowned Miss America in 1995. It was a very long road to her great moment. When she was 18 months old, she had a reaction to a vaccine. She was left deaf in one ear and has only five percent hearing in the other. Heather's family became involved in her education. Her mother decided on the acoupedic approach, where Heather was taught to use what little hearing she had and learned to speak. Her mother did this so Heather could enjoy a place in the hearing world. . . . If I had been Heather's mom, I would have taught her to sign (because I am an interpreter). However, I would not have done right by her and she might never have achieved her dream. (H. 2003)

In this narrative, the "teen hero" is Heather Whitestone. However, Barbie imagines herself not as Whitestone but as Heather's mother ("if I had been Heather's mom . . ."). Yet Barbie is certain that she would have failed the child Heather in this role: "I would not have done right by her." As a sign language interpreter, Barbie explains, she might have prevented Heather from training in oral speech. This sign language instructor assures us that Heather's mother's choice of an acoupedic approach, involving early fitting with hearing aids, auditory feedback, speech education, and no grouping with other Deaf children, was the key to Heather's success. Barbie's perspective is reinforced by Whitestone herself, who explained to her television audience that oral speech "worked for me, but it does not work for all Deaf children."[71]

Whitestone's victory and her embodiment of the moniker "Miss America with a Mission," the title of her popular biography (Wheeler 1996), were unsurprising phenomena in a decade during which Deaf culture had received substantial media attention. But what seemed to capture the imagination of Barbie and the broader listening public of this period was not simply Whitestone's status as an exceptionally talented Deaf woman. It was also her exceptional acquisition of oral speech that allowed her fuller access to the hearing culture and, importantly, the role of her mother as medium in that assimilation process.

Whitestone emerged as a national heroine almost a decade after Marlee Matlin had won national recognition as a film and television performer. Matlin's success was launched at age nineteen with her Academy Award–winning performance in the 1986 screen version (discussed above) of the 1979–1980 Tony-award winning *Children of a Lesser God*, the Broadway play that featured Deaf performers including Phyllis Frelich (who won a Tony for her performance) but was cast, in its original stage run, for hearing audiences. Like Whitestone, Matlin was virtually a child when she achieved screen fame. At nineteen, she was the youngest actress to receive the Academy's Best Actress award. Unlike Whitestone, however, Matlin had achieved stardom as an American Sign Language speaker whose deafness was regarded as a cultural and linguistic characteristic, not a disability to be medically overcome. Whereas Whitestone's status as Deaf female popular icon of the 1990s was based on her assimilation as a speaker in hearing mass culture, Matlin's initial status was gained on her stature as an insider-advocate of Deaf culture and its language of sign.

By 1995, the year Whitestone was crowned, the historical controversy concerning oral speech training versus education in sign language that had been ongoing for a century was newly refocused around the technology of cochlear implants, used by an estimated twelve thousand people worldwide in that year. Cochlear implants had been introduced experimentally to the U.S. market ten years earlier. In 1985, the year a national talent search had turned up Matlin for her role in *Children of a Lesser God*, the U.S. Food and Drug Administration had given its approval to the first of a series of cochlear implants to come under its review.[72] Approved for children aged two and older by the FDA following the recommendations of an all-hearing committee in the early 1990s, cochlear implants brought new life to an old controversy in Deaf communities and in medical and educational contexts about how Deaf children should be raised and educated. Cochlear implants introduced the potential for a medical intervention to produce the physical conditions for hearing ability in some Deaf individuals, most notably those with residual hearing.[73] By 2001, cochlear implants were the subject of broad media attention. Matlin was quoted ambiguously to suggest her support for the new technology, as in this passage from a *Business Week* article: "She [Matlin] notes that Vinton Cerf, one of the Internet's founders, helped to develop e-mail as a way to communicate with his Deaf wife, Sigrid (who has since had a cochlear implant)" (Williams 2001). Thus, by the end of the 1990s, the media icon who had embodied advocacy of ASL in her screen role in 1987 seemed to be advocating the advantages of a technology that some saw as a setback in public recognition of deafness as cultural difference not medical impairment.

The fact that the first Deaf Miss America not only used oral speech to address her public but also underwent a cochlear implant procedure after her reign[74] has not been insignificant to the ongoing public debates about the place of oral speech and sign language in education for Deaf children. Barbie's idealization of Whitestone and her mother reflects changes in public perceptions of deafness as a medical issue following FDA approval of this technology and media reports about it throughout the 1990s and early 2000s. Jack Levesque writes that when CBS aired 'Caitlin's Story' on *60 Minutes* on November 8, 1992, an episode featuring a seven-year-old "charmer" with a cochlear implant, "the Deaf community won the battle [for media coverage] but lost the war" against perceptions of deafness as an isolating and pathological condition (Levesque 2001, 40–42). The documentary *Sound and Fury* (Artistic License Productions, 2000), portraying a volatile intrafamilial controversy about the use of the technology in children, drew broad public attention to the stakes of this technology for families. The film depicts the controversy between two brothers, one married to a Deaf woman and with a Deaf daughter in her early school years, the other a hearing couple (both children of Deaf adults) with a Deaf infant. Each couple contemplates, with the input of Deaf and hearing grandparents, whether to pursue implants for their child. *Sound and Fury* demonstrates that cochlear implants have intensified the pressures and stakes in choices families have had to make for decades, even prior to the technology's availability. The

choices range between a medical and educational experience that emphasizes assimilation into hearing culture, and schooling and lifestyle options
that preserve and develop Deaf culture and language.

Maternity figures importantly in Whitestone's own choice in this regard.
Whitestone is reported to have been happy "in her silent world," as a child.
But this changed when she "became a mother and realized there were sounds
she really ached to hear" (quoted in ABC News 2002). These sounds were
the cries of her newly born sons. Her decision to pursue cochlear implants
was motivated, she explains, by her desire to become not a speaker, for
she was already that, but a listener—even if it might take years for her to
understand language, to achieve comprehension of the words that she could
newly hear. In press coverage, Whitestone moves between the positions of
mother and child. In stating that speech "does not work for all Deaf children," Whitestone conjures for her listening public an image of her deafness
as a childhood handicap overcome. Barbie also represents Whitestone to us
in a melodramatic narrative of a child in crisis, an indefatigable girl with
a dream, who achieves victory in the face of a medical tragedy. Positioned
in age between the two women she writes about, Barbie's identifications
oscillate. She idealizes Heather and identifies with Heather's dynamic hearing mother, Daphne Gray, whose biography of her daughter, *Yes You Can,
Heather!* (1995), leaves no doubt that the title's missing verb is *speak*. Oral
speech, in Gray's narrative of her daughter's life, is the marker of achievement and the organizing principle in this narrative of Heather's success.

Barbie's response, idolatry, and identification by a young woman spectator within a story of deafness as isolation and suffering surmounted,
and with the duo of an exceptional Deaf girl and her sharp-witted mother,
echoes the earlier narratives of the woman's film described throughout this
chapter.

In the next chapter, I turn to a set of examples in which caregivers like
Barbie facilitate the expression of children without oral speech. My discussion of facilitated communication brings us a step away from filmic and
textual representation, into the domain of affect and representation in embodied interactions between caregiver and child.

CHAPTER THREE

"A CHILD IS BEING BEATEN":

DISORDERS OF AUTHORSHIP, AGENCY, AND AFFECT IN FACILITATED COMMUNICATION

"Prisoners of Silence"

Writing is nothing but the representation of speech. . . .
—Jean-Jacques Rousseau, *The Social Contract* (1762)

Imagine writing a poem without being able to read it aloud.
It's like playing a record in a soundproof room—
It's going round; but no-one on the outside can hear.
If I was Deaf, would it be the same or different?
—Jan, quoted in Crossley 1997, 156

I pick up the thread from chapter 2 with more stories about children and caregivers who bring them to voice—in this case, through facilitated writing. The second of the two epigraphs above is from a poem written by Jan, an Australian teen with Down syndrome. Jan had reading and spelling skills but could speak and write only minimally. In typing this poem, Jan steadied her writing hand with a rod that she held onto with her nontyping fingers. Rosemary Crossley, innovator of the method of supported writing called facilitated communication (FC), held the other end of the rod, providing balance and resistance as Jan used one finger to select letters on a keyboard.

"Autism is frustrating," typed Lucy Harrison in her first written communication to her parents. Like Jan, Lucy wrote with the help of a facilitator, an education specialist who used her hands to support Lucy's wrists and forearms while she typed. Lucy, until she engaged in facilitated writing, had demonstrated limited verbal and expressive language abilities, but could read and spell. "When I saw the words" Lucy had typed with the support of her facilitator, Lucy's mother told Diane Sawyer in an interview televised on a *Frontline* episode titled "Prisoners of Silence" (*Frontline* 1993), "I felt like I was seeing my daughter for the first time."

It is easy to imagine the gratitude of the mother who sees her adolescent daughter "as if for the first time" when the child belatedly speaks her first words (through writing).[1] Gratitude would be directed toward both the facilitator and the method that brought the child to voice. Voice is the figurative and literal route to visibility, to becoming an autonomous subject who appears in the world. "My voice is me. Take it from me and you leave a handful of dust," wrote Anne McDonald, an adult with cerebral palsy who currently communicates through independent writing but who learned to do so with the help of a facilitator, Rosemary Crossley, who supported her body as she wrote, until Anne developed the ability to write unsupported. The sentiment of Lucy's mother echoes that of the mother of Patricia, quoted at the end of chapter 2, who felt her Deaf adopted toddler daughter was born "as if for the first time" when the girl was implanted with cochlear devices, which, for the mother, represented the ability to enter language and the (hearing) world. In the eyes of these screen mothers, to confer a means of speech ability is to confer the means of human agency—life itself—to the previously speechless child, constituting her belatedly as an autonomous subject who may enter into the realm of language and symbolic social interaction.

The *Frontline* vignette begins with this moment, when Lucy "speaks" to her mother as if for the first time through the medium of a computer—and also through the medium of a human facilitator who supports her arms and wrists as she writes. But, taking us beyond the mirror-phase-like climaxes of *Mandy* and *Miracle Worker*, Lucy's story moves forward in time, from her "prison of silence" to independent writing and college. Her progress to independence is the melodramatic success story that opens up the *Frontline* episode.

This story resonates with the narratives, fictional and documentary, recounted in chapter 2. The pages that follow offer a reading of the controversy that surrounds the method of facilitated communication documented in this episode of *Frontline*. I focus on the FC debate that is the broader context of

Lucy's story for two reasons. First, debate raged during the 1990s about the credibility of this method of assisted communication. Discussions centered on the nature and the degree of influence over written speech exercised by the human facilitator who supports the body of the writing subject, the previously "speechless" child.[2] The controversy about authorship and influence in facilitated writing allows me to consider the nature of intersubjective speech discussed thus far in a context that takes us beyond text and screen characters, as well as beyond the mirror-stage-like moment of acquisition of a means of speech—the point where the films I discussed earlier stop. Second, debate about FC's credibility heated up considerably when charges of sexual abuse were brought before the courts on the basis of allegations made through facilitated writing. This aspect of the controversy centered on the possibility of facilitator influence over the child's written text, and the potential that facilitators might, in some cases, have in fact projected abuse narratives, consciously or unconsciously, onto the unwitting child, using it as a vehicle, ventriloquist-like, to express the facilitator's own memories or fantasies of abuse (either the child's or her own). My agenda is not to take sides in debates about the validity of the method or the veracity of particular cases of FC use and abuse allegations made through this method. I am an advocate of FC despite problems that have arisen from the ways in which it has been used in some cases. Because this is a book of feminist film, media, and technology theory, my agenda in this chapter of *Moral Spectatorship* is not to position myself as an expert who sits in judgment of this method of communication, but rather to develop further, in a feminist film theory context, the concepts I've tried to build thus far: empathetic identification, affect, and the intersubjective production of agency. I examine documentation of the relationship of FC and the controversy that surrounded it as my set of examples for elaborating on these ideas. My concern is not whether the method "really works," but how it works—that is, what, besides speech, is produced in the relationships that form around facilitated writing.

The FC debate offers a well-documented controversy about the coproduction of voice belatedly in the previously speechless child. It allows us to consider the role of desire, authority, physical touch, and identification among coproducers of child voice in a context where the politics of dependency and the ideal of autonomous speech and/as agency loom large. Put forth on both sides of the FC debate was a concept of the subject as an autonomous agent. Both sides' ways of understanding the human subject and its constitution through speech, I posit, precluded a more complex understanding of human voice and agency as always coproduced, with the splitting of the subject always enacted in relationship to and in dependency upon others. The FC example is an instructive text to consider because it enacted larger controversies about the legal, cultural, and emotional aspects of the constitution of human agency in the child subject through pathways to, into, and through language that engage practices of empathy. Recall Lacan's association of entry into language with the law of the father, a process that ensues from the mirror phase (Lacan 1977a, 67). For Lacan, in being interpellated within the law of the father one enters into community with others. What matters, in the entry into the symbolic order, is the structural organization of the symbolic system, not the content symbolized through it. We can access these structures by considering the *practices* and *agencies* enacted through them, rather than by considering their contents or products. Lacan also speaks of the symbolic "father" as an agent, reducible to neither the real nor the imaginary, which promulgates the law of the father (Laplanche and Pontalis 1973, 440). In the FC context, the law of the father in this psychoanalytic sense is played out dramatically through institutional and legislative ground, across the bodies of facilitators, facilitated children, family members and friends, and professionals engaged in the child's management and protection.

Until this point, I have emphasized the structural role of shame practices in the entry of the subject into a community of others, using the writings of Tomkins and Levinas to make this case. Throughout, I have made arguments against the Lacanian model of psychic structure in order to emphasize affect and representation over language and representation, and in order to bring forward ideas from object relations and affect theory in the context of nonnormative models of development. Here I return to the Lacanian model provisionally. I do this because language, its use in conversation, and its use in speech organized around the communication of dynamics of sex and/as power, was the most important aspect of the controversy over facilitated communication. The moment of speech and voice acquisition is important in this debate, but it is not the aspect of FC on which the legitimacy of the technique and its practitioners was judged. Language and narrative, the stuff of the Symbolic (Lacan's big Other), are the terrain where facilitated communication came most dynamically into question. In the pages that follow, identification and the imaginary will play no small role in my discussion of the relationship of child to facilitator. But the performance of language and narrative is now more fully present in my discussion than it was in the earlier parts of this book.

Here I add another piece to the argument that the "speechless" child's entry into a community of others is performed through practices of shame enacted materially through intersubjective practices of touching (including physical punishment or the withholding of touch), looking (or turning away one's eyes in shame), and listening (or not). The piece added provisionally here is Lacan's proposition, adapted from Lévi-Strauss, that the symbolic is structured like a language and according to a symbolic agency that promulgates the law (Lacan 1977; Laplanche and Pontalis 1973, 440). If we look closely at what ensues from the child's progression into the symbolic, we see encounters fraught with tension about the appearance of the self to the other in which shame is consistently a product of the injunction of the law. Lacan's model allows me to move the discussion beyond the point of "coming to voice" to the practices in which the subject is understood to perform independent communication—but still with the prop, the mediation, of an other, and through the more obviously mediated form of writing, not oral speech (regarded as a more natural or conventional form of communication). Here we have an obvious double mediation: the computer and the human hand mediate speech in the place of the normative technology of speech, embodied oral voice. Regarding the organization of the child as speaking subject: how do we account for the differences that ensue from the child's speech facilitation by a caregiver as a performance of "independent" speech? Is this child's speech really more "mediated" than that of a child who speaks orally, or any other subject's oral speech, for that matter? I will suggest that, in the end, in fact it is not. All speech is mediated in the ways that the FC relationship makes uncomfortably obvious, despite claims made about independence and autonomy in unmediated oral speech performance. The case against FC was so volatile, I propose, because the method made absolutely blatant the uncomfortable fact of intersubjectivity and dependency as requisites of sociality in a culture that holds onto a notion of the autonomous subject as the proud cornerstone of democratic freedom even as technological means of mediation proliferate. The human facilitator, who can never be reduced to a mere neutral medium or instrument, became the locus of anxiety about the inevitability of dependency upon mediation in a culture desperate to hold onto the ideal of autonomy. It was on the body of the facilitator, and with regard to her imagined desires, that this debate, essentially a debate about the fate of the model of the autonomous subject, was played out in the public sphere during the 1990s, the decade associated with a revolution in digital technologies of mediation and voice.

But I have gotten ahead of myself. I introduce these questions about autonomy, agency, and voice in the structure of facilitated speech, questions about the intersubjective performance of language not discussed in previous chapters, through the example of the controversies about authorship and speech that surrounded facilitated communication in the United States during the 1990s. I mentioned the word "desire." Another concept that will be more fully investigated here, with the help of this Lacanian model and the essay by Freud quoted in this chapter's title (Freud 1955a), is the role of fantasy in the intersubjective production of agency. Previous parts of this book have focused largely on fiction film and identification between characters in film texts. I now turn to a location where we can study the intersubjective production of (typed) speech and/as agency in embodied human interactions. I show that spectatorship, fantasy, narrative, desire, and character identification are no less present and active in embodied interaction than in spectatorial relationships in and with textual representations. But this does not reduce human interaction to mental representations.

This chapter considers how we might rethink character identification and fantasy as they come into play in human interactions in which, in the words of Levinas and Merleau-Ponty, "egological isolation" is broken; when "the body of the other comes to life before me" through human interaction that involves physical touch (Levinas 1993). For Levinas and Merleau-Ponty, the model for this relationship is the intersubjective action that takes place within the individual body when one hand touches another. The copresence of two hands in the body of one subject is extended to the intersubjective unit of two bodies. In touching and in being touched by another, each body comes to life as subject in the field of the other. In facilitated writing, the tendency has been to think of the facilitator as the active one who touches. She is the one who brings the formerly passive (speechless) other, the child, to life (speech and/as writing). I wish to stress the reciprocity of this relationship. In touching the hand of another, Levinas suggests, I am also touched. Levinas weaves his own words with Merleau-Ponty's to explain that in this relationship of intersubjectivity, which is not simply one of analogy: "the other person and I 'are like the elements of one sole intercorporeity'" (Levinas 1993, 100). Sociality is thus born across both subjects "in the signifying power of sentiment" enacted in mutual touch. In this formulation, touch is not the mere symbol of love, but love itself (Levinas 1993, 101 and 113). The FC relationship makes literal this enactment of being born into the social through touch with an other.

But this model also brings into sharp relief that problematic of power and desire that arises with a model of the subject as always intersubjectively constituted, always dependent on the touch of an other to come to life with and for an other. The FC controversy made obvious the problems that ensue when it is also the adult and not only the child who "comes to life" through this relationship of helping touch, or when it is not clear precisely who speaks, the facilitator or the child, in the words typed through facilitated writing.

Yet another problem with this model of intersubjectivity is made clear in the FC example. Recall that, in the example of Lucy coming to life for her mother, the one whose supporting touch brings Lucy "to life" is the facilitator, not the mother. The intersubjective production of Lucy, who is seen by her mother "for the first time" when she speaks (writes) with the help of her facilitator, requires three bodies. This brings to mind the tripartite model of shame in the production of sociality proposed by Tomkins and described in chapter 2 in my discussion of Mandy's reunion with her mother.[3] I unfold below the problematic of a communication relationship that always includes spectators, witnesses, interlocutors, and readers, who bring further complexity to the paradigms of both the intersubjective and the autonomous subject. The group unit is bigger than two, but smaller than the models organized around audience or mass communication models available for thinking about how communication occurs.[4]

FC in historical context

Communication facilitation among nonverbal people with autism has a history that includes work with sign language, writing, and gestural communication (Goodwin and Goodwin 1969; Oppenheim 1974; Konstantareas, Oxman, and Webster 1977). Facilitated communication, the method of computer-assisted writing that Lucy used, was developed on the basis of a practice used in Australia in the 1970s by Rosemary Crossley and Anne McDonald. Crossley was then an aide at an institution in Melbourne for people with severe disabilities and profound retardation. McDonald was an adolescent with cerebral palsy who had been a life-long resident of that institution. After successfully using the technique to help McDonald communicate and then to mount and win a legal battle for deinstitutionalization, Crossley developed ways to use facilitated communication with other nonverbal children. Some, like McDonald, were youth with cerebral palsy and others were assessed with autism. This work was carried out in Melbourne at DEAL (Dignity through Education and Language), an independent nonprofit center founded by Crossley (Crossley and McDonald 1980, Crossley and Remington-Gurney 1992, Crossley 1992, Biklen 1990 and 1992b).

Crossley's method was introduced to the United States by Douglas Biklen in the early 1990s. Biklen was at that time director of the Division of Special Education and Rehabilitation at Syracuse University. In 1989, the year that the Australian government conducted the first extensive formal review of the method (Intellectual Disability Review Panel 1989), Biklen made two extended trips to Melbourne to observe Crossley's work at DEAL. In the early 1990s he published reports of his observations of autistic children with limited verbal language communicating through facilitated writing (Biklen 1990, 1992b, 1993). By then FC had come into use sporadically around the world in lay and professional contexts, either through word of Crossley's work or independent of it. A literature had begun to emerge documenting evidence of unexpected cognitive and literary competence among some people with autism using the method (Rocha 1995). But FC still did not have an organized professional base or research locus outside Crossley's nonprofit center.

Among those individuals who developed assistive writing techniques without being aware of parallel developments is the late Canadian poet David Eastham. As a child, Eastham had limited speech ability and appeared not to understand the words of others. He was believed to be nonverbal and autistic. In 1975, his tutor felt him tug on the pencil she supported in his hand as she helped him to write. She developed techniques with Eastham that paralleled those used by Crossley and McDonald. Eastham acquired some sign language and writing skills with her support and eventually progressed to independent word-board and typewriter use. Eastham's first published book of poetry (Eastham 1985) was followed by a posthumous collection coupled with a biography written by his mother after his untimely death in 1988 (Eastham 1992). Without an organized context, however, individuals like Eastham remained mostly off the radar of autism researchers, or were viewed as unique and exceptional cases.[5]

Biklen gave the method a strong if contested research base in the United States within the education and autism research communities. He introduced the method to the education field by describing cases he observed at DEAL, in which nonverbal children with autism used humor and abstraction in conversationally normal, discursive ways through typing performed with human facilitation on Canon Communicators. These were small (by 1990s standards) electronic typing devices with dot-matrix tape output (Biklen 1992b, 209). His initial skepticism that autistic children presumed to have an intellectual deficit could perform in this way was overturned by observations that led him instead to question then current ways of understanding autism. He concluded, after a review of autism research methods and principles, that autism was not well enough understood; that it is possible that some persons assessed with autism experienced "a problem with praxis" that impeded their ability to express their thoughts. He then made two propositions that would become fundamental to work with FC in the United States, and central to the controversy about it: first, this problem with speech praxis can be overcome in some individuals using the FC method; second, "we do *not* presume a deficit in understanding, but rather in expression" (Biklen 1992b, 235).

The claim that autism might be approached as a problem of expressive praxis rather than a problem of understanding flew in the face of current thinking about autism in multiple fields. Biklen's idea of a "deficit in expression" resonates throughout this chapter.[6] The location of expression is always somewhere between the one who performs and the other who witnesses. In its fundamentally ambiguous meaning, the term "expression" encapsulates the problematic of intersubjectivity. The concept of expression is fraught with ambiguity. Is expression the way I wear my face and move my body, and the manner in which I speak? Or is it what an other reads in me, or what I have expressed to the other? The gaps between what I believe I have expressed, what I have performed that escapes my conscious direction and control, and what an other perceives in or projects onto my performance is at the core of the problematic of information where it meets affect's expression in the world. What can we say about the involuntary socially contextual response such as the recoil, for example, or the motor tic that means little to me but seems to speak volumes about me to those who witness me perform it? This chapter takes up these questions of the subjective location of and responsibility for expression in dialogic situations where intersubjectivity is an explicitly marked precondition of an individual's basic ability to speak.

I use the term "expression" to characterize not just problems of autism but also the debates about FC as a reliable method of communication. The

FC controversy, I propose, was essentially a contest about the meaning and interpretation of expression in disorders involving communication impairment. But in effect, FC practice opened up the larger question about the relationship between affect and expressive representation. Biklen's claim that we presume a "deficit in expression" undercut prior and ongoing work on autism by shifting the focus from mind and intellectual ability to expressive and performative ability, foregrounding the question of the material form that communication takes in subjects who cannot speak or sign. "Expression" captures the importance of affect and agency in the performance of dialogic speech outside the boundaries of the normative. This term remains both underconsidered and highly contested in fields where communication is studied, and not just in the research and development of communication modalities for people with disabilities that impact communication. Moreover, expression, as I will show, became a most serious problem among professionals in this context of debate over FC. Moral stakes were high in the FC controversy, with careers and an entire field of practice both built and torn down in the emotion-laden conflict. How the controversy was expressed is no small aspect of the lessons about expression and agency that we can learn from looking back on the controversy about FC.

At about the time of the *Frontline* broadcast, the question of facilitator influence took a new turn. A series of articles about FC published in *Autism Research Review International* was among a spate of professional alarm bells that signaled to the autism research community the "bad news" about FC and told cautionary "horror stories" about apparent facilitator influence in false disclosures of sexual abuse in Australia (Rimland 1992a, 1992b, 1992c). *Pediatrics* published a report of three cases in which FC had been used to allege sexual abuse. The authors raised doubts about the validity of authorship of the claims, citing testing evidence in one of these cases that suggested the strong possibility of facilitator authorship (Hostler, Allaire, and Christoph 1993). They recommended that others encountering this situation test the facilitation to determine whether the child was the source of the written message. But the study they refer to that outlines a method of testing (Wheeler et al. 1993a, 1993b) failed to rule out facilitator influence in every instance. This problem of FC verification was observed in a 1994 report in the *Archives of Pediatric and Adolescent Medicine* discussing thirteen cases in which children with mental retardation, autism, and speech delay alleged sexual abuse through FC. These were all of the cases that involved disclosures through FC from among the total of 1,096 cases referred and evaluated for suspected sexual abuse between 1990 and 1993 at the Child Abuse and Referral program at the State University of New York Health Science Center in Syracuse (the city where Biklen had established the FC Institute).[7] Medical evidence of abuse was discerned in four children evaluated, and physical findings consistent with abuse were found in two. One child made the allegation verbally as well as through FC; one perpetrator confessed (Botash et al. 1994, 1282–1287). But, the authors conclude, the results neither supported nor refuted the validity of facilitation; they urge readers to examine cases where allegations are presented through FC "without bias" toward or against the method of disclosure (Botash et al. 1994, 1287).

Their advisement to regard the method without bias would seem an obvious one. However, by the time of their publication the nation was swept up in fervor over the potential for fraudulent charges in FC disclosures of abuse. Their cautionary words were written in a climate of distrust generated not only by the early evaluations of the method (Wheeler et al. 1993a and 1993b, Green and Shane 1994) but also a spate of newspaper articles published in cities around the country reporting on sexual abuse allegations made through FC and ruled by the courts to be inadmissible evidence or the product of facilitator influence. Expert naïveté regarding FC testimony and demands for retribution in cases of caregiver "torture" at the hands of court officials persuaded by FC "zealots" were some of the charges raised by journalists (Heinrichs 1992a and 1992b). In 1994, one account reported four dozen cases of sexual abuse allegations made by FC (Margolin 1994). Reader emotions were roiled by news stories such as that of the eight-year-old Virginia boy with Down syndrome who, after using the method in school for one week as an intervention for his severe communication disorder, typed an eighteen-page transcript disclosing sexual abuse at the hands of his father and sister. His vocabulary included correctly spelled terms such as "vagina," "rectum," "masturbate," and "rape" (Hostler, Allaire, and Christoph 1993). As children were placed in foster homes and parents held for questioning, the public responded in waves of indignity. First, indignity was expressed on behalf of the boy, then for the falsely accused parents, and finally on behalf of society against the facilitator and the method. A disclosure of alleged abuse by a blind autistic girl was subject to court testing that both sides agreed suggested facilitator influence. Charges were dismissed. The teacher who had facilitated the communication, however, was reported to be "distraught and confused" over the results. She remained convinced of the validity of the method and continued to use it in the classroom (Bligh and Kuperman 1993, 556).

Professional and public consternation deepened with the emergence of the profile of the confused facilitator, who remained clueless about his or her own role in authoring the disclosures, even after being shown proof of her overinvolvement in authorship. Biklen's institute was hit with three lawsuits during the 1990s.[8] The American Speech-Language-Hearing Association, during the year of the *Frontline* report's broadcast, conducted experimental studies on FC. With few exceptions, their report concluded, in testing situations the FC method failed to yield accurate messages when facilitators did not possess the information necessary to respond accurately (American Speech-Language Association 1995).[9]

Prompted by these controversies reported in education, medicine, social work, and the news media about the method's reliability in matters as serious as the abuse reports, ABC joined PBS by dedicating an episode of *Prime-time* to scrutiny of the practice (ABC 1992).

Professionals were also indignant about the snub to dedicated autism researchers who had carefully tested and evaluated techniques of assessment, only to be shown, through what some regarded as sleight of hand, that some of the children they tested had not only a theory of mind but also the capacity for normal intellectual and emotional complexity. The claims of facilitated communication, in the words of one critic, "violate conventional knowledge about the severity, chronicity, and symptomatology" of autism (Silliman 1992, 63). The prevailing logic among the professional critics of FC in psychology, speech-language pathology, and education research was that if children who simply did not have the mental capacity to communicate in writing, much less to describe the acts allegedly perpetrated upon them in the explicit terms that some of them had used in their reports, then their facilitators must be the hidden force behind the writings. In short, some of the allegations of sexual abuse could have been instances of fantasy projected by well-meaning but neurotic caregivers onto the lives of their charges, transposed from the psyche of the caregiver into the written "voice" of the previously mute child. These concerns prompted some critics to pose the question, "abuse by whom?" (Williams 1994), suggesting that the child was indeed a victim—of the well-meaning facilitator's projection of desires and fantasies, if not of the (perhaps wrongly accused) caregiver. Moreover, the accused, in this interpretation, also suffers as the potential "victim of memory" (Pendergrast 1996), in a situation where the question of whose memory is articulated looms large.

Professional controversy about FC in the United States during the 1990s was played out explicitly in the context of multiple contexts already fraught with tensions about speech and agency, truth, sexuality, and power. The importance of this dense contextual and historical framing must be fully grasped to fully understand the debates about FC and the authorship of abuse allegations.

The introduction of FC to the United States coincided with the escalated marketing of computers for home and school use. The 1990s saw fast-paced advances in research, development, and marketing in three intersecting market sectors of the computer industry: homes, schools, and areas of health and social services devoted to accommodating the everyday lives of people with a range and mix of physical, sensory, cognitive, and intellectual disabilities. "Assistive technology" took hold during the 1990s as a term describing a subcategory of products and services consolidating into a market for people with disabilities and the families and institutions responsible for making decisions about their care. "Communication disability" and "communication disorder" similarly took root during this decade as designations describing a class of people across a range and mix of categories of sensory, cognitive, and intellectual impairment or disability. Computers that could be adapted to the use of supporting people with communication disorders were morphed into products designed especially for this consolidating niche market. Crossley, in her earliest work with McDonald, used mechanical page-turners and alphabet boards. But she later introduced McDonald to the Canon Communicator, an electronic aid designed to replace speech in nonverbal users. The Communicator was introduced to the international market in 1977. This portable machine was the size of a Sony Walkman. In its earliest incarnation, its text output was a paper strip. McDonald also used, for several years, a speech synthesizer and a headstick (Crossley 1997, 29). These instruments were designed to meet the newly identified niche market of people with communication disabilities that could be accommodated with the new electronic and digital communication devices being introduced in every other domain of life, from home and industry to the arts, education, the media, health care, and social welfare. Between the late 1970s and the early 1990s, this market was boosted by the energy of the disability rights movement and the advancement of disability legislation that culminated

in the passage of the Americans with Disabilities Act (U.S. Department of
Justice 1990). The introduction of FC to the U.S. education and autism contexts by Biklen in 1990 thus coincided exactly with the global explosion
in research, development, and marketing of assistive computer devices that
built on these early devices, capitalizing on the demand created by a disability rights discourse that emphasized accommodation as a human right.
The progression of advances in assistive technologies designed for people
with communication disorders is no small subplot in the story of the digital
revolution of the 1990s.

FC thus also must be understood in the context of the larger disability rights movement, and the trend toward deinstitutionalization in North
America, Australia, and Great Britain. FC had been viewed within disability
movement politics since Crossley and McDonald's legal battle, which coincided with public scandal about squalid living conditions and inhumane
care in residential institutions in the United States such as the Bridgewater
Correctional Facility (documented in 1967 by the Boston lawyer-turned-
filmmaker Frederick Wiseman in *Titicut Follies*). The independent living and
deinstitutionalization movements have been important contextual features
of FC's profile both in Australia and in the United States. FC's introduction
to the United States coincided exactly with the launching and passage of the
Americans with Disabilities Act (ADA), and cannot be separated from the
rhetoric and ideology of that watershed as it reflected international shifts
in ideas about the rights and abilities of people with physical, cognitive,
sensory, and intellectual differences that impacted the ability to speak for
oneself.

In the United States, FC was introduced in the field of education in this
context of disability rights where the focus was, more specifically, the inclusion model. Inclusion was an outgrowth of the disability rights movement
and legislative changes (the Individuals with Disabilities in Education Act
[IDEA] and Section 504 of the Rehabilitation Act, for example) that led to
mandates to enhance the potential for children with special needs to be accommodated in mainstream classrooms. Biklen, at the time of his early FC
research, already had established himself as a proponent and noted theorist
of classroom inclusion practices. His early research into facilitated communication coincided with the publication of his book *Schooling without
Labels* (Biklen 1992a), a project that made a case for keeping children with
disabilities in the mainstream classroom. Biklen's model for the inclusive
classroom was the inclusive family—households in which parents did not in-

stitutionalize the child with a disability but instead accommodated the home
to the child's needs, maximizing the child's social interaction with the family. He offered the inclusive family as an alternative model to the segregated
special education models that were being used by school districts around the
country. In these schools, children with disabilities attended special institutions or were taught in special classrooms. Teacher training at colleges and
universities was (and still is) typically organized around a model that makes
special education a separate subfield of study within schools and departments of education. Biklen's book advanced a policy of integration and di-
versity that was in keeping with the contemporary thinking of the disability
rights movement in the watershed moment of the passage of the ADA prior,
and was framed by debates about two pieces of legislation with major implications for educational practice: Section 504 of the Rehabilitation Act of
1988 and the Individuals with Disabilities in Education Act (IDEA) of 1997.
Inclusion won a mixed response, and at this writing continues to stand as
a marginalized alternative to mainstream special education. This is in part
because inclusion would require a rethinking of the organization of schools
already fraught with problems of space and time management, and because
its implementation would disrupt the existing structure of many established
departments of higher education, requiring a rethinking of special education
training.

The interdisciplinary arena of autism research is yet another context in
which discussions about FC were situated in the United States. Definition
and classification of autism has been and continues to be subject to heavy
reformulation, driving Uta Frith, the leading historian of autism, to describe
the disorder as an "enigma" in her book's title (Frith 1989). The 1990s
saw dramatic increases in the reported incidences of autism, a condition
identified by Leo Kanner (1946) as a disturbance of affective interpersonal
contact with a biological etiology. Reports about rising case numbers, which
reflected increased diagnosis, were accompanied by changes in autism's and
related disorders' classifications. The professional and popular media speculated about the emergence of a social type characterized by an "extreme
male brain"—the socially inept, unempathetic mathematics- and computer-
oriented type of boy who finds his niche in the role of the computer geek
(Baron-Cohen 1995, Hutinger and Rippey 1997). Not surprisingly, this
emergent type coincided with the computer boom of the 1990s.

Because children with autism constitute the majority of people with
whom FC has been used and studied in the United States, this has been one

of the major professional and public contexts for the method's reception. The term "autism" was introduced in 1911 by the Swiss psychiatrist Eugen Bleuler to describe what was then regarded as an aspect of adult schizophrenia. As Uta Frith notes, the term originally described "the narrowing of relationships to people and to the outside world, a narrowing so extreme that it seemed to exclude everything except the person's own self. This narrowing could be described as a withdrawal from the fabric of social life into the self. Hence the words 'autistic' and 'autism,' from the Greek word autos meaning 'self'" (Frith 1989, 7–8).

In 1943, Leo Kanner used the term to describe eleven children he had observed who had withdrawn from human contact at very young ages. Kanner's work initiated a trend away from understanding autism as related to schizophrenia, but the tendency to interpret the autistic child as schizophrenic remained prevalent in psychiatry until the 1960s, and some (including Kristeva) continue to use the word in ways that are closer to Bleuler's meaning. Concurrently with Kanner, the Austrian psychiatrist Hans Asperger used the term "autistic psychopathy" to describe a wide range of clinical cases of children who seemed unable to have normal affective relationships with others (Asperger 1944, Frith 1989).[10] Currently the label "Asperger's" is restricted to use as a subclassification of highly intelligent and verbal autistic children, the "child professors" that Asperger had described along with a range of other kinds of cases in his 1944 report (Frith 1989, 7–8).

By the early 1990s autism as such had been the object of scientific research for a least four decades. It has had its own designated journals and specialists. But the classification and etiology of autism have continually shifted more than most other developmental disability classifications, and this pattern continues to the degree that in 2002 leading researchers were still describing autism as probably the most enigmatic form of developmental disability, echoing Frith's characterization of the disorder's status throughout its history (Herbert, Sharp, and Gaudino 2002). Various features and models of the disorder have been emphasized over the years. These have included the presence of intellectual deficit or problems in the individual's theory of mind, mental processing abilities, or expressive language ability. These different understandings of the disorder have intersected and vied with one another, continually reshaping the institutional face of the autism spectrum and launching a range of subclassifications (e.g., Asperger's, pervasive developmental disorder). Distinction among these categories of developmental disability, and assignation of children to the right classification, is elusive. This is frustrating not only to parents and to autism researchers but also to autism professionals in clinical and education contexts who require clear assessment documentation in order to devise and gain approval for educational and medical plans for their clients. What FC findings seemed to suggest is that the already fraught realm of assessment might be even more of a problem than anyone had realized.

Another context in which FC found itself entangled is the "memory wars" of the 1990s (Campbell 2003). Multiple cases in which allegations of child sexual abuse were disclosed through facilitated writing coincided with broader controversies in the 1990s about therapeutic processes in clinical psychology in which adult clients remembered and reported childhood experiences of sexual and physical abuse. Controversies concerned the truth and accuracy of the narratives of previously repressed memories of abuse reported by adult clients in therapy. Skeptics raised the concern that therapists were asking leading questions, steering clients, who were in the majority of cases discussed female, to experience as recovered memories what were in fact fantasy constructions prompted by the therapist's suggestion and influence. Professional and lay concerns about the possibility that the therapist might make leading statements, or that fantasy constructions might be felt so powerfully to be true by the suggestible client in these therapeutic contexts escalated with therapy cases of families divided by conflicts played out in homes, therapy sessions, and the court system. In 1992 professionals in law, psychology, psychiatry, social work, and education worked with family members impacted by accusations that were alleged, by some implicated in the conflict, to be "false memories" induced by overzealous therapy to form the False Memory Syndrome Foundation (FMSF). This nonprofit organization, funded by donations, is dedicated to the understanding and prevention of what has come to be called "false memory syndrome," as well as to the cause of helping "victims of memory" and of "bad therapy" to generate "retractor stories" as a corrective to the damage done by the circulation of false memories (Pendergrast 1996). One goal of the foundation is the reconciliation of families fractured by legal, therapeutic, and public media controversies over allegations proven to be false.[11]

Abuse of children in orphanages overseas was a major rallying issue for U.S. viewers of television news journalism in the early 1990s (Cartwright forthcoming). Stories about human rights abuses of children overseas were matched by concern about hands-on therapy out of control in the abuse and killing of the postinstitutionalized child (Mercer, Sarner, and Rosa 2003). Abuses occurring in home care through the United States foster system also came under scrutiny during the 1990s. The allegations of sexual abuse by children with communication disorders using FC resonated in this context. They also echoed social service findings and publicized documentation of vulnerability to abuse among disabled populations (Diamond and Jaudes 1983). At the same time, the social services professions were addressing the issue of sexual and physical abuse in contexts including daycare, schools, private homes, foster homes, and a range of institutional and home care settings.

But as professional discussion in journals and conferences unfolded, problems of truth in reporting emerged. These included the possibility of underreporting by victims and staff. Widely noted in the sexual abuse literature is the problem of fear of retribution, not only among child victims of abuse but also among family and staff members who witness abuses of other parties but fear they will lose their safety or jobs if they speak up. Interviews with Chinese orphanage employees cited in a Human Rights Watch (1996) report on abuses in that context vividly illustrate this problem of employees being "without voice" in this context. Around this problem, social workers and psychologists forged a professional apparatus designed to offer therapy and care for victims of abuse, on the one hand, and to discern cases of false memory, and to elicit and test the accuracy of narratives of abuse, on the other.

At the basis of the concept of false memory is the question of the validity of women's words, the reliability of their memory, and the degree of their suggestibility. This issue of credibility extends to feminized caretaker jobs performed by men. As the Canadian feminist philosopher Sue Campbell notes, skepticism regarding women's authority and trustworthiness in the telling of self-narratives is the implicit subtext of the FMSF's skepticism about abuse memories newly reported in therapy (Campbell 2003, 47–68). Memory, Campbell notes, in one of the key mechanisms through which personhood is afforded, and through which subjects become members of a moral community (Campbell 2003, 17). To contest a person's memories is to politically undermine that person's status as moral agent (Campbell 2003, 17).

Questions about authorship in the intersubjective production of narrative between client and therapist—a central problematic of the memory wars—were present in the discussions about FC in ways that echoed the recovered memory context. The facilitator, a person who might be male or female but who occupies a feminized caretaker role, whether as professional or family member, occupies the position of the therapist insofar as his or her participation in authorship may be regarded as overly influencing, leading, or suggestive. As I will explain, the facilitator also occupied the role, in the minds of FC skeptics, of one who speaks out of place, at the expense of a child victim.

The most publicized aspect of FC was the controversy about abuse allegations made by children through facilitated writing. The question of trusting children's claims is, of course, different from that of trusting women's words in narratives about their own experiences of abuse. In the early part of the twentieth century children were rarely allowed as witnesses into the courts, except in Europe. Only a few studies were conducted assessing the reliability of children as witnesses and investigating their susceptibility to suggestion or leading comments by adults (Ceci and Bruck 1993 and 1995, Goodman et al. 2003, Wakefield and Underwager 1988). *The Fallen Idol* (Carol Reed, England, 1948) is a compelling capsule of mid-century British thinking about the unreliability of child witnesses and child testimony.[12] In this film drama, the child's viewpoint is dismissed by authorities brought in to investigate the cause of death of the wife of the family butler. The child's words are regarded as fantasy and fib—the very stuff with which the butler, whom the boy idolizes, has filled the boy's mind in order to entertain him and enlist his help in concealing an extramarital affair. But this skepticism about the word of the child appears to have been less prevalent in the courts. By the 1970s, increases in the public allegation and reporting of abuse of children led to more frequent admissibility of child testimony in the courtroom. Throughout the 1980s and into the 1990s, research into the reliability of children's statements increased dramatically, with the testimony of children at first widely accepted as trustworthy (Faller 1984, Summit and Kryso 1978). But the question of children's susceptibility to leading questions became more pressing through the 1990s. This shift in the regard of the child as reliable witness was concordant with the emergence of the memory wars and their foregrounding of concerns about therapeutic influence, as well as questions about the reliability of adult women's memories and their ability to tell the truth without augmentation or clouding of the facts. What seems to have occurred is not that children per se were regarded as less trustworthy, but that attention to the potential for child suggestibility under adult questioning and influence became more pronounced. The testimony of children was more closely scrutinized for the potential of influence by well-meaning teachers, parents, therapists, and legal investigators who, even with the best of intentions, might plant ideas that might be transformed into false memory by the suggestible child. This increased concern about suggestibility and the reliability of the interrogative process of the child interview by adult professionals was concordant with the debates about the reliability of FC. As we shall see, that controversy centered on the credibility and reliability of facilitators, not children, with regard to their role as mediators of truth.

At issue were the facilitator's reliability as a mediator of the child's words, and the actual extent of her influence over the child's writing process. Prior to the "Prisoners of Silence" episode's airing, at least two such cases had been heard. In Kansas, a jury had found the accused guilty (Randall 1993). In the second case, a precedent was set. The New York Supreme Court ruled that for facilitated testimony to be admissible as evidence, a procedure must be implemented not only to determine whether the witness's autism "constitutes such a mental impairment as to render her competent to testify," but also to determine "whether the facilitator is accurate and reliable" (*Matter of Luz P.* 1993). Thus testing of the facilitator's reliability became a major feature of courtroom process in each case where facilitated writing was introduced as potential evidence. In many of the media reports about these cases, the question of the reliability of the facilitator was the locus of the story, overshadowing the case itself (Martin 1993). We might say, then, that it was the facilitator who was placed on trial first, before evidence could be admitted into a case.

In placing the facilitator on trial in this way, a shame narrative unfolded in the public eye where these cases were chronicled and judged on moral grounds. The picture will be familiar to those who followed the adult childhood memory wars of the 1990s: the facilitator, like the therapist in the memory wars, first had to be cleared of prior suspicion of influencing client speech to the point of generating stories—indeed, stories that might in fact be her own fabrication, and not even an interpretation of the child's plight. Her potential projection of an abuse narrative, it was feared, might even be unconsciously performed. This view of the facilitator suggested that she might inhabit the role of the hysterical adult speaking through the body of the child. The child, like the hapless adult client swayed by her therapist's leading questions, is cast as unwitting victim. In this sense, the facilitator became the paradigm—we might even say the specter—of affective disorder in an era when mediation was widely accepted as an aspect of communication. Like the science fiction specter of the machine come to life, the facilitator was the personification of the fantasy of technologies of mediation gone out of control. Or, to return to the model of intercorporeity described by Levinas (1993), the facilitator embodies the threat that desire poses to the autonomous subject in its intersubjective relationship to others. In this picture of the facilitator as hidden author of the child's words, it is not the child whose egological isolation is broken through intersubjective touch. Rather, it is the facilitator who "borrows" her identity from the other (the child), using the child's "voice" (written words) as a technology to project her own fantasies cum memories. This is precisely the kind of power dynamic that Levinas does not really address in his discussion of intersubjectivity, and which the FC controversy brought to the fore.

Thus FC was received in the U.S. context as a player in multiple domains fraught with ethical and legal contestation about dynamics of power in practices of mediated speech. Truth and accuracy in determining not only who speaks in facilitated communication but also whose mediation can be trusted, and what models of mediation are trustworthy, became matters of major importance beyond the actual cases themselves.

The perception of FC as seductive and untrustworthy preceded this rash of cases. Professional responses to the observations recorded in Biklen's 1990 essay were initially enthusiastic, but this enthusiasm itself made the method appear suspicious to some researchers including Eric Schopler, the editor of the *Journal of Autism and Developmental Disorders*. Less than a year after Biklen's first article on the method was published, Schopler described FC as a "new fad," noting with consternation that Biklen's (1990) report was merely preliminary, published without supporting data. He expressed concern that the report had "triggered enthusiasm" among "a surprising number of the journal's Professional Advisory Board members experienced with autism" despite the lack of data (Schopler in an editorial preface to Bettison 1991, 561). An essay and editorial commentary responding to Biklen in the *Harvard Education Review* called for the need for double-blind testing of FC and raised the specter of a "cult of deception" forming around the method (Cummins and Prior 1992, Prior and Cummins 1992, Schopler 1992). FC thus had the taint of unreliability, even before its association with abuse allegations. The technique was not to be trusted.

Biklen chose to frame his response most explicitly in the rhetoric of disability rights rather than taking up the scientific testing issue as his main ground. "Autism orthodoxy v. free speech" was the title of his rejoinder

(Biklen 1992a). Thus far, doubts about autism's definition and assessment protocols had been merely inferred by Biklen's findings about the potential of people with autism to communicate. But even Sue Bettison, chief executive officer of the Autism Association of New South Wales and, like Schopler, a skeptic of the FC method, took note that the positive view of the person inherent in Biklen's FC model was a welcome counter to the "depersonalization and devaluing" inherent in most disability treatment models (Bettison 1991). The title of Biklen's rejoinder made explicit his previously inferred position that established thinking about autism potentially stood in the way of the basic human rights of children with autism by failing to acknowledge the possibility that intellectual deficit might be overdiagnosed in some children assessed with autism; that flaws in assessment methods closed doors to educational strategies for those with intellectual potential masked by problems of expression and praxis. Biklen's view was correctly read by the autism research community as a direct challenge to the very foundations of the field: its theories of autism and its assessment methods. To accept FC would be to accept that the tenets of autism research needed to be rethought and changed from the ground up.

The Australian FC pioneer Rosemary Crossley's published contribution to the professional debates opening up in the United States (Crossley and Remington-Gurney 1992) and reports that drew in detail from the writings of FC users with autism in the United States were closely followed by a flurry of reports on independent tests of the method in the United States. Some of these reports suggested that individuals using the method were unable to demonstrate that they were communicating their own thoughts without the influence of their facilitators (Eberlin et al. 1993, Wheeler et al. 1993a and 1993b). In the midst of this immediate challenge to the validity of the method, Biklen founded an institute devoted to FC research and training at Syracuse University in upstate New York. With this institutional grounding, he launched a program in training and an annual FC conference that attracted researchers, clients, facilitators, family members, and prospective trainees from around the world. Thus the view that FC was too seductive, was a method "spread[ing] like wildfire," was shared among some educators and autism specialists who held fast to the position that further scientific testing of the method should precede its dissemination (Siegel 1995),[13] even as the method gained a firm institutional center that would support its development internationally.

So in 1993, *Frontline*'s motivation, in airing "Prisoners of Silence," was not really just to celebrate the good news about Lucy, a "prisoner of silence," coming to voice, or to praise facilitated communication for liberating Lucy from her speechless world. Rather, the heartwarming opener was a set-up to position viewers at an emotional high with Lucy and her mother, from which they could then be plunged into a moral quandary about the reliability of this method and the credibility of its advocates, along with the method's critics. FC users and advocates were cast, in the broadcast, on the side of affect, feelings, and faith. Its skeptics were portrayed as the level voices of reason and science. By the time that "Prisoners of Silence" had aired, three empirical studies had demonstrated the method to be a reliable means of communication (Intellectual Disability Review Panel 1989, Calculator and Singer 1992). However, the segment about Lucy was followed by an interview with speech pathologist Howard Shane, a colleague of Biklen's at Syracuse and a scathing critic of FC who was undertaking studies that would be used to discredit the method (Green and Shane 1994, Shane and Kearns 1994).[14] Shane's interview was pitted against the personal testimony of Arthur Schawlow, a world-renowned Stanford physicist. Schawlow had observed FC use in Stockholm and brought the technique back to the United States for his son Artie, a child with autism, who used the method to progress to independent writing. With his wife Aurelia, Schawlow documented Artie's experience with FC (Schawlow and Schawlow 1985). The scientist's seven honorary doctorates, Nobel Prize in physics and Presidential Medal for Science were not noted in the broadcast. Rather, as Australian FC advocate Chris Borthwick (1998) observes, *Frontline* instead emphasized that critics saw the method Schawlow advocated as dangerously unscientific.

"Prisoners of Silence," then, was positioned to duplicate in spectators of the episode the same split that existed throughout the autism and education communities, where the method was viewed by some as liberating and by others as dangerously open to fraud. Support for the method was equated with emotionalism and idealism even in cases where trusted scientists like Schawlow advocated for it. And finally, to get to my primary concern, the controversy was framed in such a way that human facilitators emerged as the locus of this emotionalism and idealism. In short, facilitators were made to embody affect and all of its problems. Giving a perverse twist to Marshall McLuhan's famous dictum that the medium is not only the message but also the entity that massages truth (McLuhan 1994, McLuhan and Fiore 2001), some education and autism researchers raised the specter of the medium—in this case the human facilitator and not the computer—as potential manipulator or massager of the truth of the child. Their concerns were organized around the fear that the facilitator might be, in effect, engaged in a kind of unwitting game of ventriloquism. The words of that most vulnerable of subjects, the speechless child with limited expressive abilities and with cognitive differences, might actually be the facilitator's own fantasy-memory in projection. The climate was thus set for a trial of judgment, moral and ethical, of the person of the facilitator, and not just an assessment of the reliability of the method. The split was organized, for many who observed the controversy, around the pull to believe the facilitator's work was just and noble, wanting to believe she allowed the child to speak of its own free will, on the one hand; and nagging doubt about both the motives and the method designed to achieve this goal, on the other. This split seemed to be populated by individuals who occupied one or the other side of the divide, but in fact for many involved the split was experienced internally, in the form of wanting to trust, but also wanting scientific proof. While FC advocates celebrated the speechless child's belated coming to voice and upending of diagnostic classification as a humanist victory, FC critics stewed in consternation: such a miracle that upturned research paradigms required scientific proof that these were not fraudulent victories of independence and agency, charades that made a mockery of the very humanist principles of child and disability rights.

I have emphasized thus far that it was not so much the architects of the method as the facilitators who became the central figures around whom skepticism was organized, and who became the subjects on trial in the FC controversy. Even where the method and its advocates (Biklen for example) have been the targets of heated criticism, the issue at stake is, fundamentally, the role of the human mediator in bringing the child to voice in any particular case. This is fundamentally a question about the right structure of symbolic interaction, which should situate the child as the speaker and the caregiver (in a feminized role) as neutral mediator in the production of the child's speech. Questions about authorship and the intersubjective relationship between a caregiver and a disabled child subject were not new when they were raised with regard to the work of those trained through Biklen's institute. The role of the human facilitator had been at the center of controversies about FC since the McDonald court case, and they continued to be raised with reference to Crossley's subsequent use of the method at

DEAL (Crossley and McDonald 1980, Intellectual Disability Review Panel 1989, Catonese 1988).

In the next section I discuss *Annie's Coming Out*, the motion picture film of 1984 that chronicles the story of Anne McDonald and Rosemary Crossley. I will be emphasizing the ways in which the film presents a drama that sets up the same issues that would become controversial in the U.S. context: the question of the trustworthiness of the female caregiver and facilitator, and the issue of abuse allegations escalating the importance of this question of the facilitator's role in the production of the child's speech. This segue through a film will lead us back to the U.S. context, where I focus more closely on the figure of the facilitator in debates about the authorship of abuse allegations, and the question of intersubjectivity and touch in the production of child voice through facilitated writing that this topic allows us to examine.

Annie's Coming Out *(1984)*

Public debates about facilitated communication can be traced to events twenty years prior to the *Frontline* segment, with the circumstances that prompted the production of the successful Australian biopic *Annie's Coming Out* (U.S. release title *A Test of Love*, Gil Brealey/Australian Film Commission, 1984). The film, winner of a Best Film Award from the Australian Film Institute, was based on the bestselling autobiography of the same title (Crossley and McDonald 1980). The book documented a pivotal case in the Australian disability rights movement. It chronicled the institutional experience and legal battle of Anne McDonald, a resident of St. Nicholas, a state residential facility in Melbourne, Australia, for people with severe mental and physical disabilities, from the age of three through eighteen. McDonald, a girl with cerebral palsy introduced in the film at age thirteen, had been assessed as severely mentally retarded and without the motor capacity to communicate verbally or through expressive movement. The film reveals, through the stunned and pitying eyes of Rosemary Crossley, a new administrative employee touring the institution, the child's twisted and growth-stunted body lying on a cot.[15] The early shots of *Annie's Coming Out* in which we see McDonald for the first time through the eyes of Crossley set the stage for a narrative of rescue that foregrounds the agency and emergent voice of the child subject. Crossley, in a role reminiscent of Christine Garland in *Mandy*, dispenses with pity and, in 1977, gets down

8. Rosemary Crossley (Angela Punch McGregor)
facilitating Annie McDonald (Tina Arhondis) during
a home visit. *Annie's Coming Out* (U.S. release title:
A Test of Love) (1984).

to a rigorous plan of work that entails teaching McDonald and other St.
Nicholas residents to read and to communicate using an alphabet board
and page turner. She later devises a means for McDonald to use a typewriter
(later substituted by a computer), with Crossley providing hand-over-hand,
wrist and arm support. By taking her on outings to museums and home
with her for weekend visits, Crossley schooled McDonald in the ordinary
day-to-day experiences of a typical child, experiences that McDonald had
missed since age three, when her family had her "put away." Throughout
this narrative of Anne's schooling, McGregor builds up Crossley's character
as a neurotically driven, intelligent, and impassioned teacher, a dynamic and
attractive young woman of the seventies, who commits herself to the liberation of the children of St. Nicholas through actions that place at risk her
career and personal life. Crossley faces vitriolic workplace skepticism and
jealousy from her peers and the (mostly female) nursing staff and scathing
questions from the press.

An Australian High Court decision was the proving ground for the challenge that the film's U.S. release title characterizes as a "test of love." With
Crossley's help, McDonald, at age eighteen, launched a legal battle for deinstitutionalization. In this controversial and widely publicized case, Mc-
Donald and Crossley made allegations of widespread, systematic abuses of
residents at St. Nicholas. Among these charges was an allegation that would
echo years later in the facilitated reports of sexual abuse mentioned above.

Through facilitated writing, McDonald described an attempt against her life by a member of the nursing staff.

In the film, the nurses of St. Nicholas are depicted as a corps of pale, small-minded women. Their dreary uniforms and lives are offset by the color and vibrancy brought to the institution by the fiery Crossley, an attractive woman in youthful street clothes. The nurses show condescension and pity toward McDonald and the other children, repeatedly missing communicative cues from the children as they force-feed and bathe them. Crossley is met with disdain when she insists that the nurses address the children as cognizant, feeling individuals. The nurses express envy and contempt toward Crossley, voicing annoyance and resentment about the attention (negative and positive) garnered from the doctors and administrators by this outsider. The changes Crossley tries to implement in workplace routine are regarded as annoying at best, a violation of reason and truth at worst. The staff's petty conversations reveal that they nurse low expectations not only for their charges but also for their own success: they believe they cannot have much of an impact on the lives of the children to whom they devote their hours of labor each day. The film dramatizes the murder attempt described in McDonald's court documents. In the film, an older, embittered nurse seizes a private moment to attempt what she regards as an act of mercy. She enters the children's sleeping ward and places a pillow over McDonald's mouth. But the attempted suffocation is foiled by the other children, who watch and listen to the scene unfold from their nearby cots. These spectators to the crime shriek loudly in protest, attracting other staff members to the scene. However, the children don't have the ability to report what they saw and heard. It is McDonald's written report to the courts that finally brings the terrible crime of compassion to light, raising the specter of other like deeds witnessed but tragically unreported by the cognizant children, who remain "prisoners of silence," unable to speak what they know, in institutions like this one all across Australia.

Foremost among the controversies stirred by the case McDonald brought against St. Nicholas was the question of whether, and to what degree, Crossley was influencing the written statements produced by McDonald in the process of facilitating her writing. Skepticism was also strong among members of the medical community concerning Crossley's claim that this girl with cerebral palsy was of normal intellect and could read and think within a normal intellectual range, but simply lacked the means of expressive praxis required to demonstrate this. McDonald's institutional records included an

assessment indicating the possibility of brain damage and suggesting she had
the mental capacity of an infant. Physician testimony about McDonald's
medical condition and assessment records figured importantly in the case,
vying against evidence from Crossley's work with McDonald. The film dramatizes the initial failure of an independent test of the FC method during
which McDonald stubbornly refused to comply, botching the outcome. But
McDonald had already aced two tests of her ability to read. Administered by
psychologists, these assessments established that she had independent reading skills. In 1979 McDonald was given two other assessments, one with and
one without facilitation, that were the basis for the judgment of the High
Court of Australia that she had the capacity to make decisions on her own
and to manage her own affairs (Bettison 1992). These tests were the basis for
the film's dramatization of the court-administered test that led McDonald
to snub her nose at the audacity of the courts to question her autonomy. By
willfully failing the test, she administered her own "test of love" to Crossley.
The film suggests that she willfully failed to comply with the test procedure,
refusing to answer as directed as a matter of pride. Her refusal to listen and
answer questions as instructed defies the dictum, if you can't measure it, it
isn't there. She makes the point, by refusing to cooperate, that this test is
an insult to her integrity as a person, and the integrity of her relationship to
Crossley. To recall this same point made in another poem by Jan, the author
of the stanza of poetry that is one of the epigraphs at the beginning of this
chapter, and which was written through facilitation:

> Can anyone hear the voice inside?
> Give me some light and I can see.
> Give me some pain and I can feel.
> Give me a call and I will hear.
> But give me credit—
> *That's for some too hard.*[16]

In the testing scene, what is tested is not accuracy or reliability, but love.
Recall that, for Levinas, in touch "the other person and I 'are like the elements of one sole intercorporeity'" (Levinas 1993, 100). Sociality is enacted
in mutual touch. And touch is not the mere symbol of love, but love itself
(Levinas 1993, 101 and 113). What McDonald takes issue with is not the
test of reliability of her words, but the test of a bond that constitutes her
as human—that enters her into sociality. The fact of social belonging, she
rightfully believes, is nothing that any human subject should be asked to

prove. This scene thus depicts, presciently, the tension that will emerge again and again in the scientific testing of facilitated communication in the United States throughout the 1990s. Again and again, whereas "failed" tests prove to scientific observers the invalidity of the method, they in many cases constituted for the facilitated subject a failure to be recognized and admitted into the world as cognizant, feeling social subject.

Although the film relies on the formula of mixing melodrama with the social problem film used in *Mandy* and *The Miracle Worker*, *Annie's Coming Out* is more firmly tied to the facts of a particular biographical and historical narrative. Marketing copy emphasized ties to the historic legal case—noting, for example, the film's "performances by real-life patients from Australia's rehabilitation centers, including Tina Arhondis as Annie." At the same time, star billing went to Australian star Angela Punch McGregor (as Crossley), guaranteeing the film a mainstream theatrical release. The orchestration of agency across the Crossley-McDonald (McGregor-Arhondis) unit echoes the relationship of Sullivan-Keller (Bancroft-Duke) dramatized two decades earlier in *The Miracle Worker*.

Like the Keller-Sullivan biographies and films, the Crossley-McDonald story occupies an important place in the disability rights movement. First, it documents the battle for independence of a person with a severe physical disability during the 1970s, a decade alive with patients' rights activism and with film and news media exposés of and subsequent reforms in residential institutions and the health and social welfare systems. McDonald's legal case and the publicity that surrounded it were important elements in a broader movement begun in the 1970s toward deinstitutionalization and an increase in outpatient and community mental health services for people with developmental disabilities and psychiatric illnesses in places including Australia, North America, and Great Britain. The book and film both documented and contributed to the international literature of a disability rights movement that was advocating for deinstitutionalization and for changes in health and social welfare funding structures that would allow for the federal support of people with disabilities in independent and group homes.[17]

Second, the news reports, book, and movie surrounding McDonald's case brought attention to the emergent discourses of communication disorders or disabilities, and assistive technologies. Communication disability is an interestingly imprecise category because it crosses assessment and diagnostic categories, describing instead relational conditions in a variety of disability classifications that can be accommodated by making changes in praxis and the environmental settings in which the individual interacts with others. Anne McDonald's diagnosis was cerebral palsy, and Lucy Harrison's was autism, but they had in common a set of conditions that precluded the performance of spoken and manual (signed) speech. The term "communication disability" describes the subjects' relationship to a social context and their ability to communicate in it, not their medical classification or diagnosis. This relational understanding of disability allows us to shift the focus from the body as the entity requiring a fix or cure to praxis, which may be accommodated.

However, as I have indicated, the shift in usage of FC from clients with cerebral palsy primarily to those with autism in Australia and the United States made a world of difference in the method's subsequent reception and use in professional and lay contexts. The use of FC among people with autism opened up thorny questions about the nature of autism vis-à-vis expressive communication during a decade fraught with controversy about the nature of that disorder and its right management. This decade, the 1990s, was also fraught with questions about human mediation and new communication technologies that extended well beyond the autism and disabilities contexts. Because "expression" was itself a category surrounded by ambiguity, as noted above, a method that featured facilitation of expressive performance among those whose expressive capacity was in question was deeply fraught from the start.

In my reading of *Mandy, Johnny Belinda*, and *Miracle Worker* in chapter 2, I was able to consider the politics of caregiving and the revered and disparaged intersubjective relationship of hearing mother (or substitute caregiver) and Deaf daughter as the latter comes to voice in the postwar years. In *Annie's Coming Out* we encounter yet another "Annie" narrative that unfolded through news stories, nonfiction bestseller, and biopic, another series of texts that can be mined for analysis of the intersubjective, assisted production of voice and/as agency in the speechless child and through her caregiver in the context of a full-blown disability rights movement. As I have argued in the earlier chapters, my concern is not only with the child and her achievement of voice and/as agency, but also with the female figure, the facilitator, as agent of her own liberation as well as her child's. As in the narratives recounted earlier, it is this figure that makes it possible for the "child" to "come out," to emerge as an autonomous social subject. But this selfless act is also the ticket to the caregiver's own emergence as a professional figure with a voice that is heard and respected in the public sphere.

The title *Annie's Coming Out* clearly evokes a phrase used to denote the act of publicly naming and performing a formerly subjugated identity. The closet from which the child emerges, however, is not that which traps identity within the normative binary terms of sexual difference or language and the law, but that which recognizes authentic expression as emanating from the individual, autonomously speaking body.

The FC narratives and controversies are stories for our times that perform a very contemporary crisis about the mediation of the human subject and its independent performance in affective relationships, through doubles and others in interconstitutively supportive roles. In the new century's human rights discourses, as in its global trade liberalization rhetoric, dependency is deplored and independence is revered. Borders are dissolved and distances are collapsed, not in order for subjects (nation-states, citizens) to shed their status as individuals but to facilitate fantasies of cultural incorporation—the bringing close of the other. The dream of borderlessness enacts Levinas's concept of the rights of man as originally the rights of the other and not of the self, the rights upheld through an attachment to the other that grants the other priority over me (Levinas 1999, 149), but it also makes clear all of the problems with this formula as regard power and agency. As I will explain below, the "test of love," the aphorism that serves as the U.S. release title of *Annie's Coming Out*, is not only the test that a child puts to its caregiver by "not listening," not obeying authority. It is also the test a skeptical public administers to those in the feminized role of caregiver of the other, demanding a degree of subjugation of self one might expect from a machine, but at the same time decrying the collapse of boundaries between self and other that results from this relationship. On one level this is a test of the caregiver's ability to be the mediating agent of change who puts the other before herself. But on another and more crucial level what is "tested" is the contemporary notion of boundaries in human feeling during an era of heightened mediation where we always take for granted, wrongly, that our mediators are neutral machines.

Touch and affect in FC

Although the computer is often featured as the key component in FC, the method's most distinctive and salient technological component, I stress, is the human facilitator. It is the facilitator who plays the chief role as a technology of mediation in the subject's generation of written messages on the computer. We now turn to examine more closely the aspect of this technology that I wish to emphasize. This is the *affective* role of the facilitator as technology. The physical support provided by the facilitator is the feature most questioned by critics. Their main question has been this: how and to what extent does physical support become physical guidance and influence? My goal here is to shift the emphasis to the factor of the emotional or affective nature of this physical support as it comes into play in the production of expression through writing. I will argue that it is affective support, affective mediation, that is the most distinctive aspect of facilitated communication, but also the part least considered in analyses of the method.

Facilitator involvement typically entails light hand-over-hand guidance and support. The objective is to help the subject isolate the index finger for letter selection, or and/or to provide manual support under the wrist or forearm to help steady the typing hand and slow down the pace of activity. Of course touch provides physical support, but it is also a medium of emotional support. Ideally, in the FC relationship touch is decreased over time to become as minimal as a reassuring hand on the shoulder. A good example of this ideal progression from touch as support to touch as symbolic contact is found in Sabin and Donnellan 1993. They describe the case of Dan, a boy who began with a facilitator providing support to his entire body as he wrote. Six months into his training he required only the trusted facilitator's hand on his shoulder while he wrote independently. For some who use the FC method, touch is phased out to the degree that the physical presence of the facilitator nearby is all that is required for the subject to feel at ease communicating on the computer. Touch, Sabin and Donnellan note, was described by participants in their FC study as being a more vital part of their experience with facilitated communication than the use of letterboards or computers (Sabin and Donnellan 1993, 205).

It cannot be emphasized enough that the facilitator provides a degree of emotional support that makes expression possible for the child, and it is this aspect of the facilitated relationship, not the mere technical aspect of physical support, that is at the core of the skepticism that surrounds FC. Because the emotional aspects of facilitation tie in with cognitive support, suggestion or influence may be an inevitable aspect of any facilitated writing relationship. Biklen and other FC advocates have noted this factor from the beginning of the method's dissemination, citing it not as a problem to be overcome, but as a necessary condition of the practice. Problems noted by critics arise when affective cognitive and emotional support can be described as suggestive or leading. The facilitator may, for example, remind the subject to look at the keys or screen, or may generally provide an organizing sense of emotional stability to a subject who struggles with attention and focus, or may provide cues to orient an individual who has an unclear or shifting sense of the boundaries that constitute the self as distinct from others and objects. Or, the facilitator may help to center someone who struggles to perform the motor activity required of the eyes, the head, and the hands in communication settings. Degree and type of support varies from case to case. Although widely described as wrist, hand, and arm support, the nature of this relationship is far more complex, including eye cues, gesture, verbal cues, and all of the components of interaction one finds in any conversation setting. Ideally, physical support diminishes and with some subjects may even be phased out completely over months or years, as was the case for Lucy Harrison.[18] In other cases, physical support may be necessary indefinitely. And in others, I emphasize, the emotional and cognitive aspects of support, which are not reducible to physical propping of limbs, may also be necessary to sustain even after physical support is phased out.

It is hard to disaggregate independent voices when questions are posed regarding who authors a message, and where the line is drawn between support and influence. It is the emotional aspect of this relationship, the dynamic of trust, love, hope, and desire between facilitator and facilitated subject conveyed through touch, and the relationship between support and "influence" that give the method qualities that critics characterized as "unreliable" and "unverifiable" (Schopler 1992, 331). Controversy over the emotional aspect of facilitation—what we might call the facilitation of the child's affective abilities and expression—lies at the core of the controversy about facilitated communication.

Recall once again André Green's definition of the affective process as *the anticipation of a meeting between the subject's body and another's body, real or imaginary* (Green 1999b, 289, his italics). The FC relationship brings us, finally to an instance where the psychical, social, and legal differences in stakes between a meeting that is real (physical) and a meeting that is imaginary (filled with expectation, hope, and projection) become clear.

At stake in this controversy about FC was not simply a method of communication and its reliability. Rather, the framing question was where and how empathy comes into play in communication during a decade in which computers were paradoxically upheld as a means of personal freedom, on the one hand, and of enslavement to an emotionally removed life lived on

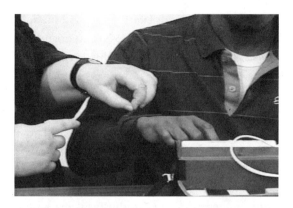

9. Hand suspending wrist, using sleeve as support. *State of the Art: Every Step of the Way toward Independent Communication* (1994).

10. Hand-on-shoulder facilitator support. *State of the Art: Every Step of the Way toward Independent Communication* (1994).

the screen, on the other. During this same period assistive technologies were both touted and doubted as a means of facilitating autonomous agency in children, the developmentally disabled, and those who require assistance or accommodation to speak. The FC controversy of the 1990s was, at bottom, a struggle among concepts of human agency and the individual subject during a period of dramatic changes in the means of the performance of the individual, not only by those disabled at the level of affect but also among neurotypical subjects experiencing affective disorders in their newly networked emotional lives. Whereas debates about networked computers have played up the role of the machine as medium that enhances human agency and connectivity, the controversy about FC has driven home the simple fact that human facilitators (teachers, health care workers, technicians, parents) have always stood between the child and speech, as well as between the subject and the computer—and the subject and the interlocutor reached with a computed message.

Frances Tustin (1981), Margaret Mahler (Mahler with Furer 1968) and, most famously, Bruno Bettelheim (1967) had raised the problem of caregiver influence over development. They described the psychoanalytic specter of the unloving, demanding mother as the pathological figure who produces autism as a psychological state in the child. These accounts, which include Bettelheim's infamous call for a therapeutic practice of "parentectomy" that would free the child from the alleged source of his autism for an extended healing period, launched a mid-century wave of maternal blame and shame. A wave of remorse, later in the century, about the false accusation of the mother, now viewed as the victim of a discredited science of the mind, coincided with the turning of the tide away from the psychoanalytic and toward the biological model of etiology (Roser 1996, Gardner 2000, Metzl 2003). Embrace of the biological aspects of the account that had been initiated by Kanner helped to facilitate vindication of the wrongly accused mother. But this hindsight view that reverses the pathological mother image into the kitsch icon of mother-as-victim of an overzealous postwar psychoanalysis has left researchers with no plausible legacy of theory through which to build a model of the actual role of caregiver involvement in the expression of the autistic child who comes to voice through supported writing. The facilitator controversy of the 1990s, then, was the displaced site where anxiety about the historically vexed status of the caregiver in the coming into being of the ambiguously "delayed" speechless autistic child subject is played out in professional discourse. The facilitator is the substitute for the pathological mother who "produced" the autistic child. But this time the caregiver is the "poorly trained" pseudo-professional (Rimland 1992a) who produces a preposterous miracle that she herself believes: the nonverbal child who miraculously comes to voice in writing.

Judith Duchan noted in 1993 that FC critics seemed to be embracing the outmoded view of communication as a system of passing information over an invisible conduit (Duchan 1993, 1108). Critics of FC seemed to be faulting facilitators for not performing as invisible conduits of messages. In the spirit of Duchan, who offered a multidimensional, contextual, and collaborative view of communication, I consider in greater depth the place of the facilitator as empathetic medium vaunted by FC advocates and vilified by FC critics. I also examine the vying concepts of the "unempathetic" autistic mind vis-à-vis communication and the empathetic facilitator. Battles over the nature of autism, affective life in the autistic subject, and the right mode of communication with and caregiving for autistic people who cannot speak were at the core of this controversy about what constitutes meaningful expression, beyond information plain and simple.

Research in computer-mediated communication following from McLuhan's dictum about the agency of the medium has tended to emphasize machine influence and agency in conveying information remotely. To talk about FC is to reopen the old, unresolved problem of the maternal or feminine subject as representational medium of "expression" as feeling and affect in child voice and agency. As noted earlier, I do not agree with the idea of Carol Gilligan (1982) that women have a moral affinity with relationships of care, and articulate this ethic of care "in a different voice" from that of men. Affective facilitation is a pink-collar category of labor insofar as it is a job typically performed by women and men in underpaid or unpaid feminized categories of work (as teachers, tutors, personal aides, speech pathologists, mothers, fathers). My emphasis is upon the feminization of this position within a category of practice, and not the actual gender of the person who performs it.

What is facilitated is feelings, not just needs (in this case, the need to communicate independently) or messages. Facilitation is by necessity a process, I propose, that involves projective identification as well as empathy. Shamed and blamed for not performing the impossible role of neutral conduits of meaning in bringing others to voice, FC facilitators were the icon of a nostalgic fantasy in which it is imagined that a child might achieve the freedom of autonomous expression unrehearsed, uninflected by the expectant and projective gaze of an other, a moral spectator whose selfless gifts of compassion and empathy (I am speaking only partly ironically here) bring the subject to life. In other words, facilitators became the paradigm of the ethical caregiver who ultimately fails at her task of performing wholly for the other.

Facilitated communication: desire and power
in the intersubjective relationship

When Biklen brought Crossley's technique to the United States, the method was greeted with excitement by parents, professionals, and the lay press, particularly in its potential use with children with autism who had severe nonsensory communication impairments. Metaphors of visibility and/as liberation abounded. In late 1991 the *New York Times Magazine* described the technique as "unlocking the door to language" (Makarushka 1991, 32). In 1992, the *Washington Post Magazine* reported that FC provided a "window on the mystery of autism" (Spake 1992). Advances in portable home and school computer technology during the years of these reports played no small part in the method's wide proliferation in homes, schools, and residential facilities informally, by lay practitioners and self-trained or minimally trained professionals. Biklen's Facilitated Communication Institute at Syracuse University sponsored workshops and training sessions offering comprehensive guidelines (Biklen and Chadwick 1999), and the American Speech-Language Association invested efforts in the generation of its own comprehensive usage guidelines even as its journal published articles questioning the method. The kind of oversight and regulation more typically imposed with the introduction of a new drug treatment or a new clinical therapy was impossible to enforce with a method whose components were mothers, teachers, and computers.

Following a widely cited study (Wheeler 1993a, 1993b) suggesting facilitator influence in authorship, two supportive qualitative studies demonstrated the need for a new way of understanding authorship, emphasizing that authorship never resides solely with one subject or another (Sabin and Donnellan 1993, Duchan 1993). Sabin and Donnellan are quite explicit in their observation that facilitators influence control over decisions in the communication process at multiple levels. They conclude that it is the power relationship in FC that requires deeper investigation, and not the question of which subject is the author of any given statement. The controversy, then, was not whether or not the facilitated subject speaks for itself: FC advocates were quite ready to admit that some level of facilitator involvement is inevitable. The controversy, then, should have focused on the question of what constitutes communication and how communication works, and not the question of which individual truly speaks a given utterance. FC critics posited that communication is an interaction among independent subjects who exchange statements that are each independently constructed. Among FC advocates, the concept of communication is well characterized in an analogy suggested by Duchan: communication is like a dance in which partners perform each given movement together (Duchan 1993, 208).

But, we might ask, is facilitated communication best characterized as a dance between two interlocutors, the (facilitated) speaking child and the facilitator as the dance partner of the child? How does the conversational partner with whom the child communicates—a third subject—figure into this model? In other words, is the dance constituted in the conversation with others that the facilitator merely mediates, or is it constituted in the construction of one person's expressive speech through the double unit of facilitator and child? To disaggregate this further, if we regard the facilitator as a dance partner, does she lead, or is she simply the mediator of the child's solo dance (speech)? And to take this another step, how do we account for the spectators of the dance—those who observe its orchestration and judge its form? Is the facilitator not also a spectator of the facilitated subject's speech? Finally, what is the dynamic of projection? If we wish to view the FC communication relationship as a dance, it is first necessary to understand that all communication occurs in dynamics of power in which are invoked multiple subjects and technologies, and multiple individuals who each may occupy different and shifting roles in the dance, whether we conceive the dance as the individual's speech or as conversation occurring between two or more subjects and involving spectatorship and dynamics of projection. A single individual's role may be that of mediator, listener-spectator, speaker, and observer—or may shift among all of the above. This is the case even when we imagine the most conventional paradigm of communication, the interpersonal dyad that posits conversation as occurring between two speakers. In short, the intersubjective model of two people proposed in dance, and discussed throughout this book thus far, is inadequate to the task of describing the complex situation in which "independent" voice is achieved. The unit of two is not adequate to the complexity of the coproduction of voice.

Despite arguments like Duchan's and Sabin and Donnellan's, the American Psychological Association delivered a major blow to the FC method in 1994 when it released a position paper citing studies demonstrating the prevalence of facilitator influence. This was, coincidentally, the same year that the American Psychiatric Association had provided a refined definition of autism—a move in the parallel controversy over which professional body (psychiatrists, psychologists, or educators) would control the definition and management of autism, that burgeoning enigmatic classification. Citing studies conducted in the early 1990s, the American Psychological Association's position paper described FC as "a controversial and unproved communicative procedure with no scientifically demonstrated support for its efficacy" (American Psychological Association 1994). What made the association's position paper a watershed was its status as a field-wide condemnation of the method, and its characterization of it in terms of human rights. Against the Association for Persons with Severe Handicaps, which was supporting access to FC as a human right, the American Psychological Association condemned the method outright. Recall that in the McDonald case twenty years earlier, facilitated communication had been championed as a technique through which McDonald achieved recognition of her autonomous agency and individual human rights. The Psychological Association's regard of the method turned this claim about liberation on its head. FC, the association charged, involved activities that "contribute immediate threats to the individual and human rights of the person with autism or severe mental retardation" (American Psychological Association 1994). Thus, in its passage from Australia to the United States and from cerebral palsy to autism, the technique went from tool of free speech and liberation to emblem of child exploitation and human rights abuse among the disabled.

Context, a factor noted earlier, was no small factor in this reversal of interpretations. Lessons from the ongoing memory wars were not lost on the American Psychological Association in their reception of FC. Professional skepticism against FC was fueled also by the intellectual backlash in the early 1990s against scholarship in the humanities and social sciences using qualitative methods variously identified as cultural, relativist, deconstructionist, and postmodern to analyze knowledge production in the sciences. These debates were fueled by the publication in 1994 of *Higher Superstition*, a scathing critique of left and feminist scholarship in academic science studies. Paul Gross and Norman Levitt's book earned laudatory mainstream op-ed and press reviews of the book, and journalists spun critiques based on its assertions. In debates that would later be dubbed the science wars, some scientists and others who wished to defend empiricism and related cornerstones of modern scientific truth methods criticized those humanities and social science scholars who questioned scientific empiricism and the ability to make firm truth claims, advocating various methods grouped by Gross and Levitt under the rubric of postmodern relativism. This "war" extended beyond the academy and did not follow clear-cut political lines.

This climate of backlash against postempirical thought was simultaneous with debates about autism: what constitutes it and how its variants should be classified, an issue touched on briefly above. Regarding the autism question: In 1994 the American Psychiatric Association adopted a system of distinct subtypes in its *Diagnostic and Statistical Manual of Mental Disorders* (DSM-IV, American Psychiatric Association 1994). The World Health Organization followed suit in the tenth edition of its *International Classification of Diseases* (ICD-10, World Health Organization 1995). Asperger's syndrome was listed by both sources as a subtype of pervasive developmental disorders (PDD). In this, it joined the list of spectrum disorders alongside autistic disorder, atypical autism, Rett disorder, and childhood disintegrative disorder. Amidst debates about the nature and classification of autism, which included controversy over ideas about theory of mind among persons with autism (now contested) as well as debates about the potential for normative affective expression in cases of nonverbal autism, the celebrated neurologist Oliver Sacks published *Awakenings* (1987), a popular account in which he uses the term "accommodation" to describe human supports developed with his postencephalitic Parkinsonian patients to help them overcome movement problems as they temporarily came "back to life" through a new drug therapy. FC entered the limelight in the midst of these controversies as well as the climate of delight in neurological miracles that was wrought by Sacks's book and the spin-off film (directed by Penny Marshall in 1990). These texts celebrated the belated and temporary "awakenings" of the human mind locked in elderly residents of an institution who suffered from Parkinson's-induced catatonia. Claims about FC's paradigm shift in autism research were dismissed by critics who, invoking Thomas Kuhn, argued that "FC must be measured against the same standards for treatment effectiveness, prediction and control that have allowed researchers and clinicians to work and communicate within the conventional scientific paradigm" (Jacobson, Mulick, and Schwartz 1995). Ultimately held up as an example of modern-day pseudoscience in psychology textbooks, FC was seen as having an emotional appeal that compared to that of the Ouija board phenomenon and water-witching (Bligh and Kupperman 1993, 554; Dillon 1993; Siegel

1995, 325; Twachtman-Cullen 1997, 140–146). Fueled by *Higher Superstition*, Jacobson, Mulick, and Schwartz used the widely read *American Psychologist* to lambast FC proponents for being in the "postmodern camp" that sees language as a relational activity with indefinite referents (Jacobson, Mulick, and Schwartz 1995). They tied postmodern linguistic relativism to the independent living movement and the shift toward deinstitutionalization, which they saw as deplorable elements of the 1980s. Twachtman-Cullen, too, describes the sentiments of the facilitators she interviewed as being in favor of a politics of deinstitutionalization and human rights, suggesting that these sentiments were evidence of an overzealous desire to see the disabled speak (Twachtman-Cullen 1997). A method as shaky as FC could only have gained credence, Jacobson, Mulick, and Schwartz argued, only in the post-1970s political climate of deinstitutionalization. This trend, they argued disparagingly, spawned "deprofessionalization" in the management of developmentally disabled people. With changes in the structure of care for developmentally disabled peoples, new, interdisciplinary, and less carefully trained and regulated paraprofessionals were given responsibility for the management of people who had been shifted from institutions to community-based and integrated habilitation programs. FC, these authors propose, could only have emerged in a professionally uncontrolled context such as this. FC's professional proponents are described by these authors as "complacent," and its parent and paraprofessional advocates and users "receptive and vulnerable" to fad treatments due to the "hopelessness and despair" they were prone to feel in response to the overwhelming task of managing their child's developmental disability without adequate institutional guidance (Jacobson, Mulick, and Schwartz 1995).

Let us put aside this critique's troubling nostalgia for the "quality" professional control over the disabled afforded by institutional warehousing before the 1980s and lost through the shift toward independent living among the developmentally disabled. And let us also put aside this article's patronizing characterization of parents as dupes, desperate for solutions and therefore vulnerable to quacks. I turn instead to the question posed by Sabin and Donnellan in 1993. This is not the question of *whether* the facilitator influences a given communication, for FC advocates had conceded this point all along. Rather, we must ask with Sabin and Donnellan, *how*, psychologically speaking, does this occur? The prospect of disentangling facilitator desires from the facilitated subject's willful act is not pleasant, because it entails asking questions about adult desires and the will to manipulate that arise in almost any pedagogical situation involving a relationship of emotional influence and hope for success (and which do not?). These questions about influence and subsequent projections of blame were the downfall of psychoanalysis in its worst developmental moment—its blame-the-mother phase. Behind this is the broader question of power as it is enacted through relationships among subjects, an issue that also goes under the rubric of the self, the very core term of humanist social science that the *American Psychologist* essay faulted postmodernism scholarship for eroding.

In the previous chapter, I noted that this charge of ventriloquism repeatedly surfaced against the Anne Sullivan-Helen Keller dyad in the last century, as when skeptics asked how a blind woman could possibly express herself in metaphors of sight such as color (Ozick 2003). The Deaf girl-child's body, in the films I examined, channeled the desires and fantasies of the mother and teacher, who gained personal gratification and professional recognition from bringing the speechless child to voice. In that discussion, I criticized a feminist position that afforded privilege to speech as a signifier of agency. Here I wish to resolve my own uneasiness about that implied moral critique of voice facilitation and the women who offer this service. This implied position hangs over this book from previous chapters as well, where my tone shades at moments toward critique of the roles played by caregivers like Daphne Gray (the maternal force behind Miss America Heather Whitestone's acquisition of voice), the fictional Christine Garland, and the filmic Anne Sullivan. By examining more closely the public contempt of the facilitator in the FC controversy, I will try to shift away from the moralizing direction of criticisms of the caregiver. I begin by repeating my disengagement from a notion of power as something that might be held by a single individual or class of persons (caregivers) over another person or group (children). And I emphasize again the complexly distributed, intersubjective articulation of the dynamic of power in the FC relationship. To read power as *necessarily* distributed across subjects, and to read speech as *always* the product of intersubjective power dynamics, is to allow that it is inevitable for caregivers to influence their subjects in the choice of what they speak and even, at times, to speak their own minds and fantasies through the children they bring to voice. Ethically troubled as this claim may be, my argument is that speech is always performed intersubjectively, at the behest of another and in the imagined space of the other's multisensory gaze. The facilitator performs a fact that sits uncomfortably with those who uphold the dictum of the right of the individual to free speech in an era that demands boundary collapse at the most subjective of expressive levels, and not just at the borders of nations geographically and economically defined. A person who comes to voice needs a screen, and that screen needs to be an empathetic human body that looks and feels—or, a body that listens and hears, to recall the recorder metaphor offered by Heinz Kohut in his work with blind children (Kohut 1971, 116 and 118). The facilitator is like the magnetic tape of Kohut's maternal recorder, a medium that is not without its own artifactual elements. Just as recording tape stretches, producing the "wow" effect noted earlier, and is scratched, producing a persistent hiss that haunts the voice, so the facilitator becomes the troublesome artifact whose unconscious noise, and whose role as moral witness, cannot be erased in the process of bringing the nonverbal autistic child to voice.

Authorship and shame in the FC controversy

Shame and blame were the dominant themes of the U.S. facilitation debates of the 1990s. By trading between them the roles of victim and perpetrator, liberator and oppressor, advocates of FC and their critics tacitly avoided the difficult question of how to theorize communication as an intersubjective process entailing relationships of power and influence.[19] From the *Harvard Educational Review* exchange forward, both sides of the debate held up the child as the entity it sought to protect and liberate from the other's appropriating claims. Advocates of FC regarded the child as an entity to be liberated through speech. This liberation was not only from silence and/as lack of agency. It was also from the oppressive beliefs of a body of special education and psychology research that cast certain autistic children as indisputably unable to communicate with the degree of expressive complexity FC demonstrated was possible in some children. This was a battle about free speech and the liberation of those with developmental disability from the binds of low expectations and mistaken assessments. However, because the FC paradigm emphasizes progression to autonomous speech, the caregiver role must always be understood, in this model, to remain as secondary as possible, and to fade out of view entirely in cases where the child is able to progress to independent writing. Independence of the facilitated speaker is the ultimate goal.

Critics of FC also saw the child as an entity in need of protection. But what they protected the child against was the fate of acting as witless puppet to those who believed they had the power to bring intellectual ability and voice to the intractably speechless child. Imputing agency to the child, according to some critics, was misguided if not delusional and constituted nothing less than a violation of the child's human rights. Thus to condemn FC was to protect the rights of cognitively disabled and nonverbal peoples from well-meaning quacks who imagined themselves to be wonder healers. The reality of facilitator authoring of some abuse allegations heightened the dynamic of shame and blame in which facilitators ultimately could not satisfy either model of personhood offered, because both demanded that they deliver the child as an autonomous being. This, I propose, was an impossible goal.

We may allow that facilitators had indeed in some cases either willfully or unconsciously imposed their will and their fantasies upon their charges. The identification of autonomous voice and authorship in highly mediated contexts is a complex one even when those involved in the authoring do not have communication impairment, and even when the mediating device is a machine. In "What Is an Electronic Author?" Richard Grusin brings Michel Foucault's and Roland Barthes's questions about authorship and agency into the context of digital textual production (Grusin 1994, Barthes 1977, Foucault 1977). Foucault's and Barthes's essays question the historical focus on the individual as the agent whose subjectivity is articulated in his or her textual productions. Grusin takes this question into the realm of the digital by stressing the multiplicity of voices and subject positions afforded in the formal structure of texts in which technologies and human subjects jointly produce meaning. Embracing the familiar notion of machine agency forwarded by Bruno Latour (1999) and Donna Haraway (1999), Grusin brings the idea of the author into the discourse of the production of networked subjectivity.

In the case of FC, the question of authorship is key because the goal of facilitated communication, advocates and critics agree, is to foster independent voice. But, as Grusin points out, the very nature of networked communication suggests that autonomous authorship is, and has always been, an unrealizable ideal. Duchan's insistence on a collaborative model aside (Duchan 1993), both critics and some advocates of FC share a strong resistance to the idea that voice is always mediated and intersubjective, upholding the goal of independence. Both groups justify their claims about the autonomous speaking subject, in different ways, through a model of liberal democracy that insists upon the right of each individual to autonomous speech. Whereas in the critical view of FC the individual who is "spoken for" by an other (the facilitator) is the hapless victim of a misguided maternal impulse, the advocate's view situates the facilitator in the role of medium of the individual's free speech (Biklen 1992a) without adequately examining the kind of power relations and intermixed subject positions that arise under this relationship, as Sabin and Donnellan (1993) begin to suggest. Ideally, in the FC trajectory, dependency is a stop along the way to the kind of independence demonstrated in the cases of Anne McDonald, Lucy Harrison, and Artie Schawlow.

But for many who use FC, communication dependency upon a mediating other remains a constant reality of everyday life, and the trust relationship with a particular facilitator may become a bond of influence and feeling from which it is hard to disaggregate independent voices, as we saw in the case of Keller and Sullivan. One shortcoming of the FC advocacy discourse, then, is its failure to provide the clear analysis, called for by Sabin and Donnellan and suggested by Duchan, of the relationship of authorship relative to personhood that constitutes sustained close relationships of facilitation. Developmental, cognitive, and physical limitations to communication are real factors that may not in all cases go away even with the best and most compassionate implementation of the FC method. As proponents insist, the method does not work with all children with whom it is tried. Reading is a key prerequisite that some cannot achieve, and other limitations exist as well. To suggest that independence is the goal is to set up a developmental divide that excludes those who cannot achieve written speech from viability as subjects—as *interdependent* subjects—even within FC discourse.

The intersubjective, interdependent relationship that FC entails is a key source of skepticism about the method's validity as a communication technique, but this interdependency is typical in all teaching and learning relationships. Facilitation may be initiated with children from preschool to teen age, years during which one would not typically expect to see a child publicly engaged in direct and sustained physical contact with a caregiver or teacher during communication with another party. The various developmental theories of Mahler, Bowlby, Freud, Lacan, and others regarding ego formation all share the general idea that a progressive process of separation initiated in infancy and continuing through the early preschool years results in an individuated subject whom we would not expect to require extended physical contact in later years. A relatively stable concept of self in an individuated body is required for normal functioning. Like the "holding" therapy for attachment-disordered, postinstitutionalized children (discussed in

Cartwright forthcoming), FC involves the school-age child in a relationship of physical and emotional dependency that one would expect the mother to engage in at home, during the early years. This gives the facilitator a socially prohibited degree of physical contact with the child she tutors.

With increased concerns about abuse allegations in childcare and any other context where subjects of care are regarded as vulnerable, touch became an increasingly fraught matter during the 1980s and 1990s. In settings in which hands-on care is given, the difference between a firm touch and a disciplinary hand is crucial. In FC, the difference between a supportive, guiding touch and a suggestive, leading touch is similarly crucial. Does the facilitator guide the child's fingers in a given interaction, or would that "guidance" more accurately be described as a push of the child's hand toward particular letter choices (Kezuka 1997)? Is physical contact with the body simply supportive, is it suggestive, or is it overtly leading? Is the body held or propped? In the case of Jan facilitated by Crossley, described at the beginning of this chapter, touch is mediated by a rod that is held by both the facilitator and the child. Answers to these questions about the nature of touch are difficult to discern with certainty through observation and testing. This is not because we need better observational means, assessment tools, or measurement scales to tell the difference between qualities of touch as they correspond to degrees of influence, but because the relationships between touch and meaning, touch and interpretation, and touch and emotion are extremely variable within and across situations. To return to the idea of suggestibility noted above in my discussion of child witnesses and the memory wars: can we speak of variations in suggestibility to touch? To support or prop, whether directly or through a mediating instrument (the rod), is, inevitably, to give direction, to one degree or another. Assessments of the method have, for these reasons, emphasized verifiability of information source, not the apparent behavioral or physical aspects of support.

Yet the fact remains that little work has been done to understand the nature of the kind of emotional and cognitive transmission that occurs in the relationship of touch that occurs between facilitator and child, whether or not the text produced can be verifiably traced back to the child. To get to the core of this problematic of the touch relationship, I look back to the use of touch as a communicative practice in Freud's early work on affect. There we find a clear connection between facilitative work with the hands and the articulation of abuse memories and fantasies.

Freud: Touch, memory, and fantasy

Touch has a long association with hysteria. Freud, in his early work on hysteria, elicited bodily signs in the patients he touched. He believed, at this early point in his work, that the bodily symptoms he described as hysterical were the product of repressed memories of childhood traumatic experiences. Working with his hands on the patient's body, Freud tried to facilitate the irruption of memories from his patients' bodies. By touching his patients, he hoped to elicit their expression of words and physical actions. "At times when relevant thoughts were not forthcoming" from the analysand, writes Allen Esterson, Freud

> placed his hand on the patient's forehead and encouraged him or her to report any images or ideas that came to mind. In the event that nothing occurred to the patient, Freud took this as a sign of resistance and repeated the pressure on the forehead while insisting that a picture or an idea would emerge. In this manner he endeavored to set in motion a chain of associations that he believed would lead eventually to the pathogenic idea (*S.E.*: II, 270–2). The ideas and images obtained from the patient by this procedure generally emerged in a piecemeal fashion, with the essential elements missing (281–2). The task of the physician was "to put these [fragments] together once more into the organization which he presumes to have existed"; i.e., to piece together the fragments to produce a coherent event or narrative, rather like the process of solving a picture puzzle (291). (Esterson 1998)

Freud's physical contact with his patients coincides with his early focus on affect.[20] Importantly, Freud's early work on affect entailed hands-on work with patients, an aspect of his technique that would be dropped, along with the focus on affect, as he sought a more scientific profile for psychoanalysis. Affect, hands-on work with patients, and belief in abuse memories as true accounts are present, hand in hand, in Freud's "Heredity and the Aetiology of the Neuroses" and "Further Remarks on the Neuro-Psychoses of Defence." In the first, Esterson notes,

> Freud claimed that for all his thirteen cases diagnosed as hysteria he had uncovered repressed memories of sexual traumas in early childhood. The assailants were nursemaids, governesses, domestic servants, teachers, and brothers slightly older than the victim (*S.E*: III, 152, 164).

In his six cases of obsessional neurosis, the patients had engaged in an *active* pleasurable sexual experience around the age of eight or ten, and all of them had also been subjected to sexual molestation in infancy (155, 168–69). The third seduction theory paper ("The Aetiology of Hysteria") contained a more detailed presentation of Freud's thesis. The number of cases of hysteria had increased to eighteen (six men and twelve women), and the culprits now included adult strangers and close relatives in addition to the categories listed in the previous papers (*S.E.*: III, 207–8). (Esterson 1998)

As is well known, Freud later contested what came to be called his seduction theory, attributing these patients' memories to fantasy—a point I will consider shortly.

Freud's classic early seduction theory and his later abandonment of it, like facilitated communication, have been subject to passionate debate. Jeffrey Masson's *Assault on Truth: Freud's Suppression of the Seduction Theory* (Masson 1984a) has been at the heart of that controversy since the book's publication in 1984 (see also Eissler 2001). In a contempt-ridden review that casts doubt on Masson's authority, British psychoanalyst Charles Rycroft takes Masson to task for assaulting Freud in making the claim that the founding father had retreated from the truth in his claim that memories of childhood sexual abuse were in fact fantasies (Rycroft 1984). Masson replies to Rycroft that what he had in fact argued in his book is that Freud believed that some seductions had occurred even as he posited that most seduction memories were fantasy constructions. "Between 1897 and 1903," Masson writes in a passage that opens the conclusion of his book, "Freud came to believe that the case of his early patient Emma Eckstein was typical: most (though not all) of his women patients had deceived themselves and him" (Masson 1984a, quoted in Masson 1984b).[21] The point he emphasizes throughout his book is not that Freud assailed the truth by denying the fact of seduction, but that Freud, despite his recognition of some accounts as accurate descriptions of childhood experience, "declined to give theoretical significance to sexual abuse and no longer discussed its importance in the genesis of neurosis in any of his later works" (Masson 1984b). Masson provides evidence that shows Freud oscillated much more than previously believed regarding his belief in the accuracy of some allegations of paternal seduction. The assault documented in Masson's book, then, is an assault on the ideal of truth as an absolute term.

This misunderstanding resonates remarkably with the critique of FC proponents as postmodern relativists who fail to acknowledge the importance of absolute truths and proof when they acknowledge that facilitator influence is present. What was suppressed by Freud and rose up to complicate his position on seduction was the problem of how to account for "some cases" that were clearly factual as against the majority of cases that he believed to be the products of fantasy. Since Freud was not a man of quantitative science, surely even these exceptional cases would have resonated in his thinking, even if their implications were not explicitly incorporated (and were suppressed as evidence) in his theoretical formulations about seduction as fantasy. Masson reports that he himself is "inclined to accept the view of many recent authors, Florence Rush, Alice Miller, Judith Herman and Louise Armstrong, among others, that the incidence of sexual violence in the early lives of children is much higher than generally acknowledged (Judith Herman believes it to be as high as one in every three women in the general population . . .)" (Masson 1984a, 189). His book does not fault Freud for disregarding numbers, but rather for disregarding the theoretical and practical implications of those cases that were not in the majority.

I quote from Masson's book and his reiteration of its points to emphasize that it is two different things to believe a story is true and to theorize a model of subjectivity that takes into account the real experience as it is articulated through memory years later. Freud's classic essay on abuse, "A Child Is Being Beaten" (Freud 1955a), read within its own terms, is a useful text whether or not Freud believed the child was truly "beaten" (seduced, abused), because this essay helps us to understand how experience can be expressed in the form of a screen memory that displaces agency and action onto other subjects and bodily regions. What matters most in using that essay, I emphasize, is not the potential facticity of the account, but the fact that memory of experience demands a story (requires the creative use of fantasy) no more or less than "pure" fantasy. Recall Mulvey's famous quip that "sadism demands a story" (Mulvey 1975, 14). This is not to diminish the importance of discerning fact from fantasy in addressing accounts of abuse, but rather to recognize the complexity and the demand for story that drives any retrospective account, whether it is based in experience or fantasy alone, and whether or not it entails explicit elements of sadism. (Indeed, we might reverse Mulvey's dictum to argue that narrative demands the structure of sadism even in its most banal forms.) I propose to use Freud's "A Child Is Being Beaten" as a medium through which to consider the FC relationships

in which sexual narratives are offered as public and intersubjective performances of the beating fantasy. In light of what I have just argued, I use this
essay not to make a judgment about authorship and truth in the FC abuse
narratives, but to underscore the intersubjective nature of the production
of these testimonies, and to emphasize the importance of interpreting what
these stories do tell us about the facilitator and child relationship, rather
than to look to them only as evidence.

In "A Child Is Being Beaten," Freud describes findings based on his analysis with adult women, a group later revealed to include his own daughter
Anna. In effect, then, he begins with three subjects (or, a fragmented subject): the adult woman who speaks her memories of childhood, the child
remembered by the woman, and the spectator: Freud. The woman's screen
memory begins with the conscious content of herself as a girl herself being
beaten, a fantasy that Freud characterized as expressing repressed incestuous genital wishes toward the father. What previously in Freud's thought
had been a terrible memory was now understood to be a wish. Guilt drives
the fantasy into a state of repression, and the woman regresses libidinally to
the anal phase. Her desire for sex with the father, in Freud's reading, is thus
expressed in the fantasy of being (or, having been) beaten by him.

Fantasies of being physically beaten, in Freud's account, typically origi-
nate in the preschool years, are repressed and, in "a construction of analysis," reemerge as screen memory later, in the form of adult fantasies that
figure the father as the one who administers the beating. Later Freud would
see this fantasy as belonging to the pre-Oedipal stage and as an expression of
the bond between mothers and children of both sexes. The second stage of
the fantasy, in which the child is being beaten by her father, is so deeply unconscious that it can never be remembered: "This second phase is the most
important and the most momentous of all. But we may say that in a certain
sense it has never had a real existence. *It is never remembered*, it has never
succeeded in becoming conscious. *It is a construction of analysis*, but it is no
less a necessity on that account" (Freud 1955a, 179–180, my emphasis).

The second phase, though regarded by Freud as most important of all, is
deemed to have no basis in the real. In a third phase of the classic beating
fantasy, subject positions are crucially altered: a third term is introduced to
the fantasy in the form of another child. In this phase, the woman relates, in
present tense, "My father is beating the child, [but] he loves only me" (Freud
1955a, 190). It is this phase that may help us to understand the psychical
displacement of the "beating" (sexual act) from the woman as the child

who remembers/fantasizes onto the third party, the other (facilitated) child; and the temporal condensation and complex identification circuit that takes place in this phase of the fantasy.

But first, to play the devil's advocate and use this story to create a possible explanation for circumstances in which facilitators unconsciously script such narratives for the children whose writing they support. For the facilitator whose unconscious is fraught with repressed memories of abuse, perhaps the professional role of mediator may open up an opportunity for her to unconsciously seize the facilitated child as this third term, as the other child who receives the "beating" the facilitator herself desires (in Freud's version) or has experienced but repressed. By writing through the body of the speechless child, the facilitator may thus bring forth unconscious fantasies or memories of abuse, using the child as the displaced site of her father's outburst even as the father may still approve (he beats the other, but "he loves only me"). In other words, the facilitator may perform an act of projective identification. As noted earlier, projection entails the expulsion (projection) of whatever within itself becomes a source of unpleasure to the subject. This dynamic is expressed in the language of the oral instinct (Laplanche and Pontalis 1973, 349–353). One reading of the facilitator who unconsciously guides the hand of her subject to write accounts of her own abuse, or her own fantasies, is that she has thrust her own bad objects (whether memories or fantasies) out into the child. It is helpful to recall the interconstitutive and transformative potential of projection here. Recall Elizabeth Bott Spillius's observation that projection "often, although not always, affects the recipient" (Clarke 2001b, 10), and Simon Clarke's point that projective identification may involve "a forcing of such feelings into the recipient" (Clarke 2001b, 8). In the case of facilitation, we have an interesting reversal of the classic projection scenario. In the classic paradigm, projection is an infantile act performed upon the mother or her substitute as recipient. Here we are faced with the problematic of a projective relationship in which the one who performs the regressive act of projection is an adult, and the recipient impacted by the expression is a child, a figure who is also regarded as doubly vulnerable because of its communication impairment and any intellectual, cognitive, or emotional disability it is believed to have.

To suggest that this exploitation through the projective relationship might occur in a professional context of giving care would understandably engender indignity among facilitators who rightly uphold their humane professional intentions and their adult ability to maintain psychic boundaries between themselves and their vulnerable subjects. Facilitators who did not maintain such boundaries were, the argument goes, exceptional and sad cases who tainted the professional role. My interpretation does not rest, however, with this tongue-in-cheek portrait of the bad-seed facilitator as the projector and the child victim as unwilling bearer of one misled woman's fantasy. There are subject positions missing in this dual model of projective identification, positions across which we can also locate responsibility for desire and for the coproduction of fantasies that were wildly shared, in the expressive registers of horror, contempt, and anger, within professional contexts and publicly, through the media circus that surrounded these cases.

The beating fantasy described by Freud represents what Ruth Lax describes as "a genitally debased love for the father and, simultaneously, punishment for the incestuous wishes" (Lax 1992, 456). For Freud, this fantasy, which affords its subject sexual pleasure, is "the essence of masochism." Lax expresses her surprise that Freud describes this fantasy only in women when in fact "beating fantasies are most likely universally present in the life of every person" (Lax 1992, 455). Lax's point is not simply to say that boys also have masochistic fantasies, but to emphasize that sexualized beating fantasies, and masochism, though coded as feminine in Freud's account are within the realm of normal behavior for men and women alike. For our purposes I will describe the fantasy as being of a feminine order irrespective of the sex of the subject who experiences it.

Lax analyzes the role of the fantasy in the development of the female superego. She retells the classic fantasy through cases in which the mother (a figure who does not figure in Freud's essay) and not the father is the locus of power. In the "average expectable environment," Lax writes, "the girl's usual interactions with the father during the positive Oedipal phase . . . culminate in incestuous desires the girl *knows* are prohibited by the mother. It is thus the mother, *not* the father, who establishes the 'Oedipal law' for the girl and its moral foundation" (Lax 1992, 469).

In Freud's account, the father is equated with Oedipal law. For Lacan, submission to the rules of language, the law of the father, are required to enter into the symbolic order through which agency can be assumed. The symbolic father is a function of the linguistic structure, and hence entry into language is linked to the Oedipal phase (Lacan 1977a). In Lax's account, it is the mother who administers the law even if it is the father who administers the beating. Whereas Freud gave us a third term, the other child, Lax offers yet another subject position: the mother as imagined moral spectator. In the narrative, she is the figure of prohibition and judgment situated in the mind's eye of the adult (child) who fantasizes or recalls a beating (hers, or another child's) at the hands of the father. This phallic mother is a structural element in the entry into the symbolic order, language, and agency. Her figure demands adherence to the law of the father, and witnesses this adherence.

In narratives of facilitation it is often the mother who is represented as the figure who voices the imperative for the child to speak (write), as we saw in the case of Lucy. It is through parental, and often maternal, eyes and ears that we appreciate the child's success with sign or facilitated writing. She is the figure through whom speech is established as the foundation for progression into language and human agency. Her desires are projected and enacted through the facilitator, as in the case of the transposition of Kate Keller's responsibility and desire for her daughter's sociality onto Anne Sullivan, discussed in the previous chapter. I stress the intersubjective relationship between "mother," who in this case may be a parental figure of authority of either sex, and facilitator, also a feminized role that may be occupied by a person of either sex, who together engage in the public enactment of this desire. Recall the scene in *Mandy* where the child first vocalizes the labial phoneme "b-b-b." Mandy demands that Miss Stockton bring her to her mother, Christine, who waits in the hall. Another teacher, one who is awash in shame about her failure to make a difference, looks on while Mandy communicates her achievement to the mother. Shame is transformed, in a dynamic of empathetic identification that propels across these three figures, into pride. The mother feels, hears, and sees that the child can speak; she is moved from shame to pride. The teacher hears and sees that the method of Deaf oral language instruction can be successfully taught; she too is moved from shame to pride. And the child enters into the social space her mother has opened for her in her act of projective and empathetic identification, mirroring pride, as a kind of free radical that affixes as and where shame also sits, back into the child. In my previous discussion of that scene I emphasized the relationship between Mandy and Christine, but I also noted the presence of the teacher whose professional pride is newly restored by the performance she voyeuristically witnesses from the wings. The teacher-mother identificatory relationship is as crucial to the dynamic of this scene as the bond between mother and child. I highlight this triad, which takes the form of the "hall of mirrors" described by Tomkins—an intersubjective experience of shame (or pride) constituted across "three heads" (Tomkins

1963, 214; see also Benin and Cartwright 2006, 5–6). But instead of shame, we have pride constituted in a manner that is dramatically intersubjective.

Identification between mother and facilitator does not curtail the facilitator's ability to identify with the plight of the child at the same time, sometimes even against the protective feelings of the family, as we saw in the case of Anne Sullivan. Overweening identification with the child as against the parent(s) was the very factor facilitators were so maligned for letting leak into the facilitated-communication relationship and into the facilitated text in false allegations of abuse. It is the facilitator's projective identification with the child as imagined silent victim that makes possible this enactment of a ventriloquist-like unconscious desire to speak out and seek justice through the mediating figure of the child. Keeping in mind Lax's proposition about the maternal figure as the purveyor of the law, I propose that it is this structure that allows the law of the father to be levied from the voice of a maternal figure or figures (male or female), and which allows this disciplinary process to unfold through a series of identifications across mother, child, and facilitator. The father, in this model, is law—an organizing principle, and not necessarily an embodied singular figure. In the end, ironically, it is the facilitator herself who is identified within the terms of the law as the figure who has beaten (that is, who has violated the rights of) the child in cases where facilitator influence is shown to be likely. Yet standing behind the facilitator and looking on are always the mother and the father, or any other caring figures who wait in the wings for the child to speak, and who are so often represented as covictims, with the child, of the facilitator's projective excesses, her failed performance as medium.

My point here is not that mothers or parents should therefore also be blamed for the failure of facilitated communication, because their desires for the child to speak outstrip the medium's ability to perform in a neutral manner. Rather, my argument is that desire for the child to speak is constituted among subject positions beyond those of the facilitator and the parents. This desire is structurally constituted across a moral social apparatus that demands the autonomous production of voice in the child—demands the child's entry into the symbolic order as a condition of its recognizability as subject. This desire cannot be located in any one subject position, such as the mother or the idealist misguided facilitator, but is structurally constituted across all the figures who have the child's best interests at heart in trying to bring the child to individual voice and/as agency.

This problem of the location of desire gets us to the core of the problem in the concept of the subject constituted through touch that is so basic
to the writings of Levinas described earlier in this discussion of facilitated
communication. "The other person and I 'are like the elements of one sole
intercorporeity'" (Levinas 1993, 100). Sociality is born across both subjects
"in the signifying power of sentiment" enacted in touch. But in the end we
demand that the child stand alone, to experience its corporeity as unitary
and free of the mediating subject whose touch makes entry into sociality
possible. This brings us to the question of the desire of the child. In all of the
many writings on FC, pro and con, written throughout the 1990s, the question of what constitutes the desire of the *child*—not its desire *to speak*, but
simply its *desire*—was never, to my knowledge, broached. It is as if the child,
not having entered language, could not possibly be constituted relative to
desire. Even Freud avoided this question. In the Freud beating essay, which
is ostensibly focused on the child, concern rests not with the child's desire at
all, but with the adult's recollection or fantasy of its desires through screen
memory (fantasy) of itself as a child. The adult analysand's narratives are,
importantly, adult fantasies about a child-self in past tense. In the narratives
of facilitation, the desire of the child, when represented, is usually couched
in expression of desires on behalf of the child, desires the child is expected to
experience later, after entry into language. Desire to be independent is first
imagined for the child by adult caregivers, and projected onto the child.

Another important distinction must be noted. For Freud, what is prohibited is not the beating but the (adult) child's past (screen) memory, which
is narrativized as a current or future event: in these narratives, either the
child *is being* beaten, or the narrator speaks of *anticipating* a beating that
will then take place as the story unfolds. Temporality is both mutable and
condensed: this is a memory that "is happening" in the telling, or that is
about to happen, dramatically enacted before the analyst's eyes. Furthermore, neither Freud nor Lax addresses the fact that the roles of characters,
like temporality, are both mutable and condensed. In other words, not only
temporality but also positionality with respect to identification and projection in the scenario of the beating are less adequately disaggregated in both
accounts. Subject positions, like time frames, shift even within a single telling. These processes of identificatory and spectatorial mutability occur interconstitutively, *in multiple directions and across multiple stages of a single
subject's life*, among children and adults present in the fantasy, through

the individual's narrative point of view. This is especially confusing when these fantasies are reconstructed in a public sphere such as the FC legal cases played out in the eyes of a viewing public, for whom positionality—who did what, to whom, and when—makes the difference between fantasy and memory, guilt and innocence.

Here I will turn to an example of a public performance of the beating fantasy enacted in the media surrounding FC to make clear the implications of this point. Tito Rajarshi Mukhopadhyay (1999, 2000, 2003), a young adult who is autistic, recounts in publication his experiences of being beaten by his mother into making eye contact with her. This ability to look that is beaten into him, he explains, makes it possible for him to participate in lessons that result in his ability to produce written speech. The mother occupies the position of the law. She is the structuring term through which the child achieves entry into the symbolic and language. When Mukhopadhyay's grandmother made public accusations of child abuse, hoping to bring the law down on her daughter for abusing the child, Mukhopadhyay publicly denied that he was a victim. He countered his grandmother's charges by avowing devoted complicity with the mother who beat him into speech (or, more precisely, who beat him until he could achieve the directed eye gaze that made speech acquisition possible for him). Beating, in this narrative, is administered by the mother, the figure who in Lax's account upholds the prohibition against the child's pleasure in the act at the hands of the father. In the case of Mukhopadhyay, as in Freud's account, the parent who embodies the law also administers the beating. And through this process the child enters language and sociality, with pleasure, against the prohibition of the grandmother. What from the grandmother's perspective is a beating is, for the child, a gift of love. Mukhopadhyay's avowal of pleasure in the beating rationalizes the equation of beating with love and entry into language through the body of the mother or her substitute, as I proposed was the case in *Miracle Worker*. What Freud did not take into account is the possibility of a kind of love that is not genital, and that involves a maternal authority, figuring into the screen memory of the beating. It is not necessary to regard the relationship of facilitated communication in sexual terms in order to understand that it is structured around a dynamic of physical discipline and control that is charged with emotions such as love, fear, joy, shame, and pride.

We find an example of this in Sabin and Donnellan's observation of a facilitator, Maryann, who used her control over the child's communication to make him perform obediently. Maryann refused to facilitate an exchange between Dan and a classmate because she preferred that Dan complete an assignment before fraternizing. Sabin and Donnellan conclude that whereas Dan is dependent on the facilitator, "speaking persons are not dependent on someone else to decide when they will talk or the speed of their speech" (Sabin and Donnellan 1993, 206). But in a classroom, speaking students are always dependent on someone else, usually the teacher, to decide when they may talk. To perform otherwise is to invite discipline and punishment. Speed of speech is regulated by the teacher as well, as in circumstances where the student is asked to speak more slowly, more softly, more calmly or otherwise modify expressive volume and speed to levels deemed appropriate for the classroom. There is no setting where a speaker is not dependent on conventions and expectations that are regulated and controlled by other individuals, imagined or present. Sabin and Donnellan's suggestion that to speak without facilitation is to be in possession of a freedom the facilitated child does not have is based in an ideal model of the subject and voice that has no basis in experience. All pedagogical and caregiving relationships involve dynamics of power, discipline, and authority over aspects of speech and listening. No child and, we might add, no adult ever speaks freely, without the influence of others, even if that influence is imagined in the form of a set of conventions for speaking internalized within the subject. What distinguishes facilitated and nonfacilitated speech is not simply the degree of control (or, degrees of dependency and freedom), but the sort of emotional and physical disciplinary *practices* exercised in the coproduction of speech.

What Sabin and Donnellan miss is that *in those relationships something is produced besides speech.* With this in mind, it is essential to analyze this relationship in a manner that goes beyond the active-passive binary—beyond the idea that speech autonomy is something one has or does not have, or that one must have to a certain degree to be a free and independent agent. We must instead discern exactly how both parties perform, with an emphasis on the *how*, rather than reducing the interaction to a simple dynamic of what is produced (speech) and by whom. As well, we must shift our focus from the binaries of subject-object, active-passive, perpetrator-victim—or, to put this in the language of object relations, simple projector-recipient, in order to understand the complexity of positions and modalities at play.

Sabin and Donnellan's example of facilitator authority over the facilitated subject pales in comparison to the vivid accounts of facilitator-client power dynamics provided by Twachtman-Cullen in her book-length denunciation of the method (Twachtman-Cullen 1997). The author, a speech pathologist who directs a center for autism, went to great lengths to immerse herself, she explains, in FC culture. What she presents is a narrative of facilitator self-deception, client coercion and control, and the production of shame. The facilitator emerges as perpetrator and the client as victim in the majority of the spectator accounts that Twachtman-Cullen narrates. I note this study in order to emphasize the role of the observer as a third term, a third subject in the intersubjective relationships described. Twachtman-Cullen's observations are based on facilitation between three sets of facilitator-clients. Close attention is paid to the details of exchanges that occur between the members of the pairs. I turn to this account with the purpose of elaborating on this idea of the beating fantasy and the intersubjective relationship around desire, law, and agency that it invokes not because I see proof of these dynamics in the account provided, but because the narrative itself invests the relationship with these qualities. Twachtman-Cullen's account is a bit like a screen memory insofar as it reads as a variant of the beating narrative. A term I will introduce into this discussion once again is shame.

Twachtman-Cullen tests the hypothesis that facilitators may be predisposed to view their clients as especially vulnerable to sexual abuse, and this may be a factor in the projection of abuse narratives onto clients through facilitated writing. She directly asks the three facilitators she interviews about their views on this issue. All three facilitators claimed that people with developmental disabilities are candidates for sexual abuse more readily than their nondevelopmentally disabled peers. Though studies lend support to the facilitators' statements on this issue, Twachtman-Cullen uses this testimony to speculate about "what effect the expectation of victimization may have on the interpretation of facilitated messages" (Twatchman-Cullen 1997, 43). Her subsequent account of facilitator-client interactions, however, flips around the subject positions within the constellation of abuse. Her accounts of facilitated writing sessions are rife with descriptions that suggest a dynamic of control over the client by the facilitator. Thus the facilitator is tacitly cast in the exploitative role, even as these very same facilitators are documented as having made explicit their concerns about the potential of client exploitation. The point of these accounts seems to be that even as the facilitator imagines her clients to be potential victims, it is in fact the facilitator who victimizes the child through a flawed pedagogical approach.

One of Twachtman-Cullen's strongest and most noteworthy points, in her accounts of problematic facilitator-client interactions over the keyboard, is that the facilitator's goal of getting the client to type may overshadow her willingness to recognize forms of communication other than speech in which the client tries to engage the facilitator. Success is measured in the client's typed words. The client's communicative looks, utterances, and gestures are not recognized by the facilitator, according to Twachtman-Cullen. She observes a relationship in which writing is the locus of disciplinary practice. This was especially obvious in cases where looks and gestures were used to indicate the client's displeasure in typing. For example, in one interaction, Twachtman-Cullen writes, "C2 [Client 2] did not appear to be paying attention to his typing. Rather, he was mumbling to himself and smiling, again as though in his own private world" (103). The facilitator's attempts to engage him in typing, Twachtman-Cullen explains, involve her repeated corrections of his spelling choices: "No. You want one e." C2 looks away from the keyboard and toward someone who has entered the room and begins to engage in what Twachtman-Cullen calls "interfering behaviors." He clenches his jaw and repeatedly grabs at his shirt, then launches a series of "agitated vocalizations" that increased in intensity as the session progressed. As C2 jabs at keys, growling in sync with each jab, his facilitator increases her resistance to his arms. "I'm not sure where you're going," she observes as she pulls his hand back and rests her head on her own shoulder, miming exhaustion. Twachtman-Cullen observes that C2 rarely looks at the keyboard while typing. She does not, however, describe the possibility that C2 experiences visual disinhibition (an inability to inhibit automatic eye movement toward disturbances or movements in the visual field). She remarks that she is "disconcerted" by the mismatch between his demeanor (agitation, intensity, inattention to the keyboard) and the content of the questions he was apparently posing through the typewriter. She does not note the possibility that problems with inhibiting or initiating movement, or with muscle tone, might be factors in his behavior. When C2 made an explicit and clearly intelligible request of his facilitator ("Go back to work!"), she observes, his utterance is ignored until he types it out (Twachtman-Cullen 103–104). Her point is that C2 is not heard by his facilitator outside the context of his written speech.

Should we really consider this failure of the facilitator to recognize the gestures and vocalizations of C2 an expressive failure—a failure not on the part of C2, but on the part of the facilitator? Twachtman-Cullen suggests as much. But she too can be faulted for a deficit in affective interpretation. Twachtman-Cullen fails to recognize differences in ways of looking, and in the meaning of patterns of looking, among subjects with autism as a factor in decoding C2's eye gaze. She does not, for example, consider the wandering eye gaze of C2 within the context of peripheral or disinhibited vision. Nor does she take into account the view held by many in the FC community that writing is a more reliable indicator of the client's true intentions than his or her gestures and speech. Biklen relates that one of his students sometimes spoke out loud while writing on his computer with a facilitator's support, but his utterances often contradicted what he wrote on the computer. This student insisted, through facilitated writing, that his interlocutors disregard the words he uttered and instead attend to the written text. "Imn not a utistivc on thje typ," he wrote (Biklen et al. 1991). In this formulation, the "not autistic" subject expresses himself through the computer, while the "autistic" body is the body that performs without aids, and, by this student's report at least, without an accurate match of feeling or intention and expression. If we take this young man at his written word, he experiences himself as a split subject: the disciplined, typing subject is the normal self, the one who can achieve a social life; the autistic subject lies outside of the dynamic of social life and controlled communication. The latter subject's expressions are to be ignored. Taking this case at its word, we might say that this boy experiences a psychically split self. There is discordance, in his own mind, between two internal partners in the self that constitute him in a psychic dance between normal and autistic expressive selves.

What Twachtman-Cullen produces is a detailed document of a failed interaction between client and facilitator, a discordant dance, if we may borrow Duchan's phrase again. The dance she observes is a study in tension over control between two partners. "Discordance," "asynchrony," and "mismatch" are some of the words Twachtman-Cullen uses to describe the relationship. Her conclusions, based on her observations and her own facilitation with the C2, are that the client required active physical guidance to type; and that he probably felt inadequate and pressured to succeed, responses she regards as familiar ones in situations where clients fail to perform in facilitated communication (Twachtman-Cullen 1997, 108).

One can only wonder if C2, like Biklen's student quoted above, felt that he might be "not autistic" on the keyboard. If Twachtman-Cullen is correct in interpreting his behavior to mean that he felt frustration and perhaps even shame over his inability to type without guidance, it would probably be reasonable to examine the primacy placed on the written word among other possible sources of facilitated interaction as the source of this shame. Like

Mandy, who was pressured to use oral speech to achieve voice, C2 is pressured to use writing to achieve his autonomous voice. I offer a comparison between the entry hall scene in *Mandy* with Twachtman-Cullen's account of this scene. Like the teacher who stands in the wings looking on as Mandy interacts first with her teacher then with her mother, Twachtman-Cullen is explicitly positioned as the moral spectator who witnesses C2 coming to voice—or, in her interpretation, failing in this goal. In Twachtman-Cullen's account, the shame that crystallizes most clearly is not the boy's, but the facilitator's. It is the facilitator whose method and efforts fail, in her interpretation of the scene. But we must also note that the "failure" must also be experienced by C2, whose experience and performance are the measure of success or failure, and by Twachtman-Cullen herself, who is a participant as witness to this scene, visible to all involved. Her book shames the FC method. Unlike the scene in *Mandy*, which produces a constellation of pride, this scene demonstrates shared shame. C2 is cast as someone who fails to perform, and who is failed by his facilitator, who misses his gestural and verbal cues. Twachtman-Cullen, too, is disappointed. The facilitator avoids the oral and gestural expressions of her client, whose frustration, in Twachtman-Cullen's account, is so palpable. The facilitator tries to stay on task, frustrating her client. An awkward dance indeed, but a three-way dance and one that is not untypical of many interactions in which learning occurs. The tragedy, in this account, is not that the facilitator might be leading the client, guiding his fingers (whether or not this was so), but that the threat of shame in failure under Twachtman-Cullen's watchful gaze overshadowed this relationship to the point that both participants would continue in their lesson without acknowledging the need to recognize and incorporate other forms of expression, or simply the need to stop. In the end, the scenario Twachtman-Cullen describes is not just about speech facilitation, but also about teaching and learning. The child resists and the teacher perseveres in a disciplinary scene in which the lesson must and will go on, because its success is under review. Spectatorship places a moral demand on the scene. Twachtman-Cullen's criticism of the facilitator is reminiscent of Jimmie Keller's humane admonition to Sullivan: "You won't open her. Why not just let her be?"

The question of degree of influence aside, the jury is still out on the question of student pleasure and pedagogical persistence and force in all domains of teaching. The measure of success should not be, did the client speak independently? But, rather, what was produced in this interaction among client, facilitator, and observer? Was it shame (no speech), or pride (speech)? For as long as we stick to those two poles, however, the controversy about FC will rage on. Surely there must be something else of meaning and value to the child's being beyond the production of speech that occurs in this intersubjective relationship between individuals who use touch, eye gaze, gesture, and vocalization together. For this, I turn back to the question of touch and the affective bond.

Representation without affect? The facilitator, body image, and touch

I want to pursue the scenario in which the facilitator helps to make possible sociality, being in the world, for the child subject even in cases where she overtly influences the writing. In *Thinking in Pictures* (1996), Temple Grandin explains the phenomenon that she and some other people with autism experience in which they have difficulty thinking in concepts and language, but rely on and even excel at constructing what she describes as mental files of visual data. She uses the metaphor of video documentation. One aspect of this sort of video databank thinking, according to Grandin, is that images are filed away and can be retrieved as a whole, sometimes at will. The process of retrieving representations, however, isn't accompanied by the same sorts of affective responses (nostalgia, sadness, happiness) associated with visual memory in nonautistic subjects. The video databank model shared by some people with autism carries the connotation that the autistic mind is like a representational technology in the double sense that it privileges visual models, and it "mechanically" records and plays back these images. This is a stereotype that I wish to pursue, because it suggests a place where representation splits off from affect. But I do so cautiously, because it too readily encodes a process that is experienced as much more complex than analogies to the visual image and media technologies allows.

Donna Williams, an author and lecturer who has also written autobiographical and reflexive accounts of the representation and experience of autism, qualifies this stereotype of the autistic person's mind as affectless representation machine. She describes the many different channels and characteristics of emotion she and others designated autistic do in fact experience (Williams 1999). Yet the characterization of the autistic mind as a machine of the visible was dominant in the popular imagination at the time of Biklen's first publications on FC. Thus reports about the method further introduced the ideas that communications technologies like the computer could play a uniquely appropriate role as communication prosthetic for people with autism—and perhaps could even perform a role in the understanding and treatment of autism, because of the parallels between the machine and the autistic mind.

Sue Rubin, who first communicated through facilitation at the age of thirteen, introduces yet another model: not mental pictures, but writing as the mode of agency. She describes the process of computer writing as facilitation engendered her own emergent subjectivity: "It was only after I started typing, and my brain somehow started working, that I began to think. Before that I merely reacted to my immediate environment. I must have been absorbing a lot of information because awesome words were at my disposal, but I didn't know what I knew until I was able to type fully."

It would be easy to see this as testimony about the power of speech and/as writing, and about the powerful impetus of the prosthetic technology of the computer not as a mental image machine, but as a text prosthesis. But we can also shift our focus, as I have tried to do throughout this chapter, to the human facilitator who stands behind the expressive action of writing in these first instances of starting to type. The facilitator, I propose, remains behind in the mind of the independent speaker (writer) just as the parent remains in the mind of the speaking child, as screen memory. Furthermore, she remains behind, as both a body image and as a figure that is constituted not only visually but, more important, through a cognitive memory of the affective routing of touch.

Williams (1999) describes the trust function of the facilitator and the way physical and visual support intersects with emotional support in the FC relationship. Her example is an activity other than communication: a hypothetical process wherein the facilitator gives and then gradually withdraws support of the facilitated subject's performance as he or she learns a task—opening a kitchen cabinet—through facilitation, as a step toward making a meal alone. In the first phase Williams describes, the facilitator takes the person's hand and guides it to the cupboard. The first component thus involves touch. Next, the facilitator just stands nearby while the person independently opens the cabinet and withdraws items. In this case, the facilitator can be seen and heard but does not touch the learner. Finally, the facilitator stays in an adjacent room while the learner goes about the task of fixing a meal, well aware of the nearness of the facilitator and therefore emotionally able to perform. In this third phase, the facilitator is present as an emotional support, incorporated as presence in the subject's mental schema, though not literally felt, seen, or heard while the activity is performed.

The term "body image" suggests the mental picture concept that Grandin describes as part of the autistic memory. But body images consist not only of mental imagery but also of memory of touch, as Elizabeth Grosz (1994), Laura U. Marks (2002) and Vivian Sobchack (2004) have so beautifully explained. Tomkins emphasizes this point: "The body image appears to be primarily constituted of a set of kinesthetic and vestibular messages" (Tomkins 1992, 255).[22] The body image Tomkins discusses is that of the subject's own body, and not the body of an other. It occurs in a discussion about why it is that there is the phenomenon of phantom limbs in people who lose appendages. The phantom is present, he proposes, not simply because there has been past experience—that it previously had been touched, seen, and given pain, for example. Rather, the phantom is present because there has been "voluminous, continuous stimulation from the inner receptors preceding and following purposive action" (Tomkins 1992, 257). The "touch" Tomkins describes, then, is not precisely a memory of feeling, but an inner imprint of a structure that knows and expects touch—that is structurally in waiting for it.

I wish to propose an analogy from this: perhaps the "missing" facilitator is experienced as a presence for the subject not because the memory of her touch and appearance remains as content, but because this structure of stimulation experienced with and through her remains in the form of a structure for waiting in anticipation of the other. The facilitator thus exists as phantom, much like a limb that was experienced and leaves residual memory of stimulation from inner receptors. When Tomkins describes this structure of inner reception as a "memory image," the term "image" refers not simply to "mental picture," as Grandin's analogy suggests, but to the structure in place that allows for the affective experience. This is more like the broader meaning of "gaze" that incorporates a field of experience including touch, hearing, and sight. There is a pathway that both remembers and anticipates stimulation, affective response at the impetus of another's touch. This gives us an understanding of touch heretofore lacking in what I have taken from the account of intersubjectivity described by Levinas (1993). It is not literally or primarily physical touch, then, on which intercorporeity is based, but touching in the sense of the kind of feeling that comes together across the senses and between subjects, leaving behind a structural memory, a pathway through which a subject may anticipate the touch of an other, real or imagined (to recall, one more time, the line André Green [1999b] used to describe affect).

Consider this hypothetical example of graduated presence and then withdrawal of the facilitator in two ways. First, this example clearly demonstrates that the facilitator plays a role beyond physical support had been, and in an activity that does not entail writing. Her presence as an imagined body image is as crucial to the success of the process as her actual physical support. Indeed, body image presence is the key factor as physical support is phased out altogether in later phases. Second and relatedly, the facilitator's physical presence is first as a tangible and visible force in the process, and then as memory image. Here we see enacted the transition from real to imagined in the affective coming together of subject and other. But "imagined" no longer holds the literal association of "image." "Imagined" connotes the ability to receive an other in the mental space of the self, through contact and memory of feeling.

Let us return to Sue Rubin's statement "it was only after I started typing . . . that I began to think." This is a remarkable claim because it suggests that Rubin experienced herself as a fully social, thinking subject—cognizant of herself as such—seemingly for the first time when typing. Although she does not note this, in beginning to type she was engaged with a facilitator. Although Rubin leaves out mention of the facilitator (her mother) in describing this process of beginning to think, it can be surmised that her experience of herself as an embodied, discrete, and self-willed being was at least initially contingent on the facilitator's physical presence and touch. In other words, Rubin came into being as a social subject through an apparatus that allowed her to perform as a self in relationship to others. Rubin's failure to mention her facilitator as an agent in her process of "beginning to think" underscores the fact that her facilitator, presumably positioned behind her and hence out of sight, would likely be most present not only through the sense of touch but through an incorporated body image, in Rubin's mental structure, where, as a discrete self, she anticipates engagement with others. The facilitator thus facilitates the very structure of the order of language, her organizing activities having left a structural change in the way the psyche processes the input and output of feeling rather than simply existing there in the psyche as remembered content of someone who has been there, touching.

What is imparted, then, is perhaps a blueprint for bodily delimitation and control. The prosthesis of the facilitator is a training ground for future anticipation of self-controlled action with an other. Williams (1999) describes her profound sense of lack of control over her own body as a fundamental aspect of her experience with autism. She noted lack of control over volition and self-directed expressive action, and problems with self-perception, with a sense of being in a unitary, discrete body. She describes fragmented perceptions of her own body and its environment. Communication comes into play relative to these aspects of autism both as problematic and as a potential source of management or tutoring in subjectivity. An experience Williams describes as "exposure anxiety" helps me to demonstrate what I mean by this: "Exposure anxiety is about feeling your own existence so excruciating that it causes you to have an instinctive aversion to conscious awareness of your own expression. . . . I would not initiate anything [communication] because I could not command myself" (Williams 1999).

Later, Williams links this lack of command over and recognition of self as embodied even more directly to speech communication. Exposure anxiety, she explains, "is a matter of expressive volume. [It is] a problem of enacting self-initiated, unprompted comprehensive movement, speech, action." This description echoes another she uses to describe communication: It is the act of "making yourself notice you have noticed." To put this in a manner more familiar to film and media studies readers, making yourself notice you have noticed is also to apprehend oneself in the act of seeing oneself—the very formula Metz introduced, and the formula so widely criticized for its inflated, self-aggrandizing notion of the spectator. This kind of reflexive apprehension must take place through some sort of intermediary or screen. The cinema, in apparatus theory, is the classic paradigm for the act of self-apprehension and subject formation as a process that implicates vision fundamentally. It is precisely this sort of self-apprehension that Williams and others have described as so elusive to some people with autism. Williams describes at length the strategies she and others use to gain control over their bodies in social settings where one is seen by others. Mimicry, a process involving visual recording and performance—two processes close to the cinematic heart, is a key technique for gaining self-regulation. Williams explains how she stores away in memory visual and auditory patterns of bodily action and speech observed in others, then replicates them later in what she hopes are the appropriate settings. In this way, a semblance of a normal life is carried out on the model of patterns previously observed and filed away for mimetic repetition. She explains mimesis as a need driven by a fundamental inability to perform as self not other: "Can't do it for, by, or as myself," she states. (Note the absence of an "I" thus far.) "*I*," she continues, "will do it *as you.*"

This strategy of performing as other, *as you* (and I deliberately refrain from using the phrase "by rote" to describe this process) entails empathy. What Williams describes, I propose, is a form of empathy training. However, Williams explains, this process of representational patterning on the model of the other sometimes misses the correct pathways of affect and action. An example is the case Williams describes of a child who gets the words right for the context, but uses the wrong affective tone and inflection for the context. Another example she offers: going to kiss someone, but biting the person instead.

"Exposure anxiety," Williams explains, is a term she uses to describe will and the mental contortions one has to go through to allow expressions to come out of one's body in the form one intended them to take—and in a form that is appropriate to the context. Pushing beyond levels of tolerance, she explains, results in involuntary aversions (saying the wrong thing, or the right thing but in the wrong voice) and involuntary retaliatory responses (which can be directed against oneself—head-banging—or against others, as in biting the person one reaches out to in order to kiss).

Affective mimicry and/as empathy: "I will do as you do"

Although not all people with autism engage in mimicry as Williams describes it, this practice deserves be taken into account in terms of the FC relationship of trust and safety—and, importantly, in terms of its affective dimensions, rather than the usual emphasis on the representational aspects of mimicry.

The emphasis on the representational in mimicry can be traced back to Lacan's 1949 version of the mirror stage discussion, in which he draws from the animal camouflage model described in Caillois 1984. In his description of "depersonalisation by assimilation to space" (Caillois 1984, 30), animal camouflage provides an analogy to the mimetic nature of identification, in which the subject's body image is constituted in a manner that draws from the photographic to appear in the visual field of the other. To appear and survive, one must also blend in. Yet to mimic is not to become alive as subject. For Caillois, mimicry entails "a sort of instinct of renunciation that orients it toward a mode of reduced existence, which in the end would no longer know either consciousness or feeling" (Caillois 1984, 32).

Although I will not develop this point further here, the account of Donna Williams described above suggests that to "blend in" is not simply a matter of representational likeness, but involves in addition the affective registers of performance that are not solely representational in nature. To appear with accuracy but with the "wrong" affect spoils the blend. Through affective distortion of mimetic representation, the subject's cover is blown. It goes to pieces in the optical space of the other. The kind of mimicry Williams describes, then, requires an affective dimension not as an add-on to the representational but as a conjoined part of the process of "making yourself notice you have noticed."

If we listen to Williams's account, we hear that mimicry is not a rote, mechanistic, camera-like operation of reproduction. Rather, it is a deeply empathetic operation, involving projection and introjection. We might ask then, does mimicry play a part in the autistic subject's incorporation of the facilitator's presence as he or she progresses to independent typing, communication, and social participation? Williams clearly explains that to mimic is not to perform as a fully social subject. It is to pose "as if" one were a normally functioning individual.

The performance of acts associated with normalcy through mimicry reported by Williams and others with autism that use this strategy is a far cry from the experience of subjective expression and self-recognition reported by those who successfully use FC. Does the FC relationship provide this sort of delimited behavioral training ground, with mimicry as a passageway to empathy, rather than as a form entailing empathy? Or, does facilitation allow an alternative to mimicry in which the facilitator deflects some of the heat of being caught in the multisensory gaze of the other? It may be that the facilitator relieves some of the social pressure of communication by mediating the relay of eye gaze, gesture, voices, and touch that add to that painful experience of "noticing oneself noticing." In this process, the facilitator deflects and triangulates the reflexive process, serving as protective *affective* cover (and not representational cover) for the subject she facilitates and mediating his or her place in the exchange of verbal, visual, and gestural aspects of gaze that comprise communication with others. In this way, what is facilitated is not simply the content of speech but the structure of the affective expression and affective experience itself, diverting its intensities.

I witnessed facilitated exchanges in which people with autism and other communications disabilities communicated with audiences at the 1997 conference of the Facilitated Communication Institute at Syracuse University and on other occasions in the late 1990s. I was struck by the range of modalities and relationships performed there. In addition to performing rote physical support and mediation, facilitators performed and interpreted the presentations and responses authored by panelists through typed words, gesture, eye gaze, and speech. In most cases, text was read aloud by facilitators even when audience members could see the type of the projection screen, with comments and elaboration. Facilitators frequently filled in background details, made interpretive remarks, or responded on their own to audience remarks, always interjected and mediated by the people they facilitated. It is this interactive and multimodal aspect of facilitation in action that I suspect Duchan was after in her analogy of the dance. Sometimes facilitator remarks were an interpretation of the facilitated person's facial expression or spoken (but presumed to be either inaudible or incomprehensible) remarks, and at other times facilitator comments seemed to come from a perceived need to maintain the affective flow of dialog, not adding much in the way of information. I saw most of these interjections by the facilitator not as evidence of their cooptation of the speaker's voice or stage, but as realistic evidence that what was being performed was the coformulation of expression by and between members of an integrated unit within which subject positions and authority shifted continually and fluidly. Rosemary Crossley's own writing and social presence leave no doubt that she was far from a receding personality in her interactions as a facilitator to Anne McDonald. This is not to say that McDonald therefore does not speak in a voice of her own, but that her speech when facilitated is always mediated and therefore intersubjective, a coperformance in which the position of authority continually shifted. The performative and interpretive dimensions of facilitation provide further insight into the function of the FC apparatus as a multimodal and multisubject relationship in which subjectivity is complexly interconstitutive.

The FC structure underlies relationships of caregiving among children who perform affective expression and communication in nontypical ways across the spectrums of categories of developmental, neurological, and cognitive disorders and disabilities. Facilitation of the child is, in more or less overt ways, the story behind all of the cases addressed in this book. I have looked back to the facilitated communication controversy of the 1990s to see what was missed in characterizing the turn to the digital and to networked interaction as a matter of information authorship and computer agency.

An era that network theorists have characterized as the information age (Castells 1996, 1997, 1998) might also be described as an age of affective disorder. Returning to information's root meaning, to inform is to give shape to the mind. Information has come to be associated with a divergent set of terms. On the one hand, information constrains and controls, and is fundamental to those basic objects of critical theory: knowledge and meaning. On the other hand, information is subject to all of the ambiguities and specificities of affect, representation, and perception, both intrapsychically and intersubjectively. One must engage in expressive performance to inform and to be informed. The lesson we learn from Donna Williams is that one's expressive performance must match representational expectations in order to be received in the sensory gaze of an other, and in order to overcome the anxiety of being constituted there in one's own body. To put this another way: just as affect and representation are fundamentally interconstitutive, so affect is interconstitutive with information. No feeling, no meaning. No affect, no representation.

Recall these lines from the stanza of a poem by Jan that I began this chapter with:

> Imagine writing a poem without being able to read it aloud.
> It's like playing a record in a soundproof room—
> It's going round, but no-one on the outside can hear.

I have tried to show throughout this chapter that the emphasis on speech, voice, and language has involved a neglect of the affective aspects involved in appearing in the field of the other's multisensory gaze. We might say that in this poem Jan anticipates a meeting between her body and another's body (Green 1999a, 312) through the reception of her speech represented in writing. Whether the object, the one who is "on the outside" hearing her poem is "imaginary or present" (Green 1999b, 289) depends largely on praxis. By this I mean *expressive* praxis and not the representational praxis of writing speech. The work of praxis always involves the receiving object, Jan's listener and facilitator, as projective, and not just receptive and incorporative subject. To listen involves a spectator's projection of desire to hear the other's voice. Desire to be constituted as medium in the sense of listener amplifies the subject who projects its voice outside the "soundproof room" of the communication-impaired body. What is projected is always a record, a copy played in anticipation of appearing in the gaze of the other. As Tomkins and Green both have so clearly shown us, without affect, representation, whether as voice or as image, fails to have the power to move or to touch the other. If there is an aspect of facilitation that was forgotten on both sides of the FC debate, as in film theory prior to the 2000s, it was affect, and, most important, the facilitator as partner in the amplification of feeling one's way into the world with the facilitated subject.

ON EMPATHY AND MORAL

SPECTATORSHIP

Heinz Kohut defines empathy as the capacity to think and feel oneself into the inner life of another (Kohut 1984). For Kohut, analysis does not cure by way of making the contents of the unconscious known to the subject. It cures through transmuting internalization, in which the analyst's empathy is internalized (Alford 1991, 27; Kohut 1984). Does this account of moral spectatorship advocate the sort of empathetic looking and listening introduced in the first chapter and described in the textual readings that followed? No. Does it therefore critique and condemn moral spectatorship? No. Moral spectatorship is a set of practices film theory can use to work on and through. But to work on a set of practices critically means neither to advocate for that sort of practice nor to denigrate its terms and its agents. If the tone, throughout this volume, seems ambivalent, and sometimes even sympathetic, toward its objects and actors, this is the effect of a wish that film theory might move beyond performing at either end of the critical spectrum of advocacy and derision with regard to viewing practices.

To put in order some of the ideas behind the readings of empathetic looking and listening described in the previous chapters, this conclusion offers a more extended discussion of the meaning of "moral" in *Moral Spectatorship*, and the concept of empathy that informs the model of empathetic identification introduced in this book.

Morality's links to spectatorship have a long history in moral philosophy. Anthony Ashley Cooper (the earl of Shaftesbury) linked moral perceptions to sensory perception in the body of the spectator: "The Mind, which is Spectator or Auditor of other Minds, cannot be without its Eye and Ear" (Shaftesbury 1699). Francis Hutcheson, writing about the idea of the greatest happiness for the greatest numbers, made distinctions among the roles of the observer, the agent of an observed action, and the person or persons upon whom the action is performed:

> In comparing the moral Qualitys of Actions, in order to regulate our Election among various Actions propos'd, or to find which of them has the greatest moral Excellency, we are led by our moral Sense of Virtue to judge thus; that in equal Degrees of Happiness, expected to proceed from the Action, the Virtue is in proportion to the Number of Persons to whom the Happiness shall extend; . . . so that, that Action is best, which procures the greatest Happiness for the greatest numbers; and that, worst, which, in like manner, occasions Misery. (Hutcheson 1725, sec. 3.8)

David Hume and, later, Adam Smith extended this triadic structure of the spectator, the agent, and the one who is acted upon, continuing to compose scenes of moral judgment through the paradigm of the senses, and particularly through sight. The concept of a moral "sensibility" is somewhat literal in its reference to the senses, for one could easily say that one must always rely on one's senses of sight or hearing to make moral judgments. But still, this does not account for the interjection of the "sensibilities" of others into one's judgments. The disaggregation of moral sensibility from the immediacy of internal sense experience, and an insistence that moral sensibility and moral judgment are always mediated by custodial and facilitative relationships with others who are real or imagined—relationships that go by the names of projection, interpretation, communication, care, and love—are perhaps the most important general ideas that *Moral Spectatorship* introduces to film theory.

In his *Theory of Moral Sentiments*, Adam Smith described the spectator as an individual who must lack involvement with the object of his look. "The unfortunate who suffers and the person who views him are," Luc Boltanski explains in his discussion of Smith's concept, "nothing to each other" (Boltanski 1999, 37). Smith, however, makes it clear that this distance is not only intersubjective, taking place between the spectator and the one who suffers. It occurs also between the spectator and "the inmate," the intrapsychical other(s) who is our imaginary interlocutor in the internal conversations that shape personal moral judgments. Smith wrote:

> We can never survey our own sentiments and motives, we can never form any judgment concerning them; unless we remove ourselves, as it were, from our own natural station, and endeavour to view them as at a certain distance from us. But we can do this in no other way than by endeavouring to view them with the eyes of other people, or as other people are likely to view them. Whatever judgment we can form concerning them, accordingly, must always bear some secret reference, either to what are, or to what, upon a certain condition, would be, or to what, we imagine, ought to be the judgment of others. (Smith 1966, 3:1)

Smith, in this passage, suggests the spectator must assume detachment from its own "natural station." In other words, the function of my self-regulating "inmate" is to detach me from my feelings in response to "the one who suffers" and to assess the propriety of my response with the imagined eyes of yet another who witnesses my response. This suggests a kind of intrapsychic split that, I argue, is closer to Lacan's notion of the split subject than one might at first think. Smith's idea is not that the subject will "see as the (internal) other sees," but that it will *judge* from the standpoint of an imagined other. I, in other words, assess my feelings and actions from the perspective of another who embodies the moral tenor of a social order, in order that I may modify my feelings and actions in relation to it.

Normalcy—*compulsory* normalcy—is a key component of this internal comportment in which I regulate my response to the other. The spectator may be inclined to regulate and express feelings within the range of what "one would expect" in response to a given scene. Tacit social norms are relevant on both sides of the equation. Normal behavior in the scene is linked to particular expressions (of pleasure, approval, interest). Spectators may feel that a normal response-expression is demanded of them, no matter what their internal response to the scene may be. If spectators deem their own internal feeling about a scene to be abnormal (as in the case where a spectator feels pleasure in witnessing suffering), shame may induce them to perform, against their own sense of pleasure, a more normative range of affects (concern, pity, grief). According to Silvan Tomkins (1963), the one who feels ashamed may imagine that others who witness his actions silently pass negative judgment upon him. As in Smith's model of the figure whom he refers to as the "inmate of the breast," judgment may thus be generated in response to an imagined projection or fantasy of an other's sentiments toward oneself. Here we may recognize shades of Christian Metz's self-reflexive spectator who sees itself seeing. That formulation of Metz's was rejected because it expressed an idealist vision of the subject as a contained and unified self. However, we might revisit it differently, in the light of Smith's theory of moral sentiments. In this way, we can see this reflexive process of "seeing oneself" as being organized around a fundamental split already performed within the subject. The subject's most basic moral sensibility is experienced through the internal and imagined eyes of others whose demands may outstrip and overrule the most "selfish" basic impulses and desires (as Levinas shows).

Feminist theories of spectatorship have given little attention to this morally incorporative aspect of the spectator's internally responsive and self-regulatory process, except to read them in the terms of a repressive apparatus that produces normative articulations of illicit desires that are repressed then expressed differently or indirectly, through symptomatic words and deeds. The concept of repression is not adequate, however, to understanding relationships characterized by responsibility, and the kinds of "selfless" pleasures involved in the practices of custodial care described in the texts discussed in this book. To condemn selfless care of others as simply maternalistic or masochistic, for example, has been a normalizing move in psychoanalytic feminism. The tendency to disparage practices of care as selfless altruism makes it difficult to find a means to describe in adequate detail the complexity of the psychic interrelationship, and the pleasures, of care that go beyond the maternal and the sentimental. The intensity and complexity of caring that characterize so many social relationships that are not primarily, or are not only, either sexual or maternal in nature deserve a more thorough analysis. It may be useful, in this regard, to introduce the concept of a desiring custodial gaze that is disaggregated from the concept of the maternal, and to read this gaze as one that is highly engaged in complex degrees and kinds of feelings besides the sexual.

In her classic work on the woman's film, Mary Ann Doane famously described the female gaze in terms of the kind of closeness and proximity that I have indicated underpin the adult-child relationships described throughout this book. I turn to a rereading of her text.

In this text, Doane makes it clear that female spectatorship and male spectatorship, like masculinity and femininity, do not refer to actual members of cinema audiences, but to psychic alignments within this binary division. She describes the problematic of an absence of a psychic position of feminine identification that coincides with female spectators (Doane 1986, 8). Women do not have the same access to the fiction of the film as men, and therefore to the terms for constructing a coherent female sexual identity in and through the text (Doane 1986, 11). Women are not outside desire, but are constituted differently than men in relationship to it. In classical accounts of spectatorship (Metz's in the *Imaginary Signifier*, for example) the relationship of voyeurism in the primary identification process entails seeing at a distance (Metz 1982, 60). As Rodowick notes, distance figures as an epistemological figure in these practices of looking (Rodowick 1991, 23), which are encoded as male.

The female look negates this gap that is so basic to voyeuristic looking, impacting female access to the classic relationship of desire constituted through distance between subject and object. This is echoed in André Green's (1999b) description of affect as a seeking of object, present or imaginary, by subject. The object, necessarily, stands at a distance. In the passing of the Oedipus complex is performed a separation from the body of the mother that makes possible the optic of distance that structures voyeuristic and other forms of looking. As Doane explains, this "distance from the origin (the maternal) is the prerequisite to desire; and insofar as desire is defined as the excess of demand over a need aligned with the maternal figure, the woman is left behind (Doane 1986, 12).

Doane reads the proximal relationship of female spectatorship as one characterized by primary narcissism. My intention throughout this book has been to try to offer a different view on relationships of proximity that are not constituted, at least not solely, through narcissism and the failure of maternal separation. I have tried to push the envelope of narcissism to the boundary limit where self is not so much radically loved as violently repudiated, or let go in the name of an other who requires selfless care. Projection and incorporation, I have argued in these pages, are key to this process. While these concepts find their articulation in British object relations theories of infancy and maternal care (Klein, Winnicott, Bálint, Fairburn), they find their expression in everyday humanism expressed and performed by male and female individuals and groups. What I have tried to show is that what is achieved is not the fundamental rent that achieves the requisite distance for desire (enacted in part through voyeuristic looking) but the production of being through intersubjectivity in the real and present world. The subject is thus neither mirrored nor mediated but produced in a split that requires the presence of the other for the speaking self to perform in the world. The trauma is entailed in forcing that intersubjectivity to be performed, not in tearing apart some preexisting closeness. For the cases discussed in this book, proximity was made to happen as a precondition of belated entry to language, via affect. Proximity was not there in the first place because of the sensory failure that made experience of the other (and therefore of moral sensibility) difficult. If there is a difficulty of difference (Rodowick 1991) in these relationships of subject production, it is a sensory difference hence a moral difference overcome by the selfless giving over of the other to an identity that is constituted intersubjectively, in dependence on an other.

Historically, moral spectatorship has been theorized in terms of an optics of distance. Thomas Brown, writing about Hume's moral theory, describes the relationship between agent and spectator as one that requires distance for the performance of calm contemplation: "In every moral action that can be estimated by us, these two sets of feelings may be taken into account; the feelings of the agent when he meditated and willed the action; and the feelings of the spectator, or of him who calmly contemplates the action at any distance of space or time" (Brown 1820, Lect. 77).

Calm contemplation of action at a distance of space and time suggests a kind of detachment on the part of the spectator that is utterly lacking in many of the relationships described throughout this book. As I have noted earlier, André Green describes analysis as a process that aims at control of the affects of suffering by detachment from the drives that are the cause of suffering (Green 1999a, 229). The analyst, therefore, is on some level compassionate toward the analysand, insofar as the analyst aims to remediate the analysand's suffering even as the analyst must practice with distanced reserve and aims to produce dispassionate detachment in himself and the analysand alike. Proximity entails suffering, distance provides cool relief but at the expense of movement toward satisfying the drives. The detached personality, Green explains, turns to tasks that differ from those to which it is better adapted: namely, the scrutiny of the environment excluding the self. Insecurity, loneliness, and a sense of abandonment are the price of becoming detached from the drives (Green 1999a, 229). Empathy, I suggest, provides a route for the self to reattach to the drives, without reducing the subject and the object to sameness.

Green's 1999 modification to his concept of affect, in which he asserts that the object sought may be imaginary or present (Green 1999b, 289), is crucial to keep in mind in interpreting this relationship of empathy—not because we need to recognize the hard difference between the two terms, "imaginary" and "present," but because fantasy and action are always interconstitutive.

Empathy and moral responsibility

Carolyn Dean, in her 2004 book on the broad perception of empathy's states of fragility and decline in postwar culture, notes that scholars have identified a gap between representation and responsibility, a gap that opened up after World War II. In this breach, some would say, consists a depletion of empathy (Dean 2004, 6–7). Whereas George Steiner, she explains, would call for "a renewal of human feeling," Slavoj Žižek and Giorgio Agamben would argue that those qualities of feeling belong to a moral framework that defines suffering and persecution in tragic terms, relying on themes of heroism and redemption already exhausted by twentieth-century crimes (Dean 2004, 7). Read through these two positions, the humanist and the postmodern, empathy is a faculty defined according to an economy of presence and absence. Like an identification card, empathy can expire. In Steiner's hopeful view, it can also be renewed. As Agamben (1999) suggests, the social frameworks for the performance of empathy (narratives of heroism or redemption, for example) can be foreclosed by historical events that enter us into practices in which we may no longer be inspired to have or to exercize our capacity for empathy—to feel for others. Dean recalls Jean Baudrillard's famous claim that desire, empathy and pleasure are media effects with no referent to a real. All forms of affect are engineered responses generated by the media's "habitual social control" (Baudrillard 1987, 24). Dean also cites Jonathan Boyarin's concept of "the repressive effects of empathy on those who remain beyond the pale." Boyarin writes: "We can only empathize with—feel ourselves into—those we can imagine as ourselves" and "the space of the other" is therefore not really expanded (Boyarin 1992, 86–88).

My concept of empathy differs from Boyarin's in that I argue that spectators may also "feel themselves into" those they can imagine not as themselves but as *theirs* or, rather, as their responsibility. Moreover, they may imagine themselves as part of a "we" that shares that responsibility. This kind of empathy is at the core of sociality, and of shame. Dean notes that Luc Boltanski links empathy to contagion, suggesting a contamination of the general "we," infected with feeling for an other who is not part of the compassionate "we" but whose suffering is source of the infection of feeling that spreads so widely. The space of the other is thus expanded, though not in the direction of the body we imagine to be the source of feelings. It is through Boltanski that we turn to Hannah Arendt's thoughts on affect, expressed in her interpretation of a text, Herman Melville's *Billy Budd*. Her reading helps me to explain what I mean in suggesting a more radically intersubjective model for empathetic identification.

Arendt provides a reading of a key scene in *Billy Budd* that illustrates the empathetic field in which compassion for an other is projected with a force likened by Melville to "vocal electricity" among spectators, perpetrator, and victim.[1] This concept of vocal electricity is akin to "contagion" (Boltanski's term, which recalls a phobic media effects moment) and "amplification," a term Tomkins used to account for the movement of affect (1980, 1991). I extend Arendt's brief reading into a discussion that incorporates attention to affect in the politics of compassion played out in this scene. Billy Budd, an orphan whose morality, like his speech ability, undergoes lapses, awaits punishment by hanging for murder on the military ship to which he has been dispatched from his previous post on the *Rights of Man*. Budd's compassion for his fellow man harbors a degree of violence that rivals that of his cold-blooded superiors. The doomed man, unimpeded by his stutter and in sound likened to that of a singing bird, in Arendt's words, "expresses compassion for the compassionate suffering felt for him by the man who has doomed him" (Arendt 1963, 81):

> Billy stood facing aft. At the penultimate moment, his words, his only ones, words wholly unobstructed in the utterance were these—"God bless Captain Vere!" Syllables so unanticipated coming from one with the ignominious hemp about his neck—a conventional felon's benediction directed aft towards the quarters of honor; syllables too delivered in the clear melody of a singing-bird on the point of launching from the twig, had a phenomenal effect, not unenhanced by the rare personal beauty of the young sailor spiritualized now thro' late experiences so poignantly profound. (Melville 1962, 123)

Billy Budd's words, "God bless Captain Vere," Arendt observes, are closer to gesture than to speech (Arendt 1963, 81). Their tone speaks straight to the hearts of the sailors assembled on deck to witness the hanging. Melville likens their resonantly compassionate response to a "vocal electric current": "Without volition as it were, as if indeed the ship's populace were but the vehicles of some vocal current electric, with one voice from alow and aloft came a resonant sympathetic echo: 'God bless Captain Vere!' And yet at that instant Billy alone must have been in their hearts, even as in their eyes" (Melville 1962, 123).

Through this scene, we can trace the electric movement of a response of compassion from Billy Budd, who feels sorry not only for himself but also for the man who condemns him to death and must live to suffer guilt and grief. He projects his own compassionate response outward, where the distance between himself and the men collapses in fellow feeling (as Arendt notes). Compassion enters the sailors assembled on deck. Billy Budd, situated "in their eyes" as spectacle of impending death, is also "in their hearts." He is the embodiment of their struggle with moral right that has brought him to this end. Billy Budd's stutter, entailing disfluency, a blockage of words, repetition—a palpable bodily tension in the production of words, has already cast him as object of empathetic identification. The men feel for him, not like him. This is the position he holds in the spectacle of his struggle to perform, to speak out, or to be still and silent among sailors and under the eye of the captain. Gilles Deleuze wrote of the stutter: "It is when the language system overstrains itself that it begins to stutter, to murmur, or to mumble, then the entire language reaches the limit that sketches the outside and confronts silence" (Deleuze 1994, 28).[2] The sailors' collective empathetic response in this final moment is to echo Billy Budd's self-effacing compassion for the captain, whose system of governance has overstrained itself, reaching its limits and instilling a sense of guilt and remorse in Captain Vere that will stay with him to his death, at which moment he will utter Billy Budd's name. The sailors' collective response to Billy Budd's call reverberates throughout the empathetic field and, finally, is thrust into Captain Vere with dramatic force: "At the pronounced words and the spontaneous echo that voluminously rebounded them, Captain Vere, either through the stoic self-control or a sort of momentary paralysis induced by emotional shock, stood erectly rigid as a musket in the ship-armorer's rack" (Melville 1963, 123–124).

Vere's momentary paralysis: is this akin to Tomkins's concept of surprise, a resetting affect, or is this a paralysis born of fear in the face of another's death that one has willed, steeling oneself for the wave of unassailable remorse? The bold selflessness of an act in which the victim and his empathetic witnesses confer compassion on the perpetrator would trigger fear in the perpetrator, to be certain: to confer compassion is to strip the recipient of agency, of the secure position of control, by making public his pathetic state. Captain Vere is perhaps shocked to be situated as abject object of compassion by his victim at the very moment that a punishment by death that he has ordered is about to be executed. For this is a performance meant to demonstrate his absolute authority over his men. The sailors have reversed the relationship of authority central to the act of benediction, a prayer that ends a service typically by entreating God for his blessing. Instead the sailors draw their leader close into their circle of suffering, enveloping him in their emotional field and paralyzing him with their projected empathy. At the moment of death, Billy Budd's body is as if paralyzed: he uncannily fails to exhibit the nerve-related shuddering of the corpse that is the physiological signal of the ending of life. This failure of a life sign is accommodated by the collectivity of spectators who have drawn so close to him in spirit: a spontaneous verbal shudder resonates among the men, as if in compensation—an inarticulate murmur that Melville suggests could perhaps be grieving consternation: a spontaneous gasp signaling retraction of the compassionate sanction they had only just expressed for Vere.

Compassion, notes Arendt, in abolishing distance, remains irrelevant and without consequence because it cannot establish "lasting institutions" (Arendt 1963, 81). The rights of subjects to act on their own behalf is at stake in the distinction between compassion and a politics of pity, on the one hand, and a politics of rights and freedoms, on the other. The following quote from Arendt resonates with discussions in each of my earlier chapters about the nature of seeing and hearing, speaking and appearing, in these politics and in the ground between them: "compassion speaks only to the extent that it has to reply directly to the sheer expressionist sound and gestures through which suffering becomes audible and visible in the world" (Arendt 1963, 82).

Can "fellow feeling" establish the grounds for a relationship that would allow the other the autonomy and agency requisite for exercising rights and freedoms? Throughout *Moral Spectatorship* I have interpreted cases of practices in which compassion is the response to subjects whose sensory, motor, and cognitive ability may exclude the potential to engage in the registers of the audible and the visible, either as actors or as spectators. To ask for more empathy is to ask for more proximity. But as Arendt warns us, this relationship may entail a violence that exceeds that wrought by the distanced practices of pity.

My proposal throughout this book has not been to suggest that we identify and practice a "right optics" of empathy, or a moral politics of right looking and right feeling. Rather, my suggestion is that we regard empathy in terms of its varieties of quality and dynamic, modality, temporality, and directionality, rather than subjecting it to measurement by degrees to assess the moral economy's ebb and flow relative to good and bad, pride and shame. In order to arrive at an understanding of empathy's production in and through media texts, it is useful to read more closely the relational practices of empathy through a system that allows us to track the qualities and directions of its movement across texts, subjects, and social contexts. Interpretation of representations finds a new use here, for it is one means of tracking flows of what Lacan identified as the unstable cargo of affect, the emotional burden he so carefully avoided.

Introduction

1 See Mulvey 1975 and 1989; Doane 1982, 1987, and 1988–1989; Doane and Bergstrom 1990; Hansen 1986; Diawara 1988; Silverman 1988, 1992, 1996, and 2000; de Lauretis 1984; Mayne 1990, 1993, and 1994; hooks 1992; Stacey 1994; and White 1999.
2 The vast literature on melodrama includes the essays collected in Gledhill 1990, Cook 1978, Brooks 1985, Modleski 1982 and 1987; Heung 1987, Doane 1987, Kaplan 1992, Klinger 1994, Gledhill 2000, Kozloff 2000, and Williams 1988, 1990, and 1998.

1. Moral Spectatorship

1 For example, Anthony Elliot's introduction to psychoanalytic theory (2002) describes Mitchell's *Psychoanalysis and Feminism* (1975) as a study of Lacanian and Freudian psychoanalysis "as a means of fusing discussions of gender power with an Althusserian-Marxist account of capitalism" (143). He does not mention the large sections of Mitchell's book devoted to Laing and Reik.
2 Psychoanalyst and feminist psychologist Elizabeth Wilson makes the point that there was an added problem, in that it seemed that the Lacanian approach could be split off from clinical practice. Lacan could be treated as theory in a way that would be harder to do with Klein, whose work was more empirical. Many of the Lacanian feminists at this time were not or had not been in analysis or therapy themselves yet, and paradoxically were rather indifferent to psychoanalytic or psychotherapeutic practice (personal written communication).

3 On Sigmund Freud's's references to the bearing of psychoanalysis on psychosis, see Bion 1957, 220–222. Kristeva 1982, 1984, 1989; Mannoni 1972, and Green 1986 are exceptions to this point.

4 See Lenneberg 1967 on the theory that the ability to learn language, like the ability to learn to walk, is typically innate and there is a critical period of childhood (ages two to seven) during which a language may be acquired, hence belated entry of the child into language constitutes a special problem. Lenneberg's theory is that the fundamental basis of primary language is acquired between two and three and after puberty the cognitive and physiological ability to acquire verbal behavior quickly declines and the subject may remain deficient for life even if exposed to learning contexts.

5 Klein's biographer Hanna Segal wrote of Dick as "the little boy who in his fantasy made such a sadistic attack on the inside of his mother's body that it became an object of horror and such paralyzing anxiety that it could not be symbolized in the external world. All symbol-formation came to a stop" (Segal n.d.). This work of Klein's, Segal suggests, inaugurated the study of "inhibition or deformation in the development of the capacity to symbolize—[an area] central to the understanding particularly of psychosis" (Segal n.d.). Kristeva continues to use "autism" as a descriptive not diagnostic term, as in her interpretation of Proust's *À la recherche du temps perdu*: "I put forward the hypothesis that there is a *latent compensatory autism* featured in this dream of the 'second apartment', out of which the frontal dream, but even more the work of writing cumulative metaphors and syntactic clauses, aspires to bring out the intensity, and succeeds" (Kristeva 2000, 771).

6 In the years between 1973 and 1999 Green, influenced by Wilfred Bion and Donald Winnicott, introduced concepts that expanded the field of practice to borderline patients and shifted the focus from repression and narcissism to decathexis and negativity. See "The Dead Mother" (in Green 1986). Although this aspect of Green's work will not be pursued here, it is useful to consider what these texts might offer to film theory, a field that has emphasized narcissism and, importantly, repression in the production of fantasy.

7 See Irigaray 1977, 1985a, 1985b. For critiques of essentialism, see Plaza 1978, Moi 1985, Jardine 1985, Silverman 1988, Fuss 1990, Whitford 1989 and 1991, and Butler 1990.

8 The French publication of that influential book, translated into English in the United States eight years later (Irigaray 1985b), coincided with an English-language interview with Irigaray in the same journal that published Plaza's critique (Irigaray 1977).

9 In *New Maladies of the Soul* Kristeva writes that the drives are a "pivot between 'soma' and 'psyche,' between biology and representation" (Kristeva 1995, 30).

10 I do not believe that he means the term "intentional" to suggest consciously willed action.

11 For this critique of Chodorow, see Alford 1989, 186–190.

12 Kristeva and Green intersected through their mutual engagement with the work of the psychoanalyst Wilfred Bion. Janice Doane and Devon Hodges (1992) write that in addition to sharing Green's concern that Lacan did not pay enough attention to psychosis and affect, Kristeva draws heavily on Green's essay "The Dead Mother" in *Black Sun: Depression and Melancholia* (Kristeva 1989), and shares his view that affect exists at the border between the maternal unnameable and the paternal Symbolic. They propose that Kristeva's case histories make Green's point that a psychotic structure is produced in the child in whom the mother wipes out the trace of the father (Doane and Hodges 1992, 54–64).

13 In *On Private Madness* (1986) Green makes a distinction between madness and psychosis.

14 From a different pride discourse, a U.S. Marines bumper sticker encountered in 2004 proclaims: "Pain is temporary. Pride is forever."

15 For influential analyses of mothering influenced by Klein, see Dinnerstein 1976, who analyzes the pathological fear of and contempt for women that results from their maternal function, and Chodorow 1978, who postulates that mothers and daughters experience a prolonged narcissistic bond that leaves daughters more prone than sons to "feminine" qualities such as empathy and emotional sensitivity.

16 Rodowick's preface to *The Difficulty of Difference* (1991, vii–xii) makes a case for interrogating our theories and for a new theory of *reading*. *Moral Spectatorship* is an attempt to do both, in keeping with a project largely dropped after Rodowick's book.

17 Although Rodowick does not make reference to the work, Sedgwick's classic exposé of axiomatic claims about sexuality, identity, and representation supports his case. A given representation (a performed act or a fantasized scene described or imagined by a subject) may have different meanings, may be differently motivated, and may be differently productive (of affect) by different subjects in ways that are not always neatly congruent with the behaviors, desires, and responses believed to belong to a given class of sexual being. Fantasized behavior may be congruent with one's sexual identity, or not. Fantasy may be the model for action, or it may not. The fantasy may incorporate oneself as actor, or not. In the end, one simply cannot make axiomatic claims that link identity to certain kinds of performance, fantasy, and desire. Although Sedgwick does not state this, her discussion about axioms is very much about the complexity of identification in fantasy relative to the affective register. This is a connection brought to life years later in her engagement with the writings of Silvan Tomkins (Sedgwick 1990, 163; Sedgwick and Frank 1995, introduction).

18 "Interanimation" is a term used by Mikhail Bakhtin to describe the process of covering the ground between specialized, monologic language use and everyday

speech. In "The Problem of Speech Genres" he identifies the concept of the Logos in Western traditions as acknowledging only one speaker. I extend this concept to the problem of identification as acknowledging only one subject as active, with the other occupying the passive role described in Bakhtin's paradigm of monologic speech as listener. See Bakhtin 1986, 67.

19 Hanna Segal more recently captures refinements of this concept, explaining that "projective identification has manifold aims: it may be directed toward the ideal object to avoid separation, or it may be directed toward the bad object to gain control of the source of danger. Various parts of the self may be projected, with various aims: bad parts of the self may be projected in order to get rid of them as well as to attack and destroy the object, good parts may be projected to avoid separation or to keep them safe from bad things inside or to improve the external object through a kind of primitive projective reparation" (Segal 1964, 27–28).

20 See Wilson 2004a and 2004b.

21 For Kleinian interpretations of society and political violence, see Segal 1987 on warfare and nuclear arms proliferation, Rustin 1991 on the critical humanization of individuals in communities, and Alford 1996 on prisoners' concepts of violence and evil.

22 Projective identification, according to Bion, is "unburdening the psyche of accretions of stimuli" (Bion 1962, 31). Susan Isaacs (1948), in "On Fantasy," emphasizes that the projection is an abstraction in the observer's mind.

23 A simple way to put this is that affect is projected, and that representations are not neutral mediators of abstract affective meaning. This was a point that brought Tomkins up short and drove him and his successors to use visual documentation such as cinema and video.

24 I am tempted to use the Deleuzian concept of lines of flight.

25 Green notes Freud's observation that "the unconscious speaks more than one dialect" (Green 1999a, 178). Green calls this multiplicity of dialects, which include gesture, body language, and writing in addition to speech, "discourse." Green's concept of discourse is far more heterogeneous than Lacan's (see Green 1999a, 179).

26 It is perhaps ironic that a system that takes energy and motility as its basis finds its earliest theorization by Freud in his writing on paralysis ("Organic and Motor Paralysis," 1893, written in 1888, and cited by Green 1986, 175).

27 Whereas Freud began with touch, hands placed on the heads of his patients, clinical psychiatry now largely emphasizes distanced treatment through psychotropic drugs and talk, and only rarely employs manual contact. As we will see in chapter 3's discussion of touch in facilitated communication, contact is an extreme measure subject to deep suspicion.

28 The cybernetic origins of affect theory are discussed in Wilson 2002, 2004a, and 2004b and noted in Sedgwick and Frank 1995.

29 For an excellent secondary reading of this concept in Kristeva's work, see Oliver 1993.

30 Tomkins distinguishes between "dismell," a neologism he generates to distinguish between a response in which one pulls up and back one's nose, as if to withdraw from proximity with something that generates a bad smell, and disgust, an expulsive act after the noxious situation has been taken in (Tomkins 1991, 21).

2. The (Deaf) Woman's Film

1 Key texts on melodrama and the mid-century woman's film include Doane 1987; Gledhill 1990; Byars 1991; Klinger 1994; Bratton, Cook, and Gledhill 1994; and Williams 1998. Key texts on feminism, maternal care, and disability include Hillyer 1993, Weiss 1994 and 1998, Press and Browner 1997, Feder Kittay 1999 and 2001, Landsman 1999, Das and Addlakha 2001, and Ginsburg and Rapp 2001.

2 There is an extensive literature in psychology and the social sciences on late acquisition of speech that for reasons of space cannot be discussed in this book. For some of the foundational texts, see Itard 1962, a work about Victor, the "wild boy" of Aveyron. Itard was the first to argue that late socialization could compensate for early deficits. Also see Betterheim 1959, Gesell 1941, Lenneberg 1964 and 1967, and Curtiss 1977, texts in linguistic theory discussing the idea that there is a critical period of development after which language cannot fully be acquired. Also noteworthy is the film based on Itard's case: L'Enfant sauvage (François Truffaut, 1970, British release title The Wild Boy, U.S. release title The Wild Child).

3 An anxiety disorder in which the child has the ability to understand speech and to speak but does not speak or speaks only to a select few, making its needs known through gesture, pointing, and other means.

4 On the social meaning of sound and its instrumentation, see Sterne 2003 and Thompson 2002.

5 On the multimodal, distributed production of meaning and agency in dialogic practices see these linguistics and cognitive science microanalyses: Goodwin 2003a, 2003b, 2003c; Hutchins 1996; and Alač 2005. On the concept of the human body as technology and the constitution of agency across bodies and artifacts there is a broad literature in science studies. See, for example, Latour 1999, Haraway 1991.

6 See my discussion of Rodowick's critique of spectatorship in the previous chapter.

7 This is discussed at length in Cartwright forthcoming.

8 The term "self" is used here because this is Kohut's preferred language. As noted in this first section of Moral Spectatorship, although Kohut refused to define the

self and considered it unknowable, he devoted most of his work to a psychology of self, describing instead the forms in which it appears. His work emphasized intersubjectivity and empathy in the constitution of the self, and reframed the concept of narcissism. Readers tied to the nuanced and complex concept of the subject are encouraged not to dismiss Kohut's concept because of its appropriation in the more reductive self psychology that emphasizes cohesion. See Kohut 1971 and the biography by Strozier (2001). See especially C. Fred Alford's very useful decentering of Kohut's concept of the self through Lacan's concept of the mirror phase and splitting (Alford 1991, 24–47).

9 See also Cartwright 2003.

10 The film won an Oscar for best short in 1954. Anderson, a prolific documentary director, is a noted Free Cinema director. His work on children includes a series of three neorealist-influenced films produced for the National Society for the Prevention of Cruelty to Children in 1955: *Green and Pleasant Land*, *Henry*, *The Children Upstairs*, and *A Hundred Thousand Children*. *O Dreamland* (1953) is an ironic-poetic exposition of the sad realities of amusement park fantasy culture, conceived while shooting *Thursday's Children*. On Anderson's film career see Silet 1998, Sussex 1970, and Graham 1981.

11 The article "Ex-Schoolgirl a Bit Dazed by Success" (*Herald-Tribune* 1940) epitomizes Wright's public persona at age twenty.

12 This familial, mother-tongue allegiance would echo in the British decision to join the United States in the war on Iraq more than half a century later.

13 See the official fan site: http://www.officialpattyduke.com/60s.htm (accessed June 2005). It applauds Duke's career while also repeatedly affirming her reclaimed identity as Anna.

14 TenBroek contrasts Cutsforth's defeatist notion of the "neurotic blind" with the notion of the "neurotic public" offered by Hector Chevigny and Sydell Braverman (1950), a concept he finds equally troubling. I will return to this concept later in this chapter, in my discussion of Penn's *The Miracle Worker*, a film that followed tenBroek's reading of Cutsforth and Chevigny by only a few years.

15 Baynton (1996), Padden and Humphries (1988, 2005), and others offer accounts of the manualist-oralist controversy showing that it is much more complicated than a two-sided debate. The documentary *Sound and Fury* discussed in the conclusion to this chapter also makes this clear.

16 See Doane 1986 and Silverman 1988.

17 I refer to the white abolitionist (1805–1879) who was great-aunt to the black lesbian poet Angelina Weld Grimké (1880–1958). See Lerner 1998 and Perry 2003.

18 The literature on the film includes Cook 1978, Walsh 1986, Williams 1988, and Kaplan 1992.

19 See U.S. Veterans Administration n.d. and 2002.

20 On public citizenship in the British welfare state, see Lister 1997, especially 169–171.

21 The Academy is a nonprofit organization established to advance the industry's strength by promoting unity among the studios through sharing of creative innovations. See Slide 1986, 1–2.

22 For a later version of this essay and a more extended discussion of the first sound transition, see Lastra 2000.

23 See also Fletcher 1934, which is part of a collection of essays in a special issue on auditory perspective in the journal *Electrical Engineering*.

24 See, for example, Mueller 1940 and Harris 1940.

25 Paul Zydel from an interview with Vincent LoBrutto (1994, 102).

26 On the Fantasound system and *Fantasia*'s rereleases see Garity and Hawkins 1941, Blake 1984a and 1984b, and Klapholz 1991. On Stokowski and hi-fidelity, see McGinn 1983.

27 On this problem, see Fletcher 1934; Steinberg and Snow 1934; Wente and Thuras 1934; Scriven 1934; Affel, Chesnut, and Mills 1934; and Bedell and Kerney 1934. See also Steinberg, Montgomery, and Gardner 1940; and Fletcher 1941.

28 See Thom n.d.

29 See the interview on the increased specialization of music recording and mixing after 1950 in Cameron 1980.

30 The question how many and which Deaf children can acquire speech does not have a simple answer. Ken Kurlychek of Gallaudet University's Laurent Clerc National Deaf Education Center writes: "When it comes to understanding and producing spoken language, it seems investment and outcomes continue to vary greatly from child to child...Intelligibility scores of Deaf children vary considerably depending on a wide range of factors and have shown little or no improvement over many years." He cites the work of Deaf educator Daniel Ling, who noted in 1976 that "speech errors of children attending special education for the Deaf today are much the same as they were 40 years ago. Advances in acoustic phonetics, speech science, psychology, hearing aid technology, and other related fields appear to have made no significant impact on standards of speech production" (Ling, 1976, p. 11) (Kurlychek 1997).

31 On the function of muteness in stage melodrama, see Brooks 1985.

32 It is noteworthy that *Johnny Belinda*, a film considered later in this section, depicts communication in sign language in a positive light. Its setting in a remote island fishing village (shot on location at Fort Bragg in Northern California) perhaps was intended as a reference to the famous northern Atlantic island Deaf community of Martha's Vineyard. But its presentation of a single, isolated Deaf subject allows viewers to see Belinda's as an isolated case, and to ignore oralism's status as the dominant instructional paradigm in the urban and suburban mainland

cultures of the United States, Canada, and England in which this Hollywood studio film would be exhibited.

33 Although the name of *Mandy*'s fictional Bishop David School for the Deaf would suggest it is meant to be one of these religious establishments, the film provides scant demonstration of BSL.

34 On the films of Robertson, Anna Freud's writings on film, and the work of Dorothy Burlingham with blind children, see Cartwright forthcoming.

35 However, such speculation would come dangerously close to Harry Harlow's troubling claims about the sufficiency of the mechanical mother surrogate in infant monkey development. See Harlow 1961, 1963, 1971.

36 The poet Susan Stewart makes a similar point when she states that "we love the voice as we love the eyes—as vessels of that presence we call the soul" (Stewart 2002, 107). She does not specify whose soul is captured there, the looker's or the one who is looked upon, or (as I am proposing) a subject position somewhere in between.

37 See Doane's full discussion of sound-body relationships (1986); the Bonitzer text she references (1975); Bonitzer 1976; Silverman 1988, Dolar 1996, 13–14 for different accounts of this function of the voice in self-apprehension.

38 Bonitzer 1976, 32. Translated and quoted in Silverman 1988, 163.

39 In the words of Anderson's biographer Allison Graham (1981, 49).

40 This technique of using celebrities to invoke paternal or maternal authority is widely replicated in later decades across texts such as the television documentary spin-offs of the popular television series *An American Family* (*Frontline*, 1973) titled *Who Are the DeBolts and Where Did They Get 19 Kids?* (John Korty, 1977) and its sequel, *Stepping Out—The DeBolts Grow Up* (Pyramid Films, 1981), narrated by Henry Winkler and Kris Kristofferson, respectively ("20 kids, different races," different nationalities, some handicapped, some not. Some adopted, some not"); and the appointment of Susan Sarandan, following her starring role in *Stepmom* (Tristar/Chris Columbus, 1988), as special representative to the United Nations Children's Fund for the year 2000 (UNICEF 1999).

41 On the pity response, see Cartwright 2004 and forthcoming.

42 On the child film studies of René Spitz, see Cartwright 2004 and forthcoming.

43 The concept of the mirror phase as an element in the child's entry into the symbolic order is the cornerstone of Lacan's writing and references to it are many. The concept can be traced back to a nonpsychoanalytic essay of philosopher Henri Wallon (1931) and was described in the psychoanalytic context by Lacan in a 1936 lecture before the 14th Congress of the International Psychoanalytical Association ("Le Stade du miroir: Théorie d'un moment structurant et génétique de la constitution de la réalité, conçu en relation avec l'expérience et la doctrine psychanalytique"). A later version of the concept was delivered at the 16th International Congress of Psychoanalysis, in Zürich, July 17, 1949, and it is this essay which is the basis for Jacques Lacan, "The Mirror Stage as Formative of

the Function of the *I* as Revealed in Psychoanalytic Experience" (Lacan 1977a, 1–7).

44 See Itard 1962, Curtiss 1977, and the film *L'Enfant sauvage*, François Truffaut, 1970 (British release title *The Wild Boy*, U.S. release title *The Wild Child*).

45 Sources are sparse, but it seems this goal went largely unrealized.

46 Account of an unidentified informant interviewed by Pullen and Sutton-Spence 1993, quotation from 175–176.

47 On the history of Deaf culture and American and European sign languages, see Gannon 1981, Padden and Humphries 1988 and 2005, Baynton 1996, and Lane et al. 1996. From the eighteenth century, when the first schools for the Deaf were founded in Europe, until the 1860s, hearing educators of the Deaf often used some form of manual sign to teach their Deaf students, and various sign languages functioned as the indigenous and spontaneous forms of communication within Deaf communities. But by the 1860s and 1870s, a campaign against signing and manualist methods of Deaf education gained momentum among those oralists favoring education in speech for the Deaf in Europe and the United States. In 1880 at an international conference in Milan it was mandated that sign language be banned from Deaf education. This was a watershed in a complex and heated debate. Methods of communication and education all along the spectrum between sign and speech never disappeared, but the overall scene of Deaf education shifted dramatically in favor of mainstreaming Deaf children into hearing culture by sending them to institutions where they would be trained to speak. Speech education for the Deaf was by and large the norm in schools for the Deaf throughout Britain, the United States and much of Europe at the time of these films' production; this would remain the case until late in the twentieth century. While the arguments against signing varied, some of them were based on theories of evolution and the rise of eugenic thinking. Alexander Graham Bell was a vehement oralist in the eugenic tradition. Prohibitions against sign language were sometimes linked to arguments against intermarriage among the Deaf, and campaigns arose in favor of the sterilization of Deaf people during the early twentieth century. One charge against sign was that it damaged the minds of Deaf people and interfered with their ability to develop higher levels of thinking; manual speech was a primitive form of communication. Sign languages were nonetheless passed down within Deaf cultures. Deaf parents taught their Deaf children to sign in communities bypassed by the push toward institutionalization due to geographic isolation or poverty; residents of Deaf institutions continued to communicate in sign among themselves; and some teachers persisted in using finger-speech despite opposition to it.

48 The *New York Times* (Crowther 1953) described child actress Mandy Miller as "remarkably fluent" in her performance of deafness, and *Sight and Sound* singled out the performances of the Deaf children at the school for their "unnaturally alert faces, their quick trust and extraordinary patience."

49 See Trumpbour 2001, 179–180. On the issue of British film culture and child audiences, Trumpbour reports that Mary Field, the director of Gaumont-British Children's Education Films and the future director of UNESCO's International Centre of Films for Young People, speculated as to whether "Britain, which leads the world in documentary, will be the pioneer and acknowledged leader in the field of children's films" (quoted in Trumpbour 2001, 180). On female adolescent spectators, see Scheiner 2000.

50 For more on Spitz, see Cartwright 2004 and forthcoming.

51 The concept of introjection was introduced by Sandor Ferenczi in his 1909 paper "Introjection and Transference" (republished in Ferenczi, *Sex in Psychoanalysis*, 1950). The term is described in shorthand by Nicholas Abraham and Maria Torok as "an explicative synonym for transference" (Abraham and Torok 1994, 111). Ferenczi describes introjection as "the ego's extension" and as the "growing onto," or "including of the loved object in, the ego" (cited in Abraham and Torok 1994, 112).

52 On the place of shaming practices in the production of sociality in the human subject, see Benin and Cartwright 2006.

53 This is a characterization that will be borne out in Bancroft's next pedagogical role, as Mrs. Robinson, *The Graduate*'s bespectacled faculty spouse, who removes her glasses to help the film's young protagonist graduate to sexual maturity. On girls who wear glasses in film, see Doane 1982.

54 See Tomkins in Sedgwick and Frank 1995, 208–210, on anger and racism on American southern plantations. See Clarke 2001b, Segal 1987, and Young 1994 on projective identification and racial hatred. Scalia 2002 most succinctly brings together theories of affect and object relations in the analysis of "intimate violence."

55 The problem of understanding the boundaries that divide touch, restraint, and force are demonstrated all too powerfully in the tragic case of Candace Newmaker, the attachment-disordered child who was literally suffocated by "holding therapy" with her parents under the guidance of a therapist. See Mercer, Sarner, and Rosa 2003.

56 Burlingham 1972, 327.

57 Lash 1980. See also Keller 1985 and Braddy 1933.

58 On emotional impairment in the postinstitutionalized child, see Cartwright 2003.

59 Negulesco's concern that an accurate representation of Belinda's voice might be heard as a "subnormal rattle" suggests that the esthetic guiding his hearing imagination with regard to Deaf voice is gendered, a point to be taken up at the end of this chapter.

60 Ayres was Dr. Kildare in all the films from the 1938 *Young Dr. Kildare* up to World War II, when as a conscientious objector he fell into disfavor. He was offered the same role in the television series that spun off of the movies; however,

that proposition was nixed when he stipulated that he would do it only if no cigarette ads were aired during the show.

61 There are numerous accounts of de L'Épée. Through his efforts the manual language of the Parisian Deaf could be used in instruction in French literacy, and could be adapted for teaching the manual method of sign as a language, allowing for the education of the Deaf as a social class. In 1755 de L'Épée established a school near Paris, using up his inheritance to support his students and those trained as teachers with him. His first book on the method was published twenty years later. His method was approved by the French Academy, and in 1791 his school was adopted by the state. See Best 1993, 380–381.

62 De L'Épée is popularly described as a priest, Best explains, but in fact he was a deacon barred from the priesthood because unwilling to espouse certain political beliefs, hence his entry into other professions (e.g., law) before teaching the Deaf (Best 1993, 380–81).

63 Diana Fuss makes note of this in her essay on Keller's hands (Fuss 2004, 127 and 137).

64 Steiner is regarded as the dean of Hollywood film scoring who produced 185 scores for Warner Brothers and whose credits include *Gone with the Wind* and *King Kong* (Marks 1996, 255).

65 See the interview with Herrmann in Cameron 1980, 117–135. On Hitchcock's use of sound, see also Weis 1982.

66 Negulesco specifically chose not to subtitle Belinda's signing of the prayer, but to interpret the prayer through the voice of the psychiatrist. In prior films in which sign language is represented, Schuchman (1988) reminds readers, the nonsigning hearing audience is excluded through a lack of captioning or voice interpretation, making Deaf viewers the audience to whom privilege is conferred. *Johnny Belinda*'s prayer scene was relatively unique as a Hollywood text accessible to Deaf spectators.

67 On telepathy see Freud 1955b and 1955c and the contributions of Burlingham, Helen Deutsch, Sigmund Freud, Paul Schilder, and others in Devereux 1953, a comprehensive volume on psychoanalysis and the occult.

68 This song was voted by *Penthouse* as one of the top twenty-five songs to "get it on" with.

69 From among his numerous films he was best known for portraying World War II officers in films such as *Bridge on the River Kwai* (1957) and *League of Gentlemen* (1959).

70 On linguistic assimilation in the United States, see Fishman 1966.

71 From the *Sound and Fury* Deaf Culture History Timeline, link at http://www .pbs.org/wnet/soundandfury/culture/deafhistory.html, accessed March 2003.

72 On the FDA review see http://www.fda.gov/cdrh/cochlear/index.html. Matlin was a performer in the Chicago run of the stage play in the minor role of Lydia. The movie was adapted by Hesper Anderson and James Carrington

(uncredited) from the play by Medoff. Matlin won the Academy Award for Best Actress and Hurt was nominated for Best Actor in a Leading Role, as was Piper Laurie for Best Actress in a Supporting Role. It was also nominated for Best Picture and Best Writing, and Best Screenplay Based on Material from Another Medium.

73 The statistic is from a National Institutes of Health Consensus Development Conference Statement, May 1995. See National Institutes of Health 1995.

74 As reported on the Web site of the Washington Speakers Bureau for Heather Whitestone McCallum, "First Hearing Impaired Miss America 1995." See Washington Speakers Bureau n.d.

3. "A Child Is Being Beaten"

1 On the relationship of speech to writing see Jacques Derrida's *On Grammatology* (1974). The quotation from Rousseau, used as the first epigraph to this chapter (from his Fragment inédit d'un essai sur les langues, *The Social Contract* [1762]), is quoted in Derrida 1974.

2 *Speechless: Facilitating Communication for People without Voices* is the title of the major book on the method by its founder Rosemary Crossley (1997). The method has been used with people with cerebral palsy, Down syndrome, autism, and other conditions in which individuals have communication disorders that include limited speech ability and difficulty writing without guidance or support. Reasons for speech and writing impairment vary, are often mixed, and are not always clearly ascertainable. They may include motor, neural, cognitive, and emotional factors.

3 See chapter 2 on *Mandy*.

4 Although there is not space to consider this topic here, the psychoanalyst Wilfred Bion's concept of group would be a starting point for this work (Bion 1955, 1961a).

5 For an example of the degree of awe that the late-emerging independent communication of severely autistic children can inspire even among professional witnesses writing in the early 2000s, see Tito Rajarshi Mukhopadhyay (2003). Especially noteworthy are the jacket blurb by Oliver Sacks and the additional professional testimony that prefaces the U.S. edition.

6 "Information" is another term worthy of consideration here. I return to this point at the conclusion of this chapter.

7 Sexual abuse accounted for 15 percent of the 2,694,000 cases of abuse and neglect reported in the United States in 1991, according to the National Resource Center on Child Sexual Abuse 1991. Jaudes and Martone (1992) state that an estimated 250,000 new cases of sexual abuse were being reported each year.

8 In 1992 two cases in which sexual abuse was disclosed through FC went to trial. In both (*Matter of M.Z.* and *Department of Social Services v. Mark and*

Laura S.), it was ruled that the attorney had failed to prove FC reliable. Because evidence based on scientific or clinical innovations must be shown to be reliable in order to be admitted, evidence that fails to be proven reliable can be excluded. Thus FC was not found to be unreliable; it was simply not demonstrated to be reliable. A year later, however, in *Matter of Luz P.*, the court ruled that FC was not subject to the requirement of proof of reliability because the facilitator should be viewed as an interpreter, and interpretation does not fall under the category of scientific or clinical innovation.

9 The association's response was to draft guidelines for pathologists who wished to use the method and cautioned that the method be used with training and attention to the matter of facilitator influence over message authoring.

10 Frith (1989) clearly outlines the distinctions between Asperger's and Kanner's research and findings regarding conditions they both described using the term "autism" in the 1940s.

11 The FMSF publishes its own newsletter, which can be accessed online at http://www.fmsonline.org/ (accessed June 2005). For an account of the debate, see the collection edited by Pezdek and Banks (1996). For feminist discussions of the memory wars, see Campbell 2003, Crews 1995, Enns et al. 1995, Haaken 1996 and 1998, and Park 1997.

12 Compared to Mandy in *Sight and Sound, The Fallen Idol* stars Jack Hawkins, the actor who played the headmaster of the school for the Deaf in *Mandy*, and whose voice was dubbed by other actors in his later sound film career after he lost his ability to speak following an operation for throat cancer (Lambert 1952, 78).

13 Sources consulted in this narrative include Biklen 1990, 1992a, 1992b, 1992c, and 1993; and Crossley 1997.

14 Shane has since developed an electronic media environment involving an "intelligent agent" (a computer) as medium in assistive speech (Caves, Shane, and DeRuyter 2002).

15 The film's scene of Annie's discovery by Crossley is dramatically echoed years later in the shots within "Shame of a Nation," discussed in *Images of Waiting Children* (Cartwright forthcoming) that introduce viewers (and filmmaker John Upton) to Elena Rostas, the adolescent orphan whose emaciated and twisted body was discovered by the camera crew reclining listlessly on a filthy cot at a destitute Romanian institution. Like Rostas, McDonald would become a symbol of disabled children warehoused out of sight and wasting away in the nation's institutions.

16 Quoted in Crossley 1997, 286. My italics.

17 For an overview of legal issues and justice matters for people with severe disabilities in the United States, Australia, and New Zealand during this period, see Dwyer 1996.

18 A detailed account of the FC technique can be found in Duchan 1993. Also see Biklen 1992a, 237–238; and Biklen 1993, 20–23.

19 To be clear, I believe that Crossley and many other facilitators are quite explicit in their writing about their own authority and their personal involvement and influence in eliciting writing from the people they work with. In facilitated conversations and presentations that I have witnessed, it is common for the facilitator to reflexively comment upon his or her own interjections and clarifications based on an established relationship with the facilitated subject. In the most effective examples of facilitation I have witnessed, the facilitator performs as a participant in a conversation in which he or she is included, and not as if he or she were expected to serve as a neutral conduit.

20 See chapter 1 above for a review of André Green's account of Freud's turn away from affect and toward representation. Green hypothesizes that in turning away from affect, Freud was hoping to gain credibility for psychoanalysis as a science.

21 Masson also notes that "on December 22, 1897, Freud writes to Fliess about a two-year-old girl who was brutally raped by her father, nearly died, and then ends the letter by saying that he has a new motto for psychoanalysis: 'What have they done to you, poor child?'" These words were removed from the public record by Anna Freud and Ernst Kris in their edition of the Freud-Fliess letters (Masson 1984b).

22 See also Wallon 1984, Schilder 1978; Grosz 1994, Weiss 1999, and Hanley 2005.

Conclusion

1 For other readings of *Billy Budd*, see Sedgwick 1990, 91–130, and especially Moruzzi 2001, 23–32 and 63–66, which offers a discussion of Arendt's reading of the text.

2 For Deleuze on the concept of the stutter, see *Difference and Repetition* (Deleuze 1995) and "He Stuttered" (Deleuze 1994).

REFERENCES

ABC News. 1992. Autism: Interviews with Diane Sawyer. *Primetime Live*. Aired January 23.

———. 2002. Symphony of Sound: After 29 Silent Years, Ex-Miss America Hears Again. *Good Morning America*, September 20.

Abraham, Nicholas, and Maria Torok. 1994. *The Shell and the Kernel: Renewals of Psychoanalysis*. Vol. 1, ed. and trans. Nicholas T. Rand. Chicago: University of Chicago Press. (Orig. pub. 1968.)

Adams, Parveen and Elizabeth Cowie. 1983. Feminine Sexuality: Interview with Juliet Mitchell and Jacqueline Rose. *m/f* 8: 1–16.

Affel, H. A., R. W. Chesnut, and R. H. Mills. 1934. Auditory Perspective: Transmission Lines. *Electrical Engineering* 53: 214–216.

Agamben, Giorgio. 1999. *Remnants of Auschwitz: The Witness and the Archive*. New York: Zone Books.

Alač, Morana. 2005. Widening the Wideware: An Analysis of Multimodal Interaction in Scientific Practice. *Proceedings of the 27th Annual Meeting of the Cognitive Science Society*, ed. B. G. Bara, L. Barsalou, and M. Bucciarelli. Hillsdale, N.J.: Lawrence Erlbaum, 85–90.

Alford, C. Fred. 1989. *Melanie Klein and Critical Social Theory*. New Haven: Yale University Press.

———. 1991. *The Self in Social Theory*. New Haven, Conn.: Yale University Press.

———. 1996. *What Evil Means to Us*. Ithaca, N.Y.: Cornell University Press.

American Psychiatric Association. 1974. *Diagnostic and Statistical Manual of Mental Disorders*. 3rd ed. (DSM-III). Washington, D.C.: American Psychiatric Association.

———. 1994. *Diagnostic and Statistical Manual of Mental Disorders*. 4th ed. (DSM-IV). Washington, D.C.: American Psychiatric Association.

American Psychological Association. 1994. Resolution on Facilitated Communication by the American Psychological Association. Adopted in Council August 14. Los Angeles, CA. See http://www.apa.org/divisions/div33/fcpolicy.html (accessed June 2007).

American Speech-Language Association. 1995. ASLA Position Statement on Facilitated Communication. *Facilitated Communication Digest* 3, no. 2: 4.

Anzieu, Didier. 1976. L'Enveloppe sonore du soi. *Nouvelle revue de psychoanalyse* 13: 161–179.

Arendt, Hannah. 1963. *On Revolution*. New York: Viking Press. (Orig. pub. 1961.)

Asperger, Hans. 1944. Die "Autistischen Psychopathen" im Kindesalter. *Archiv fur Psychiatrie und Nervenkrankheiten* 117: 76–136.

Ayato, John. 1990. *Dictionary of Word Origins*. New York: Arcade; Little, Brown.

Bader, E., and P. T. Pearson. 1988. *In Quest of the Mythical Mate: Developmental Stages of Couplehood*. New York: Brunner, Mazel.

Bakhtin, Mikhail M. 1986. The Problem of Speech Genres. *Speech Genres and Other Late Essays*, 60–102. Austin: University of Texas Press.

Baron-Cohen, Simon. 1995. *Mindblindness: An Essay on Autism and Theory of Mind*. Cambridge: MIT Press, Bradford Books.

Barthes, Roland. 1977. *Image-Music-Text*, ed. and trans. Stephen Heath. New York: Hill and Wang.

Baudrillard, Jean. 1987. *The Evil Demon of Images*. Sydney: Power Institute of Fine Arts, 1987.

Baynton, Douglas C. 1996. *Forbidden Signs: American Culture and the Campaign against Sign Language*. Chicago: University of Chicago Press.

Bedell, E. H., and Iden Kerney. 1934. Auditory Perspective: System Adaptation. *Electrical Engineering* 53: 216–219.

Benin, David and Lisa Cartwright. 2006. Shame, Empathy and Looking Practices: Lessons from a Disability Studies Classroom. *Journal of Visual Culture* 5, 155–171.

Benjamin, Walter. 1992. Work of Art in the Age of Mechanical Reproduction. In *Illuminations*, trans. Harry Zohn. London: Fontana, 211–244. (Orig. pub. 1936.)

Berman, Emanuel. 1997. Hitchcock's *Vertigo*: The Collapse of a Rescue Phantasy. *The International Journal of Psychoanalysis* 78, 975–996.

Best, Harry. 1993. *Deafness and the Deaf in the United States*. New York: Macmillan.

Best, Joel. 1990. *Threatened Children: Rhetoric and Concern about Child-Victims*. Chicago: University of Chicago Press.

Bettelheim, Bruno. 1959. Feral Children and Autistic Children. *American Journal of Sociology* 64, no. 5: 455–467.

———. 1967. *The Empty Fortress*. New York: Free Press.

Bettison, Sue. 1991. Informal Evaluation of Crossley's Facilitated Communication. *Journal of Autism and Developmental Disorders* 21, no. 4: 561–562.

———. 1992. Letter to the Editor: Correction to Previous Evaluation of Facilitated Communication. *Journal of Autism and Developmental Disorders* 22, no. 3: 451–452.

Biklen, Douglas. 1990. Communication Unbound: Autism and Praxis. *Harvard Educational Review* 60: 291–314.

———. 1992a. Autism Orthodoxy v. Free Speech: A Reply to Cummins and Prior. *Harvard Educational Review* 62: 242–256.

———. 1992b. Communication Unbound: Autism and Praxis. *Hospital Practice* 27, no. 4 (April 15): 209–250.

———. 1992c. *Schooling without Labels*. Philadelphia: Temple University Press.

———.1993. *Communication Unbound*. New York, N.Y.: Teacher's College Press.

Biklen, Douglas, and Marilyn Chadwick. 1999. Foundation Workshop in Facilitated Communication Training and Introductory Skills Workshop: Learning to be a Facilitator. Photocopied document distributed at training workshops of the Facilitated Communication Institute, Syracuse University, New York, March 8 and 9.

Biklen, Douglas, M. W. Morton, S. N. Saha, J. Duncan, D. Gold, M. Hardardottir, E. Kama, S. O'Connoir, and S. Rau. 1991. Imn not a utistivc on thje typ (I'm not autistic on the typewriter). *Disability, Handicap and Society* 6: 161–180.

Bion, W. R. 1955a. Group Dynamics: A Re-view. In *New Directions in Psycho-Analysis*, ed. Melanie Klein, Paula Heimann, and R. E. Money-Kyrle, 440–477. New York: Basic Books.

———. 1955b. Language and the Schizophrenic. In *New Directions in Psycho-Analysis*, ed. Melanie Klein, Paula Heimann, and R. E. Money-Kyrle, 220–239. New York: Basic Books.

———. 1961. *Experiences in Groups and Other Papers*. New York: Basic Books.

———. 1962. *Learning from Experience*. London: Heinemann.

Blake, Larry. 1984a. Mixing Dolby Stereo Film Sound. In *Film Sound Today: An Anthology of Articles from Recording Engineer/Producers*, ed. Mel Lambert, 1–10. Hollywood, Calif.: Reveille Press.

———. 1984b. Re-Recording and Post Production for Disney's Fantasia. In *Film Sound Today: An Anthology of Articles from Recording Engineer/Producers*, ed. Mel Lambert, 19–24. Hollywood, Calif.: Reveille Press.

Bligh, Sally, and Phyllis Kuperman. 1993. Brief Report: Facilitated Communication Evaluation Procedure Accepted in a Court Case. *Journal of Autism and Developmental Disorders* 23, no. 3: 553–557.

Boesky, D. 1982. Acting Out: A Reconsideration of the Concept. *International Journal of Psycho-analysis* 63: 39–55.

Boltanski, Luc. 1999. *Distant Suffering: Morality, Media and Politics.* Trans. Graham D. Burchell. Cambridge: Cambridge University Press.

Bonitzer, Pascal. 1975. Les Silences de la voix. *Cahiers du cinema* 256 (February–March): 22–33.

———. 1976. *Le Regard et la voix.* Paris: Union Générale d'Éditions.

Borthwick, Chris. 1998. Prisoners of Silence: What *Frontline* Didn't Tell You. DEAL. http://home.vicnet.net.au/~dealccinc/FrantA.htm (accessed June 1998; site discontinued).

Botash, Ann S., Diane Babuts, Nancy Mitchell, Maureen O'Hara, Laura Lynch, and JoAnn Manuel. 1994. Evaluations of Children Who Have Disclosed Sexual Abuse via Facilitated Communication. *Archives of Pediatrics and Adolescent Medicine* 148 (December): 1282–1289.

Boulous Walker, Michelle. 1998. *Philosophy and the Maternal Body: Reading Silence.* New York: Routledge.

Bowie, Malcolm. 1991. *Lacan.* London: Fontana.

Boyarin, Jonathan. 1992. *Storm from Paradise: The Politics of Jewish Memory.* Minneapolis: University of Minnesota Press.

Braddy, Nella. 1933. *Anne Sullivan Macy.* New York: Doubleday, Doran.

Bratton, Jacky, Jim Cook, and Christine Gledhill. 1994. *Melodrama: Stage, Picture, Screen.* London: British Film Institute.

Brooks, Peter. 1985. *The Melodramatic Imagination: Balzac, Henry James, Melodrama, and the Role of Excess.* New York: Columbia University Press.

Brown, Thomas. 1820. *Lectures on the Philosophy of the Mind.* W. &. C. Tait, Edinburgh.

Burlingham, Dorothy. 1972. Some Problems of Ego Development in Blind Children. In *Psychoanalytic Studies of the Sighted and the Blind.* New York: International Universities Press. (Orig. pub. *The Psychoanalytic Study of the Child* 20 [1965]:194–208.)

Burris-Meyer, Harold. 1941. Development and Current Uses of the Acoustic Envelope. *Journal of the Society of Motion Picture Engineers* 37, no. 1: 109–114.

Butler, Judith. 1990. *Gender Trouble: Feminism and the Subversion of Identity.* New York and London: Routledge.

———. 2004. *Precarious Life: The Powers of Mourning and Violence.* London: Verso.

Byars, Jackie. 1991. *All That Hollywood Allows: Re-reading Gender in 1950s Melodrama.* London: Routledge.

Caillois, Roger. 1984. Mimicry and Legendary Pyschaesthenia. Trans. John Shepley. *October* 31: 16–32.

Calculator, S. N. and K. M. Singer. 1992. Preliminary Validation of Facilitated Communication. *Topics in Language Disorders* 12, no. 6: ix–xvi.

Cameron, Evan William, ed. 1980. *Sound and the Cinema: The Coming of Sound to American Film*. Pleasantville, N.Y.: Redgrave.

Campbell, Sue. 2003. *Relational Remembering: Rethinking the Memory Wars*. Lanham, Md.: Roman and Littlefield.

Cartwright, Lisa. 2003. Photographs of "Waiting Children": The Transnational Adoption Market. *Social Text* 73: 83–109.

———. 2004. "Emergencies of Survival": Moral Spectatorship and the "New Vision of the Child" in Postwar Child Psychoanalysis. *Journal of Visual Culture* 3, no. 1: 35–49.

———. Forthcoming. *Images of Waiting Children: The Visual Culture of Transnational Adoption*. Durham, N.C.: Duke University Press.

Castañeda, Claudia. 2002. *Figurations: Child, Body, World*. Durham, N.C.: Duke University Press.

Castells, Manuel. 1996. *The Information Age: Economy, Society and Culture*, vol. 1, *The Rise of the Network Society*. Cambridge, Mass.: Blackwell. 2nd ed., 2000.

———. 1997. *The Information Age: Economy, Society and Culture*, vol. 2, *The Power of Identity*. Cambridge, Mass.: Blackwell. 2nd ed., 2004.

———. 1998. *The Information Age: Economy, Society and Culture*, vol. 3, *The End of the Millennium*. Cambridge, Mass.: Blackwell. 2nd ed., 2000.

Catonese, A. T. 1988. DEAL *Communication Centre Operations: A Statement of Concern*. Dame Mary Herring Special Project. Interdisciplinary Working Party on Issues in Severe Communication Impairment. Melbourne, Australia: DEAL.

Caves, K., H. C. Shane, and F. DeRuyter. 2002. Connecting AAC Devices to the World of Information Technology. *Assistive Technology* 14: 81–89.

Ceci, Stephen J., and Maggie Bruck. 1993. The Suggestibility of the Child Witness: A Historical Review and Synthesis. *Psychological Bulletin* 113: 403–439.

———. 1995. *Jeopardy in the Courtroom: A Scientific Analysis of Children's Testimony*. Washington, D.C.: American Psychological Association.

Ceci, S. J., E. F. Loftus, M. D. Leichtman, and M. Bruck. 1994. The Possible Role of Source Misattributions in the Creation of False Beliefs among Preschoolers. *International Journal of Clinical and Experimental Hypnosis* 42: 304–320.

Chevigny, Hector, and Sydell Braverman. 1950. *The Adjustment of the Blind*. New Haven, Conn.: Yale University Press.

Chion, Michel. 1982. *La Voix au cinema*. Paris: Éditions de l'Étoile.

Chodorow, Nancy. 1978. *The Reproduction of Mothering*. Berkeley: University of California Press.

Clarke, Simon. 2001a. The Kleinian Position: Phantasy, Splitting and the Language of Psychic Violence. *Journal for the Psychoanalysis of Culture and Society* 6, no. 2: 289–297.

———. 2001b. Projective Identification: From Attack to Empathy? *Journal of Kleinian Studies* 2: 1–30.

Cohan, Steven. 2000. Case Study: Interpreting *Singin' in the Rain*. In *Reinventing Film Studies*, ed. Christine Gledhill and Linda Williams, 53–75. New York: Oxford University Press.

Coleman, L. 1986. False Allegations of Child Sexual Abuse: Have the Experts Been Caught with Their Pants Down? *Forum* (Jan.–Feb.): 12–21.

Conte, J. R., E. Sorenson, L. Fogarty, and J. D. Rosa. 1991. Evaluating Children's Reports of Sexual Abuse: Results from a Survey of Professionals. *American Journal of Orthopsychiatry* 61: 428–437.

Cook, Pam. 1978. *Duplicity in Mildred Pierce*. In *Women in Film Noir*, ed. E. Ann Kaplan. London: British Film Institute.

———. 1986. Mandy: Daughter of Transition. In *All Our Yesteryears: Ninety Years of British Cinema*, ed. Charles Barr. London: British Film Institute, 355–61.

Cooper, Anthony Ashley. 1699. *An Inquiry Concerning Virtue or Merit*. London.

Crews, Frederick. 1995. *The Memory Wars: Freud's Legacy in Dispute*. New York: New York Review of Books.

Crossley, Rosemary. 1992. Getting the Words Out: Case Studies in Facilitated Communication Training. *Topics in Language Disorders* 12: 46–59.

———. 1997. *Speechless: Facilitating Voices for People without Voices*. New York: Dutton.

Crossley, Rosemary, and Anne McDonald. 1980. *Annie's Coming Out*. New York: Penguin.

Crossley, Rosemary, and J. Remington-Gurney. 1992. Getting the Words Out. *Topics in Language Disorders* 12, no. 4: 29–45.

Crowther, Bosley. 1953. Review of *The Story of Mandy*. *New York Times* 21, no. 3: F24.

Cummins, R. A., and M. P. Prior. 1992. Autism and Assisted Communication: A Response to Biklen. *Harvard Educational Review* 62, no. 2: 228–240.

Curtiss, Susan. 1977. *Genie: A Psycholinguistic Study of a Modern-Day "Wild Child."* New York: Academic Press.

Cutsforth, Thomas D. 1925. The Role of Emotion in a Synaesthetic Subject. *American Journal of Psychology* 36: 527–543.

———. 1951. *The Blind in School and Society: A Psychological Study*. New York: American Foundation for the Blind.

Dann, Kevin Tyler. 1998. *Bright Colors Falsely Seen: Synaesthesia and the Modern Search for Transcendental Knowledge*. New Haven, Conn.: Yale University Press.

Dass, Veena, and Renu Addlakha. 2001. Disability and Domestic Citizenship: Voice, Gender, and the Making of the Subject. *Public Culture* 13, no. 13: 511–531.

Davis, Lennard. 2000. *My Sense of Silence: Memoirs of a Childhood with Deafness*. Urbana: University of Illinois Press.

Dean, Carolyn. 2004. *The Fragility of Empathy*. Ithaca, N.Y.: Cornell University Press.

De Lauretis, Teresa. 1984. *Alice Doesn't.* Bloomington: Indiana University Press.

Deleuze, Gilles. 1994. "He Stuttered." In *Deleuze and the Theater of Philosophy,* ed. Constantin V. Boundas and Dorothea Olkowski. New York: Routledge.

———. 1995. *Difference and Repetition.* New York: Columbia University Press. (Orig. pub. 1968.)

Department of Social Services v. Mark and Laura S. 1992. 593 N.Y.S. 2d 142 (NY Family Ct.).

Derrida, Jacques. 1974. *On Grammatology.* Baltimore, Md.: Johns Hopkins University Press.

Deuchar, Margaret. 1984. *British Sign Language.* London: Routledge.

Devereux, George. 1953. *Psychoanalysis and the Occult: A Symposium.* New York: International Universities Press.

Diamond, L. J., and P. K. Jaudes. 1983. Child Abuse in a Cerebral-Palsied Population. *Developmental Medicine and Child Neurology* 25: 169–174.

Diawara, Manthia. 1988. Black Spectatorship: Problems of Identification and Resistance. *Screen* 29, no. 4 (Autumn): 66–76.

Dillon, Kathleen M. 1993. Facilitated Communication, Autism, and Ouija. *Skeptical Inquirer* 17, no. 3: 281–287.

Dinnerstein, Dorothy. 1976. *The Mermaid and the Minotaur.* New York: Harper and Row.

Doane, Janice, and Devon Hodges. 1992. *From Klein to Kristeva: Psychoanalytic Feminism and the Search for the "Good Enough" Mother.* Ann Arbor: University of Michigan Press.

Doane, Mary Ann. 1982. Film and the Masquerade: Theorising the Female Spectator. *Screen* 23: 3–4 (Sept.-Oct.): 74–87.

———. 1984. The "Woman's Film": Possession and Address. In *Re-vision: Essays in Feminist Film Criticism,* ed. Mary Ann Doane, Patricia Mellencamp, and Linda Williams, 67–80. Frederick, Md.: American Film Institute / University Publications of America.

———. 1986. The Voice in the Cinema: The Articulation of Body and Space. In *Narrative, Apparatus, Ideology: A Film Theory* Reader, ed. Philip Rosen, 335–348. New York: Columbia University Press. Also in *Film Theory and Criticism: An Introductory* Reader, 5th ed., ed. Leo Braudy and Marshal Cohen, 363–375 (New York: Oxford, 1999). (Orig. pub. in *Yale French Studies* 60 [1980]: 33–60.)

———. 1987. *The Desire to Desire: The Woman's Film of the 1940s.* Bloomington: Indiana University Press.

———. 1988–89. Masquerade Reconsidered: Further Thoughts on the Female Spectator. *Discourse* 11, no. 1 (Fall): 42–54.

Doane, Mary Ann, and Janet Bergstrom, eds. 1990. "The Spectatrix." Special issue of *Camera Obscura* 20–21.

Dolar, Mladen. 1996. The Object Voice. In *Gaze and Voice as Love Objects*, ed. Renata Salecl and Slavoj Žižek, 7–31. Durham, N.C.: Duke University Press.

Duchan, Judith Felson. 1993. Issues Raised by Facilitated Communication for Theorizing and Research on Autism. *Journal of Speech and Hearing Research* 36 (December): 1108–1119.

Duke, Patty, and Gloria Hochman. 1995. *A Brilliant Madness: Living with Manic Depressive Illness*. New York: Bantam, 1995.

Duke, Patty, and Kenneth Turan. 1988. *Call Me Anna: The Autobiography of Patty Duke*. New York: Bantam.

Dwyer, J. 1996. Access to Justice for People with Severe Communication Impairment. *Administrative Law Review* 3, no. 2: 73–120.

Eastham, David. 1985. *Understand: Fifty Memowriter Poems*. Ottawa: Oliver Pate.

Eastham, Margaret. 1992. *Silent Words: Forever Friends*. Ottawa: Oliver Pate.

Eberlin, M., G. McConnachie, S. Ibel, and L. Volpe. 1993. Facilitated Communication: A Failure to Replicate the Phenomenon. *Journal of Autism and Developmental Disorders* 23, no. 3: 507–530.

Eissler, K. R. 2001. *Freud and the Seduction Theory: A Brief Love Affair*. Madison, Conn.: International Universities Press.

Enns, Carolyn Zerbe, Cheryl L. McNeilly, Julie Madison Corkery, and Mary S. Gilbert. 1995. The Debate about Delayed Memories of Child Sexual Abuse: A Feminist Perspective. *Counselling Psychologist* 23, no. 2: 181–279.

Erikson, Erik. 1965. *Childhood and Society*. London: Penguin.

Esterson, Allen. 1998. Jeffrey Masson and Freud's Seduction Theory: A New Fable Based on Old Myths. *History of the Human Sciences* 11, no. 1 (February): 1–21.

Etchegoyen, R. Horatio. 1991. *The Fundamentals of Psychoanalytic Technique*. New York: Brunner/Mazel.

Faller, Kathleen Coulborn. 1984. Is the Child Victim of Sexual Abuse Telling the Truth? *Child Abuse and Neglect* 8: 473–481.

Feder Kittay, Eva. 1999. Not *My* Way Sesha, *Your* Way, Slowly. In *Mother Troubles*, ed. Julia E. Hanigsberg and Sara Ruddick, 1–27. Boston: Beacon Press.

———. 2001. When Caring Is Just and Justice Is Caring: Justice and Mental Retardation. *Public Culture* 13, no. 13: 557–580.

Ferenczi, Sandor. 1950. *Sex in Psychoanalysis*. New York: Robert Bruner.

Fishman, Joshua. 1966. *Language Loyalty in the United States*. The Hague, Netherlands: Mouton.

Fletcher, Harvey. 1934. Auditory Perspective: Basic Requirements. *Electrical Engineering* 53: 9–11.

———. 1941. The Stereophonic Sound-Film System—General Theory. *Journal of the Acoustical Society of America* 13, no. 2 (October): 89–99.

Fliess, Robert. 1973. *Symbol, Dream, and Psychosis*. New York: International Universities Press.

Foucault, Michel. 1977. *Language, Counter-Memory, Practice*, trans. Donald F. Bouchard and Sherry Simon. New York: Cornell University Press.

Fraiberg, Selma. 1977. *Insights from the Blind*. New York: Basic Books.

Freud, Anna, and Dorothy Burlingham. 1962. *Infants without Families: The Case for and against Residential Nurseries*. New York: International Universities Press.

———. 1973. Infants without Families: Reports on the Hampstead Nurseries. In *Writings of Anna Freud, vol. 3 (1939–45)*. New York: International Universities Press.

Freud, Sigmund. 1955a. A Child Is Being Beaten: A Contribution to the Study of the Origins of Sexual Perversion. In *The Standard Edition of the Complete Works of Sigmund Freud*, trans. James Strachey, vol. 17: 175–204. London: Hogarth Press. Also in *Collected Papers*, trans. Alix Strachey and James Strachey, vol. 2: 172–201 (London: Hogarth Press). (Orig. pub. 1918.)

———. 1955b. Psycho-Analysis and Telepathy. In *The Standard Edition of the Complete Works of Sigmund Freud*, trans. James Strachey, vol. 18: 177–193. London: Hogarth Press. (Orig. pub. 1921.)

———. 1955c. Dreams and Telepathy. In *The Standard Edition of the Complete Works of Sigmund Freud*, trans. James Strachey, vol. 18: 195–220. London: Hogarth Press. (Orig. pub. 1922.)

———. 1957. A Special Type of Object Choice Made by Men. In *The Standard Edition of the Complete Works of Sigmund Freud*, trans. James Strachey, vol. 11: 163–175. London: Hogarth Press. (Orig. pub. 1910.)

———. 1958a. Remembering, Repeating, and Working Through. In *The Standard Edition of the Complete Works of Sigmund Freud*, trans. James Strachey, vol. 12: 145–155. London: Hogarth Press. (Orig. pub. 1914.)

———. 1958b. Observations on Transference Love. In *The Standard Edition of the Complete Works of Sigmund Freud*, trans. James Strachey, vol. 12: 157–171. London: Hogarth Press. (Orig. pub. 1915.)

Freud, Sigmund and Josef Breuer. 1957. Studies on Hysteria. In *The Standard Edition of the Complete Works of Sigmund Freud*, trans. James Strachey, vol. II: 48–106. London: Hogarth Press. (Orig. pub. 1895.)

Frith, Uta. 1989. *Autism: Explaining the Enigma*. London: Blackwell.

Frontline. 1993. Prisoners of Silence. Televised news program. Arlington, Va.: Public Broadcasting Service.

Fuss, Diana. 1990. *Essentially Speaking: Feminism, Nature, and Difference*. New York: Routledge.

———. 2004. *The Sense of an Interior: Four Rooms and the Writers that Shaped Them*. New York: Routledge.

Gannon, Jack R. 1981. *Deaf Heritage: A Narrative History of Deaf America*. Silver Spring, Md.: National Association of the Deaf.

Gardner, Martin. 2000. The Brutality of Dr. Bettelheim. *Skeptical Inquirer* 24, no. 6: 12–14.

———. 2001. Facilitated Communication: A Cruel Farce. *Skeptical Inquirer* 25, no. 1: 17–19.

Garity, William E., and J. N. A. Hawkins. 1941. Fantasound. *Journal of the Society of Motion Pictures Engineers* 37, no. 2 (August): 127–146.

Garland-Thomson, Rosemarie. Forthcoming. *Staring: How We Look*. New York: Oxford University Press.

Gesell, Arnold. 1941. *Wolf Child and Human Child*. New York: Harper and Brothers.

Gilligan, Carol. 1982. *In a Different Voice*. Cambridge, Mass.: Harvard University Press.

Ginsburg, Faye, and Rayna Rapp. 2001. Enabling Disability: Rewriting Kinship, Reimagining Citizenship. *Public Culture* 13: 533–556.

Gledhill, Christine, ed. 1990. *Home Is Where the Heart Is: Studies In Women's Melodrama and The Woman's Film*. London: British Film Institute.

———. 2000. Rethinking Genre. In *Rethinking Film Studies*, ed. Christine Gledhill and Linda Williams, 221–243. London: Arnold.

Glickman, Neil S., and J. C. Carey. 1993. Measuring Deaf Cultural Identities: A Preliminary Investigation. *Rehabilitation Psychology* 38: 275–283.

Goodman, Gail S., S. Ghetti, J. A. Quas, R. S. Edelstein, K. W. Alexander, A. D. Redlich, I. M. Cordon, and D. P. Jones. 2003. A Prospective Study of Memory for Child Sexual Abuse: New Findings Relevant to the Repressed/Lost Memory Controversy. *Psychological Science* 14: 113–118.

Goodwin, Charles. 2003a. Conversational Frameworks for the Accomplishment of Meaning in Aphasia. In *Conversation and Brain Damage*, ed. Charles Goodwin, 90–116. Oxford: Oxford University Press.

———. 2003b. Pointing as Situated Practice. In *Pointing: Where Language, Culture and Cognition Meet*, ed. Kita Sotaro, 217–241. Mahwah, N.J.: Lawrence Erlbaum.

———. 2003c. The Semiotic Body in its Environment. In *Discourses of the Body*, ed. Justine Coupland and Richard Gwyn, 19–42. New York: Palgrave / Macmillan.

Goodwin, M. S., and T. C. Goodwin. 1969. In a Dark Mirror. *Mental Hygiene* 53: 550.

Graham, Allison. 1981. *Lindsay Anderson*. Boston: Twayne.

Grandin, Temple. 1996. *Thinking in Pictures and Other Reports from My Life with Autism*. New York: Vintage.

Gray, Daphne. 1995. *Yes You Can, Heather!* Grand Rapids, Mich.: Zondervan.

Green, André. 1970. L'Écran bi-face, un oeil derrière la tête. *Psychanalyse et cinema* 1 (January): 15–22.

———. 1978. Potential Space in Psychoanalysis: The Object in the Setting. In *Between Reality and Fantasy*, ed. S. Grolnick. New York: Aronson.

———. 1986. *On Private Madness*. London: Hogarth Press.

———. 1999a. *The Fabric of Affect in the Psychoanalytic Discourse*. Trans. Alan Sheridan. London: Routledge. (Orig. pub. as *Le Discours vivant*, 1973.)

———. 1999b. On Discriminating and Not Discriminating Between Affect and Representation. *International Journal of Psycho-analysis* 80: 277–316.

Green, G., and H. Shane. 1994. Science, Reason and Facilitated Communication. *Journal of the Association for Persons with Severe Handicaps* 19, no. 2: 151–172.

Grimké, Angelina E. 1836. *Appeal to the Christian Women of the South*. New York: Anti-Slavery Society.

Gross, Paul R., and Norman Levitt. 1994. *Higher Superstition: The Academic Left and Its Quarrels with Science*. Baltimore, Md.: Johns Hopkins University Press.

Grosz, Elizabeth. 1990. "Lacan and Feminism," *Jacques Lacan: A Feminist Introduction*. London: Routledge.

———. 1994. *Volatile Bodies: Toward a Corporeal Feminism*. Bloomington: Indiana University Press.

Grusin, Richard. 1994. What Is an Electronic Author? Theory and the Technological Fallacy. *Configurations* 2, no. 3: 469–483.

H., Barbie. 2003. Heather Whitestone. *Teen Ink*, February 2003.

Haaken, Janice. 1996. The Recovery of Memory, Fantasy, and Desire: Feminist Approaches to Sexual Abuse and Psychic Trauma. *Signs* 21, no. 4: 1069–1094.

———. 1998. *Pillar of Salt: Gender, Memory and the Politics of Looking Back*. New Brunswick, N.J.: Rutgers University Press.

Hanley, Francine Teresa. 2005. The Dynamic Body Image and the Moving Body: A Theoretical and Empirical Investigation. Ph.D. dissertation, Victoria University Melbourne, Victoria, Australia.

Hansen, Miriam. 1986. Pleasure, Ambivalence, and Identification: Valentino and Film Spectatorship. *Cinema Journal* 24, no. 4: 6–32.

Haraway, Donna. 1991. *Simians, Cyborgs and Women: The Reinvention of Nature*. New York: Routledge.

Harlow, Harry Frederick. 1961. The Development of Affectional Patterns in Infant Monkeys. In *Determinants of Infant Behavior*, ed. B. M. Foss, vol. 1. London: Methuen.

———. 1963. The Maternal Affectional System. In *Determinants of Infant Behavior*, ed. B. M. Foss, vol. 2. Methuen.

———. 1971. *Learning to Love*. San Francisco: Albion Publishing.

Harris, Elmer. 1988. *Johnny Belinda: A Play in Three Acts*. Dramatist's Play Service.

Harris, Sylvan. 1940. The Control of Sound. *Journal of the Society of Motion Picture Engineers* 35, no. 2 (August 1940): 111–125.

Haskell, Molly. 1973. *From Reverence to Rape*. Chicago: University of Chicago Press.

Heinrichs, P. 1992a. State "Tortured" Family: Landmark Case Finds Experts' Naivety "Tragic." *Sunday Age*, February 16, B1.

———. 1992b. Suffering at the Hands of the Protectors. *Sunday Age*, February 16, A1.

Herald-Tribune. 1940. Ex-Schoolgirl a Bit Dazed by Success. *New York Herald-Tribune*, June 9, 1940, VI-2.

Heung, Marina. 1987. "What's the Matter with Sara Jane?": Daughters and Mothers in Douglas Sirk's Imitation of Life. *Cinema Journal* 26, no. 3: 21–43.

Hillyer, Barbara. 1993. *Feminism and Disability*. Norman: University of Oklahoma Press.

hooks, bell. 1992. The Oppositional Gaze: Black Female Spectators. In *Black Looks: Race and Representation*, 115–131. Boston: South End Press.

Hostler, S. L., J. H. Allaire, and R. A. Christoph. 1993. Childhood Sexual Abuse Reported by Facilitated Communication. *Pediatrics* 91: 1190–1192.

Hutcheson, Francis. 1725. *Inquiry Concerning Moral Good and Evil*. Edinburgh.

Hutchins, Edwin. 1996. *Cognition in the Wild*. Cambridge: MIT Press.

Hutinger, Patricia, and Robert Rippey. 1997. *How Five Preschool Children with Autism Responded to Computers*. The Early Childhood Comprehensive Technology System, funded by the U.S. Department of Education, PR H180U50039, Fall 1997. http://scott.mprojects.wiu.edu/~eccts/articles/autism1.html.

Intellectual Disability Review Panel. 1989. *Report to the Director-General on the Reliability and Validity of Assisted Communication*. Melbourne, Australia: Community Services, Victoria.

Irigaray, Luce. 1977. Women's Exile: Interview with Luce Irigaray. *Ideology and Consciousness* 1: 62–76.

———. 1985a. *Speculum of the Other Woman*. Trans. Gillian C. Gill. Ithaca, N.Y.: Cornell University Press. (Orig. pub. as *Speculum de l'autre femme*, 1974.)

———. 1985b. *This Sex Which Is Not One*. Trans. Catherine Porter. Ithaca, N.Y.: Cornell University Press. (Orig. pub. as *Ce Sexe qui n'en est pas un*, 1977.)

Isaacs, Susan. 1948. On the Nature and Function of Phantasy. *International Journal of Psychoanalysis* 29: 73–97. Reprinted in *Developments in Psycho-Analysis*, ed. Melanie Klein, Paula Heimann, Susan Isaacs, and Joan Riviere, 67–121 (London: Hogarth, 1952).

Itard, J. M. G. 1962. *The Wild Boy of Aveyron*. Trans. G. Humphrey and M. Humphrey. New York: Appleton-Century-Crofts. (Orig. pub. 1801.)

Izard, Carroll E., ed. 1982. *Measuring Emotions in Infants and Children*. Cambridge: Cambridge University Press.

Jacobson, John W., James A. Mulick, and Allen A. Schwartz. 1995. A History of Facilitated Communication: Science, Pseudoscience, and Antiscience. Science Working Group on Facilitated Communication. *American Psychologist* 50, no. 9: 750–765.

Jardine, Alice. 1985. *Gynesis: Configurations of Woman and Modernity.* Ithaca, N.Y.: Cornell University Press.

Jaudes, J. K., and M. Martone. 1992. Interdisciplinary Evaluations of Alleged Sexual Abuse Cases. *Pediatrics* 89: 1164–1168.

Jay, Martin. 1993. *Downcast Eyes: The Denigration of Vision in Twentieth-Century French Thought.* Berkeley: University of California Press.

Jones, Ernest. 1927. The Early Development of Female Sexuality. *International Journal of Psycho-analysis* 8, no. 4: 459–472.

Kanner, Leo. 1946. Autistic Disturbances of Affective Contact. *American Journal of Psychiatry* 103: 242–246.

Kaplan, E. Ann. 1990. Introduction to *Psychoanalysis and Cinema*, ed. E. Ann Kaplan. London: Routledge.

———. 1992. *Motherhood and Representation: The Mother in Popular Culture and Melodrama.* London: Routledge.

Keller, Helen. 1985. *Teacher: Anne Sullivan Macy.* Westport, CT: Greenwood Press.

Kempe, Henry. 1962. The Battered-Child Syndrome. *Journal of the American Medical Association* 181 no. 1: 7–24.

Kempley, Rita. 1986. Children of a Lesser God. *Washington Post*, October 3.

Kezuka, Emiko. 1997. The Role of Touch in Facilitated Communication. *Journal of Autism and Developmental Disorders* 27, no. 5: 571–593.

Klapholz, Jesse. 1991. Fantasia: Innovations in Sound. *Journal of the Audio Engineering Society* 39, nos. 1–2: 66–70.

Klapper, Joseph T. 1960. *The Effects of Mass Communication.* New York: Free Press.

Klein, Melanie. 1952a. Notes on Some Schizoid Mechanisms. In *Developments in Psycho-Analysis*, by Melanie Klein, Paula Heimann, Susan Isaacs, and Joan Riviere, 292–320. London: Hogarth. Also in *Envy and Gratitude and Other Works, 1946–1963*, by Melanie Klein, 1–14 (1957; London: Vintage, 1997). (Orig. pub. *International Journal of Psycho-Analysis* 27 [1946]: 99–110.)

———. 1952b. Some Theoretical Conclusions Regarding the Emotional Life of the Infant. In *Developments in Psycho-Analysis*, by Melanie Klein, Paula Heimann, Susan Isaacs, and Joan Riviere, 198–236. London: Hogarth. Also in *Envy and Gratitude and Other Works, 1946–1963*, by Melanie Klein, 61–93 (1957; Vintage, London, 1997).

———. 1955. On Identification. In *New Directions in Psycho-Analysis*, ed. Melanie Klein, Paula Heimann, and Roger Money-Kyrle, 309–345 (London: Tavistock).

———. 1975a. The Importance of Symbol-Formation in the Development of the Ego. In *The Writings of Melanie Klein*, vol. 2. London: Hogarth Press. (Orig. pub. *International Journal of Psychoanalysis* 11 [1930]: 24–39.)

———. 1975b. The Psychoanalysis of Children. In *The Writings of Melanie Klein*, vol. 2. London: Hogarth Press. (Orig. pub. 1932.)

Klinger, Barbara. 1994. *Melodrama and Meaning: History, Culture, and the Films of Douglas Sirk*. Bloomington: Indiana University Press.

Kohut, Heinz. 1971. *The Analysis of the Self: A Systematic Approach to the Treatment of Narcissistic Personality Disorders*. New York: International Universities Press.

———. 1984. *How Does Analysis Cure?* Chicago: University of Chicago Press.

Konstantareas, M. Mary, Joel Oxman, and Chris D. Webster. 1977. Simultaneous Communication with Autistic and Other Severely Dysfunctional Nonverbal Children. *Journal of Communication Disorders* 10: 267–282.

Kozloff, Sarah. 2000. *Overhearing Film Dialogue*, Berkeley: University of California Press.

Kristeva, Julia. 1982. *Powers of Horror: An Essay on Abjection*. Trans. Leon S. Roudiez. New York: Columbia University Press. (Orig. pub. as *Pouvoirs de l'horreur*, 1980.)

———.1984. *Revolution in Poetic Language*. Trans. Margaret Waller. New York: Columbia University Press. (Orig. pub. as *La Révolution du langage poétique*, 1974.)

———. 1989. *Black Sun: Depression and Melancholia*. Trans. Leon S. Roudiez. New York: Columbia University Press.

———. 1995. *New Maladies of the Soul*. Trans. Ross Guberman. New York: Columbia University Press.

———. 2000. From Symbols to Flesh: The Polymorphous Destiny of Narration. *International Journal of Psychoanalysis* 81.

———. 2001a. *Melanie Klein*. Ross Guberman. New York: Columbia University Press.

———. 2001b. *Hannah Arendt*. Trans. Ross Guberman. New York: Columbia University Press.

Kuhn, Annette. 1992. *Mandy* and Possibility. *Screen* 33, no. 3 (Autumn): 233–243.

Kurlychek, Ken. 1997. A First Language: Whose Choice Is It? Laurent Clerc National Deaf Education Center, Gallaudet University. http://clerccenter.gallaudet.edu/products/Sharing-Ideas/afirst/emphasis.html (accessed March 2006).

Lacan, Jacques. 1977a. The Mirror Stage As Formative of the Function of the *I* As Revealed in Psychoanalytic Experience. In *Écrits: A Selection*, by Jacques Lacan, trans. Alan Sheridan, 1–7. New York: W. W. Norton. (Orig. a paper for the 16th International Congress of Psychoanalysis, Zürich, July 17, 1949.)

————. 1977b. On a Question Preliminary to Any Possible Treatment of Psychosis. In *Écrits: A Selection*, by Jacques Lacan, trans. Alan Sheridan. New York: W. W. Norton. (Orig. pub. 1957.)

————. 1988. Seminar I. In *The Seminars of Jacques Lacan*, book 1, *Freud's Papers on Technique, 1953–1954*, ed. Jacques-Alain Miller, trans. J. Forrester. New York: W. W. Norton. (Orig. pub. 1954.)

Lambert, Gavin. 1952. Mandy (review essay). *Sight and Sound* 22, no. 2: 77–78.

Landsman, Gail. 1999. Does God Give Special Kids to Special Parents? Personhood and the Child with Disabilities as Gift and as Giver. In *Transformative Motherhood: On Giving and Getting in a Consumer Culture*, ed. Linda L. Layne. New York: New York University Press.

Landy, Marcia. 1991. *British Genres, 1930–1960*. Princeton, N.J.: Princeton University Press.

Lane, Harlan L., Robert Hoffmeister, and Benjamin J. Bahan. 1996. *A Journey into the Deaf-World*. San Diego, Calif.: Dawnsign Press.

Laplanche, J., and J.-B. Pontalis. 1973. *The Language of Psycho-analysis*. Trans. Donald Nicholson-Smith. New York: W. W. Norton. (Orig. pub. as *Vocabulaire de Psychoanalyse*, 1967.)

Lastra, James. 1994. Standards and Practices: Aesthetic Norm and Technological Innovation in the American Cinema. In *The Studio System*, ed. Janet Staiger, 200–222. New Brunswick, N.J.: Rutgers University Press.

————. 2000. *Sound Technology and the American Cinema: Perception, Representation, Modernity*. New York: Columbia University Press.

Latour, Bruno. 1999. *Pandora's Hope: Essays on the Reality of Science Studies*. Cambridge, Mass.: Harvard University Press.

Lax, Ruth F. 1992. A Variation on Freud's Theme in "A Child Is Being Beaten" — Mother's Role: Some Implications for Superego Development in Women. *Journal of the American Psychoanalytic Association* 40: 455–473.

Lazarsfeld, Paul and Herbert Menzel. 1963. Mass Media and Personal Influence. In *The Science of Human Communication*, ed. Wilbur Schramm, 94–115. New York: Basic Books.

Lenneberg, Eric. 1964. The Capacity of Language Acquisition. In *The Structure of Language: Reading in the Philosophy of Language*, ed. Jerry Alan Fodor and Jerrold Katz. Englewood Cliffs, N.J.: Prentice Hall.

————. 1967. *Biological Foundations of Language*. New York: John Wiley and Sons.

————. Lerner, Gerda. 1998. *The Grimké Sisters from South Carolina*. New York: Oxford University Press. (Orig. pub. 1967.)

Levesque, Jack. 2001. CBS Hurt Deaf Children with *Caitlin's Story*. In *Deaf World: A Historical Reader and Sourcebook*, ed. Lois Bragg, 40–42. New York: New York University Press.

Levinas, Emmanuel. 1999. *Alterity and Transcendence*. Trans. Michael B. Smith. New York: Columbia University Press.

Light, Alison. 1991. *Forever England: Femininity, Literature and Conservatism between the Wars*. New York: Routledge.

Ling, Daniel. 1976. *Speech and the Hearing-Impaired Child*. Washington, D.C.: The Alexander Graham Bell Association for the Deaf.

Lister, Ruth. 1997. *Citizenship: Feminist Perspectives*. New York: New York University Press.

LoBrutto, Vincent. 1994. Interview with Paul Zydel. In *Sound-on-Film: Interview with Creators of Sound*, ed. Vincent LoBrutto, 101–108. Westport, Conn.: Praeger.

London Times. 1952. New Films in London: An Unusual Theme. August 4: 9.

Lorber, Howard Z. N.d. The Abusive Male: Affect Hunger and the Loss of Self. http://allbluescounseling.com/abusive_male%20and%20affect%20hunger .htm (accessed June 2007).

Macalpine, Ida, and Richard A. Hunter. 1956. *Schizophrenia 1677: A Psychiatric Study of an Illustrated Autobiographical Record of Demoniacal Possession*. London: William Dawson and Sons.

Mahler, Margaret S. 1963. Thoughts about Development and Individuation. *Psychoanalytic Study of the Child* 18: 307–324.

———. 1966. Notes on the Development of Basic Moods: The Depressive Affect. In *Drives, Affects, Behavior*, ed. M. Schur, vol. 2, 161–169. New York: International Universities Press.

———. 1972. On the First Three Phases of the Separation-Individuation Process. *International Journal of Psychoanalysis* 53: 333–338.

Mahler, Margaret S., with M. Furer. 1968. *On Human Symbiosis and the Vicissitudes of Individuation*. New York: International Universities Press.

Makarushka, M. 1991. The Words They Can't Say. *New York Times Magazine*, October 6, 32.

Mannoni, Maud. 1972. *The Backward Child and His Mother: A Psychoanalytic Study*. Ed. R. D. Laing, trans. A. M. Sheridan Smith. World of Man: A Library of Theory and Research in the Human Sciences. New York: Pantheon Books. (Orig. pub. 1964.)

Mannus, Margaret. 2001. What's in a Word: Studies in Phonosemantics. Ph.D. dissertation, University of Trondheim, Norway.

Margolin, K. N. 1994. How Shall Facilitated Communication Be Judged? FC and the Legal System. In *Facilitated Communication: The Clinical and Social Phenomenon*, ed. Howard C. Shane, 227–258. San Diego, Calif.: Singular Press.

Marks, Laura U. 2002. *Touch: Sensuous Theory and Multisensory Media*. Minneapolis: University of Minnesota Press.

Marks, Martin. 1996. The Sound of Music. In *The Oxford History of World Cinema*, ed. Geoffrey Nowell-Smith, 248–258. New York: Oxford University Press.

Martin, E. 1993. Facilitation Theory Tested. *Times Herald Record*, July 31: 1, 18.

Masson, Jeffrey. 1984a. *The Assault on Truth: Freud's Suppression of the Seduction Theory*. New York: Farrar, Straus and Giroux. (New ed. 1985.)

———. 1984b. In Response to a Case of Hysteria (April 12, 1984). *New York Review of Books* 31, no. 13, August 16.

Matter of Luz P. 1993. 92–07565, New York State Supreme Court Appellate Division, Second Judicial Department, Opinion and Order, January 14, 1993, 189 A.D. 2d 274, 595 N.Y.S. 2d 541.

Matter of M.Z. 1992. 590 N.Y.S. 2d 390 (Fam. Ct.).

Mayne, Judith. 1990. *The Woman at the Keyhole: Feminism and Women's Cinema*. Bloomington: Indiana University Press.

———. 1993. *Cinema and Spectatorship*. New York: Routledge.

———. 1994. *Directed by Dorothy Arzner*. Bloomington: Indiana University Press.

McGinn, Robert E. 1983. Stokowski and the Bell Telephone Laboratories: Collaboration in the Development of High-Fidelity Sound Reproduction. *Technology and Culture* 24, no. 1 (Jan.): 38–75.

McLuhan, Marshall. 1994. *Understanding Media: The Extensions of Man*. Cambridge: MIT Press. (Orig. pub. 1964.)

McLuhan, Marshall, and Quentin Fiore. 2001. *The Medium Is the Massage: An Inventory of Effects*. Corte Madera, Calif.: Gingko Press (Orig. pub. 1967.)

Melville, Herman. 1962. *Billy Budd: Sailor*. Chicago: University of Chicago Press. (Orig. pub. 1924.)

Mercer, Jean, Larry Sarner, and Linda Rosa. 2003. *Attachment Therapy on Trial: The Torture and Death of Candace Newmaker*. Westport, Conn.: Praeger.

Metz, Christian. 1982. *The Imaginary Signifier: Psychoanalysis and the Cinema*. Bloomington: Indiana University Press. (Orig. pub. as *Le Significant imaginaire*, 1977.)

Metzl, Jonatha. 2003. *Prozac on the Couch*. Durham, N.C.: Duke University Press.

Miller, Alice. 1985. The Political Consequences of Child Abuse. *Journal of Psychohistory* 26, no. 2 (Fall).

Miller, William. 1993. *Humiliation*. Ithaca, N.Y.: Cornell University Press.

———. 1997. *The Anatomy of Disgust*. Cambridge, Mass.: Harvard University Press.

Mitchell, Juliet. 1975. *Psychoanalysis and Feminism: Freud, Reich, Laing, and Women*. New York: Vintage. (Orig. pub. 1974.)

Modleski, Tania. 1982. *Loving with a Vengeance: Mass-Produced Fantasies for Women*. Hamden: Archon.

———. 1987. Time and Desire in the Woman's Film. In *Home Is Where the Heart Is: Studies in Melodrama and the Woman's Film*, ed. Christine Gledhill, 326–338. London: BFI.

Moi, Toril. 1985. *Sexual/Textual Politics: Feminist Literary Theory*. New York: Routledge.

Montrelay, Michele. 1978. Inquiry into Femininity. Trans. Parveen Adams. *m/f* 1: 83–101.

Moruzzi, Norma Claire. 2001. *Speaking through the Mask: Hannah Arendt and the Politics of Social Identity*. Ithaca, N.Y.: Cornell University Press.

Mueller, W. A. 1940. Audience Noise as a Limitation to the Permissible Volume Range of Dialog in Sound Motion Pictures. *Journal of the Society of Motion Picture Engineers* 35 (July): 48.

Mukhopadhyay, Tito Rajarshi. 1999. When Silence Speaks: The Way My Mother Taught Me. Paper delivered at the Autism 99 conference. http://trainland .tripod.com/rajarshi.htm (accessed October 2005).

———. 2000. *Beyond the Silence: My Life, the World and Autism*. London: National Autistic Society.

———. 2003. *The Mind Tree: A Miraculous Child Breaks the Silence of Autism*. New York: Arcade. (Rev. ed. of Tito Rajarshi Mukhopadhyay, *Beyond the Silence*, 2000.)

Mulvey, Laura. 1975. Visual Pleasure and Narrative Cinema. *Screen* 16, no. 3 (Autumn). Reprinted in *Narrative, Apparatus, Ideology: A Film Theory Reader*, ed. Philip Rosen (New York: Columbia University Press), 1985.

———. 1989. *Visual and Other Pleasures*. Bloomington: Indiana University Press.

National Institutes of Health. 1995. Cochlear Implants in Adults and Children. National Institutes of Health Consensus Development Conference Statement, May 15–17. See http://consensus.nih.gov/1995/1995cochlearimplants100html .htm (accessed June 2007).

National Resource Center on Child Sexual Abuse. 1991. *Current Trends in Child Abuse Reporting and Fatalities: Results of Annual 50 State Survey 1991*. Chicago: Deborah Daro.

Negulesco, Jean. 1984. *Things I Did and Things I Think I Did*. New York: Linden Press, Simon and Schuster.

Nussbaum, Martha. 2004. *Hiding from Humanity: Disgust, Shame and the Law*. Princeton, N.J.: Princeton University Press.

Oliver, Kelly. 1993. *Reading Kristeva: Unraveling the Double-bind*. Bloomington: Indiana University Press.

Oppenheim, R. 1974. *Effective Teaching Methods for Autistic Children*. Springfield, Ill.: C. C. Thomas.

Ozick, Cynthia. 2003. What Helen Keller Saw. *The New Yorker*, June 16 and 23, 188–196.

Padden, Carol, and Tom Humphries. 1988. *Deaf in America: Voices from a Culture*. Cambridge, Mass.: Harvard University Press.

———. 2005. *Inside Deaf Culture*. Cambridge, Mass.: Harvard University Press.

Park, Shelley M. 1997. False Memory Syndrome: A Feminist Philosophical Perspective. *Hypatia* 12, no. 2: 1–50.

Pelka, Fred. 2001. Helen Keller and the FBI. *Ragged Edge Online* 5, September. http://www.ragged-edge-mag.com/0901/0901ft3.htm.

Pendergrast, Mark. 1996. *Victims of Memory: Sex Abuse Accusations and Shattered Lives.* 2nd ed. Hinesburg, Vt.: Upper Access. (Orig. pub. 1995.)

Perelberg, Rozine Jozef. 1999. The Interplay of Identifications: Violence, Hysteria, and the Repudiation of Femininity. In *The Dead Mother: The Work of André Green*, ed. Gregorio Kohon. London: Routledge.

Perry, Mark. 2003. *Lift Up Thy Voice: The Grimké Family's Journey from Slaveholders to Civil Rights Leaders.* New York: Penguin.

Pezdek, Kathy, and William Banks, eds. 1996. *The Recovered Memory/False Memory Debate.* San Diego, Calif.: Academic Press.

Plaza, Monique. 1978. "Phallomorphic Power" and the Psychology of "Woman." *Ideology and Consciousness* 4.

Press, Nancy A., and Carol H. Browner. 1997. Provisional Normalcy and "Perfect Babies": Pregnant Women's Attitudes toward Disability in the Context of Prenatal Testing. In *Reproducing Reproduction: Kinship, Power and Technological Innovation*, ed. Sarah Franklin and Helena Ragone, 46–65. Philadelphia: University of Pennsylvania Press.

Prior, Margot, and Robert Cummins. 1992. Questions about Facilitated Communication and Autism. *Journal of Autism and Developmental Disorders* 22, no. 3: 331–338.

Pullen, Gloria, and Rachel Sutton-Spence. 1993. The British Deaf Community During the 1939–1945 War. In *Looking Back: A Reader on the History of Deaf Communities and Their Sign Languages*, ed. Renate Fischer and Harlan Lane, 171–176. Hamburg: Signum Press.

Rado, Sandor. 1956. *Psychoanalysis of Behavior: Collected Papers.* New York: Grune and Stratton.

Randall, G. 1993. Live-in Aid Convicted of Sexual Abuse. *Wichita Eagle*, March 30: 1a; March 31: 8a.

Reiskind, H. I. 1941. Multiple-Speaker Reproducing Systems for Motion Pictures. *Journal of the Society of Motion Picture Engineers* 37, no. 2 (August): 154–163.

Renov, Michael. 2004. *The Subject of Documentary.* Minneapolis: University of Minnesota Press.

Rimland, B. 1992a. Facilitated Communication: Now the Bad News. *Autism Research Review International* 6, no. 1: 3.

———. 1992b. Facilitated Communication: What's Going On? *Autism Research Review International* 6, no. 4: 2–3.

———. 1992c. A Facilitated Communication "Horror Story." *Autism Research Review International* 6, no. 1: 7–8.

Rocha, Adriana. 1995. *A Child of Eternity*. New York: Ballantine Books.

Rodowick, D. N. 1982. The Difficulty of Difference. *Wide Angle* 5, no. 1: 4–15.

———. 1991. *The Difficulty of Difference: Psychoanalysis, Sexual Difference, and Film Theory*. New York: Routledge.

Rosalato, Guy. 1974. La Voix: entre corps et langage. *Revue française de psychoanalyse* 38, no. 1 (January): 75–94.

Rose, Jacqueline. 1986. *Sexuality in the Field of Vision*. London: Verso.

Roser, K. 1996. A Review of Psychoanalytic Theory and Treatment of Childhood Autism. *Psychoanalytic Review* 83: 325–341.

Rupp, Leila J., and Verta Taylor. 1987. *Survival in the Doldrums: The American Women's Rights Movement, 1945 to the 1960s*. New York: Oxford University Press.

Rustin, Michael. 1991. *The Good Society and the Inner World*. London: Verso.

Rycroft, Charles. 1984. A Case of Hysteria. *New York Review of Books* 36, no. 6.

Sabin, Laural A., and Anne M. Donnellan. 1993. A Qualitative Study of the Process of Facilitated Communication. *Journal of the Association for Persons with Severe Handicaps* 18, no. 3: 200–211.

Sacks, Oliver. 1987. *Awakenings*. New York: E. P. Dutton.

Salecl, Renata, and Slavoj Žižek. 1996. *Gaze and Voice as Love Objects*. Durham, N.C.: Duke University Press.

Scalia, Joseph. 2002. *Intimate Violence: Attacks upon Psychic Interiority*. New York: Columbia University Press.

Schawlow, Arthur T., and Aurelia L. Schawlow. 1985. The Endless Search for Help. In *Integrating Moderately and Severely Handicapped Learners: Strategies That Work*, ed. M. F. Brady and P. Gunther. Springfield, Ill.: Charles Thomas Publishing.

Scheiner, Georganne, 2000. *Signifying Female Adolescence: Film Representation and Fans, 1920–1950*. Westport, Conn.: Praeger.

Schiff, A. W., and J. L. Schiff. 1971. Passivity. *Transactional Analysis Journal* 1, no. 1: 71–78.

Schiff, J. L., A. W. Schiff, K. Mellor, E. Schiff, S. Schiff, D. Richman, J. Fishman, L. Wolz, C. Fishman, and D. Momb. 1975. *Cathexis Reader: Transactional Analysis Treatment of Psychosis*. New York: Harper and Row.

Schilder, Paul. 1978. *The Image and Appearance of the Human Body*. New York: International Universities Press. (Orig. pub. 1935.)

Schopler, E. 1992. Editorial commentary. *Journal of Autism and Developmental Disorders* 22: 337–338.

Schuchman, John S. 1988. *Hollywood Speaks: Deafness and the Film Entertainment Industry*. Urbana: University of Illinois Press.

Scriven, E. O. 1934. Auditory Perspective: Amplifiers. *Electrical Engineering* 53: 25–28.

Sedgwick, Eve Kosofsky. 1990. *Epistemology of the Closet*. Berkeley: University of California Press.

———. 2003. *Touching Feeling: Affect, Pedagogy, Performativity*. Durham, N.C.: Duke University Press.

Sedgwick, Eve Kosofsky, and Adam Frank. 1995. *Shame and Its Sisters: A Silvan Tomkins Reader*. Durham, N.C.: Duke University Press.

Segal, Hanna. 1964. *Introduction to the Work of Melanie Klein*. London: Hogarth. (Reprint, Karnac, 1988.)

———.1980. *Melanie Klein*. New York: Viking Press.

———. 1981. *The Work of Hanna Segal: A Kleinian Approach to Clinical Practice*. Aronson. (Reprint, Free Association Books / Maresfield Library, 1986.)

———. 1987. Silence is the Real Crime. *International Review of Psycho-Analysis* 14: 3–12. Reprinted in *Psychoanalysis and the Nuclear Threat: Clinical and Theoretical Studies*, ed. J. B. Levine et al., 35–58 (Hillside, N.J.: Analytic Press, 1988); and in Hanna Segal, *Psychoanalysis, Literature and War: Papers 1972–1995*, ed. John Steiner. (Routledge: London, 1997).

———. N.d. Biography written for the Romanian edition of *The Writings of Melanie Klein* in four volumes. Binghamton, N.Y.: *Esf* Publishers. http://vatlin.chat.ru/ Klein_biography_eng.htm (accessed April 2005).

Shane, Howard C., ed. 1994. *Facilitated Communication: The Clinical and Social Phenomenon*. San Diego: Singular Press.

Shane, Howard C., and K. Kearns. 1994. An Examination of the Role of the "Facilitator" in "Facilitated Communication." *American Journal of Speech-Language Pathology* 3: 48–54.

Siegel, Bryna. 1995. Brief Report: Assessing Allegations of Sexual Molestation Made through Facilitated Communication. *Journal of Autism and Developmental Disorders* 25, no. 3: 319–326.

Silet, Charles L. P. 1998. *Lindsay Anderson: A Guide to References and Resources*. Boston: G. K. Hall.

Silliman, E. R. 1992. Three Perspectives on Facilitated Communication: Unexpected Literacy, Clever Hans, or Enigma? *Topics in Language Disorders* 12, no. 4: 60–68.

Silverman, Kaja. 1983. *The Subject of Semiotics*. New York: Oxford University Press.

———. 1988. *The Acoustic Mirror: The Female Voice in Psychoanalysis and Cinema*. Bloomington: Indiana University Press.

———. 1992. *Male Subjectivity at the Margins*. New York: Routledge.

———. 1996. *The Threshold of the Visible World*. New York: Routledge.

———. 2000. *World Spectators*. Stanford, Calif.: Stanford University Press.

Slide, Anthony. 1986. *American Film Industry: A Historical Dictionary*. New York: Greenwood Press.

Smith, Adam. 1966. *The Theory of Moral Sentiments*. London: Henry G. Bohn. (Orig. pub. 1759.)

Sobchack, Vivian. 2004. *Carnal Thoughts: Embodiment and Moving Image Culture*. Berkeley: University of California Press.

Spake, A. 1992. It Is Like Wishing I Could Be Normal. *Washington Post Magazine*, May 31, 16–30.

Spitz, René. 1955. The Primal Cavity: A Contribution to the Genesis of Perception and its Role for Psychoanalytic Theory. *The Psychoanalytic Study of the Child* 10. New York: International Universities Press, 215–240.

———. 1959. *A Genetic Field Theory of Ego Formation*. New York: International Universities Press.

———. 1965. *The First Year of Life: A Psychoanalytic Study of Normal and Deviant Object Relations*. New York: International Universities Press.

Spitz, René and Katherine M. Wolf. 1972. The Smiling Response: A Contribution to the Ontogenesis of Social Relations. In *Facial Expression in Children: Three Studies*, ed. Ruth Washburn, René Spitz and Frances Goodenough. New York: Arno Press.

Spitzer, R. L. 1981. The Diagnostic Status of Homosexuality in DSM-III: A Reformulation of the Issues. *American Journal of Psychiatry* 138: 210–215.

Spruiell, Vann. 1972–73. Thinking Blind. Unpublished paper presented at the Fourth Annual Maurice Friend Lecture, New York, 1984.http://www.analysis .com/vs/vs84b.html (accessed June 2006).

Stacey, Jackie. 1994. *Star Gazing: Hollywood Cinema and Female Spectatorship*. London: Routledge.

Stam, Robert, Robert Burgoyne, and Sandy Flitterman-Lewis. 1992. *New Vocabularies in Film Semiotics: Structuralism, Post-Structuralism, and Beyond*. New York: Routledge.

Steinberg, J. C., and W. B. Snow. 1934. Auditory Perspective: Physical Factors. *Electrical Engineering* 53: 12–17.

Steinberg, J. C., H. C. Montgomery, and M. B. Gardner. 1940. Results of the World's Fair Hearing Test. *Journal of the Acoustic Society of America* 12 (October): 291–301.

Stepansky, Paul E., comp. and ed. 1988. *The Memoirs of Margaret S. Mahler*. Hillsdale, N.J.: Analytic Press.

Stern, Daniel. 1985. *The Interpersonal World of the Infant*. New York: Basic Books.

Sterne, Jonathan. 2003. *The Audible Past: Cultural Origins of Sound Reproduction*. Durham, N.C.: Duke University Press.

Stokoe, William. 1960. *Sign Language Structure: An Outline of the Visual Communication Systems of the American Deaf*. Buffalo, N.Y.: Department of Anthropology and Linguistics, University of Buffalo.

Strozier, Charles B. 2001. *Author, Heinz Kohut: The Making of a Psychoanalyst*. New York: Farrar, Straus and Giroux.

Summit, R., and J. Kryso. 1978. Sexual Abuse of Children: A Clinical Spectrum. *American Journal of Orthopsychiatry* 48: 237–251.

Sussex, Elizabeth. 1970. *Lindsay Anderson*. London: Praeger.

tenBroek, Jacobus. 1995. The Neurotic Blind and the Neurotic Sighted, Twin Psychological Fallacies. National Federation of the Blind. http://www.blind.net/bpba1951.htm.

Thom, Randy. N.d. Are Movies Getting Too Loud? FilmSound.org. http://www.filmsound.org/randythom/loud-movies.htm (accessed June 2004).

Thompson, Emily. 2002. *The Soundscape of Modernity: Architectural Acoustics and the Culture of Listening in America, 1900–1933*. Cambridge: MIT Press.

Tomkins, Silvan. 1962. *Affect, Imagery, Consciousness*, vol. 1, *The Positive Affects*. New York: Springer.

———. 1963. *Affect, Imagery, Consciousness*, vol. 2, *The Negative Affects*. New York: Springer.

———. 1980. Affect as Amplification: Some Modifications in Theory. In *Emotion: Theory, Research, and Experience*, vol. 1, *Theories of Emotion*, ed. R. Plutchik and H. Kellerman, 141–164. New York: Academic Press.

———. 1991. *Affect, Imagery, Consciousness*, vol. 3, *The Negative Affects: Anger and Fear*. New York: Springer.

———. 1992. *Affect, Imagery, Consciousness*, vol. 4, *Cognition, Duplication, and Transformation of Information*. New York: Springer.

Trumpbour, John. 2001. *Selling Hollywood to the World: US and European Struggles for Mastery of the Global Film Industry, 1920–1950*. Cambridge: Cambridge University Press.

Tustin, F. 1981. *Autistic States in Children*. Boston: Routledge.

Twachtman-Cullen, Diane. 1997. *A Passion to Believe: Autism and the Facilitated Communication Debate*. Boulder, Colo.: Westview Press.

U.S. Department of Justice. 1990. Americans with Disabilities Act of 1990. Pub. L. 101-336, 104 Stat. 327 (July 26, 1990), 42 U.S.C. § 12101.

U.S. Veterans Health Administration. 2000. *Audiology and Speech Devices*. VA Handbook 1173.7. Washington, D.C.: U.S. Department of Veterans Affairs.

———. 2002. Prescribing Hearing Aids and Eyeglasses. Directive VHA DIR 2002–039 (July 5, 2002). Washington, D.C.: U.S. Department of Veterans Affairs.

———. N.d.(a). *Hearing Aids Information Bulletin* no. 90-3. Washington, D.C.: U.S. Department of Veterans Affairs.

———. N.d.(b). Network 2 Provision of Hearing Aids and Other Assistive Listening Devices. Network Memorandum 10N2–98–00. Washington, D.C.: U.S. Department of Veterans Affairs.

Vetlesen, Arne Johan. 1994. *Perception, Empathy and Judgment: An Inquiry into the Preconditions of Moral Performance.* State College, Pa.: Penn State University Press.

von Senden, Marius. 1932. *Space and Sight: The Perception of Space and Shape in the Congenitally Blind before and after Operation.* London: Methuen.

Wakefield, Hollida Z., and Ralph C. Underwager. 1988. *Accusations of Child Sexual Abuse.* Springfield, Ill.: C. C. Thomas.

———. 1994. The Alleged Child Victim and Real Victims. In *Handbook of Forensic Sexology*, ed. James J. Krivacska and John Money, 223–264. Buffalo, N.Y.: Prometheus Books.

Wallon, Henri. 1984. Kinesthesia and the Visual Body Image in the Child. In *The World of Henry Wallon*, ed. G. Voyat, 115–131. New York: Jason Aronson. (Orig. pub. 1954.)

Walsh, Andrea. 1986. *Women's Film and Female Experience, 1940–50.* Boston: Praeger.

Warfield, Frances. 1957. *Keep Listening.* New York: Viking.

Washington Speakers Bureau. N.d. Heather Whitestone McCallum: First Hearing-Impaired Miss America. http://www.washingtonspeakers.com/speakers/for_print.cfm?Speakerid=1582 (accessed June 2007).

Weis, Elizabeth. 1982. *The Silent Scream: Alfred Hitchcock's Sound Track.* Madison, N.J.: Fairleigh Dickinson University Press.

Weiss, Gail. 1999. *Body Images: Embodiment As Intercorporeality.* New York: Routledge.

Weiss, Meira. 1994. *Conditional Love: Parents' Attitudes toward Handicapped Children.* Westport, Conn.: Bergin and Garvey.

———. 1998. Ethical Reflections: Taking a Walk on the Wild Side. In *Small Wars: The Cultural Politics of Childhood*, ed. Nancy Scheper-Hughes and Carolyn Sargent, 149–162. Berkeley: University of California Press.

Wente, E. C., and A. L. Thuras. 1934. Auditory Perspective: Loud Speakers and Microphones. *Electrical Engineering* 53: 17–24.

Wheeler, D. L., J. W. Jacobson, R. A. Paglieri, and A. A. Schwartz. 1993a. *An Experimental Assessment of Facilitated Communication.* Tech. Rep. No. 92-TA1. Schenectady, N.Y.: O. D. Heck, ER Developmental Disabilities Service Office.

———. 1993b. An Experimental Assessment of Facilitated Communication. *Mental Retardation* 31, no. 1: 49–60.

Wheeler, Jill C. 1996. *Heather Whitestone: Miss America with a Mission.* Edina, Minn.: Abdo and Daughters.

White, Patricia. 1999. *Uninvited: Classical Hollywood Cinema and Lesbian Representability.* Bloomington: Indiana University Press.

White, Tony. 1997. Symbiosis and Attachment Hunger. *Transactional Analysis Journal* 27, no. 4: 300–304.

Whitford, Margaret. 1989. Rereading Irigaray. In *Between Feminism and Psycho-analysis*, ed. Teresa Brennan. London: Routledge.

———. 1991. *Luce Irigaray: Philosophy in the Feminine*. London: Routledge.

Williams, Barry. 1994. Abuse by Whom? *The Skeptic* (Australia) 14, no. 3: 27–29.

Williams, Donna. 1999. Lecture delivered at the annual conference of the Facilitated Communication Association. Portland, Oregon, May 9–10.

Williams, John. 2001. Marlee Matlin's World of Possibilities. *BusinessWeek online*. May 23. http://www.businessweek.com/bwdaily/dnflash/may2001/nf20010523_563.htm (accessed June 2004).

Williams, Linda. 1988. *Feminist Film Theory: Mildred Pierce and the Second World War*. In *Female Spectators: Looking at Film and Television*, ed. Dierdre Pribram. London: Verso.

———. 1990. Something Else Besides a Mother: Stella Dallas and the Maternal Melodrama. In *Issues in Feminist Film Criticism*, ed. Patricia Erens, 137–162. Bloomington: Indiana University Press.

———. 1998. Melodrama Revised. In *Refiguring American Film Genres: Theory and History*, ed. Nick Browne. Berkeley: University of California Press.

Wilson, Elizabeth. 2002. Imaginable Computers: Affects and Intelligence in Alan Turing. In *Prefiguring Cyberculture: An Intellectual History*, ed. D. Tofts, A. Jonson, and A. Cavallaro, 38–51. Cambridge: MIT Press.

———. 2004a. Gut Feminism. *Differences* 15, no. 3: 66–94.

———. 2004b. *Psychosomatic: Feminism and the Neurologic Body*. Durham, N.C.: Duke University Press.

Winnicott, Donald W. 1965. The Capacity to Be Alone. Reprinted in *The Maturational Processes and the Facilitating Environment*, by Donald W. Winnicott, 29–36 (New York: International Universities Press). (Orig. pub. 1958.)

———. 1971a. Mirror-role of Mother and Family in Child Development. Reprinted in *Playing and Reality*, by Donald W. Winnicott, 111–118. London: Tavistock. (Orig. pub. 1967.)

———. 1971b. Playing: Creative Activity and the Search for the Self. In *Playing and Reality*, by Donald W. Winnicott, 53–64. London: Tavistock.

———. 1971c. *Playing and Reality*. London: Tavistock.

———. 1971d. Transitional Objects and Transitional Phenomena: A Study of the First Not-Me Possession. Reprinted with additions in *Playing and Reality*, by Donald W. Winnicott, 1–25. London: Tavistock. Also reprinted in *Through Paediatrics to Psycho-analysis: Collected Papers* (New York: Basic Books, 1975). (Orig. pub. 1953.)

———. 1971e. The Use of an Object and Relating through Identifications. Reprinted in *Playing and Reality*, by Donald W. Winnicott, 86–94. London: Tavistock. (Orig. pub. 1969.)

———. 1974. Fear of Breakdown. *International Revue of Psychoanalysis* 1: 103–107.

———. 1975a. Hate in the Countertransference. Reprinted in *Through Paediatrics to Psycho-analysis: Collected Papers*, by Donald W. Winnicott, 194–203. New York: Basic Books. (Orig. pub. 1947.)

———. 1975b. *Through Paediatrics to Psycho-analysis: Collected Papers*. New York: Basic Books.

———. 1984. *Deprivation and Delinquency*. Ed. Clare Winnicott, Ray Shepherd and Madeleine Davis. London: Tavistock.

———. 1989. The Fate of the Transitional Object. In *Psycho-Analytic Explorations*, by Donald W. Winnicott, 53–58. London: Karnac.

Wolff, Larry. 1988. *Child Abuse in Freud's Vienna: Postcards from the End of the World*. New York: New York University Press.

Wolff, Lothar. 1970. *Rock A Bye Baby*. Time Life Documentary.

World Health Organization. 1995. *International Classification of Diseases*, 10th ed. Geneva: World Health Organization.

Young, Robert. 1994. *Mental Space*. London: Process Press.

Žižek, Slavoj. 1992. *Enjoy Your Symptom! Jacques Lacan in Hollywood and Out*. London: Routledge.

Lisa Cartwright is a professor of communication and
science studies and a faculty member in critical gender
studies at the University of California, San Diego.
She is the co-author, with Marita Sturken, of *Practices
of Looking: An Introduction to Visual Culture* and
author of *Screening the Body: Tracing Medicine's
Visual Culture.*

Library of Congress Cataloging-in-Publication Data
Cartwright, Lisa, 1959–
Moral spectatorship : technologies of voice and
affect in postwar representations of the child /
Lisa Cartwright.
p. cm.
Includes bibliographical references and index.
ISBN-13: 978–0-8223–4177–2 (cloth : alk. paper)
ISBN-13: 978–0-8223–4194–9 (pbk. : alk. paper)
1. Children in motion pictures. 2. Deaf in motion
pictures. 3. Motion picture audiences—Psychology.
I. Title.
PN1995.9.C45C37 2008
791.436'3523—dc22
2007043857